The Pocket Lawyer
for Filmmakers

The Pocket Lawyer for Filmmakers

A Legal Toolkit for Independent Producers

Second Edition

Thomas A. Crowell, Esq.

Focal Press
Taylor & Francis Group

NEW YORK AND LONDON

First published 2007
This edition published 2013 by Focal Press
70 Blanchard Road, Suite 402, Burlington, MA 01803

Simultaneously published in the UK
By Focal Press
2 Park Square, Milton Park, Abingdon, Oxon OX14 4RN

Focal Press is an imprint of the Taylor & Francis Group, an informa business

Notices

Practitioners and researchers must always rely on their own experience and knowledge
in evaluating and using any information, methods, compounds, or experiments
described herein. In using such information or methods they should be mindful of their
own safety and the safety of others, including parties for whom they have a professional
responsibility.

To the fullest extent of the law, neither the Publisher nor the authors, contributors, or
editors, assume any liability for any injury and/or damage to persons or property as a
matter of products liability, negligence or otherwise, or from any use or operation of
any methods, products, instructions, or ideas contained in the material herein.

Library of Congress Cataloging-in-Publication Data
Crowell, Thomas A.
The pocket lawyer for filmmakers : a legal toolkit for independent producers / Thomas A. Crowell.—2nd ed.
    p. cm.
ISBN 978-0-240-81318-9 (pbk.)
1. Independent filmmakers—Legal status, laws, etc.—United States. 2. Motion pictures—Law and
legislation—United States. 3. Copyright—Motion pictures—United States. I. Title.
KF4298.C76 2011
343.7309'9–dc22   2010045052

British Library Cataloguing-in-Publication Data
A catalogue record for this book is available from the British Library.

ISBN 13: 978-0-240-81318-9 (pbk)

CONTENTS

Disclaimer	*xiii*
Dedication	*xv*
Acknowledgments	*xvii*
About the Author	*xix*

PART I. OVERVIEW OF THE POCKET LAWYER

INTRODUCTION   3

The Audience for This Book   3

Why This Is Not a Contract Form Book   4

How to Use This Book   4

Legal Issues   6

Structure of the Book   6

E-Z Tabs   9

Filmmaker FAQs   9

Key Issues at a Glance   13

PART II. LEGAL BUILDING BLOCKS: CONTRACT AND INTELLECTUAL PROPERTY

1. COPYRIGHT AND INTELLECTUAL PROPERTY   23

What Is a Copyright?   23

Exclusive Rights Under Copyright   24

The Film Property   24

2. ISSUES IN FILM CONTRACTING   27

Deal Points   27

Who Are the Parties?   28

What Are You Getting?   28

What Are You Giving in Exchange for What You're Getting?   29

What Rights Do You Have or Are You Giving Up?   29

What Promises, Representations, and Warranties Are Being Made?   30

What Protections Do You Have?   30

What Rules Govern the Business Relationship Between the Parties?   31

What Happens When Something Goes Wrong?   31

PART III. THE PRODUCTION COMPANY AND FINANCING YOUR MOVIE

Filmmaking Is a Business   *34*

3. SETTING UP THE PRODUCTION COMPANY   35

Business Concepts   35

Types of Business Entities   37

Loan-Out Companies   42

4. YOUR PROFESSIONAL TEAM   43

Attorneys   43

Accountants   47

Insurance   49

5. FINANCING YOUR MOVIE   53

Pay for the Film Out of Pocket   54

Debt   54

Equity   55

Investors and Securities Laws   56

Step by Step: Securities Compliance   60

6. FILM TAX CREDITS AND OTHER PRODUCTION INCENTIVES   63

Production Incentives Defined   63

Eligibility Requirements   64

Types of Production Tax Credits   66

Applying for State Tax Credits: An Overview of the Process   67

Credits into Cash   69

Working with Asset-Backed Lenders   70

Tips for Selecting a Good Tax Credit State   72

PART IV. DEVELOPMENT

Creating, Acquiring, and Managing the Film Property   76

7.   IDEA RIGHTS: PROTECTING YOUR PITCHES AND
     AVOIDING IDEA "THEFT"   77

Nondisclosure Agreements and Submission Releases   77

Goals and Deals   80

Deal Points: Submission Release   80

Deal Points: The Nondisclosure Agreement (NDA)   81

Law: Protecting Ideas and the "Novelty" Requirement   82

Business Issues: Finances and Costs   84

Negotiation Tips and Tricks   84

8.   CREATING A SCREENPLAY   87

Writing the Screenplay by Yourself (Sole Authorship)   87

Writing Collaboration (Writing Partners and Joint Authorship)   90

Deal Points   92

Step by Step: Writing Collaboration   96

The Writers Guild of America (WGA)   97

9.   ACQUIRING SCREENPLAY RIGHTS   101

Buying Rights   101

The Screenplay Option/Purchase   102

Major Deal Points: The Option Agreement   103

Major Deal Points: The Purchase Agreement   105

Hiring a Screenwriter   111

Goals and Deals   111

Major Deal Points: Writer's Services Agreement   112

Screenplay Adaptations   117

Goals and Deals   117

Major Deal Points: The Literary Property Acquisition Agreement   117

Life Story Rights   124

Major Deal Points: Life Rights Consent and Release   127

10. CHAIN OF TITLE: THE CARE AND FEEDING OF YOUR COPYRIGHT   131

What Is a Chain of Title?   131

Copyright Searches and Permissions   132

Copyright Registration   136

The Copyright Notice   139

Copyright Recordation, Assignments, and Transfers   139

Certificate of Authorship   142

PART V. PRE-PRODUCTION

Production Services Agreements   146

Product Placement   146

Hiring Cast and Crew   146

11. THE PRODUCTION SERVICES AGREEMENT   149

Getting a Network Interested in Your Project   149

Major Deal Points: The Production Services Agreement   150

Practice Tips   155

12. PRODUCT PLACEMENT   157

Product Placement Agreement   157

Legislative Restrictions on Product Placement and Endorsements   161

Contractual Restrictions on Product Placement and Endorsements   162

Tips   162

13. HIRING CAST AND CREW   165

Federal and State Labor and Employment Laws: An Overview   165

Don't Discriminate   165

Independent Contractor or Employee?   165

Working with Minors   166

Unions   167

Services Agreements   167

Checklist: Elements of a Services Agreement   168

14. THE PRODUCER'S SERVICES AGREEMENT   171

Goals and Deals   172

Major Deal Points: Producer's Services Agreement   172

Law   180

Business Issues   180

Step by Step: Hiring a Producer   181

15. THE DIRECTOR'S SERVICES AGREEMENT   183

Goals and Deals   183

Major Deal Points: Director's Services Agreement   184

Law   193

Business Issues   193

Step by Step: Hiring a Director   193

16. CREW SERVICES AGREEMENT   195

Goals and Deals   196

Major Deal Points: Crew's Services Agreement   196

Crew Member Gear   198

Law   201

Business Issues   201

17. PERFORMERS   203

Letters of Intent   203

The Screen Actors Guild (SAG)   205

The Performer's Services Agreement   212

Major Deal Points: Performer's Services Agreement   213

Law   219

Business Issues   220

How to Get a Script to a SAG Actor   222

Step by Step: Hiring Actors   225

PART VI. PRODUCTION

Quiet on the Set! *228*

18. EXTRAS AND DEPICTION RELEASES   229

   Depiction Releases   229

   Caution: No Fraud or Misrepresentations Allowed!   233

19. LOCATIONS   235

   Where Are You Shooting?   235

   Why You Need a Location Release   235

   Getting Permission to Use a Location   237

   The Location Agreement   238

   Major Deal Points: Location Agreement   239

   Tips   241

20. WHAT'S ON THE SET?   243

   On-Set IP Infringement   243

   Copyrights on the Set   245

   Major Deal Points: Artwork License   248

   Representations and Warranties: Authorized Person   248

   Trademarks on the Set   250

   E&O and Other Contractual Obligations   256

PART VII. POST-PRODUCTION

It's in the Can   *260*

21. POST-PRODUCTION STAFF   261

   Hiring Post-Production Artists and Technicians Directly   261

   Artists and Technicians Provided by Post-Production Facilities   261

22. MUSIC   263

   Music Licensing   263

   Goals and Deals   267

   Major Deal Points: Music Licensing Agreement   267

   Step by Step: Prerecorded Music Licensing   270

   Stock and Royalty-Free Music   270

Commissioned Music   271

Major Deal Points: Composer's Services Agreement   272

Inducement (If Dealing with a Loan-Out Company)   277

Law   277

23. FILM CLIPS AND STOCK FOOTAGE   279

Stock Footage Companies   280

Movie Studio Footage   280

Major Deal Points: The Film Clip License Agreement   281

The National Archives   283

Step by Step: Film Clips   283

24. CREDITS AND COPYRIGHT NOTICE   285

Copyright Notice and Disclaimer   285

PART VIII. DISTRIBUTION

Selling Your Film   288

25. TRADITIONAL DISTRIBUTION   289

What Distributors Do   289

Types of Traditional Distribution Deals   290

The Money Pipeline   291

How Does the Money Get from a Movie Theater to the
   Producer?   292

Distribution Rights Acquisition Agreement (Distributor's
   Fee Deal)   295

Major Deal Points: Distribution Agreement   295

Law: Copyright Issues   303

Business Issues: Distributor's Expenses   304

Tips for Attracting a Distributor   305

26. DIY DISTRIBUTION   307

Your DIY Plan   308

DIY Theatrical Distribution   309

The Four-Wall Agreement   311

DIY DVD Distribution   314

DIY Online Distribution   317

The Content Aggregator Deal   318

YouTube   320

PART IX. CONCLUSION

Law Library Appendices A–E   325

The Law Library   326

APPENDIX A: A FILMMAKER'S GUIDE TO INTELLECTUAL PROPERTY LAW   327

Copyright Law   328

Right of Publicity   354

Violation of Privacy Rights   356

Libel and Defamation   359

Moral Rights   366

APPENDIX B: A FILMMAKER'S GUIDE TO CONTRACT LAW   367

Contract Law: An Overview   367

APPENDIX C: THE CLAUSE COMPANION   375

APPENDIX D: A FILMMAKER'S GUIDE TO LABOR AND EMPLOYMENT LAW   393

Employee or Independent Contractor?   393

Employee Responsibilities   399

Child Labor Laws: California and New York   400

APPENDIX E: STATE FILM COMMISSION OFFICES   407

BIBLIOGRAPHY AND RESOURCES   419

NOTES   423

INDEX   433

DISCLAIMER

This is a book written by a lawyer, so of course it has to open with a disclaimer. Here goes:

As you will note by its rectangular shape and paper pages, this is a book and *not* an attorney. Nothing in this book is intended as legal advice or to substitute for the personalized advice of a lawyer. Only your lawyer can tell you which laws apply to your particular situation. Laws change all the time and may be subject to numerous exceptions that are not covered by this book. There are no guarantees as to the accuracy or applicability of the information presented herein.

Furthermore, this book uses examples that feature character and company names. These names are fictitious and any similarity to actual people, living or dead, or actual companies is purely coincidental. I have also used several real trademark and business names to illustrate certain legal issues. The use of these names and marks does not imply any approval, sponsorship, endorsement by, or affiliation with the owners of these trademarks. All views expressed are mine and do not necessarily reflect those of either the publisher or anyone I consulted while writing this book.

DEDICATION

To my wife, Natali; my sons, Connor and Xander;
my parents, Caleb and Sheila; and to frustrated filmmakers everywhere.

ACKNOWLEDGMENTS

This book has been shaped by many people.

First, I could not have written this book without the help of two very special people: my parents. As published authors many times over, they inspired in me a love of writing and a love of the law; as experienced editors they read and redlined the numerous drafts of my manuscript. Thank you for your hard work on this book and for your love and support over the years.

My warmest thanks go out to my beautiful wife Natali for fighting through the various drafts of my manuscript and for putting up with the crazed schedule of a lawyer/author/husband. The experiences she and I shared when we were producing films became much of the substance of the book and of our wonderful life together.

Special thanks should be accorded to my sons, Connor and Xander, for keeping me sane. They faithfully reminded me that no matter how much work I have, I must always take time out to play.

I'm grateful for the help of my publisher, Elinor Actipis; my acquiring editors, Chris Simpson and Anaïs Wheeler; my project manager, Sarah Binns; and everybody at Focal Press. Elinor, thank you for handing me the reins on this book and trusting me to write the book I envisioned.

I am forever indebted to Sheafe B. Walker, Esq., whose tireless research and writing skills and passion for the law shaped the sections of the book that focus on employment and labor law.

I'm grateful for the help of my reviewers: Dom Caristi, Tom Rondinella, and Ivan A. Saperstein, Esq. Dom's comments gave me the fresh perspective I needed to produce the final draft of my book. Tom, a vibrant and tireless film producer, supplied me with his practical producer's-eye view of the manuscript. Ivan's help has been invaluable, both with this manuscript and in my law practice. He is one of those truly great attorneys: knowledgeable, hardworking, and generous. Many thanks to John W. Cones, Esq., for his sharp editorial eye and excellent advice.

My heartfelt thanks go to my old friend, theatrical agent Victoria Kress, who heads up the youth division of the Don Buchwald & Associates agency. Victoria provided valuable insight, tips, and humor on how to handle actors and their agents. Special thanks should be accorded to Jason Anderman, Esq., a great lawyer and trusted friend, for his encouragement and comments on the various drafts of this manuscript.

Thanks to William Patry, Esq., for inspiring in me a love of copyright law, and to Roz Lichter, Esq., and the Benjamin N. Cardozo School of Law for providing an environment where the study of entertainment and intellectual property law can flourish. Many thanks to Jeffrey M. Liebenson, Esq., and my former colleagues at KMZ Rosenman, LLP, for their support during the early years of my legal career. Thanks to Jeff Sanders, Esq., for introducing me to the exciting world of entertainment law. A special shout out to Marshall M. Kolba, Esq., for showing me at an early age that you can be a lawyer and still be cool at the same time.

Entertainment attorney and friend, Matt Savare, Esq., has inspired and reviewed numerous sections of the book; thanks, Matt! I was given valuable research help on the second edition through the tireless efforts of Paolo Macchi, Esq., a young lawyer with a bright future. Three Point Capital's Michael Hansen provided me with numerous tips and tricks on production incentive lending. Elliott Kanbar, owner of the Quad Cinema in New York City, was gracious enough to provide me with tips and tricks for four-walling filmmakers, which I pass along in this edition. Thanks to reviewers Drew Fessenden, a producer who truly understands the importance of the legal department, and Sal Petrosino, an educator who instills in film students at the School of Visual Arts the skills they need to excel in the rough and tumble world of the film industry.

One of the fun things about being an attorney is that you are always learning. Every new client brings a fresh set of legal issues to explore. I am, therefore, grateful to all my clients for allowing me the opportunity to learn from them and to help them make their wonderful films.

ABOUT THE AUTHOR

Currently in private practice with Saperstein & Crowell, LLP, Thomas A. Crowell, Esq., counsels clients on a wide range of entertainment law and intellectual property rights issues.

Before becoming an attorney, Mr. Crowell was a television producer and the head of business development for one of Japan's premier satellite television news companies, The Science Technology Network. Mr. Crowell managed the company's Development and Acquisitions department and supervised the production of its weekly science news program. Mr. Crowell created the children's video series *Professor Potto's Videolabs*,™ which was awarded a National Parenting Center Seal of Approval. He has also been a recipient of the New Jersey Young Filmmakers Award.

In addition to his private practice, Mr. Crowell lectures nationally, teaching producers how to avoid common legal pitfalls in the film and television industry. He has taught film law courses at several New York institutions, including the School of Visual Arts and Film/Video Arts. Mr. Crowell is an alumnus attorney of KMZ Rosenman, one of the United States' largest law firms, where he practiced with the entertainment, intellectual property, and corporate law practice groups.

Mr. Crowell is an advocate and supporter of legal *pro bono* work for artists. He is the executive director *emeritus* of the New Jersey Volunteer Lawyers for the Arts, a New Jersey not-for-profit organization dedicated to providing legal education, representation, and other legal services to low-income artists and nonprofit arts organizations.

Mr. Crowell received his Juris Doctor degree from the Benjamin N. Cardozo School of Law, where he graduated *cum laude* and was awarded membership in the Order of the Coif, the national legal honors society. Mr. Crowell earned his Bachelor of Fine Arts degree from New York University's Tisch School of the Arts in Film and Television Production. He is admitted to the practice of law in New York and New Jersey and before the bar of the U.S. Supreme Court. He is a member of the New York Bar Association, the

New York County Lawyers' Association, and the Copyright Society of the United States of America.

For more information about Mr. Crowell, please log on to www.thomascrowell.com. For more information about Mr. Crowell's law practice, please visit www.sclawpartners.com.

OVERVIEW OF THE
POCKET LAWYER

INTRODUCTION TO THE SECOND EDITION

Since the first edition of this book was written a scant three years ago, several developments have played increasingly important roles in the way independent filmmakers raise money for their films, choose the kinds of projects to shoot, and determine how to get their movies to the right audience. In this second edition I have tried to respond to these needs by including completely new sections on tax credit and film production incentive financing, production services agreements, and do-it-yourself film distribution. I have also included lots of new case law, graphics, and a host of other updates, all aimed at making this guide topical and easy to use. There was so much I wanted to cram in between these covers that it simply wouldn't fit (not unless you wanted to carry around a guide bigger than the Manhattan phone book). Don't worry, we didn't save that material for the third edition; no, we decided to post it on the new *Pocket Lawyer for Filmmakers* website at www.thepocketlawyerforfilm.com!

INTRODUCTION

This book is intended to provide you with a grasp of many of the key legal issues you will face during the course of making your independent films. The material in this book can help you understand and negotiate crucial production contracts, steer you through the choppy waters of handling actors and their agents, and navigate your production past the perils of copyright infringement and other lawsuits. Most important, it can help you protect that most valuable of properties: the rights to your film.

When I was first approached to write this book, I wanted to create something filmmakers would use on a daily basis—something that I would have used when I was a producer. Before sitting down to write, I surveyed the market and found that books on film law generally fell into two broad categories: contract form books and textbook-style legal treatises. What was missing was a pocket guide that could help the first-time filmmaker spot critical legal issues right away, without having to first sort through a lot of legal theory or read through a stack of contracts. Filmmakers needed a quick reference to reach for when they were on the phone with an actor's agent or waiting to go into a pitch meeting. I wanted to write a book that would sit in the producer's bag just as *The American Cinematographers Manual* is carried by every camera operator.

THE AUDIENCE FOR THIS BOOK

This book is aimed at the independent filmmaker who wants to make money by selling his or her film. You, the reader, may be an industry professional, a recent film school graduate, or an amateur who wants to break into "the biz." Regardless of who you are, if you want a chance at selling your film you must have artistic passion and *you must be prepared to treat your film project as a business!*

The book's premise is simple: You can't sell something you don't own, and unless you take care of the legal aspects of filmmaking, you could wind up not owning or not being able to sell your movie.

Furthermore, paying careful attention to a film's legal housekeeping will go a long way toward convincing a distributor that the filmmaker is a professional whose project is worth considering. The opposite is especially true: A filmmaker who ignores the legal aspects of her film will almost certainly scare a distributor away from picking up an otherwise marketable film! Even if you decide to self-distribute your film, you need to safeguard against lawsuits, cost overruns, and the failure to properly protect your rights.

WHY THIS IS NOT A CONTRACT FORM BOOK

A quick thumb through this book will show you that there are few contract forms within these pages. This is intentional.

I was an independent producer for many years before I became an attorney. Like many producers, I was very hands-on: I was much more comfortable wrapping cable than reading contracts. When it came time to negotiate a contract, I would pull a contract form book from the shelf and fill in the blanks. After all, I figured, a lawyer wrote the form book, so the contracts it contained had to be good.

FAQs/
INTRO.

What I didn't realize was that these form contracts are only good for a particular deal... and no two deals are exactly the same. Contractual language that works for one situation may leave you woefully unprotected in another; contracts are *not* one size fits all.

That's where this book comes in handy. Rather than giving you form contracts, I have taken key contracts and broken them down into their important deal points. This allows you, the filmmaker, to concentrate on negotiating the deal without having to read and understand a lot of legal language.

It is also the way the pros do it. The distributor who negotiates a distribution agreement with the filmmaker is almost never the same person who drafts the contract. It is easier to come to an agreement when you are concentrating on what the deal *is* rather than on *how* to draft the agreement. (That being said, of course crafting the contract matters. "The devil is in the drafting," as they say, and the wording of a defined term or a net profit clause may make all the difference.)

Don't get me wrong: Both contract form books and textbooks are good and valuable resources in their own right. In fact, it is my sincere belief that the filmmaker is best protected by using this book in conjunction with a contract form book when negotiating contracts and by using a textbook when trying to figure out *why* the law is the way it is.

A list of useful books that contain examples of film contracts may be found at the back of this book. Books by Mark Litwak, John W. Cones, and Philip H. Miller may be particularly helpful. (See "Bibliography and Resources," p. 419.)

HOW TO USE THIS BOOK

This book is organized roughly chronologically, according to the life cycle of a film. Nevertheless, it is also intended to be a flexible resource, allowing the filmmaker to access information in a variety of ways:

- The book is designed for easy access for the filmmaker who needs to jump right in and find an answer without having to first read the book cover to cover. To help these nonlinear readers, I have repeated some key information from section to section, particularly in the sections covering contracts' deal points.

- The book may also be read straight through like any traditional book. In fact, readers may get the greatest benefit from starting at the beginning and continuing until the end. Not only will such a reader know what to anticipate, but he will have a greater understanding of how all the legal puzzle pieces fit together.

- Extensive cross-references have been included in the text. These references provide the section and page number where a related topic may be located. (See "Setting Up the Production Company," p. 35.)

- A section featuring frequently asked questions (FAQs) may help you zero in on particularly pressing issues. (See "Filmmaker FAQs," p. 9.)

- Several appendices are included at the end of the book, forming a portable law library. These sections will provide you with separate, handy guides to intellectual property, contract, labor, and employment law. Also included is a quick reference to understanding common contract clauses and a state-by-state directory of film commission offices.

FAQs/
INTRO.

  - Appendix A: "A Filmmaker's Guide to Intellectual Property Law," p. 327
  - Appendix B: "A Filmmaker's Guide to Contract Law," p. 367
  - Appendix C: "The Clause Companion," p. 375
  - Appendix D: "A Filmmaker's Guide to Labor and Employment Law," p. 393
  - Appendix E: "State Film Commission Offices," p. 407

IMPORTANT TIP: Regardless of how you use this book, you should first read the section entitled "Legal Building Blocks." This section is critical to understanding the rest of the guide. (See "Legal Building Blocks: Contract and Intellectual Property," p. 21.)

VIDEO VS. FILM

Ten years ago there were two camps: videographers and filmmakers. Today, thanks to excellent inexpensive video cameras and computer editing programs, the distinction between film and video has largely been eliminated. Many independent producers shoot on high-definition (hi-def) video and transfer to film for theatrical distribution, and every project shot on film is transferred to video at some stage of its distribution. More and more theaters have facilities for projecting DVD, Blu-Ray, smartcards, and other video media, and virtually every film has its own online trailer. Because producers tend to refer to their projects as "films" regardless of the medium in which they are shot, I have adopted that convention here. From a legal perspective, the choice of label is largely irrelevant. I have used the term *filmmaker* to describe creative artists working in either film or video, and the term *film* to describe the project or medium in which they are working, even if that medium is video.

LEGAL ISSUES

This book is designed to help you spot legal issues common to most film and video productions. Generally, these legal issues will typically fall into one or more of the following categories:

- Copyright and intellectual property law
- Contract law
- Labor and employment law
- Finance and business

Most issues involve several of these topics—for instance, working with an actor who is a member of the Screen Actors Guild (SAG) involves both contract and labor law; raising money for a film involves finance, business, and contractual legal issues; distributing a film involves contractual and copyright issues.

Although the business of filmmaking involves virtually every area of law, this figure illustrates some of the most common legal issues a filmmaker faces.

Key Areas of Law Impacting the Filmmaker

Contract Law	• Negotiating, drafting, and defending agreements
Copyright	• Protects original works of expression
Employment Law	• Federal and state labor law
Serurities Laws	• Federal and state investment and market regulations
Tax and Production Incentives	• Help film financing through tax credits and other incentivies
Rights in Ideas	• Protect unique ideas as property (tough protection to get)
Trademark	• Protects titles, labels, slogans, etc. against consumer confusion
Rights of Publicity	• Protects the right to commercially exploit likenesses
Defamation	• Liability for statements that damage a person's reputation

STRUCTURE OF THE BOOK

The book follows a roughly chronological organization that tracks the life cycle of a film. You will learn how to deal with such issues as:

- *Setting up your production company and financing your film.* Filmmaking is a business and needs to be treated like one. This section will help you:

- Choose and create the right type of company. (See "Setting Up the Production Company," p. 35.)

- Select and hire professionals such as lawyers and accountants. (See "Your Professional Team," p. 43.)

- Learn what kinds of insurance you need to have in place before you make your movie. (See "Insurance," p. 49.)

- Decide how to finance your film and watch out for common financing traps. (See "Financing Your Movie," p. 53.)

- Identify whether or not you have potential securities law issues. (See "Investors and Securities Laws," p. 56.)

- Understand how tax credits and other incentives are used in film financing. (See "Film Tax Credits and Other Production Incentives," p. 63.)

- Learn how to borrow money against tax credits in order to partially fund your film. (See "Investors and Securities Laws," p. 56.)

FAQs/
INTRO.

- *Development.* During development, the script is chosen and acquired, the writers are hired, and the film property is protected. This section will help you:

  - Protect your script ideas. (See "Idea Rights," p. 77.)

  - Work with other screenwriters. (See "Writing Collaboration," p. 90.)

  - Buy or option a screenplay. (See "Acquiring Screenplay Rights," p. 101.)

  - Adapt a book into a screenplay. (See "Screenplay Adaptations," p. 117.)

  - Acquire somebody's life story. (See "Life Story Rights," p. 124.)

  - Protect your script through copyright registration. (See "Copyright Registration," p. 136.)

- *Preproduction.* During preproduction the filmmaker is primarily concerned with hiring the cast and crew and preparing for production. This section will help you:

  - Negotiate a product placement deal. (See "Product Placement," p. 157.)

  - Become familiar with labor and employment law. (See Appendix D, "A Filmmaker's Guide to Labor and Employment Law," p. 393; "Federal and State Labor and Employment Law," p. 165.)

  - Hire a producer. (See "Producer's Services Agreement," p. 171.)

  - Hire a director. (See "Director's Services Agreement," p. 183.)

  - Hire a crew member. (See "Crew Services Agreement," p. 195.)

  - Draft an actor's letter of intent to help secure financing. (See "Letters of Intent," p. 203.)

  - Hire an actor. (See "Performer's Services Agreement," p. 212.)

  - Deal with the Screen Actors Guild. (See "The Screen Actors Guild," p. 205.)

  - Get a script to an actor. (See "How to Get a Script to a SAG Actor," p. 222.)

  - Negotiate a production services agreement. (See "Production Services Agreements," p. 149.)

- **Production.** When you shoot your film, you need to be concerned with locations, extras, and avoiding infringing other people's intellectual property. This section will help you:
  - Identify when you need a release from an extra. (See "Depiction Releases," p. 229.)
  - Negotiate a location agreement. (See "Major Deal Points: Location Agreement," p. 239.)
  - Know when you need a shooting permit. (See "Shooting Permits," p. 237.)
  - Keep your art direction from infringing someone's copyrights. (See "On-Set IP Infringement," p. 243.)
  - Negotiate a license to use someone else's artwork. (See "Artwork License," p. 248.)

FAQs/
INTRO.

- **Post-production.** When the shooting stops, the post-production begins. Here you need to be concerned with editing and scoring your film. This section will help you:
  - Hire post-production staff. (See "Post-Production Staff," p. 261.)
  - License music. (See "Music Licensing," p. 263.)
  - Hire a composer. (See "Commissioned Music," p. 271.)
  - Obtain stock footage and film clips. (See "Film Clips and Stock Footage," p. 279.)

- **Distribution.** When the film is completed, you will probably want to sell it. To do that you either need to work with a distributor or you will need to distribute your film yourself. This section will help you:
  - Learn about the different kinds of distribution deals. (See "Types of Traditional Distribution Deals," p. 290.)
  - Understand how the audience's dollars make their way from ticket sales all the way to the producer's pocket. (See "The Money Pipeline," p. 291.)
  - Learn how to negotiate a distribution agreement. (See "Major Deal Points: Distribution Agreement," p. 295.)
  - Understand how to distribute your film by yourself if you can't secure a distributor. (See "DIY Distribution," p. 307.)
  - Put your film in a theater by yourself. (See "DIY Theatrical Distribution," p. 309.)
  - Sell your DVDs without a distributor. (See "DIY DVD Distribution," p. 314.)
  - Get your film on iTunes or Netflix without a distributor. (See "DIY Online Distribution," p. 317.)
  - Make money from putting your film on YouTube. (See "YouTube," p. 320.)

The chronological portion of the book is followed by a Law Library in the form of appendixes, which provide an overview of the following:

- Copyright; rights of publicity; defamation; privacy law; and moral rights; see Appendix A, "A Filmmaker's Guide to Intellectual Property Law," p. 327.

- Contract law basics; contract formation; types of contracts; contract breaches; see Appendix B, "A Filmmaker's Guide to Contract Law," p. 367.

- Typical contract clauses found in most film and video contracts; see Appendix C, "The Clause Companion," p. 375.

- Independent contractors and employees; legal requirements for employers; dealing with child labor laws particular to the film industry; see Appendix D, "A Filmmaker's Guide to Labor and Employment Law," p. 393.

- The state film commission offices, which help filmmakers find local crew and supplies and provide information on state permits, production incentives, and public land location regulations; see Appendix E, "State Film Commission Offices," p. 407.

FAQs/
INTRO.

E-Z TABS

New to this edition are the E-Z tabs, which allow you to quickly locate the section you're looking for. The tabbed sections are:

Part 1: FAQs and Introduction

Part 2: The Production Company

Part 3: Development

Part 4: Pre-Production

Part 5: Production

Part 6: Post-Production

Part 7: Distribution

Part 8: Intellectual Property

Part 9: Contracts

Just put your thumb over the appropriate tab on the back cover and flip until you find the section you need. No muss. No fuss. No endless searching. It's just a pity I couldn't make it lemon-scented for you…

FILMMAKER FAQs

Do you have a burning legal question that needs to be answered right now? The following frequently asked questions (FAQs) are designed to help you jump right into the book and get answers.

However, to get the most from this book, you should first read the section, "Legal Building Blocks: Contract and Intellectual Property," on p. 21.

Business and Finance

Starting a production company and financing a movie are critical first steps to any successful production. As you begin, you might have one or all of the following questions:

- Why do I need a company? Can't I just make a movie? (See "Setting Up the Production Company," p. 35.)
- What kind of business should I set up? What's the difference between a corporation and an LLC? (See "Types of Business Entities," p. 37.)

FAQs/
INTRO.

- Do I need a lawyer? An accountant? (See "Your Professional Team," p. 43.)
- What kind of insurance do I need when I make a movie? (See "Insurance," p. 49.)
- What are the different ways to raise money for my film? (See "Financing Your Movie," p. 53.)
- I am going to be raising money from investors. What do I need to know? (See "Investors and Securities Laws," p. 56.)
- I have an actor interested in my project, but the film isn't funded yet. How do I use the actor's interest to help secure funding? (See "Letters of Intent," p. 203.)
- I want to work with an actor who has his or her own "loan-out" company. Can you tell me more about that? (See "Loan-Out Companies," p. 42.)
- I heard that film tax credits are a great way to finance my film. How do I take advantage of them? (See "Film Tax Credits and Other Production Incentives," p. 63.)

Development

Development is the stage in a film's life cycle that deals with the creation and acquisition of the script, life story, and other rights needed to make your picture.

- I haven't written a script yet and I want to pitch a few ideas to a production company. How do I protect my ideas so the production company won't steal them? (See "Idea Rights," p. 77.)
- How do I copyright my script? (See "Copyright Registration," p. 136.)
- I want to write a script with somebody else—what do I need to do? (See "Writing Collaboration," p. 90.)
- How can I base my script on a comic book or novel or other work that somebody else has written? (See "Screenplay Adaptations," p. 117.)
- How do I hire a writer? (See "Hiring a Screenwriter," p. 111.)
- I want to buy another writer's script; how do I do that? (See "Acquiring Screenplay Rights," p. 101.)

- I'm still raising money. Is there any way I can reserve the right to a script so that no one else can buy it first? (See "The Screenplay Option/Purchase," p. 102.)

- Can I base my script or movie on someone's life story? (See "Life Story Rights," p. 124.)

- I was inspired by someone else's work. How do I determine whether I can be sued for copyright infringement? (See "Copyright Infringement," p. 353.)

- I want to work with a writer who's a member of the Writers Guild of America. What is that? (See "Writers Guild of America," p. 97.)

Pre-production

In pre-production you should be concerned with preparing for the shoot. A huge part of that is hiring the cast and crew:

- How do I get money for putting a company's product in my film? (See "Product Placement," p. 157.)

- Someone wants to hire my production company to shoot a program for them. How do I do that? (See "Production Services Agreement," p. 149.)

- When I hire cast and crew, what legal areas do I need to worry about in addition to the contracts? (See "Hiring Cast and Crew," p. 165; Appendix D, "A Filmmaker's Guide to Labor and Employment Law," p. 393.)

- How do I hire an actor who is a member of the Screen Actors Guild? (See "The Screen Actor's Guild," p. 205.)

- How do I hire a director? (See "The Director's Services Agreement," p. 183.)

- How do I hire a producer? (See "The Producer's Services Agreement," p. 171.)

- How do I hire a crew member? (See "Crew Services Agreement," p. 195.)

- I want to work with a famous actor. How do I get the actor interested in my project? (See "How to Get a Script to a SAG Actor," p. 222.)

- Can I hire only independent contractors and not employees? (See "Independent Contractor or Employee?," p. 165.)

- I need to cast children in my film. Are there any special legal requirements I have to worry about? (See "Working with Minors," p. 166; Appendix D, "Child Labor Laws: California and New York," p. 400.)

Production

Production is the stage in a film's life cycle when you shoot the film:

- I need to shoot in a restaurant/store/house. How do I get permission? (See "Getting Permission to Use a Location," p. 237.)

- I just want to shoot a couple of scenes on the streets. Do I need to get permission from anybody? (See "Shooting Permits," p. 237.)

- Why do I need a location release or permit? What happens if I don't get one? (See "Why You Need a Location Release," p. 235.)

- I want to film passersby on the street or patrons in a business. Do I need them to sign releases? (See "Depiction Releases," p. 229.)

- My art director wants to decorate the set with a really cool poster/statue/painting he bought. Do I need to get permission from somebody to use it? (See "On-Set IP Infringement," p. 243.)

- I am shooting a scene in a kitchen/grocery store. Do I have to get permission from the manufacturers every time I show a product label on screen? (See "Trademarks on the Set," p. 250.)

FAQs/
INTRO.

Post-Production

Post-production is the stage in a film's life cycle when you edit, score, and assemble all the pieces into a finished film:

- Do I need contracts when I work with editors and engineers? (See "Post-Production Staff," p. 261.)

- I want to use a popular song in my movie. Whose permission do I need? (See "Using Prerecorded Music," p. 263.)

- I want to hire a composer. How do I do that? (See "Commissioned Music," p. 271.)

- Can I rerecord my own version of a popular song? (See "Rerecording an Existing Song," p. 266.)

- I want to insert footage from another movie. How do I do that? (See "Film Clips and Stock Footage," p. 279.)

Distribution

Distribution is the stage in a film's life cycle when you license and sell the film. This is the money-making stage (hopefully):

- How does a film make money? (See "The Money Pipeline," p. 291.)

- What kind of contract will a distributor offer me? (See "Distribution Rights Acquisition Agreement," p. 295.)

- I've worked with a SAG actor. Are there any distribution concerns? (See "Assumption Agreement," p. 304.)
- I think I got all the copyright permissions I needed when I made the film. If I didn't, will there be any problems with distribution? (See "Law: Copyright Issues," p. 303.)
- Help! I can't get a distributer to pick up my film! What do I do now?!? (See "DIY Distribution," p. 307.)
- How do I get my film into a movie theater? (See "DIY Theatrical Distribution," p. 309.)
- How do I sell DVDs of my movie? (See "DIY DVD Distribution," p. 314.)
- I want to get my film on iTunes or Netflix without a distributor; how do I do that? (See "DIY Online Distribution," p. 317.)
- Can I make money by putting my film on YouTube? (See "YouTube," p. 320.)

FAQs/
INTRO.

Copyright

Copyright law protects artistic works such as films, books, paintings, etc.:

- If I own the copyright to my film/script what rights do I have? (See Appendix A, "Copyright Rights," p. 329.)
- How long does my copyright last? (See Appendix A, "Copyright Duration," p. 351.)
- Does copyright protect every part of my film? (See Appendix A, "What Is Not Protectable Under U.S. Copyright Law?" p. 332.)
- How do I hire a cast or crew member and ensure that I keep the copyright to their work? (See Appendix A, "Work Made for Hire," p. 344.)
- What is "fair use"? Can't I just use anybody's work in my film as long as I don't sell the film? (See Appendix A, "Fair Use," p. 335.)
- Aren't there certain books/films/photographs that aren't protected by copyright law? (See Appendix A, "Public Domain," p. 332.)

KEY ISSUES AT A GLANCE

The following flowcharts will help you see at a glance where you are in your film's legal framework and where you need to go.

FAQs/
INTRO.

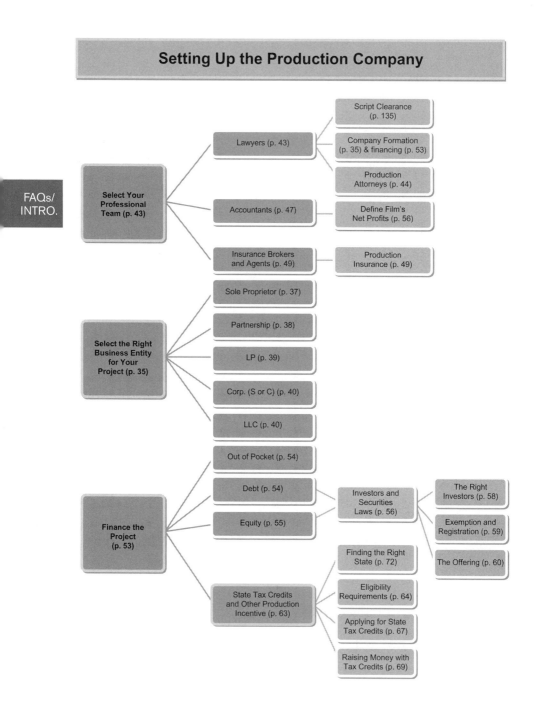

Setting Up the Production Company

Development – Getting the Rights

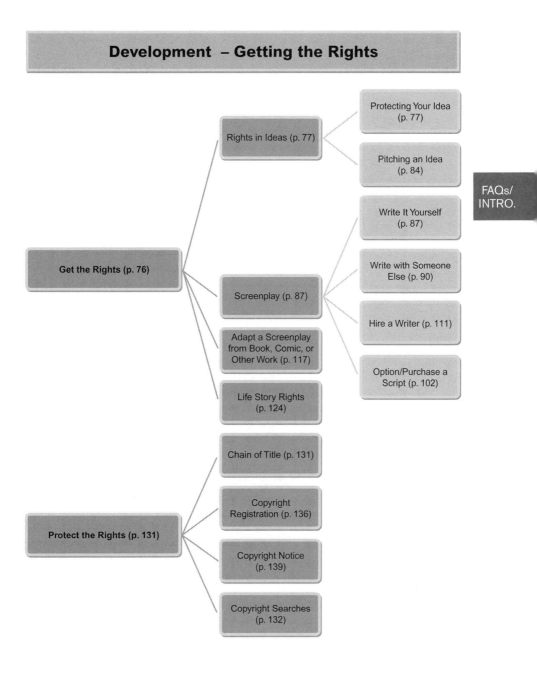

- **Get the Rights (p. 76)**
  - Rights in Ideas (p. 77)
    - Protecting Your Idea (p. 77)
    - Pitching an Idea (p. 84)
  - Screenplay (p. 87)
    - Write It Yourself (p. 87)
    - Write with Someone Else (p. 90)
    - Hire a Writer (p. 111)
    - Option/Purchase a Script (p. 102)
  - Adapt a Screenplay from Book, Comic, or Other Work (p. 117)
  - Life Story Rights (p. 124)

- **Protect the Rights (p. 131)**
  - Chain of Title (p. 131)
  - Copyright Registration (p. 136)
  - Copyright Notice (p. 139)
  - Copyright Searches (p. 132)

FAQs/ INTRO.

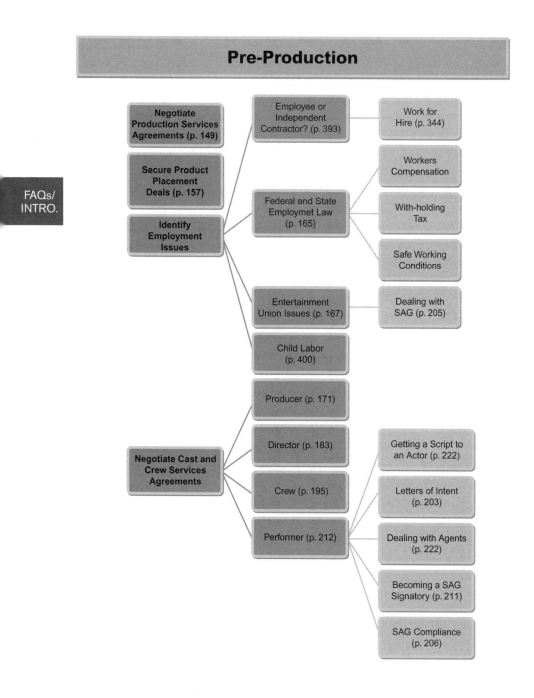

Pre-Production

Negotiate Production Services Agreements (p. 149)

Secure Product Placement Deals (p. 157)

Identify Employment Issues

Employee or Independent Contractor? (p. 393)

Work for Hire (p. 344)

Federal and State Employmet Law (p. 165)

Workers Compensation

With-holding Tax

Safe Working Conditions

Entertainment Union Issues (p. 167)

Dealing with SAG (p. 205)

Child Labor (p. 400)

Negotiate Cast and Crew Services Agreements

Producer (p. 171)

Director (p. 183)

Crew (p. 195)

Performer (p. 212)

Getting a Script to an Actor (p. 222)

Letters of Intent (p. 203)

Dealing with Agents (p. 222)

Becoming a SAG Signatory (p. 211)

SAG Compliance (p. 206)

Production

FAQs/
INTRO.

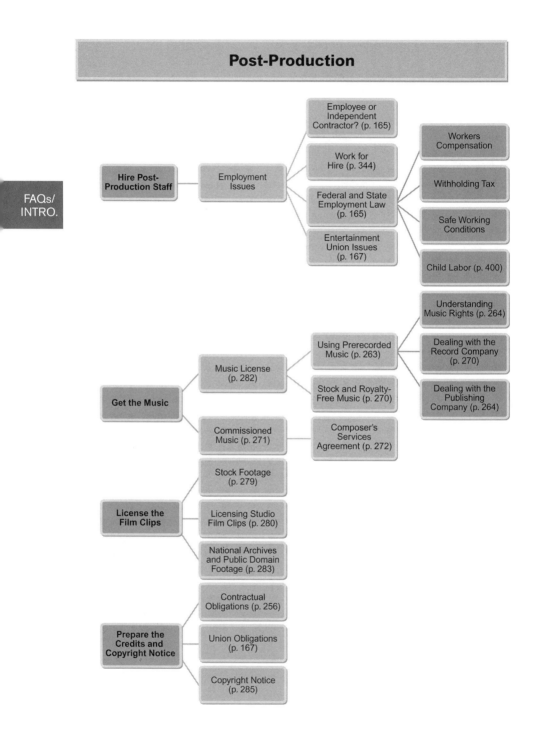

FAQs/ INTRO.

Post-Production

Hire Post-Production Staff
- Employment Issues
  - Employee or Independent Contractor? (p. 165)
  - Work for Hire (p. 344)
  - Federal and State Employment Law (p. 165)
    - Workers Compensation
    - Withholding Tax
    - Safe Working Conditions
    - Child Labor (p. 400)
  - Entertainment Union Issues (p. 167)

Get the Music
- Music License (p. 282)
  - Using Prerecorded Music (p. 263)
    - Understanding Music Rights (p. 264)
    - Dealing with the Record Company (p. 270)
    - Dealing with the Publishing Company (p. 264)
  - Stock and Royalty-Free Music (p. 270)
- Commissioned Music (p. 271)
  - Composer's Services Agreement (p. 272)

License the Film Clips
- Stock Footage (p. 279)
- Licensing Studio Film Clips (p. 280)
- National Archives and Public Domain Footage (p. 283)

Prepare the Credits and Copyright Notice
- Contractual Obligations (p. 256)
- Union Obligations (p. 167)
- Copyright Notice (p. 285)

Distribution

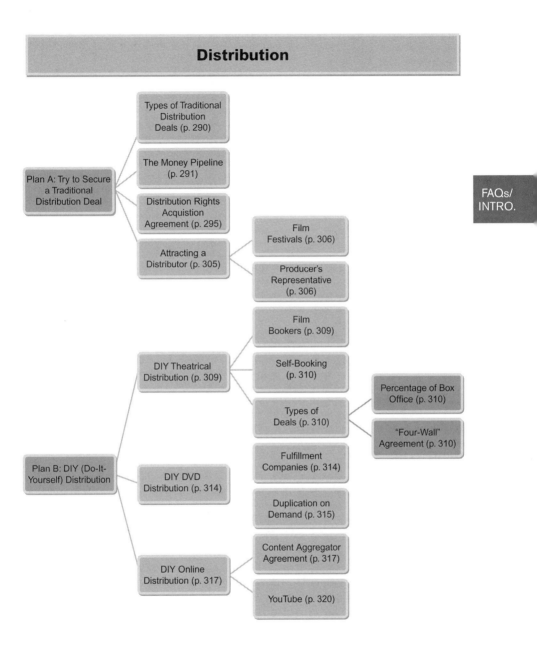

Plan A: Try to Secure a Traditional Distribution Deal
- Types of Traditional Distribution Deals (p. 290)
- The Money Pipeline (p. 291)
- Distribution Rights Acquistion Agreement (p. 295)
- Attracting a Distributor (p. 305)
  - Film Festivals (p. 306)
  - Producer's Representative (p. 306)

Plan B: DIY (Do-It-Yourself) Distribution
- DIY Theatrical Distribution (p. 309)
  - Film Bookers (p. 309)
  - Self-Booking (p. 310)
  - Types of Deals (p. 310)
    - Percentage of Box Office (p. 310)
    - "Four-Wall" Agreement (p. 310)
- DIY DVD Distribution (p. 314)
  - Fulfillment Companies (p. 314)
  - Duplication on Demand (p. 315)
- DIY Online Distribution (p. 317)
  - Content Aggregator Agreement (p. 317)
  - YouTube (p. 320)

FAQs/ INTRO.

2

LEGAL BUILDING BLOCKS: CONTRACT AND INTELLECTUAL PROPERTY

FAQs/
INTRO.

READ THIS SECTION FIRST!

Two key legal areas every filmmaker must become acquainted with are *intellectual property law* and *contract law*. These are the building blocks of every agreement used in motion picture and video production. You will get the most benefit from this book if you first read the following section before diving into the rest of the book.

A more detailed discussion of intellectual property and contract law can be found at the back of the book in:

Appendix A: "A Filmmaker's Guide to Intellectual Property Law," page 327, and

Appendix B: "A Filmmaker's Guide to Contract Law," page 367

1

COPYRIGHT AND INTELLECTUAL PROPERTY

All film deals are built on the foundation of intellectual property. Film contracts are used to protect and/or effectively transfer such intellectual property rights as copyrights, trademarks, rights of publicity, or rights in ideas.

> **WHAT IS INTELLECTUAL PROPERTY?**
> The term *intellectual property* refers to a collection of laws that protect products of the mind or personality, such as copyright, trademarks, rights in ideas, rights of publicity, and privacy rights. The laws that protect patents and trade secrets are also part of intellectual property, but these are generally less important to the filmmaker. Intellectual property is often referred to by its abbreviated label, IP.

WHAT IS A COPYRIGHT?

The most important intellectual property law for filmmakers is *copyright law*. Copyright is actually a collection of legal rights, all of which protect "original works of authorship fixed in any tangible medium of expression."[1]

Copyright protects all of the following:

- Literary works, such as screenplays, novels, magazine articles, and poems
- Motion pictures, television shows, and other audiovisual works
- Musical works, including any accompanying words
- Dramatic works, including any accompanying music
- Pantomimes and choreographic works
- Pictorial, graphic, and sculptural works
- Sound recordings
- Architectural works
- Websites
- Other works of original authorship fixed in a tangible medium of expression

Copyright is one of the easiest forms of intellectual property protection to obtain: just create an original work of authorship, write it down or record it in some way, and you have a copyright in that work. Only a minimum amount of creativity is required. You don't even have to fill out a form or put a "C" in a circle to get copyright protection; however, you get more legal protection if you do. (*See* "Copyright Registration," p. 136.)

EXCLUSIVE RIGHTS UNDER COPYRIGHT

FAQs/
INTRO.

For filmmakers, copyright law gives the copyright owner the *exclusive* right to take his or her work and:

1. *Make copies of it.* Zeus Pictures, Inc., owns the copyright to the film *Wombats in Love*. Only Zeus Pictures, or someone with that company's permission, can authorize Dupe Co. to press DVDs of that film.

2. *Distribute it.* Once the film prints for *Wombats in Love* are made, only Zeus Pictures, or someone with that company's permission, can authorize Dingo Distributors, LLC, to license the picture for domestic theatrical distribution. However, once a video or DVD copy is sold (as opposed to licensed), Zeus Pictures has no more control over to whom that particular copy can be sold.

3. *Publicly perform that work.* Only Zeus Pictures can authorize an exhibitor or broadcaster to show *Wombats in Love* to the public.

4. *Publicly display that work.* Only Zeus Pictures can authorize a website or other public display of production stills from *Wombats in Love*.

5. *Make derivative works based on the original work.* Only Zeus Pictures can commission a remake or sequel to *Wombats in Love* or authorize the manufacture of action figures, video games, and other licensed products based on the movie.

Of course, Zeus Pictures can *license* or *sell* any of these rights to a third party.

THE FILM PROPERTY

When you own intellectual property, you have the exclusive right to sell, license, dispose, possess, and exploit it. When you sell intellectual property, you are really selling these rights. This holds true for all forms of property, whether you're selling your house, your car, or the copyright to your screenplay. If you plan to sell or publicly exhibit your film, you must treat it and protect it as the valuable property it is.

The *film property* is the collection of property rights in the film and the screenplay on which it is based. The term usually refers to a collection of rights necessary for owning a motion picture, which includes:

- The copyright to the screenplay
- Ownership of treatments and synopses on which the screenplay is based

- The right to adapt the screenplay from another work, such as a book
- The copyright and other property rights in the resulting motion picture
- Any trademark rights in the film's title or images of its characters
- The right to authorize the use of clips or likenesses of the film's actors for promotional tie-ins
- The right to create another work (e.g., a video game, television series, action figure, etc.) based on the film property

These rights, especially copyright, can be divided up and licensed in a number of ways. Typically, rights are granted and divided up by the following categories:

FAQs/
INTRO.

Medium, such as:

- Film
- Television
- Literary
- Theater
- Video game
- Digital
- Home video
- Merchandising

Means of exhibition and distribution, such as:

- Theatrical exhibition
- Cable
- Video on demand (VOD)
- Pay-per-view (PPV)
- Satellite
- Free over-the-air broadcast
- In-flight movie
- Closed circuit
- Internet download
- Internet streaming video

Duration, such as:

- Perpetual
- Specified time
- Specified number of broadcasts, performances, exhibitions

Territory, such as:

- North America
- Europe
- The universe

As a result, it is possible for a screenwriter to convey the theatrical rights in a script to a production company while retaining the rights to write a novel from the screenplay. That is why it is critical for filmmakers and writers to be aware of exactly which rights they are receiving and granting.

FAQs/
INTRO.

Being able to control the property rights to a screenplay is the foundation on which you will construct your film property. To sell, distribute, or exhibit most films, you must first have secured the property rights to the screenplay on which they are based.

You protect your film property by ensuring that you:

1. Own or control the copyright to the screenplay. (*See* "Creating a Screenplay," p. 87; and Hiring a Screenwriter, p. 111.)

2. Don't infringe on someone else's copyright. (*See* "Copyright Infringement," p. 353; Clearances, p. 244.)

3. Register and maintain a clean copyright chain of title. (*See* "Chain of Title," p. 131.)

GOT A FEW MINUTES? GET SOME COPYRIGHT LAW UNDER YOUR BELT!

Now might be a good time to acquaint yourself with the basics of copyright law; after all, you will be dealing with copyright issues at every stage of your film project. Get yourself up to speed by reading through the copyright law section in the "Law Library" portion of this book. (*See* Appendix A: "Copyright Law," p. 328.)

Because copyright is such a tricky subject, it is easy to get into trouble, either by (1) failing to adequately protect one's work or (2) inadvertently infringing somebody else's copyright. *Keep in mind that you don't have to* intend *to infringe a copyright to be held liable for copyright infringement.*

The United States Copyright Office has a very helpful website. Its FAQ page can help answer some basic questions about copyright law: www.copyright.gov/help/faq/.

2

ISSUES IN FILM CONTRACTING

DEAL POINTS

Deal points are those terms that everyone must agree on before negotiating the rest of a contract. These are the terms that would appear on a *deal memo* or short form contract. Major deal points are usually the points that are negotiated first by the producer; as a result, these are the clauses that this book will spend the most time on.

For a description of common contract clauses found in production agreements, see Appendix C, "The Clause Companion," p. 375.

> **DEAL MEMO**
>
> A *deal memo* is a short memorandum outlining the major deal points of a contract. Signed by both parties, the deal memo is usually a binding contract. It is often used as a quick agreement to get the parties working together until a more complete agreement (a *long-form agreement*) can be drafted and signed by the parties.

Before we dive into the deal points of specific contracts, it's helpful to keep in mind the issues that shape them. Try to avoid getting bogged down in legalese by keeping in mind the purpose of a particular contract clause.

Most contract clauses deal with one or more of the following topics:

- Who are the parties?
- What are you getting?
- What are you giving in exchange for what you're getting?
- What rights do you have or are you giving up?
- What promises, representations, and warranties are being made?
- What protections do you have?
- What rules govern the business relationship between the parties?
- What happens when something goes wrong?

As you'll see, these concepts are interdependent. Any given contract clause may deal with several concepts, each one affecting the other. Let's look at each of these issues in greater depth, from a producer's point of view.

WHO ARE THE PARTIES?

This is not as simple as it may seem; the actor you're hiring may, in fact, want his loan-out company to be party to the contract (see "Loan-Out Companies," p. 42), or the screenplay that you're acquiring may be based on a novel written by someone other than the author of the screenplay (see "Screenplay Adaptations," p. 117).

A contract may have more than two parties, each of whom may have a different set of duties and obligations toward the others.

FAQs/ INTRO.

WHAT ARE YOU GETTING?

What you're getting depends on the kind of deal you're negotiating. From a filmmaker's perspective, you will generally be acquiring the following:

- *Rights.* Contract clauses that deal with intellectual property rights are often the most critical part of the film contract. (See Appendix A, "A Filmmaker's Guide to Intellectual Property Law," p. 327.) They control:
  - The copyright to a screenplay. (See Appendix A, "Copyright," p. 328.)
  - The right to use a company's trademark in your film. (See "Trademarks on the Set," p. 250.)
  - The right to use a piece of music in your film. (See "Music Licensing," p. 263.)
  - The license of artwork shown in your film. (See "Artwork License," p. 248.)
  - The right to use an actor's likeness on an action figure. (See Appendix A, "Right of Publicity," p. 354.)
  - The right to shoot a scene in a particular location (See "Getting Permission to Use a Location," p. 237.)
  - The right to distribute your film to iTunes or Netflix members. (See "DIY Online Distribution," p. 317.)
- *Services.* Virtually anybody who is hired by the production company performs services for the production company. You are contracting for services when you hire or you are hired as:
  - An actor to perform. (See "Performer's Services Agreement," p. 212.)
  - A cinematographer to shoot the picture. (See "Crew Services Agreement," p. 196.)
  - A composer to write the score for the soundtrack. (See "Composer's Services Agreement," p. 272.)

- A production company to create a program. (See "Production Services Agreement," p. 149.)
- *Property.* The lease of equipment, the purchase of materials to build the set, the rental of moving vans, location releases and permits, all involve the sale, rental, or leasing of property. (See "Locations," p. 235.)
- *Money.* Money to fund the production from your investors (see "Financing Your Movie," p. 53), or from a lender, payment for your services as a producer, money from the rental of your film from the distribution company—all are situations in which one of the parties receives monetary compensation.

WHAT ARE YOU GIVING IN EXCHANGE FOR WHAT YOU'RE GETTING?

Money or the right to money is usually what you're giving in exchange for rights, services, and property. Obviously, compensation comes in many forms: fixed compensation, deferred compensation, profit participation, contingent compensation, residuals, bonuses, royalties, rental fees, licensing fees, buyouts, option prices, and so on. (See Appendix C, "Compensation," p. 376.)

Understanding *when* and *to whom* you are obligated to pay the money is just as important as understanding *how much* money you will need to pay. A producer who promises to more than one entity 100% of the first dollar the production company receives runs the risk of starring in a real-life version of *The Producers*.

In addition to money, producers often give rights, such as the right to distribute the film in a certain territory, the right to manufacture DVDs, or the right to create a television series based on their film property. One important aspect of intellectual property is that it can be assigned, which means the rights to use that intellectual property can be conveyed to persons who are not part of the initial contract between producer and artist. Accordingly, filmmakers must make sure they have the right to assign the intellectual property rights that are conveyed to them. (See Appendix A, "A Filmmaker's Guide to Intellectual Property Law," p. 327.)

WHAT RIGHTS DO YOU HAVE OR ARE YOU GIVING UP?

In addition to the rights that are granted to you under the contract, what rights do you have prior to entering into the contract?

Intellectual Property

- If you are protected by a contract, you may have rights to your idea or concept. (See "Idea Rights," p. 77.)

- If you have written an original screenplay (and no one has hired you to write it), you own a copyright. (See "Sole Authorship," p. 87.)

- Do you own the rights to that film you were hired to direct? (See "Work Made for Hire," p. 344.)

Rights with Respect to the Business Relationship

Your contract will grant you rights with respect to your relationship with the other parties. For instance, you may have a right to be the first person at the bargaining table (see Appendix C, "Right of First Negotiation," p. 389) or the right to be the last person to reject an offer (see Appendix C, "Right of Last Refusal," p. 389).

WHAT PROMISES, REPRESENTATIONS, AND WARRANTIES ARE BEING MADE?

In addition to the exchange of services or property for money, what other promises are being made by the parties? You might be promising, for instance:

- That you have the right to enter into the contract with the other party and that you have all the rights you say you do. (See Appendix C, "The Clause Companion: Representations and Warranties," p. 381.)

- That you will agree to the production company's restrictions on publicity. (See Appendix C, "Publicity," p. 389.)

- That you will not hamper the transfer of copyright. (See Appendix C, "No Encumbrances," p. 387.)

- That your film will not defame anybody or infringe anybody's rights. (See Appendix A, "Defamation," p. 359.)

- That the written contract is the entire agreement between the parties. (See Appendix C, "Merger Clause," p. 387.)

WHAT PROTECTIONS DO YOU HAVE?

Smooth business relationships require more than promises between the parties; they require each party to be able to protect his or her valuable assets. For example:

- How often can you check the other party's accounting? (See Appendix C, "Audit and Accounting Provisions," p. 383.)

- Who has approval over a creative or business decision? (See Appendix C, "Approval," p. 375.)

- Who pays the legal bill if you are sued for somebody else's mistake or breach? (See Appendix C, "Indemnification," p. 386.)

- Once the term of the contract is over, do you get to keep the copyrights transferred under the contract? (See Appendix C, "Savings Clause," p. 390.)

- If a writer has not transferred all the rights to the production company, can the production company make the writer hold off on exploiting those reserved rights for awhile? (See Appendix C, "Holdback Provisions," p. 379.)

WHAT RULES GOVERN THE BUSINESS RELATIONSHIP BETWEEN THE PARTIES?

FAQs/ INTRO.

In a sense, the entire contract is a rulebook for the relationship between the parties. That being said, many provisions determine important housekeeping functions that are separate and apart from the quid pro quo issues at the heart of the contract. For example:

- How do you communicate with the other parties? (See Appendix C, "Notice," p. 388.)

- Can you assign your rights or duties under the contract to other people? (See Appendix C, "Assignment and Delegation," p. 383.)

- How long is the contract in effect? (See Appendix C, "Term," p. 382.)

WHAT HAPPENS WHEN SOMETHING GOES WRONG?

If something goes wrong, you can always sue, right? Perhaps not. It is quite common for contracts to contain clauses limiting a person's right to sue in court, requiring that person to arbitrate instead. Several kinds of clauses govern how the parties must solve their disagreements. The following questions might be addressed, for example:

- Can the parties sue, or must they arbitrate disputes? (See Appendix C, "Arbitration," p. 383.)

- Do the parties have time to cure problems before they are in breach of contract? (See Appendix C, "Default-and-Cure," p. 384.)

- What happens if something goes wrong and it's nobody's fault (e.g., an earthquake, flood, or fire)? (See Appendix C, "Force Majeure," p. 385.)

- Where must a lawsuit or arbitration be initiated? (See Appendix C, "Choice of Law," p. 384.)

THE BOTTOM LINE: **The value of the film property lies in its copyright. Written, well-drafted, and signed contracts are the only way to safeguard the film's copyright and, by extension, the entire film property.**

FAQs/
INTRO.

GOT A FEW MORE MINUTES? GET SOME CONTRACT LAW UNDER YOUR BELT!

Now might be a good time to acquaint yourself with the basics of contract law. You might want to read through the contract law section in the "Law Library" portion of this book. (See Appendix B, "A Filmmaker's Guide to Contract Law," p. 367.)

A catalogue of common contract clauses and their definitions can be found in Appendix C, "The Clause Companion," p. 375.

3

PROD.
CO.

THE PRODUCTION COMPANY AND FINANCING YOUR MOVIE

FILMMAKING IS A BUSINESS

If you're planning on making a film for your own amusement and have no intention of trying to make money from it, you can probably skim through this section.

But if you're like most filmmakers, you would like the possibility of selling or licensing your film some day. Whether you hope to see your film in theaters, on iTunes, on cable TV, or on DVDs distributed worldwide, you'd like some return on your financial investment. It should come as no surprise, then, that if you want your film to make money, you need to treat your production as a business.

This part covers many of the key issues involved in setting up and financing your production company:

- How to choose and create the right type of company. (See "Setting Up the Production Company," p. 35.)

PROD. CO.

- How to contract with loan-out companies commonly used by actors and other artists. (See "Loan-Out Companies," p. 42.)

- How to select and hire professionals such as lawyers and accountants. (See "Your Professional Team," p. 43.)

- How to ensure your company retains ownership of the film property. (See "The Company as Owner of the Film," p. 41.)

- Learn what kinds of insurance you need to have in place before making your movie. (See "Insurance," p. 49.)

- What to do if someone threatens to sue your company. (See "Cease-and-Desist Letters and Lawsuits," p. 46.)

- Decide how to finance your film and watch out for common financing traps. (See "Financing Your Movie," p. 53.)

- Identify whether or not you have potential securities law issues. (See "Investors and Securities Laws," p. 56.)

- Raise money from tax credits and other state production incentives. (See "Film Tax Credits and Other Production Incentives," p. 63.)

- Learn how to select the right state for your production based on the state's film incentive programs. (See "Tips for Selecting a Good Tax Credit State," p. 72.)

SETTING UP THE PRODUCTION COMPANY

The first step in forming a production company is often to create a *business entity*, such as a limited liability company (LLC), limited partnership (LP), or corporation. There are many advantages to setting up a business entity:

- You can divide the financial risk among several people. The members, partners, or shareholders of a business share in the company's profits and losses.

- Your company is considered a *legal person* and as such can enter into contracts, bring lawsuits, and hold intellectual property rights, such as the copyright to a film.

- You can separate your personal finances from the company's finances.

- You may die someday, but your company doesn't have to. Some kinds of businesses can last forever, and ownership interests in those companies, such as shares or membership interests, can be passed down from generation to generation.

And perhaps most important:

- You can avoid personal lawsuits! If your company breaches a contract or infringes a copyright, it will be the company that will pay the damages, *not* the company's officers or individual members. However, this *limited liability* protection is only offered with certain kinds of business entities (see the information that follows).

BUSINESS CONCEPTS

Limitation of Liability

Some business entities, such as LLCs, corporations, and LPs, allow their members to limit their liability to the amount that they are invested in the company. The members of such companies are not personally liable for the debts or other legal claims against the company.

So, for example, if an LLC or corporation is sued for breach of contract, the most that each member or shareholder can lose is the amount of his or her investment in that company. If the company is bankrupt and has no more assets, the company's creditors cannot collect the company's unpaid debts from the personal assets of its members.

It is important to note, however, that the limitation of liability a company's owners (its members, shareholders, or partners) might enjoy is not ironclad. There are situations in which a court will allow creditors to "pierce the corporate veil" (a term used for LLCs and LPs as well as corporations) and hold the company's owners personally liable for the debts of the company. Courts may pierce the corporate veil:

- If the company's members or shareholders have used the company to commit fraud.

- If the company's members or shareholders have treated the company as their alter egos—in other words, if the members fail to keep proper company records, mix their personal finances in with the assets of the company, or undercapitalize the company, leaving it without sufficient assets to perform normal business functions.

PROD.
CO.

Respondeat Superior

Keep in mind that an employer, such as a production company or producer, is generally legally responsible for the actions of its employees and agents performed during the scope of their duties.[1] This is the *respondeat superior* doctrine.

This means that if your employee gets into a car accident while picking up cast and crew members, your company is responsible for paying the damages from any lawsuit that may arise. Similarly, if your art director infringes somebody's copyright in creating a painting for your movie set, your company is responsible. Furthermore, if your employee or agent enters into a contract with a third party on your company's behalf, your company may be bound by that contract. Here the employee vs. independent contractor distinction really matters. (See "Independent Contractor or Employee?," p. 165.) Liability for the actions of independent contractors, unlike employees, often doesn't transfer to the contracting party except for:

- Inherently dangerous activities

- Activities that can't be delegated

- Where the contracting party exercises control over the manner in which the independent contractor performs the work.[2]

If you have a limited liability entity (such as an LLC, LP, or corporation) and your company hires an employee, your *company*, and *not you personally*, will be responsible for paying the legal damages that result from your employee's actions. On the other hand, if the employee was hired by you rather than by your limited liability business, *you personally* will be responsible for paying all claims, legal costs, and damages.

It is extra work to set up and run a limited liability business, but it may save you from having to sell your house to pay for a lawsuit caused by an employee's actions.

Keep in mind that it's not always clear just who is an employee and who is an independent contractor. You may think you are working only with independent contractors, but you could in fact be managing employees. For help with these distinctions, see Appendix D, "A Filmmaker's Guide to Labor and Employment Law," p. 393.

TYPES OF BUSINESS ENTITIES

The first step in establishing your business is selecting the type of company you will establish. Producers typically do business as one of the following kinds of companies:

- Sole proprietorship
- General partnership
- Limited partnership
- C corporation
- S corporation (S corp.)
- LLC

Some business entities, such as the sole proprietorship or the general partnership, do not require any legal formalities to start up. Other kinds of businesses, such as the LLC, the LP, or the corporation (S or C corp.), can only be created by filing and registering with the state government.

TIP: **This book cannot cover all the legal requirements for creating a business; there are entire books devoted to that subject alone. The filmmaker is encouraged to seek an attorney who is experienced in setting up business organizations.**

PROD. CO.

Sole Proprietorship

The *sole proprietorship* is the default form of business. You are sole proprietor—automatically—the moment you start doing business by yourself, without having formed another kind of company.

There are some advantages to being a sole proprietor:

- Virtually no legal paperwork is involved.
- Decision making is easy because there is only one member of the company—you.

However, there is one *huge* disadvantage to sole proprietorships:

- There is no limitation of liability. If your business is sued, you are sued. If the business defaults on its debts, you personally must pay the debts.

WHAT'S IN A NAME? THE DBA CERTIFICATE

The law begins with the presumption that sole proprietors do business under their own name (e.g., "Sasha Collins"). However, if you want to operate your sole proprietorship under a name that is different from your own (e.g., "Bongo Monkey Pictures"), depending on where you live, you will need to file a *fictitious name statement* with either the city government where your business is located or with county clerk's office. These are also known as *DBA certificates* (which stands for "doing business as"). Additionally, you should also perform business name and trademark searches to make sure that your proposed name is not currently being used by another company.

General Partnership

A *general partnership* may be formed when two or more people work together to own and operate a business for profit. There is usually no government filing required to create a general partnership, although it is recommended that partners have a *partnership agreement* or other contract which lays out the partners' respective rights and duties.

A partnership carries with it certain legal implications, such as:

- *Fiduciary duty.* Each partner has a heightened legal duty of loyalty and good faith toward his or her partners.

- *Unlimited personal liability.* Generally, each partner is personally liable for the debts and obligations his partners incur within the scope of the partnership business.

- *Partnership property.* Unless there is a partnership agreement that says otherwise, the partnership—and not the individual partners—will own all property acquired by partnership funds, brought into the partnership, or contributed to the partnership.

- *Partnership proceeds.* Unless there is a partnership agreement that says otherwise, all partners will share equally in the income and losses of the partnership, regardless of the amount of work they actually do in the management of the business.

Two or more people who work together in a common business enterprise are often surprised when the court determines that they are in fact partners in a general partnership.

One variation on the general partnership is the LLP, not to be confused with the LP (discussed in a moment). Because the right to form an LLP is often restricted to professionals, such as doctors, lawyers, and architects, it will not be discussed in this book.

CAUTION! Be very careful when deciding to do business as a general partnership! Because general partners must answer for the debts of the other partners incurred during the scope of the business, choosing the wrong partner can get you into personal financial trouble.

For example, Carlos and Kim are general partners in KimCarlos Productions, a startup motion picture company hoping to find financing for their first motion picture, *Broken Beer Bottle Blues*.

For the film, Kim decides that she needs to do extensive research on the effects of drinking and depression. Over a two-month period she lives in a neighborhood bar, pounding back expensive imported beer and videotaping herself with the latest high-definition video camera, purchased with an eye toward using it for the film. Needless to say, she runs up quite a bar tab and electronics bill. When her creditors come a-knockin', they can attempt to collect the debt from Carlos personally as well as from KimCarlos Productions and Kim personally.

PROD.
CO.

Joint Venture

A *joint venture* is a special type of general partnership, one formed for a particular and limited purpose. Producers and writers often use joint ventures to combine the forces of two existing production companies for a particular project, such as coproducing a film, writing a screenplay, or creating a television pilot.

To have a joint venture, the joint venture partners must have (1) a common business purpose, such as the writing and exploitation of a screenplay; (2) shared profits and losses; (3) an express or implied contract to work together; and (4) an equal hand in controlling the relationship.

Limited Partnership (LP)

A *limited partnership* is a partnership in which *some* of its partners may enjoy liability protections:

- The business is owned by two classes of partners: *general partners* and *limited partners.*
- Only the general partners are personally liable for all the debts of the business. For this reason, there must at least one general partner.
- Only general partners may obligate the business (authorize the business to enter into contracts, authorize loans, settle lawsuits, hire and fire, etc.).
- Limited partners are liable only to the extent of their investments, but they have no management authority.
- A person may be both a general and a limited partner at the same time.
- A state government filing of articles of organization is required to form an LP.
- Though not generally required, a partnership agreement is recommended.

Corporation

There are two types of for-profit corporations: *C corporations* and *Subchapter S corporations* (aka "S corps"). The features common to both kinds of corporations are:

- The corporation is owned by its shareholders and managed by its board of directors and officers.
- Someone can be both a shareholder and a director or officer.
- Directors, officers, and managers legally obligate the business (they can cause the business to enter into contracts, authorized loans, settle lawsuits, hire and fire, etc.).
- All shareholders enjoy limited liability status.
- A corporation is created by filing articles of incorporation with the state government.
- Ownership interests are conveyed by the corporation issuing shares or by a shareholder transferring shares to another person.
- Bylaws dictate how the corporation governs itself.

The two big differences between the S corp and the C corp are as follows:

- The C corp can have an unlimited number of shareholders, whereas the S corp is limited to 75 shareholders.
- The C corp is subject to "double taxation," which means that the corporation is first taxed and then the individual shareholders are taxed. The S corp, like partnerships, LLCs, and sole proprietorships, are only taxed at the individual income level.

Limited Liability Company (LLC)

The limited liability company, also known as an LLC, has become the business entity of choice for most small film production companies. This is because it has the limited liability advantages of the corporation with the flexibility of a partnership. Its features include:

- The LLC is owned by its "members."
- The LLC may be managed directly by the members (in the case of a "member-managed" LLC) or by managers whom the members appoint (in the case of a "manager-managed" LLC).
- Like the shareholders of a corporation, the members and managers enjoy limited liability status.
- State filing, called the *articles of organization*, is required to form a LLC.
- Taxation is on the individual member level, similar to the S corp, the partnership, or the sole proprietorship.
- The rules dictating how the business is run are largely driven by the *operating agreement*, which is a very flexible and highly customizable contract between the members of the LLC.
- In addition to contributing cash, members may also agree to contribute services to the company, such as directing the movie or writing the script, or to

PROD.
CO.

contribute property, such as the copyright to the screenplay or the ownership of the camera or the use of an editing system.

FORMING AN LLC

- LLCs are typically formed by filing articles of organization with the secretary of state in the state in which your business is located. At this point, you will need to elect whether your LLC is a member-managed or manager-managed LLC.

- An *operating agreement* should be negotiated, agreed upon, drafted by a lawyer, and signed by the LLC's members. The operating agreement usually governs the company's structure, the duties and obligations of each of the company's members, the amount and manner of the members' contributions to the LLC, the way finances are handled, and the way voting is determined. Many states require the operating agreement to be signed within a certain time after the articles of organization have been filed.

- If you are planning on raising money with your LLC (usually done by offering LLC membership interests to investors), you should have your securities attorney carefully review, and preferably draft, your operating agreement. See "Investors and Securities Laws," p. 56.

- Some states have an additional formation requirements. New York, for instance, requires LLCs to publish their formation in two local newspapers within 120 days of formation, designated by the county clerk. Failure to do so results in a suspension of your ability to do business in New York![3]

PROD.
CO.

The Company as Owner of the Film

Regardless of which business entity the producers ultimately form, the filmmakers must conduct all business related to the making of the film in the name of the company. This means that:

- Everything should be paid for out of a company bank account, not a personal bank account.

- The copyright and other film assets should be transferred to and owned by the production company.

- When making the movie, it is the company that should enter into contracts required for making the film. *It is critical that you first form your LLC and execute your operating agreement before entering into contracts on behalf of the company!* Make sure to sign all contracts in your capacity as company owner, partner, member, manager, shareholder, and so forth. *Do not* sign them without indicating your company status.

    Example: "Don Simmons, Managing Member, Sprocket Films, LLC."

- The company, and not the individuals who own the company, should rent, own, or purchase all the equipment.

- The company should hire all performers and crew members.

- Records of membership, partnership, or shareholder interests must be meticulously kept. Each owner's percentage of ownership must be tracked and records adjusted as new owners join the company. Ownership interest increases and decreases each time owners invest more capital in the company.

Failure to adhere to these and other critical rules could erase the limited liability protections that the company enjoys.

LOAN-OUT COMPANIES

Loan-out companies are often used by actors and above-the-line crew members. A loan-out company is a company formed for the sole purpose of providing the services of an artist to a production company. Loan-out companies are typically either LLCs or Subchapter S corps.

PROD. CO. When a production company is hiring an artist who has his or her own loan-out company, the production company is actually hiring the loan-out company, which in turn is providing the services of the artist.

Any contract with that artist must be drafted so that the contracting party is, in fact, the loan-out company. *Example:* "Production Company, Inc., agrees to employ Lender, Actor's Loan-Out, LLC, f/s/o the Performer, Andie Actor."

Additionally, all contracts with loan-outs should include an *inducement clause* at the end of the contract. (See Appendix C, "Inducement Clause," p. 387.)

Keep in mind that loan-out companies should still be required to transfer copyrights and other intellectual property to the production company that engages them under production contracts, just as individuals are required to do. (See "Work Made For Hire," p. 344.) *Example:* Davida Director has a loan-out company, Dodo, LLC. Peanut Pictures, Inc., engages Dodo, LLC, to provide the directing services of Davida for the film *The Laughing Legume.* Under its director's services contract with Peanut Pictures, Inc., Dodo, LLC, must still agree that all work done by Davida is done as a work made for hire with Peanut Pictures as the copyright owner.

If the production company is seeking financing in the form of state production incentives, such as tax credits, hiring an actor or director through their loan-out company may require additional guarantees from those workers that their respective loan-out companies will be registered to do business in the state granting the tax credits. (See "Eligibility Requirements," p. 64.)

Loan-out company terminology:

- *f/s/o* is a common abbreviation for the term "for services of."
- *Lender* is typically the defined term that refers to the loan-out company.
- *Inducement* is a promise by the artist that she will perform the services required by the production company as though she were hired directly by the company rather than through her loan-out company.

THE BOTTOM LINE: Before you open your doors as a production company, you should form a limited liability business to protect your personal assets.

4

YOUR PROFESSIONAL TEAM

To create your company and get your business up and running, you will need to work with several different types of professionals: attorneys, accountants, and insurance agents and brokers.

ATTORNEYS

PROD. CO.

One of the first things you should do is establish a relationship with a good entertainment attorney, preferably one with experience in setting up businesses.

Although the process of forming a company is not brain surgery, creating the company's internal documents can be tricky and is a task better left for your attorney. After all, you should be worrying about developing a screenplay, not how to draft the operating agreement provision on tax treatment of membership interests. It is important to bring in your attorney early in the process of establishing your company. No, I'm not shilling for lawyers here. You will actually save money on legal fees by making sure that everything is done right from the beginning, rather than bringing in a lawyer after the fact to clean up problems.

Because film and television are highly specialized industries, you will need a lawyer who is familiar with both IP law and with the particular deals and agreements routinely used by production companies in the film and TV industries. In other words, your average general practitioner might not be the best person for the task of negotiating and drafting film contracts.

Some filmmakers prefer to use several attorneys: a general business attorney to help them set up and run their production company and an entertainment attorney to help with the legal issues involved in shooting a movie. Additionally, if a filmmaker is looking to raise money for a film from investors, she should seek the advice of an attorney who has securities law experience. (See "Investors and Securities Laws," p. 56.)

In the beginning, your attorneys can:

- Form your business with the state
- Prepare internal company documents (e.g., operating agreements, bylaws, partnership agreements, etc.)
- Help you protect movie ideas when they are still in the "concept" phase; see "Idea Rights," p. 77

- Advise you regarding employees and independent contractors
- Help you with the company's financing documents and investor solicitation process

Once your business is set up, the entertainment attorney does most of the heavy lifting during development and pre-production. Your attorneys should:

- Prepare a screenplay clearance report, alerting you to potential legal issues contained in the script (See "Screenplay Clearance Report," p. 135.)
- Negotiate or help in the negotiation of key cast and crew agreements
- Draft the cast, crew, and other necessary contracts
- Help advise on union issues and labor and employment law
- Advise you on choosing the most favorable state in which to shoot for your tax credit needs (See "Tips for Selecting a Good Tax Credit State," p. 72.)
- Work with the financiers, agents, and lending institutions in setting up and managing escrow accounts

PROD. CO.

ESCROW ACCOUNTS

An *escrow account* is a bank account set up for a special purpose, such as holding an actor's or director's salary. The money is deposited in a bank (the *escrow agent*) and released by the bank to the actor or director under the terms stated in the escrow agreement. The escrow account provides a level of reassurance to the actor or director, because the money is literally in the bank and can't be taken out by the production company in violation of the terms of the escrow agreement. With increasing frequency, filmmakers are using online transaction settlement services like the well-known Escrow.com.

Be careful here. There have been more than a few "scam" sites set up to dupe the unwary investor. These sites are often elaborately designed to look like the legit escrow sites, but once your investor's money has been wired there, neither you nor they will ever see it again. Make sure to do your research before using an unfamiliar escrow service.

How to Find the Right Attorney

The best way to select the right attorney or attorneys is through references from other producers. You can also contact your state's bar association for help in finding an entertainment attorney in your area. Findlaw.com, a great resource for legal cases and articles, has a listing of entertainment attorneys by state at http://lawyers.findlaw.com/lawyer/practice/Entertainment, as does Whichdraft.com's wdlawyer-directory: www.wdlawyerdirectory.com.

Once you've located an entertainment attorney, sit down with him and discuss your project. Don't be afraid to interview the attorney before you retain that person. Make sure that he is a good fit for you by asking such questions as:

- How much experience do you have representing production companies?
- How much of your practice is devoted to representing production companies?
- How long have you been practicing law? What law school did you graduate from?
- Have you ever worked in film or video production?
- Have you ever been sued for malpractice or brought up on disciplinary charges?
- Do you have any relationships with distributors?
- Can you estimate how much legal fees will be, given the size and nature of my production?
- Do you charge by the hour or do you offer any services at a flat rate?

PROD.
CO.

Attorney's Fees

Most attorneys either charge by the hour or as a percentage of the final film budget. It is not unusual for an entertainment attorney to charge $300+ an hour or 2–5% of the film's budget. Remember, the more information you give them and the more homework you are willing to do, the cheaper it will be for you in the long run.

After the initial conversation with your attorney, she will probably bill you every time she talks to you over the phone—and many attorneys charge in either 6- or 15-minute blocks of time.

Some attorneys can quote you a flat rate for certain services. This means that you will pay a fixed fee for the particular legal service, regardless of how long it takes the attorney to perform that service. Attorneys often charge flat fees for routine tasks such as:

- Copyright and trademark registration application filings
- Business formation (state filings)
- Simple contract preparation (where little or no negotiation is required)
- Initial consultations

TIP: **There are two phases in creating a contract: the negotiation and the drafting. If you are an experienced producer, you may save time and money by negotiating the initial deal points yourself and then turning the contract over to your attorney to draft. However, if you are uncomfortable or inexperienced with negotiating a particular deal, you may be better off having your attorney handle the negotiations. Remember to budget for both your attorney's negotiation time and her drafting time.**

If you simply can't afford an attorney, contact your local Volunteer Lawyers for the Arts Organization. These non-profit organizations provide volunteer attorneys to low-income artists and arts organizations. However, unlike paid attorneys, they are not always "on call" for you. A volunteer attorney may handle a contract or two but is unlikely to take on the arduous task of becoming a production attorney for the entire film production.

VOLUNTEER ATTORNEYS

Organizations that supply pro bono attorneys to filmmakers, such as Volunteer Lawyers for the Arts, can usually be found with a simple Internet search under your state plus the phrase "pro bono attorneys for the arts." They tend to help artists located or doing business in the organization's home state. If you're in:

- California: www.calawyersforthearts.org
- New York: www.vlany.org
- New Jersey: www.njvla.org

Check your state bar for the arts-focused pro bono legal organization nearest you.

PROD. CO.

Cease-and-Desist Letters and Lawsuits

If you are sued, don't panic. Actually, before a lawsuit is filed against you, you will probably receive a "cease and desist" letter from your adversary's attorney. This is a letter that tells you (in your adversary's opinion) what you have done wrong and what rights you have violated. The letter also lets you know what you can do to rectify the problem.

> *Example:* Let's say that you are being accused of infringing the copyright in a painting that you have used as a background prop in a scene in your film. (See "On-Set IP Infringement," p. 243.) The cease-and-desist letter will begin by telling you that the copyright to that painting is owned by your adversary. It will then inform you that you have infringed the adversary's copyright by depicting that painting in your film. In the letter, your adversary will demand that you remove any scenes containing the painting from the film, and he will then probably demand some form of payment for the unauthorized use of the painting. The letter will usually conclude by saying that you have a certain time period within which to respond, and it will threaten further legal action (a lawsuit) if you do not comply with the terms of the letter.

If you have received a cease-and-desist letter, <u>do not try to answer it yourself!</u> Unless you are an attorney, you might not know how to write your response so as to avoid admitting facts that could be used against you in a lawsuit. On more than one occasion I have personally had to clean up a mess left by a client who has responded to a cease-and-desist letter before contacting me.

Hopefully, if you follow this book's advice, you will already have a lawyer who can respond to the letter that you've received. But if you have not hired a lawyer already, now is definitely the time to do so.

If you don't respond to the terms of the cease-and-desist letter or if you can't reach an agreement with your adversary, their next step may be to file a lawsuit.

If you are sued, stop talking directly with your adversary. Let your lawyer do the talking. Once you have a lawyer, your adversary's attorney should only talk with your attorney and not to you personally (unless your attorney gives permission). If you can't afford a lawyer, try to get one through your local Volunteer Lawyers for the Arts or similar pro bono legal organization.

ACCOUNTANTS

Managing money, handling taxes, and supervising payroll is a full-time job. If you are dealing with budgets in the thousands of dollars, *especially if that money belongs to other people,* you should hire an accountant.

PROD. CO.

There are several kinds of accounting projects your production company will face: (1) general business accounting and tax preparation for the production company itself, (2) accounting for the film production, (3) audits of production and production company expenses for lenders and state production incentive agencies, and (4) audits of production company and distributor accounting records for a production's investors. Many producers choose to hire a production office accountant in addition to their company's accountant. The production office accountant keeps track of the *film's* expenses. The production company accountant keeps track of the *company's* income, expenses, taxes, and accounting to the company's investors.

You should bring in your accountant as early as possible in the creation of your business. Ideally, the accountant and the attorney will work together in forming your company.

In the beginning, your accountant should:

- Get a federal tax ID number (also called an Employer Identification Number, or EIN).
- Set up payroll and income tax withholding for employees.
- Work with your attorney to set up special bank accounts, such as escrow accounts.

As your business begins to take in money from investors, lenders, and other sources, your accountant should:

- Create and keep track of account ledgers recording everybody's investments.
- Help prepare the budgets and other financial documents needed to apply for state film production incentives. (See "Applying for State Tax Credits: An Overview of the Process," p. 67.)
- Organize and prepare cash flow schedules, financing documents, and budgets to submit to tax credit lenders. (See "Working with Asset-Backed Lenders," p. 70.)

As pre-production gears up, money is spent fast and furiously. Both your business accountant and your production office accountant should be monitoring your cash flow on a daily basis and generating weekly reports. They will need to:

- Prepare income and expense reports and create budgetary forecasts based on spending patterns.

- Keep a tight rein on costs, alerting the production company at the earliest possible moment to potential cost overages.

- Collect and record business expenses and receipts.

- Disburse payroll, possibly in conjunction with a payroll company, making sure that the appropriate withholdings have been taken into account.

- Ensure that payroll checks are sent to the appropriate parties. Often this is an agent or a manager who takes his or her commission before passing the remainder on to the actor or crew member. If this is the arrangement, you must double-check that there is language in that cast or crew member's contract permitting you to disburse the funds directly to his or her agent or manager.

The accountants will continue to work after the film is in the can. They will:

- Make sure that the production company is meeting its obligations to investors, lenders, and state production incentive-granting agencies by providing them with budget reports, tax documents, audited statements, etc.

- Track royalties, licensing fees, film rental fees, and other sources of income derived from the licensing of the film property.

- Ensure that an audited final budget is properly prepared and submitted to the state issuing any state tax incentives.

- Prepare the company's tax filings and other tax documents.

PROD. CO.

ABOVE-THE-LINE AND BELOW-THE-LINE COSTS

A film's production budget is often separated into three broad categories: above-the-line, below-the-line, and other expenses.

Above-the-line costs include all the creative elements and key personnel: salaries and fees for principal actors, producers, writers, directors; literary property acquisition; and screenplay development costs.

Below-the-line costs include other expenses required to put the film in the can: crew labor, equipment rental, studio rental, film stock, art direction, wardrobe, post-production, and so forth.

Other costs include legal expenses, insurance, publicity, contingency, overhead, and so on.

INSURANCE

Productions require several different types of insurance. Establish a good working relationship early on with an insurance broker or agent who is experienced in the film industry. The need for insurance comes into play early in the game: for instance, you'll need to have workers' compensation insurance the moment you start hiring employees.

Insurance Coverage

Production companies need to take out entertainment insurance policies covering the following:

General liability. This policy pays third parties for damage caused by the production company. For instance, if you destroy a stove while shooting on location in a restaurant, general liability insurance should pay this claim.

PROD.
CO.

Workers' compensation. This is a legal requirement if you are employing people. It covers work-related injuries to employees. Along with general liability insurance, this should be one of the first insurance packages you obtain. (See "Labor and Employment Law," p. 165.)

Errors and omissions insurance (E&O). This policy pays claims arising from intellectual property disputes, such as copyright infringement, defamation, trademark tarnishment, idea misappropriation, invasion of privacy, or the like. Although E&O is costly, distribution companies, broadcasters, and exhibitors typically require production companies to have an E&O policy in place prior to distributing or exhibiting a film. Securing an E&O policy often takes a lot of work. To get insurance, production companies are required to provide chain of title to the screenplay, copies of production agreements, proof of intellectual property licensing, and a script clearance report. (See "Chain of Title," p. 131.)

Production insurance package. Insurance brokers who service the film and television industry commonly offer production insurance packages that include some or all of the following types of insurance:

- *Negative film and videotape.* This insures the exposed film negative or videotape stock against damage. When your footage is damaged, payment on this claim will fund your reshoots.

- *Faulty raw stock and camera.* This insures faulty film, tape, and other materials prior to exposure and is usually purchased in conjunction with negative film and videotape insurance, above.

- *Talent insurance; essential element cast.* This will compensate the production company for losses incurred as a result of actor's injuries or illnesses.

- *Equipment insurance.*

- *Car insurance.*

- *Third-party property damage liability.*
- *Props, sets, wardrobe.*

Keep in mind that an insurance company will pay out a claim only up to a certain coverage limit, as defined in the insurance policy. That's why it often pays to purchase the highest limit the production company's budget can afford.

PROD. CO.

ADDITIONAL INSUREDS

During the course of your film project, you will be adding many *additional insureds* to your insurance policy. These are people or companies whose interests will also be protected by your insurance policy. For instance, when you get a shooting permit from a city, the city will be added as an additional insured to your general liability policy so that if they are sued from someone injured by your film production, the city will be covered by your insurance policy.

Completion Bonds

A *completion bond* is like an insurance policy that guarantees the film will be made on time and on budget. The completion bond is granted by the *completion guarantor* for a fee, which is often around 3–6% of the film's budget.

Prior to issuing a completion bond, the completion guarantor reviews elements of the film package, including the shooting script, the production budget, the shooting schedule, the chain of title, résumés of key cast and crew personnel, production insurance packages, critical production contracts, and bank accounts. Producers and directors may also have to sign agreements stating that they will stay within budget and on schedule and that they have secured all the necessary permissions required for making the film.

Once the completion bond has been granted, the film's investors are protected in that the film is now guaranteed against the production going over budget. Such protection, however, comes at a huge creative cost: If the film begins to go over budget or fall behind schedule, or if other requirements of the completion bond are not met, the completion bond company may seize creative control over the film, substitute its own director and producer, and finish the film in the cheapest and quickest possible way. Needless to say, the threat of being pulled off the job and replaced by a substitute whose primary concern is the film's financial bottom line gives a tremendous incentive to directors and producers to stay on budget and on time.

LOOKING FOR SOMETHING?

LA 411 and NY 411 are great print and online resources to help you find production insurance brokers, completion bond guarantors, expert tax credit accountants, and even an extra roll of gaffers tape. Check out the following resources:

- www.la411.com
- www.newyork411.com

THE BOTTOM LINE: You should have your attorneys, accountants, and insurance brokers or agents in place to help you form your business properly. Above all, don't take anybody else's money until you've hired your professional team.

PROD. CO.

5

FINANCING YOUR MOVIE

Getting the money: This is, without a doubt, the single trickiest part of making a movie. Unless you're a trust fund baby or a Hollywood movie star, finding the money to make your film will probably be the biggest barrier between you and the realization of your creative vision.

Fortunately, digital technology has enabled producers to shoot professional-quality feature films at dimestore prices. Unfortunately, given the fact that many feature films routinely cost $50 million, that "dimestore price" can still be in the tens to hundreds of thousands of dollars. Furthermore, although digital technology may give you the tools required to capture an image on tape and then edit it, it will not help you pay for locations, cast and crew, hotel and travel, meals, music licensing, rentals, or any of the other items required for making even the smallest film.

PROD. CO.

If ownership of the final project is not critical, filmmakers may get their films made by coproduction agreements or by selling the project to a third party, such as a studio.

- *Coproduction agreements*. Coproduction agreements allow filmmakers to partner with another entity, usually a production company with studio facilities and/or equipment. In exchange for providing production services and/or studio facilities to the filmmaker, the coproducer receives an ownership position in the film itself. Depending on the deal, that coproducer may own equity in the filmmaker's company, a portion of the copyright in the film, a percentage of the profits of the film, or most likely, some combination thereof.

- *Selling the film*. Filmmakers often pitch a film package—script, stars, and hot director—to a more established studio. If the studio likes the film, it will offer to buy the package. Sometimes this sale is treated as a coproduction, but the copyright to the final project and, therefore, ownership of the film itself invariably rests with the studio. Despite the lack of ownership of the final film, many filmmakers would be more than willing to sell their projects to a major studio. The problem is that you usually have to be an established film producer to attract the interest of a movie studio. However, in both the world of television and online video it can be easier to strike a deal with a media company in which you shoot your program on their dime (see "Production Services Agreements," p. 149). But like the movie studio, the television company will usually want to own all the rights to the final film or program.

None of that sits well with most indie filmmakers, who want an ownership position in their films. Therefore, they finance their films in one or more of the following ways:

- Pay for the film out of pocket
- Incur debt

- Bring in investors
- Use state production incentives, such as tax credits, to partially fund the film

PAY FOR THE FILM OUT OF POCKET

This idea is fairly straightforward: cash in some stocks and bonds, sell something to raise money, allocate a portion of your weekly paycheck, or dip into your savings account—in other words, *use money you already have to make the film*. This is the most expensive, most risky, but potentially the most lucrative route; it also has the advantage of being the least troublesome from a legal point of view. Of course, most people don't have hundreds of thousands of dollars lying around with which to fund their movies!

PROD.
CO.

Some producers decide what to write and shoot based on the resources they already have. However, some pictures don't lend themselves to that low-budget approach. Furthermore, if you want to give yourself the best chance of selling the film, you will want to have known actors in your lead roles, and, unfortunately, most name actors would rather stay in a hotel than the director's mom's basement.

DEBT

If you don't have the money lying around, you can always try to borrow it. Loans are either *secured* by collateral or *unsecured*.

- If a debtor defaults on a secured loan, the lender can take the property that serves as collateral for the loan.
- If the debtor defaults on an unsecured loan, the lender will have to sue the debtor to recover the money lent.

Independent filmmakers typically borrow money in several ways:

- *Credit cards.* Credit cards are a form of debt. The high interest rates that credit card companies charge makes them one of the most expensive forms of debt to carry. Yet filmmakers love their credit cards. Whether they're renting lights or paying for an actor's meal, the film's costs are routinely paid for by plastic. Many a tale has been told of filmmakers who pay for their feature films by racking up huge credit card bills and using new cards to float the balance as long as they can. As you can imagine, the card-financing success stories are rare, and bankruptcy is often the outcome of this approach.
- *Personal loans.* This kind of loan, typically from a bank, requires you to put up some form of collateral to guard against the possibility of your defaulting on the loan. A second home mortgage is an example of this kind of loan. If you can't repay the loan, the bank takes your car, house, or other collateral you used to secure the loan.

- *Promissory notes.* These are debt instruments that your production company may grant to another company or individual, called the *noteholder* or *lender.* A promissory note is an *unconditional promise to repay* the borrowed amount at a specific time plus interest. Even if your company has not made any money on the film—in fact, even if the company has *lost* money—your company is still obligated to repay the loan. Many filmmakers use promissory notes to avoid securities issues. (See "Investors and Securities Laws," p. 56.) Be careful here! Promissory notes may still be classified as securities, especially when the lender is given a percentage of the profits of the film.

- *Borrowing against state tax credits.* Producers who apply for state tax credits can borrow money against the resale value of the credit by working with a lender. (See "Credits into Cash," p. 69.)

EQUITY

As opposed to a loan, which obligates the borrower to return the money loaned (plus interest), an *equity* investment represents an *ownership* interest in the company. Examples of this kind of financing include shares in a corporation, units in a limited partnership, or membership interests in a limited liability company (LLC). If the company fails to make money, so do the investors, but if the company makes money, the investors share in the profits. Since net profits are so important to equity investors and other profit participants, let's spend a little time exploring that concept.

Net Profits

The term *net profits* is often seen as the illusory end product of Hollywood "creative accounting." Yet such profits do exit (sometimes), and investors expect to receive them (most of the time). In fact, the list of people who want to share in a Film's Net Profits (the *net profit participants*) also includes writers, directors, producers, and lead talent.

So what is a net profit? "Hollywood accounting" aside, in most businesses net profits are simply revenue minus expenses.

> **Example:** Glop-Pop Inc. sells $1 million worth of oatmeal-flavored lollypops. The combined costs of producing the lollypops (ingredients, salaries, factory costs, etc.) and running Glop-Pop Inc. (salaries, overhead, taxes, advertising, etc.) are $750,000 per year. At the end of the fiscal year, Glop-Pop declares its net profits: The company has made a net profit of $250,000 on the fibrous confections.

In the film industry, however, net profits are a highly defined term of art that can change from deal to deal. In other words, a Film's Net Profits are what the parties to the contract define them to be... and in the case of a movie studio, that definition can run for 40 pages or more. Furthermore, the formulae for computing net profits differ drastically depending on whether you are a vertically integrated major studio/distributor or an indie filmmaker. Since most of this book's readers are probably indie filmmakers, that is the net profit model we'll emphasize.

Indie Film Net Profits

A threshold question is, what kind of net profits are you talking about—the net from the exploitation of the film by the distribution company(s) or your production company's net profits, once all the costs of making the film have been deducted?

It might be helpful to keep two broad definitions in mind as you look at the contracts in this book:

• The *Film's Net Profits* are the monies that are given to the production company after the distributors have deducted their expenses and have been paid their distribution fees. (See "Traditional Distribution," p. 289.) This is also the level at which investors and other net profit participants usually take their cuts. *This is the net profit definition we will refer to most often in this book.*

• By contrast, the *production company's net profits* are what's left over after the production company has paid its investors, the profit participants (those people sharing in the net profits), deferred salaries, and other the costs of making and promoting the film. If such profits exist at all, they're the final pile of money left on the table. It's similar to the net profits in our earlier oatmeal-popsicle example.

> **Example:** Pizzicato Pictures has made its first picture, *Sax and Violins*, a gripping drama about a jazz musician caught up in the rough and tumble world of the chamber orchestra. When it was raising money for the film, Pizzicato promised its investors and screenwriter a portion of the *Film's Net Profits*. The film is distributed and the distribution company deducts expenses and pays itself a distribution fee. The remaining monies are sent to Pizzicato; these monies become the *Film's Net Profits*. The investors and the screenwriter(s) are paid their share from the Film's Net Profits, as are all the deferred salaries; finally Pizzicato pays the cost of production and all its other debts. Any monies left over become the *production company's net profits*.

For a detailed description of distribution expenses and other deductions, see "How Does the Money Get from a Movie Theater to the Producer?," p. 292.

INVESTORS AND SECURITIES LAWS

From the investor's point of view, an equity investment has tremendous upside potential: If you invest several thousand dollars in a company that is producing a low-budget film that turns out to be as successful as *The Blair Witch Project*, you will reap many times the value of your initial investment.

For the producer, the biggest advantage with this kind of financing is that if the film never sells and the company loses money, there is no obligation to repay the

PROD.
CO.

investor's capital. You might be thinking, "Wait a minute, let me see if I understand this: Investors put money into my company and I have no obligation to return that money unless my film makes money? Where do I sign? Better yet, where do I get my investors to sign?"

Before you rush out and offer shares or membership interests in your company, take heed: You must be extremely careful using this kind of financing, because it is quite easy to run into problems with both state and federal securities laws. Despite both your and your investor's willingness to enter into a seemingly fair deal, *failure to adhere to a complex system of state and federal securities laws may expose you and your company to civil and criminal penalties.*

What Is a Security?

When most people hear the word *security*, they think of stock in a large public company, such as a share of Microsoft. Filmmakers are often very surprised when they learn that their efforts to raise money for their films may be violating state and federal securities laws, because what the filmmaker is offering to investors is also considered a security. The reason is that virtually any kind of investment can be subject to scrutiny under these laws.

Under federal law, a security is defined as follows:

> any note, stock, treasury stock, security future, bond, debenture, evidence of indebtedness, certificate of interest or participation in any profit-sharing agreement, collateral-trust certificate, preorganization certificate or subscription, transferable share, investment contract [...].[1]

In other words, an investment doesn't have to be labeled "Stock Certificate" to be regulated as a security.

Film Investments as "Investment Contracts"

Producers typically run into problems when they offer membership interests in an LLC, units in an LP, or shares in their corporation to potential investors in exchange for money to make the film (a process called an *offering*). That exchange of money for the expectation of profits may create an *investment contract*, and thus a security.

In one famous case[2] the U.S. Supreme Court held that an investment contract (and thus a security) exists if the following elements are present:

- A person invests money in a common enterprise or scheme
- That investor expects profits
- Such profits are derived solely from the efforts of others

As a result, if a person gives you money for your film project, and if that person is expecting a profit, and if he or she does not participate in the making of the film or the management of the film company, then that person's interest is probably a security.

Example: Fred Filmmaker is trying to raise money for his feature film. He has created an LLC and is now seeking investors. The following crew members give him money in exchange for membership interests in his LLC: Carlo the cinematographer, Donna the director, William the writer, Gary the grip, and Peter the production office supervisor. Fred's Aunt Agatha and his barber, Betty, also give him money to invest in the film. Fred does not want to register his membership interests as securities or file for an exemption to securities registration. *Fred may have violated the securities laws.* Because neither Aunt Agatha nor Betty the barber contributed to the running of the business of the LLC or the making of the film itself, their membership interests were securities and as such would need to be registered or exempted from registration.

If the investment is a security, it must be either *registered* with the state and federal governments or *exempted* from registration *before* prospective investors are even asked if they want to invest in the film.

When a production company offers securities without registering or exempting them from registration, the company is probably breaking the law. If *both* state and federal securities laws are not complied with, the filmmaker can risk severe civil and criminal penalties from both the state and federal securities agencies.

> **CAUTION!** You should always seek the help of an attorney who has experience in securities law before you solicit any investors or offer any securities!

Accredited and Nonaccredited Investors

Not only do the securities laws control the registration and exemption of securities, they also regulate whom you can solicit and how. Furthermore, the amount of information that must be disclosed is affected by whether the potential investor is an accredited or a nonaccredited investor.

An *accredited investor* is an officer of the company issuing the securities or a person or institution that has a lot of money. Anyone who is not within the category of accredited investors is, by definition, a *nonaccredited investor.*

The following are among the categories of accredited investors:

• A director, executive officer, or general partner of the company selling the securities

• An individual, either alone or with his or her spouse, with a net worth that exceeds $1 million at the time of the purchase

• An individual with income exceeding $200,000 in each of the two most recent years or joint income with a spouse exceeding $300,000 for those years and a reasonable expectation of the same income level in the current year

If a potential investor is an accredited investor under the securities laws, he or she is presumed to have enough financial knowledge and experience to adequately assess the risks of the investment.

Every nonaccredited investor, however, must be given adequate information with which they can evaluate and make a decision about investing in your film. Nonaccredited investors must be given the same kinds of information that would be given by issuers of a registered security to its investors. The amount of disclosure is actually quite high: Investors must be apprised of risk factors, both with the company and of the film industry in general.

> **CAUTION!** As a rule of thumb, proceed with caution when making an offering to nonaccredited investors. You can reduce certain risks by making offerings only to accredited investors. If you do need nonaccredited investor money (and many of us do), be sure to seek the advice of an attorney who is experienced in the nuances of nonaccredited investor financing.

PROD. CO.

Exemptions from Registration

Registering securities in a film is expensive, time consuming, and usually not necessary for low-budget films. However, if you're not registering your security, you *must exempt* your security from registration. Filmmakers typically take advantage of one of the registration exemptions offered by SEC Regulation D:

- *Rule 504 offering.*[3] Under Rule 504, production companies can offer to sell $1 million of securities within a one-year period. There is no limit to the number of investors who can be brought on board with this offering; however, companies generally cannot advertise or solicit the public. Offers should only be made to persons with whom the company has a preexisting relationship.

- *Rule 505 offering.*[4] Rule 505 allows the company to offer to sell $5 million of securities within a year. There is no limit to the number of accredited investors to whom it may sell securities, but the company may not sell securities to more than 35 nonaccredited investors. Even though the company can sell securities to nonaccredited investors, it is a good practice to sell to only accredited investors. The disclosure requirements are stricter under Rule 505.

- *Rule 506 offering.*[5] Under Rule 506 there is no limit to the amount of money that the production company can raise. But the offering must only be made to offerees with whom the company has a preexisting relationship. In addition to the investors being *accredited, financial sophistication* is a prerequisite for all nonaccredited investors. Under Rule 506 the disclosure requirements are the strictest of all.

Companies seeking to exempt their securities from registration must file a Form D notice of exempt offering with the SEC. Regulation D can be found on the SEC website at www.sec.gov/about/forms/formd.pdf.

Note: Form D must be filed within 15 days after the first sale of securities in the offering![6]

NO FRAUD ALLOWED!

All securities offerings, even those exempted under Regulation D, are subject to the antifraud provisions of the securities laws. This means that any false or misleading statement made by the company offering the securities is subject to civil and criminal penalties.

The Offering

These documents contain:

PROD. CO.

- An investor questionnaire, in which, ideally, the potential investors warrant that they are accredited investors.
- A securities disclosure document, such as a private placement memorandum (PPM), which contains such key points as these:
  - An overview of the company, its managers, and their experience
  - Risk factors and disclosures—essentially telling investors that film investments are extremely speculative and they may lose their money
  - Capitalization—how the company is raising money
  - How the money raised will be used
  - How the investors' interests will be affected if other investors contribute money
  - Description terms of the securities offered
  - Audited financial statements of the company
  - An LLC operating agreement or other organizational documents
  - A "Description of Business" section, which should include information on the state of the film industry and the relevant markets in which you plan to shop your film
  - The script (or at least a synopsis)
  - Subscription agreement—the agreement for the sale of securities to the investor

STEP BY STEP: SECURITIES COMPLIANCE

To issue securities, production companies must:

- Work with an attorney experienced with private placement and securities laws, preferably film offerings

- Either register their securities or file for Regulation D exemption by submitting a Form D
- Comply with their state securities laws (called Blue Sky laws) regarding offering securities
- Identify appropriate investors—the best practices to make sure all the potential investors are accredited investors
- Have an attorney create offering documents for your film project
- Submit offering documents to potential investors

THE BOTTOM LINE: **If you plan on raising money from equity inves-tors, you should seek the advice of an attorney who is experienced in securities and private placement law—*before* you even ask anyone if they are interested in investing! This is one area where it simply does not pay to try to do it yourself.**

PROD. CO.

6

FILM TAX CREDITS AND OTHER PRODUCTION INCENTIVES

PRODUCTION INCENTIVES DEFINED

How would you like to be paid by a state (and sometimes also a city) just for shooting there?

Who wouldn't?!

One indispensible method of funding films is through the use of state *production incentives*, the most significant of which are *tax credits*. Broadly speaking, a tax credit is money paid by a state to the filmmaker for shooting (and incurring expenses) in that state. Cities and states offer these incentives to encourage film production within their borders; in fact, production incentives are conditional upon a certain percentage of the film's budget being spent in that state. In addition to tax credits, other state production incentives include relief for sales, gross receipts, use, and other local taxes. Some states also offer *rebates*, which are paid to filmmakers for certain qualified expenses incurred within that state.

Depending on the kind of tax credit, the filmmaker may use this money to:

• Put the money back into the film

• Borrow money from a lender with the credit as collateral

• Offset her state tax obligations

• Sell the credit to someone else to offset that buyer's state tax obligations

• Put the money toward the film's marketing and promotion

• Pay back equity investors

> **Example:** Jared is shooting his film, *The Wrath of Grapes*—a cross between *Sideways* and *Saw*—in which a sommelier turns psychotic killer (tagline: "Is that red wine you're drinking?"). His budget is $5 million and he shoots in New York state. If his production company spends $5 million on applicable expenses in New York, which provides a 30% tax credit, Jared will receive a check for $1.5 million from the state of New York—even if the film's production company doesn't owe any taxes there!

Production incentives have become one of the most significant factors producers consider when determining where to shoot their films.
—**Matthew Savare, entertainment attorney, Lowenstein Sandler, PC**

FINDING THE RIGHT STATE

Most states have active *film commissions* whose function is to encourage in-state film and television production by helping filmmakers find local crew and supplies, recommending production-oriented state policy and legislation, and providing information on state permits, production incentives, and regulations on the use of public land for production. These organizations will be able to give you detailed information on that state's film incentive programs and eligibility requirements and supply you with the forms you need to get the process started.

For a list of *state film commissions*, see Appendix E, "State Film Commissions."

For list of *state production incentives*, see the Screen Actors Guild website: www.sag.org/state-film-incentives. You may also want to search production company payroll websites, which typically have up-to-date information on state incentives.

Keep in mind that state production incentives are a volatile landscape. A state that granted favorable production incentives one year may no longer offer them the following year.

ELIGIBILITY REQUIREMENTS

The states that offer tax credits give them to production companies only for *qualified productions* and only for *qualified production expenses*. For instance, at the time of this writing, Hawaii won't give a tax credit to a webisode series or short film that is distributed exclusively on the Internet.[1] Nor does stock footage qualify for a Hawaiian state tax credit. So much for being able to pay for your honeymoon with state tax credits by shooting background footage!

Qualified expenses typically include only those costs incurred in the credit-granting state, such as:

• Cast and crew salaries

• Equipment rentals

• Lodging, transportation, and other location fees

• Set construction and production studio rentals

> **Example**: Jared shoots a sci-fi sequel to *The Wrath of Grapes*, called *Planet of the Grapes*, and needs a jungle location. He decides to shoot in Hawaii (who

wouldn't!?) and wants to use the state's tax incentives. He registers for business in Hawaii (a requirement), buys production insurance in New York, and flies to Maui with his cast and crew to shoot. Although the cast and crew salaries paid for services rendered in Hawaii would qualify for the tax incentives, the production insurance purchased in New York would not.

In addition to making sure your key expenses are incurred within the crediting state, you need to make sure that you spend a threshold amount within that state.

Example: Fiona is shooting in New Jersey, which requires that 60% of the production company's total production expenses, excluding post-production costs, be incurred within the state. If she spends 45% of her production budget on New York equipment and studio rentals, she will receive no New Jersey tax credit.

Here are some tips for taking advantage of state tax incentives:

- Some states do *not* let you include above-the-line costs (e.g., salaries for writers, directors, producers, principal cast) as qualifying production expenses.
- State residency requirements are important. You will often qualify for a higher tax credit if you hire state residents rather than an out-of-state crew.[2]
- Many states offer additional incentives for filmmakers who shoot in economically undeveloped areas.
- States often have specific rules regarding loan-out companies, state registration, and local taxes.
- As you might be able to gather, these credits and rebates are designed to bring film productions into a particular state and incentivize them to spend the majority of their production budgets on local crew, cast, and production expenses. For this reason, they may not be applicable for a filmmaker who is shooting all over the map.

PROD. CO.

QUALIFIED PRODUCTION EXPENSES AND LOAN-OUT COMPANIES

Be careful when an actor or director is working through a loan-out company (see "Loan-Out Companies," p. 42). Typically, payments to loan-out companies, such as an actor's salary, only count toward qualified production expenses if that actor's loan-out company is registered to do business in your production state and files an income tax return in that state. If the actor has a loan-out company, you might need to include a provision in the performer's services loan-out agreement that requires:

1. The loan-out company to register to do business and file a tax return in the production state

2. Giving your production company the power of attorney to register the loan-out company to do business in the production state if the loan-out company fails to do so within a certain period of time

TYPES OF PRODUCTION TAX CREDITS

There are three types of film tax credits that are offered by various states, some of which are more beneficial to filmmakers than others:

Refundable credits. If you have applied for and have been accepted by a state that offers filmmakers a refundable tax credit, you will receive a tax refund from that state. That's right, the state cuts you a check equal to a percentage of the qualifying expenses incurred in that state! These funds can reduce your tax liability below zero; in other words, even if you have no state tax liability, you may be eligible to get money back!

Example: On the shores of Lake Michigan, Moira is shooting her first noir feature, *Lamprey on Me*, about the adventures of a jawless detective. For filmmakers who spend at least $50,000 in Michigan, the state offers a refundable tax credit of up to 42% of the filmmaker's qualified expenses on Michigan expenditures. Assume that after Moira applies for the Michigan film production credit, she spends $100,000 in qualified expenses in Michigan. Once she files a Michigan business tax return at the end of the year, she can expect to receive a $40,000 refund check from the state of Michigan.[3]

Refundable credits are often preferred by both filmmakers and lenders; unlike *transferable* credits (see below), they don't need to be sold to a third party in order for the filmmaker to get her money. As a result, a filmmaker with a refundable tax credit will usually receive more money from a lender than if the filmmaker had a transferable tax credit.

Transferable credits. Transferable tax credits are used to offset state tax liability. They are not refundable. In other words, if you don't owe any taxes in the state in which you shot, you do not get cash back from the state. What you can do, however, is sell the transferable credit to someone else for them to offset their state tax liability. Filmmakers typically use *tax credit brokers* to sell their transferable tax credits for them. Of course, the sale is always for less than the face value of the tax credit; in fact, this credit nets a filmmaker less money than the refundable tax credit because both the broker and the lender take a cut before the filmmaker receives her money (see "Credits into Cash" later in this chapter).

Example: Moira is shooting the next film in her detective trilogy, *Lampreying Mantis*, on the other side of Lake Michigan, in Illinois. For filmmakers who spend at least $100,000 in Illinois on projects with a running time that exceed one hour, Illinois offers a transferable tax credit of 30% of the filmmaker's qualified Illinois production expenses.[4] Assume that after applying for the Illinois film production credit, Moira spends $100,000 in qualified expenses in Illinois. Unlike the refund check she received in Illinois, this time she will receive a tax credit certificate, which she can either use to offset her Illinois state taxes or sell to a third party for them to offset their Michigan state taxes.

Nonrefundable and nontransferable credits. This is the least flexible tax credit arrangement: Filmmakers don't get a refund and don't get to sell their credits.

All they get to do is to offset their own or their production company's state taxes with these credits. However, for a company that does business in a state over several years, these nonrefundable and nontransferable tax credits can carry over from year to year.

Example: Moira is shooting her last crime thriller, *Predator and Lamprey*, in an abandoned lighthouse in her production company's home state of Maine. For filmmakers who spend at least $75,000 on qualified production costs in Maine, that state offers a nontransferable, nonrefundable 5% tax credit.[5] She applies for Maine's Certified Media Production Income Tax Credit and spends $100,000 in qualified production costs. When she files her state tax return and attaches the Tax Reimbursement and Credit Certificate she's received from Maine's Department of Economic and Community Development, she will receive a tax credit of 5%, which she can use to reduce her Maine state taxes by $5,000. She must use this credit herself and cannot sell this credit to any third party.

PROD. CO.

By now you're probably thinking: "Free money from the state? What's the catch?" The catch is that due to the popularity of these programs, states can quickly run out of funds, so it pays to get applications in early in the state's fiscal year. Credits are usually offered on a first-come, first-served basis. Furthermore, state tax credit programs are in constant flux, and a state that offered a great incentive one year may end up curtailing its program simply because popularity among filmmakers has drained the tax credit funds dry. It's a constantly changing market, one that requires serious attention to financial detail and reporting. Check the production incentives of your state and its neighbors before deciding where to shoot.

APPLYING FOR STATE TAX CREDITS:
AN OVERVIEW OF THE PROCESS

Because the processes and types of incentives differ from state to state, a detailed account of each state's procedures is not possible here.[6] However, the following steps are fairly common:

1. Research the tax and rebate incentives in the states in which you may be shooting. If those states offer transferable tax credits, you might want to get in touch with a tax credit broker to understand what the market is like for selling the credits.

2. Contact the state film commission offices in states in which you will potentially be shooting (see Appendix E, "State Film Commissions," p. 407). They can supply you with information on that state's production incentive programs, how to apply for them, and which state agency administers them.

3. Most states have a minimum budget threshold and, for big budget films, a cap on the amount of credit available. Prepare a detailed budget that lists the qualified expenses you intend on incurring in your target state. Make sure to include details on hiring local cast and crew.

4. States have requirements detailing the percentage of a production or minimum number of shooting days that must take place in the target state. Prepare a shooting breakdown that lists the in-state locations and facilities where you plan to shoot, to demonstrate the percentage of the shoot that will take place in-state.

5. You will be asked to submit an application form, sometimes no less than 10 days in advance of shooting. The application form will probably ask you to submit:

   a. A budget, as in Step 3, that lists the qualified expenditures

   b. A shooting schedule

   c. Production facility and location information

   d. List of wages for both resident and nonresident employees; some states exclude above-the-line expenses (writer, director, producer, speaking performers) from the definition of qualified expenses[7]

   e. Evidence of a completion bond, if needed

6. After you submit the initial application, you may be required to schedule an appointment to discuss your application. It's important to note that you may be required to have the producer and the production office accountant at the meeting.

7. Some states, such as New York, will issue a "conditional approval" of the film. You will receive a certificate of conditional eligibility from the state. Note that this approval is *conditional* in nature, and if you fail to adhere to the very specific tax credit budgetary requirements, **your approval will be revoked, and you will be responsible for repaying any monies loaned to you by lenders (see below) based on the tax credit. You may also end up forfeiting your film itself if the film's copyright was used as collateral to secure the loan.**

8. Once you've received conditional approval, you'll be required to notify the state production office and keep them updated on your:

   a. Shooting schedule

   b. Cast and crew call sheet for first day of production

   c. Current budget

9. Once the film has wrapped, and typically after postproduction has also been completed, you will need to submit a final application to the state office in charge of administering the film incentive program. This typically includes:

   a. State government final application tax credit forms

   b. Finalized versions of the following:
   - Accounting for the film
   - Film budget
   - Shooting schedule
   - Cast and crew list
   - Payroll reports

   c. An independent audit

PROD.
CO.

Failure to submit all the proper materials at this stage can cause you to lose the film tax credit that you worked so hard to gain!

Make sure to keep copies of all records, expenses, reports, and receipts. State film offices may audit you up to several years after your production has wrapped, and many states require an audit. Be sure to hire production accountants who are familiar with the processes of the states in which you are shooting, since nuanced rules could disqualify certain expenses. This point cannot be emphasized enough!

CREDITS INTO CASH

Having an entitlement to a future tax credit is all well and good, but how do you turn it into cash you can use *now* for your production? Your quickest option is to *borrow* money against the resale value of the credit by working with a lender such as a bank or an *asset-backed lender* (ABL). Both these types of lenders evaluate your tax credit and offer you less than the face value of the credit (hey, they have to make money, too). ABLs may offer a loan of only 80% or 90% of the credit's value, whereas a bank will charge interest and processing fees. Be prepared to pay either lender's legal expenses as they set their legal team to analyzing your tax incentive and preparing the loan documents.

PROD. CO.

You may get more money borrowing against a rebate or refundable tax credit rather than a transferable one. The reason is simple: You get the rebate or refund and the bank deals directly with you. For a transferable credit, if you can't use it, you have to sell it to recoup its value. As a result, the lender may lend against 86% of the tax certificate's value. (Production companies typically receive 82–88% of the face value of the credit from the sale.)

Example: Jarrett is producing the film *The Naked Mole Rat's Revenge* in New Jersey, which, as of this writing, offers a 20% *transferable* tax credit. He submits his paperwork and receives a provisional notice that his tax credit will be $200,000, which he brings to an ABL to borrow against. The ABL agrees to lend him 90% of the value of the tax credit certificate, but because the tax credit is transferable, it will have to be sold to a New Jersey taxpaying entity, which in turn will also pay less than the face value of the tax credit certificate (perhaps only 88%). As a result, the ABL will lend Jarrett 90% against the already discounted purchase price of the tax certificate, for an up-front amount of 79.2% of the credit (88% × 90% = 79.2%). So, if he shoots in New Jersey, he will receive a loan of $158,400 for his $200,000 tax credit certificate.

Now let's assume that Jarrett had shot in Hawaii instead of New Jersey, where the tax credit is a *refundable* 20% (except in Honolulu and elsewhere on the island of Oahu, where it is only 15%). Jarrett receives his $200,000 tax credit certificate. Because the tax credit is refundable and not transferable, it doesn't have to be sold to a third party in order for the ABL to get its money. Now the ABL might issue a loan of 90% of the value of the tax certificate, with no third-party deductions. Here's the breakdown: Jarrett gets a loan of $180,000 (90% × $200,000), as opposed to the $158,400 he would have received for shooting in New Jersey… more than enough for several rounds of piña coladas at the hotel tiki bar!

Of course Jarrett must take into account the transportation and housing costs involved in shooting in our nation's tropical paradise and whether or not the swaying palm trees fit the look and feel of his film. After all, how could a naked mole rat feel vengeful after all those piña coladas?

WORKING WITH ASSET-BACKED LENDERS

ABLs are often more flexible and quicker in their lending policies than banks. ABLs will usually lend against both transferable and refundable tax credits, whereas a bank may only lend against a refundable credit. It all depends on where you are shooting, however; if you are shooting in Canada and using Canadian tax credits, a bank may be the way to go, since banks have largely dominated Canadian tax credit lending for years.

PROD. CO.

The ABL Lending Process

1. It's a good idea to establish a relationship with a lender early on. ABLs may help you with the initial stages of selecting a favorable tax credit issuing state. You should approach them at least two to three months prior to principal photography.

2. You will be asked to fill out a financing application. Be prepared to supply the lender with the following information:

   a. Production company contact info (as well as any co-production companies)

   b. Detailed information on the production itself:

      • Shooting schedule, expected start and wrap dates

      • Locations

      • Above-the-line crew

      • Estimated duration

   c. Contact information for the production company's:

      • Bank

      • Production attorneys

      • Completion guarantors, if any

      • Insurance agents

   d. In addition to the application, you will be asked to provide:

      • A complete budget

      • A detailed financing plan

- Cash-flow schedule
- Your shooting schedule
- Biographies of your producer and director
- Correspondence between the production company and the state film incentive program
- Synopsis of the project
- An estimate of the amount of tax credits being sought

3. The ABL will review your application and materials, and if you pass muster, it will issue a *term sheet* detailing the conditions of the loan. Make sure to have your attorney review this document carefully. You may also be asked to give the ABL a deposit to cover its legal expenses.

4. If you are shooting in a transferable tax credit state, the ABL usually has relationships with tax credit brokers and will facilitate the process between you and the broker.

PROD.
CO.

BE ORGANIZED AND PREPARED

Nothing will kill a potential lender's interest in you more quickly than disorganization. This is a process that requires you to work closely with accountants, financiers, lenders, and maybe brokers. It simply can't be done at the last minute or "by the seat of the pants." Remember, lenders aren't lending you money because they have a passion for your film. They are lending you money because they believe they can recoup *even more* money from the tax credits that you will receive when you successfully comply with the issuing state's requirements. If the lender gets the sense that you may fail to qualify for the state tax credits, either through your mismanagement or your lack of understanding of qualified production expenses, they will not lend you money. And nothing gives them the willies faster than a disorganized producer.

Remember:

- You should work with a qualified accountant, preferably one with experience in film production and tax credits.
- Your cash-flow schedule, financing documents, and budget should all line up. Nothing is worse than showing a lender a budget of $2 million and a cash-flow schedule of $1.75 million.
- You need to really understand the qualified production expense rules of the incentive-granting state. For instance, some states require you to order camera equipment rentals through a local vendor to qualify as a production expense. If you receive a loan from the lender and then fail to qualify for the state tax credits or you have them revoked, *the lender may be able to seize your film as collateral to satisfy the debt.*

TIPS FOR SELECTING A GOOD TAX CREDIT STATE

From a tax credit perspective, there are a number of factors you want to consider when selecting the best states in which to shoot:

- *The nature of the tax credit itself.* Refundable? Transferable? Nonrefundable and nontransferable? Bottom line: Are the tax credits sellable? In other words, does your production company need to use them itself or can it sell them to a third party?

- *Are the tax credits subject to recapture?* What happens if someone buys your tax credits and after the purchase, the credit-issuing state discovers that you've been fast and loose with your accounting or were just plain mistaken about how much money you spent in qualified production expenses? The answer depends on the state: In some states your credit may be subject to *recapture* by the issuing state, which will revoke the credit. So, not only can the state bring a claim against you, but so can the purchaser, who has effectively purchased a worthless tax credit. Since there is an inherent risk on the part of the purchaser in recapture states, film tax credits sell for less money in these states. Other states are "clean states," meaning that a good-faith purchaser for value of your film tax credit gets to keep the film tax credit you sold them while the issuing state is bringing you up on charges of fraud.

- *Is it the right location?* Don't lose sight of the fact that your audience will not see your tax credits; they will only see the location where you decided to shoot. You might like the Massachusetts tax credit program, but if you're shooting a western, you might find it hard to make Martha's Vineyard look like Montana's badlands. You also need to take into account whether it is worth the cost of transporting and lodging cast and crew just for the sake of a few more percentage points of tax credit.

- *Is my film's content right for the state?* Some states are beginning to scrutinize the content of the films seeking state production incentives to ensure that they portray the location state in a favorable light. If a state's laws stipulate that "movies underwritten by the state should help promote it as a tourist destination,"[8] a movie that (1) paints a negative picture of the location state or (2) contains patently offensive material might be rejected for production incentive funding by that state's film commission. For instance, the Michigan film commissioner rejected the film *The Women,* in large part because it depicted "realistic cannibalism."[9] I guess some states don't like films about people who love people.... [10]

- *Other incentives.* In addition to state tax credits, some states offer other production incentives such as grants to filmmakers and waiving of sales tax.

- *Contact the state film offices.* Most states have a film office set up to encourage production in that state. They're wonderful resources to find up-to-the-minute information about that state's film incentives.

- *Consider federal incentives as well.* Currently, the federal government offers a tax incentive[11] for investors who invest in films with budgets that range between

$1 million and $20 million and with at least 75% of its production completed within the United States. This incentive allows an investor to deduct money invested in a qualifying film from the investor's passive income earned in that same year.

"Incentives change every day. It is important to work with people who have up-to-the-minute information and the experience to help a producer select the right combination of incentives that will best serve the film's production and financing needs and maximize the upfront credit amount."

—Michael Hansen, managing director, Three Point Capital, an asset-backed lender

PROD.
CO.

4

DEVELOPMENT

CREATING, ACQUIRING, AND MANAGING
THE FILM PROPERTY

During development, ideas and concepts are turned into screenplays; literary rights are acquired; life stories are purchased. In short, this is the stage of a film's life cycle in which the film property first takes shape.

No matter what kind of audiovisual production a filmmaker wants to make— a narrative film, a television commercial, a documentary, an industrial video—the filmmaker will need to have the legal right to tell that particular story. To put it bluntly, this is one of the most important legal issues facing filmmakers: A distributor will not pick up a film for distribution if the story rights have not been obtained! Even if you plan on distributing your film by yourself, you will need to promise all your subdistributors and exhibitors (iTunes, Amazon.com, YouTube) that you have the necessary rights to distribute the film.

Of critical importance during development is the protection of the copyright in the screenplay. You need to make sure that the copyright is properly registered, that the script does not use anybody else's copyrighted material without permission, and that any writers whom you have hired have properly transferred their copyrights to your production company.

When you are collaborating with another writer, hiring a screenwriter, or acquiring literary, life, or other rights, you must have signed contracts. A handshake deal will not legally transfer the copyright or create a work made for hire.

This section covers legal issues concerning:

- How to protect rights in ideas. (See "Idea Rights," p. 77.)
- Writing the screenplay by yourself. (See "Writing the Screenplay by Yourself," p. 87.)
- Collaborating with other writers. (See "Writing Collaboration," p. 90.)
- Acquiring the rights to somebody's life story. (See "Life Story Rights," p. 124.)
- Optioning and purchasing a screenplay. (See "Acquiring Screenplay Rights," p. 101.)
- Adapting a screenplay from another work. (See "Screenplay Adaptations," p. 117.)
- Hiring a screenwriter. (See "Hiring a Screenwriter," p. 111.)
- Protecting the copyright in your screenplay. (See "The Care and Feeding of Your Copyright," p. 131.)

DEV.

7

IDEA RIGHTS: PROTECTING YOUR PITCHES AND AVOIDING IDEA "THEFT"

Without a doubt, a copyright is the best way to protect a screenplay from being stolen. However, a filmmaker may have only an *idea* for a film or television program—a concept that has yet to be turned into a screenplay—and copyright law *does not* protect ideas. In fact, even though they are valuable to the filmmaker, ideas can be very hard to protect *legally*: The law starts with the presumption that ideas are free for anyone to use.

Generally, for a filmmaker to protect an idea when he is pitching it to a production company or movie studio, the idea *must be novel* (see below) and *the filmmaker needs to enter into a contract* with the party to whom he is pitching the idea. In essence, the filmmaker must get the production company to agree that the filmmaker will be compensated if the production company uses the filmmaker's idea.

NONDISCLOSURE AGREEMENTS AND SUBMISSION RELEASES

If possible, the filmmaker should have the production company sign a *nondisclosure agreement* (NDA). This is a contract in which the production company will agree that:

- The idea is unique and valuable.

- The idea is the filmmaker's proprietary information.

- The production company will keep this idea confidential.

- The production company will not exploit the idea without permission.

- If the production company does exploit the idea, the filmmaker will be compensated.

> **REALITY CHECK**
>
> A filmmaker generally does not have the leverage to make a Hollywood studio sign an NDA; however, he or she may be able to convince a smaller production company or a local advertising agency to sign one.

Even if the filmmaker cannot get the production company to sign an NDA, he may still be able to create an *implied contract* or an *express contract* (see "Express and Implied Contracts," p. 371) with the production company in which the production company agrees not to use the filmmaker's idea without compensating the filmmaker.

To establish a claim for breach of implied-in-fact contract for an idea, the filmmaker must show that he or she:

DEV.

- Prepared the work

- Disclosed the work to the production company *for sale*

- Did so under circumstances from which it could be concluded that the production company voluntarily accepted the disclosure, knowing the conditions on which it was tendered and the reasonable value of the work[1]

This contract can be created orally and backed up by a written confirmation of its terms. For instance, you can reiterate your agreement in a follow-up e-mail to the person to whom you are pitching your idea.

More typically, the production company has the leverage in the situation and will require the filmmaker to sign a *submission release* before hearing the filmmaker's pitch. The submission release is a document that largely exonerates the production company if it exploits an idea similar to the one the filmmaker is pitching. Production companies generally demand that filmmakers sign a submission release covering any unsolicited material and pitches the filmmaker wants the production company to evaluate.

Be careful how you offer your idea for sale: One U.S. Court of Appeals recently held that an offer to *partner up* on producing a program based on a creator's idea did not support an implied contract claim for the sale of an idea.[2] Although this decision was later overturned, it illustrates how courts can be very strict when construing whether a contract for the sale of an idea has been formed.

***THE BOTTOM LINE:* Once you start telling people your idea without the benefit of a contract, you may have given up any property right you have in that idea.**

SAFEGUARDING SOCRATES

Adam Auteur has a great movie idea: He wants to write a movie about the secret life of the great Greek philosopher Socrates. In Auteur's story, Socrates was the same person as Confucius: an immortal being who leaves China and settles in ancient Greece. Auteur's idea is also novel in that Socrates will be played on screen at all times by three people—like the chorus in a Greek tragedy.

Auteur wants to pitch the concept to Barbara, a Major Studio, Inc., executive, with the expectation that if Barbara likes his idea, Major Studio, Inc., will hire Auteur to write the screenplay. Auteur wants to make sure that his idea is protected so that Major Studio, Inc., can't make the film without him.

Auteur can try to protect both the property right and confidentiality of his idea through an NDA. However, because he is not pitching to a small production company, he probably doesn't have the leverage to get the studio to sign an NDA.

In fact, the opposite is true: Major Studio, Inc., doesn't want to blindly agree that Auteur's idea is Auteur's personal property. Major Studio, Inc., hears pitches every day, many of which are similar to each other. It does not want to be stopped from developing another filmmaker's Socrates-based story merely because it is similar to the one it heard from Auteur. To protect itself, it may refuse to listen to Auteur's pitch until Auteur has signed a submission release, which waives the filmmaker's right to sue Major Studio, Inc., if it develops a similar movie.

Because he is pitching to a big Hollywood studio, Auteur may have to choose between signing a submission release and not pitching at all. However, if Auteur is represented by an agent or an attorney, they might be able to negotiate a waiver of the submission release requirement, letting him try to create an oral contract during the pitch. Then, during the pitch meeting, Auteur might be able to create an implied contract between him and the production company by getting the Major Studio, Inc., executive to orally agree to compensate him for his idea should the production company decide to use it.

***THE BOTTOM LINE:* From a legal perspective, to protect his idea, Auteur should get the studio to agree to his contract terms *before* he pitches. From a business perspective, Auteur had better be careful not to sound too much like a lawyer or the meeting may suddenly be canceled!**

DEV.

GOALS AND DEALS

When a filmmaker pitches to a production company, each side wants a certain amount of legal protection. Here's a snapshot of what each side wants:

- The *filmmaker* wants to ensure that he can pitch his idea without fear of it being used by the production company without his permission. Ideally, he will have the production company sign an NDA. Barring that, he wants to avoid signing the production company's submission release. As a further step, the filmmaker might try to enter into an implied or express contract with the production company during the pitch meeting, followed up by a written restatement of that contract via e-mail or certified mail.

- The *production company,* on the other hand, wants to ensure that they can use ideas similar to the filmmaker's idea without fear of being sued by the filmmaker. Ideally, they will have the filmmaker sign a submission release. If that is not possible, they should be wary of entering into any implied contracts with the filmmaker during the pitch meeting.

DEV.

DEAL POINTS: SUBMISSION RELEASE[3]

The production company usually requires a filmmaker to sign a submission release prior to hearing a filmmaker's pitch. Submission releases usually contain the following provisions.

No Liability for Exploiting Similar Ideas

The production company will not be held responsible if it exploits a similar idea to the one which the filmmaker has pitched. *Note:* In film contracts, the term *exploits* usually means "to develop or sell a property" (e.g., a production company exploits an idea by commissioning a screenplay based on it).

No Contractual or Fiduciary Relationship

The filmmaker agrees that she has not entered into a contract with the production company for the sale of the idea, nor is there a fiduciary relationship between the parties that would require the production company to act only in the filmmaker's best interests.

Representations and Warranties of Authorship and Indemnification

The filmmaker must promise that she is the sole creator of the idea and that she will indemnify the production company if the production company is sued by somebody else laying claim to the idea. (See Appendix C, "Representations and Warranties; Indemnification," p. 386.)

Free Use of Nonprotected Property

The production company may freely use anything the artist discloses that is not protectable as "literary property." Because ideas are not protected by copyright, and the production company has not agreed to a contract that protects the filmmaker's ideas, this paragraph may mean that the production company is free to use any ideas pitched or disclosed by the filmmaker!

Now let's take a look at the opposite of a submission release: the NDA.

DEAL POINTS: THE NONDISCLOSURE AGREEMENT (NDA)

NDAs are the reverse of submission releases; they allow filmmakers to protect their ideas. NDAs usually contain the following provisions.

DEV.

Confidentiality

The production company must agree to keep the disclosed ideas confidential. The production company also agrees that the confidential information is the *property of* the filmmaker. This is a critical recitation, since ideas and concepts are legally difficult to protect as property without a contract.

Definition of Confidential Material

The confidential information is usually defined in terms of both (1) those materials, oral and written, that a filmmaker submits to the production company, and (2) those materials the production company itself creates in order to evaluate the project.

Exclusions from the Definition of Confidential Material

This section defines what is *not* considered confidential or proprietary to the filmmaker (and thus is unprotected by the contract). Typically *excluded* from the definition of confidentiality in this section is:

• Material that the filmmaker discloses to others on a nonconfidential basis

• Material that the production company can show it developed independently of the filmmaker

- Material that becomes publicly known
- Material that is in the public domain (e.g., clichéd concepts, common plots, stereotypical characters, etc.)

Agreement to Evaluate

The production company agrees that it is receiving the confidential information for the purpose of evaluating the material for possible production. If the production company passes on the project, it agrees not to use the material. If the production company wants to use the material, it must agree to enter into an agreement with the filmmaker for its purchase and/or exploitation.

Representations and Warranties of Authorship and Indemnification

The filmmaker must promise that she is the sole creator of the idea and that she will indemnify the production company if the production company is sued by somebody else laying claim to the idea.

DEV. # LAW: PROTECTING IDEAS AND THE "NOVELTY" REQUIREMENT

U.S. law is very wary about protecting ideas. To receive any protection at all, even by contract, an idea must be *novel,* that is, *new* and *unique.*

If there is a contract between the producer and the production company, the producer's idea only needs to be novel to the production company or other party who is hearing the idea for the first time.[4]

> *Example:* If the producer had pitched the same idea first to another production company, which had agreed to keep the idea confidential, the idea would still be novel as far as the second production company was concerned. The producer could contract with the second production company for the idea's disclosure.

However, *without a contract* between the producer and the production company, the producer has an almost impossible task ahead of him when trying to sue a production company that has used his idea without permission. The producer must prove that his idea was so unique and original that *no one else in the world* had ever conceived of it!

To make things even tougher, some ideas are so unoriginal not even a contract will protect them.

One New York court[1] listed the following factors as among those courts will use to judge the novelty of an idea:

- The idea's specificity or generality, i.e., is it a generic concept or one of specific application?

- How common an idea is, i.e., how many people know of this idea?
- How unique the idea is, i.e., how different is this idea from generally known ideas?
- The commercial availability of the idea, i.e., how widespread is the idea's use in the film and television industry?

However, as the court pointed out, an idea will *not* be considered novel if:

- It is merely a variation on a basic theme[5] or
- It is merely a clever or useful adaptation of existing knowledge

NOT EVERY GOOD IDEA IS A "NOVEL" IDEA

One well-known case involved the idea for *The Cosby Show*.[8] A producer pitched NBC on the idea of "combining the family situation comedy theme with an all-black cast." NBC turned him down and then went on to develop *The Cosby Show*. When the producer sued, he lost. The court stated that the producer's idea was not novel and therefore not subject to legal protection from unauthorized use because he had "merely combined two ideas which had been circulating in the industry for a number of years—namely, the family situation comedy, which was a standard formula, and the casting of black actors in nonstereotypical roles."

DEV.

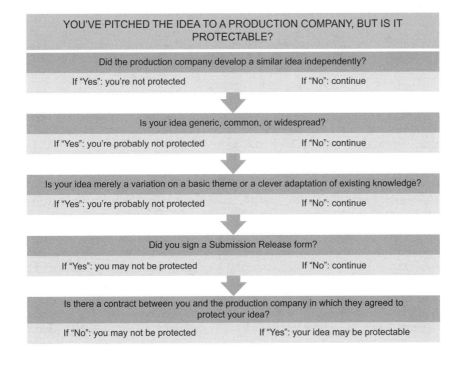

YOU'VE PITCHED THE IDEA TO A PRODUCTION COMPANY, BUT IS IT PROTECTABLE?

Did the production company develop a similar idea independently?

If "Yes": you're not protected   If "No": continue

Is your idea generic, common, or widespread?

If "Yes": you're probably not protected   If "No": continue

Is your idea merely a variation on a basic theme or a clever adaptation of existing knowledge?

If "Yes": you're probably not protected   If "No": continue

Did you sign a Submission Release form?

If "Yes": you may not be protected   If "No": continue

Is there a contract between you and the production company in which they agreed to protect your idea?

If "No": you may not be protected   If "Yes": your idea may be protectable

For instance, the "idea of a reality television show where people compete for a prize is a basic staple of modern television programming."[6]

Furthermore, just as in copyright law, the production company will not be liable to the producer if it can prove that it came up with its similar movie concept through its own initiative or through wholly independent means.[7] (See "The Doctrine of Independent Creation," p. 340.)

BUSINESS ISSUES: FINANCES AND COSTS

Whether or not a filmmaker can demand that a production company sign an NDA prior to the filmmaker's disclosure depends on the filmmaker's leverage.

Generally, neither a submission release nor an NDA requires one party to pay the other as part of that contract. However, in the case of any implied or express contract that the filmmaker may try to create during the meeting, the production company should agree to compensate the filmmaker a *reasonable amount* if it ends up using the filmmaker's idea.

Other than attorney's fees in drafting and negotiating the NDA or submission release, the only costs incurred here are the costs of sending a follow-up letter via certified mail.

DEV.

NEGOTIATION TIPS AND TRICKS

Often a filmmaker's agent or attorney can negotiate with the production company and get them to waive the requirement of a submission release.

Step by Step: Protecting an Idea

1. Put your idea into written form. Make it as full, complete, and expressive as you can, and register it with the U.S. Copyright Office. (See "Copyright Registration," p. 136.)

2. If possible, try to have the production company sign an NDA.

3. If obtaining an NDA is not possible, have your agent or attorney negotiate a waiver of the submission release form.

4. In the pitch meeting, try to create a contractual obligation contingent on the movie studio using your idea. Don't try to sound like a lawyer here, just be clear, casual, and enthusiastic. It's really a question of finesse. If you sound like you're "playing lawyer," they will bring in their own attorney or, more likely, stop the meeting right there. *Note:* I am emphatically *not* suggesting that you trick them into agreeing to anything; in fact, there needs to be a "meeting of the minds" of all parties in order for a contract to be formed. No, what I'm

saying is that now is the time be especially friendly and clear; use all your people skills here.

Example: Say something like, "I'm really excited about pitching my show to you. But, before I do, I just want to make sure that you guys are going to treat it as my property until we have a more formal deal in place… and you're not going to discuss it with anybody outside your company… and, of course, if you do decide to use it, I'm going to be paid a reasonable amount for it. We can work out the other details later."

5. If the movie studio executive agrees, you may have a contract. You should wait for the executive to show that she agrees with your requirements, either verbally or with some physically gesture, such as a nod. Generally, mere silence is not assent.

6. Follow up with an e-mail and certified letter restating the terms of the oral contract. Your claim to ownership of your idea will be strengthened if the production executive to whom you pitched agrees to your terms again after she has heard your pitch.

Example: "Thank you for taking the time to hear my pitch concerning my proposed screenplay. As we discussed, you have agreed not to use my ideas without compensating me a reasonable amount. Thanks, too, for agreeing to keep my ideas confidential. I look forward to the possibility of working with you and your company in creating the first movie to show the secret life of Socrates."

7. As a bonus, your ownership claim will be further reinforced if you can get the studio to state that they've never heard an idea like yours (notice how I rephrased the "novelty" requirement).

Example: "It was so great to hear you say that you thought my idea was unique. I think so too, but it's nice to hear it confirmed by someone whose opinion I respect." Generally, you should only introduce the issue if they've mentioned it at the meeting, after being blown away by your perfect pitch, of course.

Follow-Up

Once the filmmaker has pitched his or her idea, the next step is for the production company to either offer the filmmaker a deal or to pass on the project—that is, turn the filmmaker down.

- *If the movie studio has offered to pick up the project,* the kind of deal it will offer will depend on the nature of the project and the reputation of the filmmaker.
  - The production company might want to commission the filmmaker to write a screenplay. (See "Hiring a Screenwriter," p. 111.)
  - The production company may want to purchase a finished screenplay from the filmmaker. (See "Acquiring Screenplay Rights," p. 101.)
  - The production company may want to option the finished screenplay (an option is the exclusive right to purchase the screenplay). (See "The Screenplay Option/Purchase," p. 102.)

DEV.

- If you own a production company and have pitched to a studio, you may be offered a production services agreement. (See "Production Services Agreement," p. 149.)
- *If the movie studio has passed on the project,* the filmmaker should request the return of all his materials, or alternatively, their destruction. This helps to protect the film-maker against the uncontrolled disclosure of his materials and, he hopes, his ideas.

DEV.

> ### CAUTION
>
> - Be careful how you phrase your verbal contract; be sensitive with your approach and tone. Sometimes sounding too much like a lawyer can turn an otherwise friendly business negotiation into an adversarial relationship.
>
> - Listen and look for the production company's response; the production company must acknowledge and agree that you are disclosing the idea to them with the understanding that you expect them to pay you at least a "reasonable value" for your work, should they decide to use it.
>
> - Even to be protected by a contract, your idea must be novel to the recipient. The idea "need not reflect the flash of genius, but it must show genuine novelty and invention, and not a merely clever or useful adaptation of existing knowledge."[9]

How to Protect Your Pitch

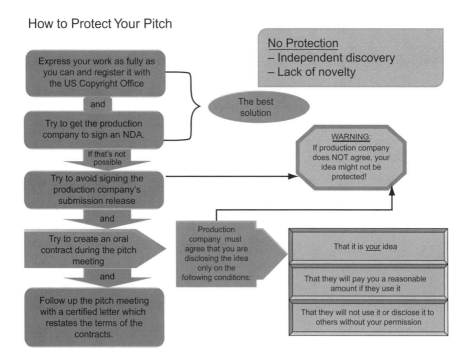

CREATING A SCREENPLAY

Creating and protecting a screenplay can be both artistically and legally challenging:

- Legally, the simplest route is to write it yourself. (See "Writing the Screenplay by Yourself," p. 87.)

- Even if you are the sole author of a screenplay, if you're adapting another person's work, you will need his or her permission to do so. (See "Screenplay Adaptations," p. 117.)

- If you are writing with another person, you should be aware of the legal implications of collaborative writing and joint authorship. (See "Writing Collaboration," p. 90.)

- If you are basing the script on someone's life story, you will need to secure the rights. (See "Life Story Rights," p. 124.)

- Regardless of how the screenplay is written, you should protect it by registering the copyright. (See "Copyright Registration," p. 136.)

    but:

- If, instead of writing the screenplay yourself, you are buying or optioning the screenplay, you have a slightly different set of concerns. (See "Acquiring Screenplay Rights," p. 101.)

WRITING THE SCREENPLAY BY YOURSELF (SOLE AUTHORSHIP)

From a legal perspective, writing a screenplay by yourself is the easiest scenario. Assuming that the screenplay is wholly original with you, meaning that you haven't adapted it from someone else's work, you haven't written it with anyone else, and you haven't been hired to write it, the question of ownership of the screenplay's copyright is simple: You own it.

- You will still need to register the copyright to your screenplay. (See "Copyright Registration," p. 136.)

- Additionally, you'll need to assign the screenplay copyright to the production company that shoots the script, even if the company is yours. (See "Copyright Recordation, Assignments, and Transfers," p. 139.)

SOLE AUTHORSHIP

Woodrow Writer is finishing up his documentary screenplay, *Food for Worms: The Exciting World of Compost.* He has not based the film on another work, such as a graphic novel or a play.

Woodrow did get the *idea* for the script from watching several farming documentaries made in the 1950s, but because he only used *ideas* from these films, rather than scenes, dialogue, or other *expressions,* Woodrow does not have to worry about those film-makers suing him for copyright infringement.

Woodrow did take a few pages of voiceover narration directly from *The Encyclopedia of Vermont Farming,* published in 1897, but because the copyright to that book has long since expired and the book is now in the *public domain,* he may freely use any part of that book (of course, so can anybody else). (See Appendix A, "Public Domain," p. 332.)

Having had a hard time finding other filmmakers interested in writing about controlled decomposition of organic matter, Woodrow has written the entire screenplay by himself. Copyright law considers Woodrow the sole author of the screenplay, and thus Woodrow is the script's sole copyright owner. In fact, anyone who wants to take the script and make a movie from it, write an article or book based on it, or turn it into a first-person-shooter video game must first get Woodrow's permission.

But:

If Woodrow had been employed by a production company when he wrote the script, and writing the script was part of the scope of his duties there, the script would be considered a work made for hire. Even if Woodrow worked as an independent contractor for the production company, the script would be a work made for hire if the company signed Woodrow to a work-made-for-hire agreement. In both these scenarios, the production company would own the copyright to the screenplay, and the company would be the only one authorized to license the screenplay for others to use. (See "Work Made for Hire," p. 344.)

Registering the Copyright to Your Work

The moment your script is finished, register it with the U.S. Copyright Office. Don't be fooled into thinking that mailing a copy of your script to yourself or depositing it with the Writer's Guild is the same as registration. It's not. Only registration with the federal government will allow you to take full advantage of copyright protection. Besides, it's only $35 if you use the new Copyright Office online registration system (www.copyright.gov/eco/).

For a guide to registering your screenplay, see "Copyright Registration," p. 136, or download Circular 45, "Copyright Registration for Motion Pictures Including Video Recordings," from the U.S. Copyright Office at www.copyright.gov/circs/circ45.pdf.

GOALS AND DEALS

As the sole author, you alone get to decide whether to sell your script or to accept or reject a particular deal. Oh, the power! Some of the deals you could face include:

- Producing your own script (see "Production," p. 227)
- Selling your script for movie production (see "The Screenplay Option/ Purchase," p. 102)
- Optioning your script (see "The Screenplay Option/Purchase," p. 102)
- Licensing your script for novelizations or other adaptation (see "Screenplay Adaptations," p. 117)
- If it's a television program and you own a production company, a television network may want to pay you to produce it (see "Production Services Agreement," p. 149)

DEV.

Step by Step: Writing the Screenplay by Yourself

1. As you write your original screenplay, be aware of the sources you are drawing your work from. It's okay to be inspired by another work, but you must always be sensitive to the line between inspiration and copying. (See Appendix A, "Copyright Infringement," p. 353.)

2. If you are copying a portion of another person's work, even in part, you should analyze your use under copyright law to see whether you need to obtain permission. (See "Copyright Law," p. 328; "Screenplay Adaptations," p. 117; "Copyright Searches and Permissions," p. 132.)

3. Once your screenplay is written, you should register its copyright with the U.S. Copyright Office. (See "Copyright Registration," p. 136.) All copies of the script should have a prominently displayed copyright notice on the cover. (See "Copyright Notice," p. 139.)

   Example: *Food for Worms: The Exciting World of Compost* © 2011 Woodrow Writer.

4. Before your film is shot, you will need to assign the script's copyright to the production company that shoots it. Be sure you understand which rights you are granting (at a minimum, the theatrical motion picture right) and which rights, if any, you are retaining. (See "Copyright Assignments," p. 139; "Option/ Purchase," p. 102.)

WRITING COLLABORATION (WRITING PARTNERS AND JOINT AUTHORSHIP)

Whether you are writing a screenplay that you plan to produce or are writing one that you hope to sell, at some point you may decide to collaborate with other writers. Writing partners can be a great way to ease the burden of creating a 120-page screenplay. They help each other through writer's blocks, share in the actual workload, and bring new and fresh perspectives to each other's material. But, as with any business relationship, working with a writing partner can create legal problems, especially if certain issues are not dealt with *before* the partners start writing together.

Problems with collaborators typically occur over issues of screenplay ownership, the sharing of profits and expenses, and how to decide whether to accept offers for the screenplay's purchase. The best way to prevent these issues from disrupting an otherwise beneficial working relationship is to have the writing relationship governed by a writers' collaboration agreement, which is a contract that defines the duties and rights of each coauthor as well as the way in which the business of selling or exploiting the screenplay is managed.

Under U.S. copyright law, unless they have a contract that says otherwise, script writers who work together writing parts of the same script can be considered *joint authors*. (See "Joint Authors and Joint Works," p. 94.) Without a writers' collaboration agreement, copyright law will supply the default provisions that govern the ownership of the script's copyright. These default provisions often run counter to the expectations of one or more of the writers. For instance, in the absence of a contract that says otherwise, if the screenplay is sold, copyright law assumes that all writers will share equally in the script's profits and ownership—even if one of the writers originated the idea and did 95% of the work!

THE BOTTOM LINE: Without a written and signed agreement between you and your cowriters, they may own more of the script than you would like and be able to license it without your permission.

JOINT AUTHORSHIP

Connor Concept has an idea for a screenplay—a comic love story about two cannibalistic Elvis impersonators he has titled *Love Me Tender... and Juicy*. Connor sees himself primarily as an idea guy, and he decides to turn his story into a screenplay with the help of William Wordsmith. Because William is an experienced writer, Connor is hoping to help him flesh out the script outline and then let William do the majority of the actual writing.

They start writing together without an agreement between them. Because the two writers are each contributing copyrightable sections to the script (in other words, not just ideas), they are joint authors.

William writes the first 12 pages, and they are brilliant. Unfortunately, he then accepts the job writing for a television series, leaving Connor to finish the other 108 pages of the screenplay. Finish it he does.

Fortunately for Connor, his idea is so strong, despite his mediocre writing, that the script sets off a heated bidding war. Big Studio, Inc., is the winner, offering Connor $1.5 million to purchase the screenplay. There was no contract between the two writers, so Connor figures William should get about 10% of the money: after all, the screenplay was Connor's idea and William only wrote 10% of the final script. William, however, demands 50%.

Unfortunately for Connor, as a joint author under copyright law, William is entitled to a full 50%. If this is not the result Connor wanted, he should have protected his interests with a contract that specified how the monies and copyright ownership should be split.

DEV.

Creating Together: Joint Author

When two or more authors work together to create a screenplay or film, copyright law may consider them to be *joint authors*.

Without a contract between the creators, **copyright law will control how the copyright is owned.**

Copyright law **does not** favor the author who did the most work; nor does it favor the author who came up with the idea.

The Writers' Collaboration Agreement: Goals and Deals

With a writers' collaboration agreement, each collaborating writer wants to establish his or her rights and obligations with respect to:

- Copyright ownership
- Screenplay sales and licenses
- Allocation of expenses
- Resolving disagreements
- Work schedule and distribution of writing tasks

For definitions and explanations of common contract clauses, see Appendix C, "The Clause Companion," p. 375.

DEAL POINTS

A writers' collaboration agreement determines the rights and duties of each writer in a writing relationship. The agreement should contain sections that determine the following aspects of the relationship.

The Ownership of Rights

The ownership of rights is often affected by which author came up with the idea on which the screenplay is based. (To keep things simple, many writers opt to share the rights equally, despite one of them being the idea person.) Ownership issues include:

- Who will own the rights to the screenplay? Do the writers intend to be joint authors?
- If the writers do *not* want to be considered joint authors, the agreement should specify that.
- If they *do* intend to be joint authors, they should include a provision saying so, as well as language stating that in the event that one of the author's contributions is deemed not to be copyrightable, the author with the copyrightable contribution assigns a copyright interest to his writing partner.
- How is the ownership of the rights divided? Is it shared equally? Are the rights shared differently (e.g., the writer who came up with the idea gets 60%, the coauthor 40%)? For joint authors, the law presumes that they share the copyright equally, no matter which author came up with the idea, unless the agreement specifies otherwise.
- Is every right shared in the same proportion? For example, the screenplay rights are split 50–50, but the right to make literary adaptations (i.e., books) is split 60–40, with the higher percentage going, again, to the idea person.
- Are any rights held by only one writer, such as the idea person retains the exclusive right to create a video game based on the screenplay?
- Who gets the rights in the event the writers can no longer work together? Does the idea person retain the exclusive right to turn her concept into another screenplay? If so, does she have to pay the other writers under this agreement?
- What if the screenplay can't be sold? Can either writer use portions of the work in their own separate works? Often writers require that their coauthor seek written permission before being allowed to use material from the joint work in separately authored, nonjoint works.

- Can either writer assign his or her own portion of the copyright? Generally, writers may want to restrict the transfer of the copyright to the transfer of the right to receive money from the copyright. Writers may want to restrict each other from granting to third parties the right to change or modify the screenplay.

- What promises are being made about the material each author contributes? Each author should represent and warrant that he created the material that he has added to the screenplay. He should indemnify the other author for a breach of this provision.

The Working Relationship

- How do the writers decide when and to whom to sell the screenplay? It is a good idea to restrict all the writers' abilities to individually grant any kind of license in the screenplay. Typically, the agreement requires the written permission of all or of the majority of the writers before the screenplay can be licensed.

- How is the income from exploiting the screenplay divided? One typical formula is to have the right to income mirror the copyright ownership interests of the writers.

- When is the screenplay scheduled to be finished? Will work be done according to a schedule? If one writer is not meeting deadlines, is that a default? If so, does the defaulting writer have time to cure the default (e.g., 10 days) before it is considered a breach of contract? It is a good idea to include mechanisms that allow the parties to cure defaults before they become breaches of contract. One method is to require a notice to be sent to the defaulting party for that party to be considered in default of their obligations. Once the defaulting party has received the notice, he or she is typically given some time to correct his or her default ("cure") before it is considered a breach of contract.

DEV.

- In the event of a breach of contract, is arbitration mandatory?

- If any writer withdraws from the agreement before the screenplay is finished, how is the withdrawing writer's ownership affected? Is his percentage reduced by the amount added by other writers to fill the gap that the departing writer leaves behind? Typically, any withdrawal requires the creation of a *termination agreement*, which redefines the rights of the respective parties in terms of what each owns in the absence of the collaboration agreement. If the parties can't agree on the termination agreement, does the dispute go to arbitration or to court?

- How long does the agreement last? You might want to assert a time limit of a year or two here; if you can't write the screenplay in that time, there may be problems with the working relationship. Of course, that time period can be extended by all parties agreeing to do so. But distinguish between the term of the writing relationship and the ownership and duties with respect to the copyright of the screenplay, both of which are usually for the life of the copyright in the work.

- How will the writing team pay for the expenses of shopping the screenplay? Usually writers pay for their own individual expenses.

- Are all business decisions decided by a majority vote? Some decisions, such as whether to admit new members into the writing team or whether to sell the screenplay, often require a unanimous vote.

- What happens if one writer's actions or unpaid debt causes the writing team to be sued (which can happen under the rules of joint and several liability)? The writer at fault should have a duty to indemnify her cowriter. (See "Indemnification," p. 241.)

- How will each writer be credited? How will writers be credited if they withdraw from the collaboration? One solution is to determine credit in accordance with the Writers Guild of America (WGA) rules. Even if none of the parties are members of the union, this way gives some structure to the formulation of writing credits. (See "WGA Credits," p. 98.)

Law: Joint Authors and Joint Works

DEV.

Joint authors have certain rights under copyright law; if the authors want to change these rights, they need to do so by a contract between them, such as a writers' collaboration agreement.

When two or more authors work together to create a screenplay, copyright law may consider them to *be joint authors.*

> *Example:* Remember William and Connor from the beginning of this section? William and Connor each wrote portions of the screenplay, with the intent that their individual contributions become part of the same screenplay. They are joint authors under copyright law and their screenplay is considered a *joint work.*

To become a joint author, each coauthor must:

1. Contribute copyrightable elements to the joint work. For example, a would-be joint author would have to contribute more than just ideas, because ideas are not copyrightable.

2. In addition to adding copyrightable elements, each potential joint author must also *intend* to merge his or her own contributions *inseparably* or *interdependently* with the contributions of the other coauthors to form a unitary whole. For example, a novel or screenplay may involve *inseparable* contributions, because the different authors' contributions generally do not stand alone, as in "Okay, Jenny, which sentences did you write again?" A motion picture, by contrast, generally has *interdependent* contributions, which can stand alone but are meant to be merged together to a new form, as in "I directed and shot the film that you wrote, and I never signed a work-for-hire agreement; I guess we're joint authors of the film."

> **CAUTION!** As a screenwriter, you want to have a say in how your screenplay is licensed, but unless there is a contract between you and your other joint authors specifying how and to whom a screenplay must be licensed, any joint author can grant nonexclusive licenses to the script without having to first seek the permission of the other joint authors!

More details on how copyright law treats joint authors are found in Appendix A, "*Joint Authors and Joint Works,*" p. 341.

Business Issues

Entering into a writing collaboration is more than just a sharing of creative capital. If you plan to sell the final screenplay, you must recognize that you are going into business with your coauthor.

Deciding on a Business Organization

The organizational form that a business relationship takes should be determined in advance. Although a writers' collaboration agreement focuses on the screenplay and defines how each writer will act with respect to the script—its creation and exploitation—there are numerous business aspects it does not cover (e.g., taxation, voting, etc.). As a result, it may be advisable for writing collaborators to also form a business. (See "Setting Up the Production Company," p. 35.)

`DEV.`

- *LLCs.* Given its flexibility, writers often create a member-managed limited liability company issuing membership interests to all cowriters. (See "Limited Liability Company," p. 40.)

- *General partnerships.* Writers who work together to create and sell a screenplay might be surprised to learn that the law may treat them as having *already* formed a partnership.

- *Joint ventures.* Alternatively, the law may treat cowriters as being part of a joint venture, especially if their relationship involves only one script or project.

Intellectual Property

Without a contract specifying otherwise, (1) each joint author owns the whole copyright—jointly with the other joint authors; (2) and each joint author can grant a nonexclusive license to the script. It is, therefore, advisable to have a contract that, at the very least, governs how the joint authors decide whether or not to accept an offer to purchase the rights to the script.

- If one author has single-handedly created the script concept (but not the script itself), that author may want to argue for a greater share of income and copyright ownership.

- The converse is also true: The screenwriter who has been brought in to write a second or third draft of an existing screenplay may want to avoid the collaboration agreement altogether and argue that he or she is a joint author, entitled to share equally with the other joint authors.

STEP BY STEP: WRITING COLLABORATION

Before Starting to Write

1. Choose your writing partners with the same care you would use to choose business partners—because that is what they are.

2. Decide whether to form a business organization. (See "Types of Business Entities," p. 37.) If you decide to form a member-managed LLC, many of the aspects of the writers' collaboration agreement can be dealt with in the agreement that governs your business entity (e.g., the LLCs operating agreement; the partnership agreement for a general partnership).

3. Negotiate, draft, and execute a writers' collaboration agreement, paying special attention to the issues of ownership of rights, resolving disputes, deadlines, marketing strategies, expenses, and profits and losses.

While Writing

1. Keep track of each author's financial contributions and expenses.

2. Together, develop a strategy for trying to sell or make the screenplay.

After Your Work is Written

1. Register the copyright with the U.S. Copyright Office. (See "Copyright Registration," p. 136.) If you and your partners have decided to form a company, assign the copyright to the company and register the assignment with the U.S. Copyright Office. (See "Copyright Recordation, Assignments, and Transfers," p. 139.)

2. Together, develop a strategy for trying to sell or produce the screenplay.

DEV.

CAUTION

- It is critical to have a collaboration agreement, signed by all authors. Without a contract to restrict them, joint authors may license the screenplay without first getting the permission of their coauthors.

- To qualify as a joint author, you must contribute something more than just the idea or concept for a screenplay.
- Choose your writing partners carefully. Not only are they your writing partners, they are also your business partners.

THE WRITERS GUILD OF AMERICA (WGA)

Working with Union Writers

The Writers Guild of America (WGA) is the union for professional screenplay, television, and certain "new media" writers. If you want to hire a writer or buy a script from a writer who is a member of the WGA, you might need to become a signatory with that union. A *signatory* is a company that has signed and therefore agreed to abide by the collective bargaining agreement of the WGA, known as the WGA Theatrical and Television Minimum Basic Agreement (MBA). If anything in your contract with the writer you hire conflicts with the MBA, your conflicting terms disappear and the MBA's terms govern in their place.

> *Example:* Even though the signatory producer wants to give three people "story by" credit, the MBA limits the number of writers able to receive that credit to two. Since the film is done under the WGA contract, only two writers may be given "story by" credits in the final film.

DEV.

In general, the MBA controls minimum deal terms. For example, it controls:

- Minimum payment for WGA writers
- Qualification for credits
- Separation of rights
- Reacquisition of the rights to the screenplay
- Rules governing "new media" projects that fall within its jurisdiction

Separation of Rights

Writers who are members of the WGA have special rights called *separated rights.* These are additional rights granted to WGA members who create original works under the WGA MBA. If a professional writer creates an original screenplay or teleplay or contributes a substantially new story to preexisting material that has been assigned to him or her, the writer may be entitled to a separation of rights.[1] Separated rights differ depending on whether the initial work was created for theatrical or television release. These rights, which stem from copyright, would not automatically flow to the writer for hire in the absence of the MBA. In fact, in nonunion films these rights are almost always reserved by the production company, leaving the writer with no separated rights or copyright interest whatsoever.

Separated rights can include:

- Publication rights
- Dramatic stage rights
- Sequel payments
- Mandatory rewrites for authors selling an original screenplay to the signatory production company
- Meeting with a production executive
- Reacquisition of the screenplay that has not been produced within five years, by repaying to the production company the amount of money the writer was paid for her services
- Sequel Movie of the Week (MOW) rights
- TV series rights
- Merchandising rights
- Radio rights

Who Receives Separated Rights?

If a WGA member writer is working for a WGA signatory company, that writer may receive separated rights as follows:

- *Motion picture.* A writer will receive separated rights if she is entitled to a "story by," "screen story by," or "written by" credit.
- Television show. A writer will receive separated rights if he is entitled to a "story by" or "written by" credit (and in some cases he may be eligible if he receives a "television story by" credit as well).

Since the award of separated rights is driven by what WGA credit the writer receives, let's turn to WGA credits.

WGA Credits

If the film is subject to the WGA rules and jurisdiction (in other words, the production company is a signatory and the writers are union members), the WGA will determine the writing credits. As the WGA points out in its handy *Credits Survival Guide:*

> *The Guild has the sole authority to determine writing credits on theatrical and television projects written under its jurisdiction. A [production] company cannot guarantee that you will receive writing credit, or any particular form of writing credit.*[2]

How a writer is credited by the WGA affects his or her right to residuals, separated rights, and other rights under the WGA MBA.

When principal photography is over, the production company must send to both the WGA and to all of the writers:

- A notice of tentative writing credits
- The final shooting script
- The production company's proposed credits
- Any source material for the script

The way writers are credited by the WGA is set out in the WGA Screen Credits Policy:

- "*Story by*" *credit* is given when the writer contributes literary material that is "distinct from screenplay and consisting of basic narrative, idea, theme, or outline indicating character development and action."

- "*Screen story by*" *credit* is given for scripts that are "based upon source material and a story […] and the story is substantially new or different from the source material."

- "*Screenplay by*" *credit* is given when there is "source material of a story nature (with or without a 'screen story by' credit) or when the writer(s) entitled to 'story by' credit is different than the writer(s) entitled to 'screenplay by' credit."

- "*Written by*" *credit* is given when the "writer(s) is entitled to both the 'story by' credit and the "screenplay by' credit."

The WGA defines a *screenplay* as "individual scenes and full dialogue, together with such prior treatment, basic adaptation, continuity, scenario and dialogue[…]."[3]

DEV.

HANDY WGA LINKS

- WGA: www.wga.org.
- WGA Separation of Rights Guide:
  www.wga.org/subpage_writersresources.aspx?id=122
- WGA Screen Credits Policy:
  www.wga.org/subpage_writersresources.aspx?id=171
- WGA Credits Survival Guide:
  www.wga.org/subpage_writersresources.aspx?id=153
- WGA Guide to New Media: www.wga.org/content/default.aspx?id=3930

9

ACQUIRING SCREENPLAY RIGHTS

If you haven't written your own screenplay, you will either have to buy one from someone who has written one or hire someone to write a script for you. You may even have to buy someone's script and hire a writer to rewrite it.

In this chapter you will learn how to:

- Purchase a screenplay. (See "The Screenplay Option/Purchase," p. 102.)

- Hire a screenwriter. (See "Hiring a Screenwriter," p. 111.)

- Adapt a script from a novel or comic book. (See "Screenplay Adaptations," p. 117.)

- Purchase the right to someone's life story. (See "Life Story Rights," p. 124.)

DEV.

BUYING RIGHTS

When you acquire literary property, such as the rights to a screenplay or the right to turn a book into a movie, you must pay special attention to the legal formalities of acquiring that property's copyright. All parties involved will need to know exactly who owns which of the many rights involved. For instance, even though the production company is buying the right to turn the screenplay into a movie, the writer of an original screenplay might want to keep a portion of the copyright rights, such as the right to turn the script into a stage play. (See "Screenplay Purchase Agreement: Reserved Rights," p. 106.) And no matter how the copyright is shared or owned, one thing is certain: The production company *must* have a signed contract granting it the right to make a motion picture (and other rights). (See "Screenplay Purchase Agreement: Rights Granted," p. 105).

It's simple: If a copyright to a screenplay or book is not properly sold or licensed to you, you don't have the right to turn that script or novel into a movie. This is not something that will "slip under the radar." When it comes time to distribute your film, the distributor will double-check that the copyright has been properly assigned to you or your production company, and if it hasn't been, you will lose the deal. Even if you're self-distributing, you could be sued by a writer who has not properly granted you the rights to her work.

Example: Pamela Producer wants to combine her passion for horror movies with her love of sophisticated desserts. She reads Waldo Writer's screenplay *Chocolate Kiss of Death* and decides to turn it into a slasher film. After all, she reasons, black-and-white films used chocolate sauce to simulate blood. Because Pamela and Waldo are such good friends, they don't bother with signing a contract. Pamela makes the movie and shops it to distributors. The distributors insist on seeing the contract between Pamela and Waldo. They need to make sure that Pamela owns the copyright to the screenplay.

When Pamela goes back to Waldo to have him sign over the copyright, she finds her old friend locked in a bitter divorce battle with his wife Wanda. One of the assets Waldo and Wanda are fighting over is the copyright to his works. Without that copyright, Pamela cannot sell the film. She should have had him sign over the copyright long before she started filming.

DEV.

THE SCREENPLAY OPTION/PURCHASE

A filmmaker who wants to make a movie using someone else's script must buy the motion picture rights to that script in order to make the movie. If you can, you should try to buy the entire copyright to the script, not just the motion picture rights. Remember, the more rights you own, the more ways you can exploit those rights. To purchase the rights to a screenplay, the filmmaker should use a *screenplay purchase agreement*.

Typically, a filmmaker doesn't want to buy a script unless he knows that he can get it made. The filmmaker needs a little time to secure funding, interest actors, and hopefully, set up a distribution deal. However, the filmmaker can't attach all those elements (financiers, talent, distributors) to the project unless the filmmaker has the right to make the film from the screenplay. This is where the *option agreement* comes in handy. An option agreement is a contract that gives the filmmaker the *exclusive* right to *buy* the screenplay copyright during a defined period of time.

If the producer *options* the screenplay, he has *not* yet purchased all the rights to the screenplay. Purchasing a screenplay during the option period is called *exercising the option*. If the filmmaker chooses not to exercise the option and the option expires, the right to sell the screenplay *reverts* back to the screenwriter.

Always Negotiate a Purchase Agreement with the Option!

When you negotiate the option agreement you must, at the same time, also negotiate the purchase price and other key terms of the screenplay sale. A filmmaker who has negotiated the option agreement to a screenplay but not the purchase agreement holds a *worthless option*. It is worthless because although the filmmaker may exercise the option, the sale terms have not been agreed on and, therefore, the screenwriter is not obligated to sell the script to the filmmaker for a certain price. In the case of a worthless option, what the filmmaker really has is not a right to *buy* the script but a right to *negotiate* for its sale. The screenwriter may demand as much money for the script as he or she wants and the only choice the filmmaker has is either to agree to pay it or not to buy the script.

FAILING TO NEGOTIATE THE SCRIPT PRICE

Wendy Writer has written a script called *King Axolotl,* a monster flick about a giant fire-breathing aquatic salamander, which Petra Producer is very interested in making.

Suppose Petra *didn't* negotiate a purchase agreement when she negotiated the option agreement for the script. It's now six months later, and Petra has a backer interested in funding the picture. Petra tells Wendy that she wants to buy the script for $65,000. Wendy, knowing that Petra has an interested financier whom she doesn't want to lose, decides to hold out for a higher purchase price–$100,000. After all, Wendy figures, she is not obligated to sell the script to Petra at any certain price, so she might as well hold out for a higher price. Petra has lost her leverage over bargaining for the purchase price.

Without a purchase agreement tied to an option, the option is worthless.

DEV.

MAJOR DEAL POINTS: THE OPTION AGREEMENT

For definitions and explanations of common contract clauses, see Appendix C, "The Clause Companion," p. 375.

The Parties

- *Producer.* The producer wants to "test drive" the script before she buys it—that is, to be able to shop the screenplay around to see if anybody is interested in making the movie before she purchases the rights to the script outright. To that end, the producer will seek to get the longest possible time (the *option period*) in which to shop the script. The producer will also seek to pay the smallest amount of money for the option and to make that amount applicable against the purchase price.

- *Writer.* It is often in the writer's interest to make an outright sale of the script, as the purchase price of a script is greater than its option price. However, the writer should also consider whether the producer can actually get the film made. The more of the writer's films that get made, the more money the writer can demand for her next film. The writer, therefore, should give the producer enough time to shop the script around to financiers, production companies, distributors, and so forth. For that reason, an option may make sense to the writer as well. The writer will seek to limit the term of the producer's option period, to give the writer some time to seek other potential buyers for the script while the screenplay is still reasonably fresh.

The writer may work for his loan-out company, which would then be a party to the agreement. (See "Loan-Out Companies," p. 42.)

Grant of Option

This is the heart of the option—it grants to the producer the exclusive right to purchase the script by a future date according to the terms of the purchase agreement. As previously mentioned, a purchase agreement must be coupled with the option. (See "Purchase Agreement," p. 105.)

Option Price

This is the amount paid for the *option, not* the purchase price for the script itself.

- Option prices range from a token amount, such as $50 on the low end, to 10% of the purchase price on the high end.
- Will the option price be deducted from the final purchase price? If so, the option price is *applicable* against the purchase price; if the option price is not deductible from the purchase price, it is *nonapplicable.*

Option Period or Term

This governs the *duration* of the option:

- Most options are for at least a year, and often for 18 months.
- Often producers are given the right to renew the option prior to its expiration. If the option is renewed, the writer usually gets an *extension payment.* This payment is typically *not* applied against the purchase price.

Exercise of Option

This clause details how the producer may exercise the option and purchase the script pursuant to the purchase agreement.

- A notice sent via certified mail is a common device for exercising options.
- This clause should reference the purchase agreement, requiring that the writer sign the purchase agreement when the producer exercises the option. Make sure to give the producer the power of attorney to execute the purchase agreement on the writer's behalf if the writer fails to exercise the purchase agreement.

- The writer should also be obligated to sign other documents such as copyright assignments and certificates of authorship that transfer the copyright and other rights in the script to the producer.

Right to Development and Pre-Production

A producer may need to develop the motion picture prior to purchasing the script. This clause gives the producer the ability to rewrite the script, commission storyboards, and produce trailers for the purpose of raising money for the film. If this clause wasn't in the agreement, any development of the film based on an unpurchased script might infringe the writer's copyright in the screenplay.

> *CAUTION!* Producers should keep in mind that they cannot sell any of the material they developed based on the script unless they purchase the script (i.e. "exercise the option").

DEV.

Reversion

This clause underscores the fact that the writer's rights will revert back to him if the option is not exercised either during the term of the option or during any renewal periods.

This clause should require the producer to grant the power of attorney to the writer for executing any documents conveying the rights back to the writer.

MAJOR DEAL POINTS: THE PURCHASE AGREEMENT

Rights Granted

This section outlines the specific rights granted to the producer. In short, the producer needs the right to make a motion picture or pictures in whatever medium, to be distributed in any manner, throughout the universe, in perpetuity.

Remember, copyright can be divided in a number of ways, so the rights must be defined in terms of their:

- *Medium* (e.g., motion picture, television).
- *Duration* (e.g., perpetual).
- *Geography* (e.g., the universe, North America).

- *Motion picture rights.* At a minimum, the producer needs the exclusive right to make a motion picture from the script. The producer needs to make sure that this right extends to all media in which that motion picture will be exploited, such as theatrical release, television, video, DVD, Blu-ray, online media, on demand, mobile devices, and "any exhibition medium, now known or hereinafter developed."

- *Merchandising rights.* The producer is granted the right to make T-shirts, action figures, and so forth from the characters and events in the script. The writer is usually granted a portion of the money the producer receives from these sales.

- *Other rights.* Other rights are subject to negotiation but frequently granted to the producer, such as the right to make derivative works such as television shows, radio plays, and sequels, remakes, video games, plays, and "novelizations" of up to 7,500 words. *Novelization* is the right to create a novel or other literary version of the movie or screenplay.

- *Right to make changes.* The producer must have the unfettered right to make changes to the script.

Reserved Rights

Reserved rights specify which rights the writer keeps. These are the rights the producer does *not* get. The rights the writer keeps are the subject of negotiation.

Often, the writer keeps the following:

- *Book rights* (the right to make a novel of the screenplay).
- *Radio rights.*
- *Comic book rights.*
- *Stage rights* (the right to turn the script into a play).
- If the writer is a WGA member and the producer is a signatory, the writer may also have *separated rights*. (See "Separation of Rights," p. 97.)
- The producer may ask for a holdback period for the *reserved rights* (often 5–7 years). This means that for the holdback period, the writer *cannot* exploit those reserved rights that are subject to the holdback.
- Even though the rights are reserved by the writer, the producer will often ask for the *right of first negotiation/right of last refusal* for any sale or exploitation of the rights. (See Appendix C, "Right of First Negotiation," p. 389.)

Copyright

This clause governs the mechanics of ownership and transfer of the script's copyright.

- It is *critical* that the producer performs a copyright search with the U.S. Copyright Office to ensure that the acquired property is not owned by anybody else other than the stated owner(s) or that it is not in the public domain.

- The script's copyright information should be listed in the agreement, including the script's title, registration number, and year of publication.
- The producer typically gets the granted rights forever, along with an agreement by the writer to transfer of any copyright renewal rights. (But see Appendix A, "Termination of Transfer," p. 350.)
- The writer must promise to execute any additional documentation necessary to transfer the copyright to the production company.

Reversion of Rights

Frequently the writer will negotiate a return of the rights granted if they are not used by the producer within a certain period of time (called a *reversion*). The writer usually wants the rights to revert back to him if the film has not begun principal photography within five years from the date of the screenplay purchase.

Purchase Price/Compensation

This is where the purchase price for the script is specified. Different rights (theatrical, television, etc.) are compensated at different rates. If the writer is a WGA member, the minimum amount the producer can pay the writer will be determined by that union's *rate schedule*. Make sure to check with the Guild to get their current rates.

DEV.

- *Rights transfer.* Should be conditional upon payment of the purchase price. Payment is usually due when the option is exercised or on first day of principal photography, whichever is earlier.
- *Sequels.* If a movie spawns a sequel, the writer typically receives 25–50% of theatrical purchase price of the script.
- *Remakes.* If the movie is remade, the writer typically receives 33–50% of theatrical purchase price of the script.
- *Net profits.* The writer commonly contracts for a portion of the Film's Net Profits—often 5%. (See "Net Profits," p. 116.)
- *Bonus compensation.* Writers sometimes get bonuses if the motion picture is produced and released.
- *Agents.* Sometimes the writer will try to negotiate a 10% increase in the fee to pay the writer's agent's commission.

Accounting

If the writer is a net-profit participant or will receive any form of deferred or contingent compensation, this paragraph will delineate how often the writer may expect to receive accounting statements. This is coupled with the right to audit the production company, usually no more frequently than once a year.

Representations and Warranties

Representations and warranties are the promises that the writer is making to the producer and are coupled with an indemnification clause in which the writer states:

- He or she is the sole owner of the screenplay and nothing in the script infringes the rights of anyone else.

- Copyright registration is up to date and accurate.

- No other motion picture, dramatic, or other version of the script has been made or authorized.

- None of the granted rights are or have ever been granted to anyone else.

- By selling the script, the writer will not be violating any third-party rights (e.g., copyrights or rights of publicity).

- Writer will not impair or encumber or otherwise do anything to interfere with the granted rights.

- The writer should indemnify the producer for breaches of representations and warranties, misrepresentations, or damages resulting from the writer's breach of contract.

DEV.

Credit

This clause specifies how the writer's credit is determined.

- If the producer is a signatory of WGA and the writer is a member of that union, the WGA will determine who gets writing credit and how they are credited. (See "WGA Credits," p. 98.)

- The producer should include a clause disclaiming liability for inadvertently making a mistake with the writer's credit. Typically, the remedy for credit error is a promise from the producer to correct the credits in future copies of the film.

No Obligation to Produce

Although the producer has the right to produce the film, he needs to be sure that he is not *obligated* to produce the film.

Publicity

The publicity clause gives the producer the right to use the writer's name and biography in connection with advertising, marketing, and publicizing the film.

- The producer needs to be able to use the writer's name, likeness, biography, and so forth in connection with the marketing of the film.

- Conversely, the producer will want to prohibit the writer from releasing any publicity about the motion picture without the producer's approval. You may want to point out to the writer that this means no unauthorized blogging or Facebook posts as well!

Remedies

The writer should waive any claim to injunctive relief arising out of a breach of the contract. Depending on the advice of counsel, producers may want any dispute to be settled through binding arbitration rather than through the courts.

◆◆◆◆◆

Law: Optioning and Selling the Screenplay

- Under U.S. copyright law, all screenplay sales, assignments, and transfers *must* be in writing to effectively transfer the copyright.
- Both sides in the transaction need to be especially careful that everybody understands which rights are granted and which rights are reserved.
- What is being purchased is the copyright to the screenplay. A producer must make sure that all the screenplay's authors and contributors sign off on the deal.

DEV.

- When you negotiate the exclusive right to buy (the option), you must also negotiate the sale (the purchase agreement).

Business Issues

Union rules may affect your negotiating range!

- *WGA member.* If the writer is a member of the WGA and the producer is a signatory, many of the deal terms, such as minimums on how much a writer can be paid, the criteria for credits, and rights that will remain with the writer after he or she has sold the screenplay, will be controlled by the WGA Minimum Basic Agreement.
- *Non-WGA member.* If the producer is not a WGA signatory, she will not be bound by the WGA rules and is free to contract with a nonunion writer on whatever terms they mutually agree to. Even if the deal is not governed by the WGA, it may still be helpful to turn to the WGA provisions with respect to determining credit and other issues. Just because a non–WGA signatory producer uses the WGA MBA to determine credit, that doesn't mean that the rest of the deal is controlled by the WGA MBA.

Finances and Costs

Remember, the producer may need to negotiate several kinds of payments with the writer:

- *An option payment.* This is for the option itself—often 10% of the purchase price of the script.

- *Option extension payments.* This is typically more money than the option payment itself.
- *The purchase price payment.* This is payment for the sale of the script, due when the option is exercised. The purchase price is usually broken down into:
  - *A fixed compensation payment.* This is the fee which is paid regardless of how much money the movie makes.
  - *Contingent compensation payments.* These payments are based on a percentage of the money the movie makes. The writer is often granted 5% of the Film's Net Profits. (Indie film deals may grant writers up to 10% because the fixed compensation paid may be lower.)
  - *Other rights payments.* If the producer wants to exploit other rights, such as turning the movie into a television series or making a play from the screenplay, he may have to pay additional fees to the writer. If the production is governed by the WGA, the producer will definitely have to pay additional fees for these rights.

THE BOTTOM LINE: **The option agreement grants the producer the exclusive right to purchase the screenplay from the writer. The purchase agreement dictates the terms of the actual sale. The option and purchase agreements should be negotiated at the same time. Once they are signed by everybody, keep them together and treat them as one contract.**

DEV.

Step by Step: The Screenplay Option Purchase

1. The producer should perform or commission a copyright search of the U.S. Copyright Office to ensure that the producer has identified all the copyright owners. The producer should pay special attention to who owns the copyrights to any underlying works on which the script is based, such as a comic book or a novel. (See "Copyright Searches and Permissions," p. 132.)

2. If the script is based on another work, the producer will have to make sure that the writer has gotten—in writing—the right to turn that underlying work into a script for production. (See "Screenplay Adaptations," p. 117.)

3. If the copyright to the screenplay has not been registered, the producer should require that it be registered prior to the option/purchase agreement being executed.

4. The option/purchase agreement should be negotiated, written, and signed by all parties.

5. The producer should record the new additions to the chain of title. Remember, the chain of title is an unbroken record of the movie's ownership and is critical to selling a film. (See "Copyright Recordation, Assignments, and Transfers," p. 139.)

   a. The producer should require the writer to execute a certificate of authorship. (See "Certificate of Authorship," p. 142.)

b. The option agreement may also be recorded with the Copyright Office.

c. When the script is sold, the writer should execute a short form copyright assignment, which is to be registered with the U.S. Copyright Office.

HIRING A SCREENWRITER

Often a writer will pitch an idea to a production company in the hopes that the production company will hire her to write the screenplay. (See "Idea Rights," p. 77.) Or a filmmaker will have an idea or own the rights to literary property and need to hire a writer to turn that idea or property into a screenplay. (See "Screenplay Adaptations," p. 117.)

At the outset it is critical that the production company that hires the writer complies with all state and federal labor and employment laws. (See "Labor and Employment Law," p. 393; "Hiring Cast and Crew," p. 146.)

GOALS AND DEALS

For definitions and explanations of common contract clauses, see Appendix C, "The Clause Companion," p. 375.

DEV.

The employment agreement that controls the relationship between the writer and the production company is called a *writer's services agreement*.

One of the most common, and most economical, ways to structure the employment arrangement is by creating a *step deal*. Like an option agreement, the step deal minimizes the production company's risk because the writer is hired and compensated in stages.

For example, the writer is first commissioned to create a treatment for which she is paid money, both when she starts writing the treatment and when she delivers the treatment to the production company. Once the production company has read the treatment during a *reading period*, the company may elect to have the writer try her hand at the first draft of the screenplay. However, on a non-WGA production, the production company is under no obligation to require the writer to continue working on the project. The production company can keep the treatment, pay the writer only for the treatment, and then turn around and hire another writer to develop the treatment into a screenplay.

Common payment and delivery stages for a step deal are:

1. Treatment
2. Revision of treatment
3. First draft of screenplay
4. First revision of screenplay
5. Second draft of screenplay
6. Polish

As always for production service contracts, it is critical that as part of the deal the writer creates the screenplay as a work made for hire, and thus the copyright to the screenplay is owned by the production company, producer, or other hiring party. (See "Work Made for Hire," p. 382.)

COMMONLY DEFINED TERMS IN A WRITER'S SERVICES AGREEMENT

- *Product form.* The results of the particular stage being worked on by the writer. For example, treatments, rewrites, and drafts are all various product forms.

- *Delivery period.* The time within which the writer must deliver each product form.

- *Reading period.* The time within which the production company has to read and review the writer's delivered product form.

- *Option period.* The time within which the production company must exercise its option on the writer's services, thereby obligating the writer to create the next step's product form.

Example: Wendy Writer has been hired by Nadir Pictures, LLC, to write the first draft of a screenplay based on the treatment she showed them during a pitch meeting. The contract calls for her to deliver the *product form*—which, in this case, is the first draft of the screenplay—within the *delivery period* of 12 weeks. Following that, Nadir will have a four-week *reading period* within which to review her screenplay, make notes, and decide whether to ask her to go on to the next step. Nadir's reading period is coupled with a four-week *option period* within which it must either tell Wendy that she's obligated to do a rewrite or let her off the hook.

MAJOR DEAL POINTS: WRITER'S SERVICES AGREEMENT

The Parties

- *Production company.* The production company is trying to hire the writer while minimizing the risk of paying for a complete screenplay before it has secured the money to make the movie. The form most favorable to the production company is the step deal.

- *Writer.* If the writer is being hired under a step deal, he will try to minimize the risk by negotiating a larger overall compensation package to offset the chance of being dismissed before the project's completion.

The writer may work for his loan-out company, which would then be a party to the agreement. (See "Loan-Out Companies," p. 42.)

Engagement or Employment

This paragraph lays out the basis for the deal, which is that the production company is hiring the writer to perform writing services as specified in the agreement. If several writers are being hired, the agreement should specify that and define them as a *writing team*.

Writer's Services

This section details the specific services the production company is hiring the writer to perform.

- The steps and product forms are specified (e.g., writing a treatment and the first draft of a screenplay) along with the delivery periods within which the writer must deliver the product form. Typical delivery and reading periods:

  - First draft of a screenplay: 12–16 weeks

  - Reading/option periods: 2–4 weeks

  - First revision of the first draft: 6–8 weeks

  - Second revision 6–8 weeks

- *Option periods.* During the reading period, the production company usually has an option on the writer's services. If this option is exercised, the writer is obligated to write and deliver the next product form. Options usually run concurrently with reading periods.

  - This section usually specifies that *time is of the essence,* meaning that even the slightest delay in delivery will result in a breach of contract. (See Appendix B, "Breach of Contract," p. 371.)

  - It is a good idea to specify that delivery must be made to a particular person in the production company.

- *Postponement of services.* The production company typically has the right to postpone the writer's services on any particular step for a period of up to two years. If such postponement occurs, the production company may ask the writer to resume writing on the condition that doing so does not conflict with any contractual obligations the writer may be under at that time.

Compensation

If the WGA MBA governs the contract, it will also dictate the minimum amount of compensation the writer must receive. Check the latest WGA schedule of minimums. There are several different ways a writer may be compensated:

- *Fixed compensation.* In a step deal, each product form is paid for separately. Usually the writer gets some money at the commencement of the writing

DEV.

of a particular product form and the remainder on delivery of that particular product form.

- *Deferred compensation.* For low-budget pictures especially, production companies may want to put more of their actual cash into the production rather than into paying the salaries of the above-line personnel. As a result, the writer may be asked to defer some or all of his salary until the picture is produced, is released, and begins to make money. The writer should attempt to negotiate a higher salary if his salary is being deferred, because a deferred salary is an inherently risky proposition; after all, if something is deferred, it is not guaranteed. (See Appendix C, "Deferred Compensation," p. 377.)

- *Contingent compensation.* Writers are often granted a portion of the net profits from the picture, typically 2–5% of the Film's Net Profits. (See "Net Profits," p. 116.)

- *Bonus compensation.* Writers often negotiate bonuses if the motion picture is produced because the number of scripts is far greater than the number of movies made from those scripts. The amount of the bonus will be greater if the writer is the only writer on the film, and it will be less if the writer shares screenplay credit with another writer. The bonus is usually paid on commencement of principal photography but subject to the writer's repayment to the production company if the writer's sole screenwriter credit status changes.

- *Additional payments.* If the motion picture is remade into another form, the writer typically gets paid for those forms as well:
  - *Sequel.* Fifty percent of the writer's fixed compensation.
  - *Remake.* Thirty-three percent of the writer's fixed compensation.
  - *Television.* Rates differ depending on the length of the television program.

DEV.

Accounting

If the writer is a net-profit participant or will receive any form of deferred or contingent compensation, this paragraph will delineate how often the writer may expect to receive accounting statements. This is coupled with the right to audit the production company, usually no more frequently than once a year.

Right of First Negotiation

Depending on the writer's leverage, she may request a right of first negotiation on any subsequent versions of the motion picture, such as remakes, sequels, and television shows. If this is agreed to, the production company should be given the power to revoke her right of first negotiation if the writer is no longer actively engaged in writing screenplays for a living. (See Appendix C, "Right of First Negotiation," p. 389.)

Pay or Play

The production company has the right but not the obligation to use the writer's work, provided that the production company pays for the work.

Results and Proceeds

- All the results and proceeds of the writer's work must be assigned to the production company, including copyright, moral rights, rights and ideas in the screenplay, and any other creative and intellectual property right in and to the screenplay, its characters, and story.

- The production company should structure this as a work made for hire, with an alternate provision stating that if a court of competent jurisdiction finds that the work is not a work made for hire as that term is defined by U.S. copyright law, then the writer assigns all copyright, title, and interest in and to the screenplay to the production company. (See "Work Made for Hire," p. 382.)

- The writer should agree to execute any other documents necessary to convey the rights to the production company. This should be coupled with a power of attorney for the production company to execute documents on the writer's behalf if the writer fails to do so within a certain period of time.

- A *savings clause* allows certain provisions to survive the termination of a contract. The production company will need to keep the copyright in all the writer's work that was produced and/or transferred under the agreement, even if the parties decide to cancel the contract.

- The writer should also agree to provide a certificate of authorship. (See "Certificate of Authorship," p. 142.)

DEV.

Representations and Warranties

Representations and warranties are the promises the writer is making to the production company and are coupled with an indemnification clause stating that:

- The writer is the sole writer of the screenplay and that nothing in the script infringes or interferes with anyone else's rights.

- No other motion picture, dramatic, or other version of the script has been made or authorized.

- By selling the script, the writer will not be violating any third-party rights.

- The writer will not impair, encumber, or otherwise do anything to interfere with the granted rights.

- The writer should indemnify the production company against any claims arising from his or her breach of the representations and warranties.

Credits

- If the contract is governed by the WGA, so are the credit provisions. (See "WGA Credits," p. 98.) As mentioned earlier, it may be a good idea to have the WGA provisions govern credit, even if the production company is not a signatory of the WGA MBA.

- The producer should include a clause disclaiming liability for inadvertently making a mistake with the writer's credit. Typically, on non-WGA films the remedy for credit error is a promise from the producer to correct the credits in future copies of the film.

Publicity

The production company typically wants to restrict the writer's ability to give interviews about the script without the permission and control of the production company.

Net Profits

DEV.

Like all profit participant contracts, the writer's services agreement should contain a rider that defines how the Film's Net Profits will be calculated.

Remedies

The writer should waive any claim to injunctive relief arising out of a breach of the contract. Depending on the advice of counsel, producers may want any dispute to be settled through binding arbitration rather than through the courts. Keep in mind that if the writer is a member of the WGA, union rules will affect the parties' ability to change the remedies available to the writer.

Step by Step: Hiring Writers

1. If your production company is considering working with a WGA writer, that company must become a WGA signatory. (See "The Writers Guild of America," p. 97.)

2. If the screenplay will be an adaptation of another work, permission to use that work must be obtained. (See "Screenplay Adaptations," p. 117.)

3. The production company must comply with the labor and employment laws when hiring any writer, regardless of whether they are in the WGA. (See Appendix D, "A Filmmaker's Guide to Labor and Employment Law," p. 393.)

4. Negotiate the major deal points.
5. Make sure that product form and delivery stages are well understood by all parties.
6. The production company should set up a payroll schedule with its accountant.
7. Ensure that each product form is delivered to the same production company representative and that the delivery time and date are logged.
8. Pay close attention to delivery, reading, and option time periods.
9. Exercise the option at each stage by having a written notice sent to the writer and the writer's representatives (i.e., agents, lawyers, etc.).

SCREENPLAY ADAPTATIONS

A filmmaker might want to write or commission a script to be based on someone else's material (e.g., a book, graphic novel, article, or play). To do so, the filmmaker must negotiate with the author of that literary property (often called the *underlying literary property*) and buy or option the rights to turn that property first into a screenplay and then into a movie.

GOALS AND DEALS

DEV.

For definitions and explanations of common contract clauses, see Appendix C, "The Clause Companion," p. 375.

In some respects, the *literary property acquisition agreement* is similar to the screenplay purchase agreement (see "Acquiring Screenplay Rights," p. 101). For instance, both contracts govern the acquisition of a property's copyright with the intention of developing it into a motion picture. However, rather than purchasing the rights to a preexisting screenplay, with a literary acquisition agreement what is being bought and sold is the theatrical motion picture rights to a novel, comic book, or other literary property. As mentioned, these rights may be optioned first rather than purchased outright.

MAJOR DEAL POINTS: THE LITERARY PROPERTY ACQUISITION AGREEMENT

The Parties

In this agreement, the owner of the literary property is conveying the motion picture and television rights to the producer.

* *Producer.* For the producer, acquiring the literary rights to a work is just the first step in preparing the screenplay. As a result, the producer does not want to be obligated to the owner of the underlying rights more than is necessary. It may be in the producer's best interest to negotiate an option. (See "Option Agreement,"

p. 103.) Additionally, the producer needs to make sure that she is dealing with all the owners of the underlying rights. Furthermore, she needs to be certain that she can acquire all the rights she needs to effectively exploit the motion picture rights.

- *Owner.* The owner of a literary property, especially a literary property of proven worth, should only sell the motion picture rights to a producer who can actually bring the film to the big screen. To help ensure that the property will be made into a film, the owner should insist on a reversion clause, which would allow the owner to recapture the motion picture rights at a certain date if the producer has not been able to make the movie. (See Appendix C, "Reversion of Rights," p. 381.) Because the producer will want other rights in addition to the motion picture rights (such as merchandising, television, Internet, etc.) to make the property attractive to producers, the owner should be cautious about conveying away too many of the rights to other parties prior to negotiating a deal with the producer. The owner should pay particular attention to his or her own legal housekeeping. A motion picture producer will not acquire rights unless the owner can prove that he is the sole owner.

Rights Granted

DEV.

The producer needs all the rights necessary to develop, produce, exploit, distribute, exhibit, publicize, and advertise the film adapted from the literary property that the producer is acquiring.

This section lays out the specific rights granted to the producer.

- *Motion picture rights.* At a minimum, the producer needs the exclusive right to make a motion picture from the property. The producer needs to make sure that this right extends to all media in which that film will be exploited (such as theatrical release, television, video, DVD, online media, and "any exhibition medium, now known or hereinafter developed").

- *Television rights.* The producer should also receive the television rights in all televised media (such as cable, satellite, free broadcast, pay-per-view, VOD, online distribution, etc.).

- *Merchandising rights.* The producer is granted the right to make T-shirts, action figures, and so forth from the characters and events in the script. The owner usually receives a portion of the money the producer receives from these sales.

- *Trademarks.* If the property has any trademarks associated with it, the right to use those trademarks in association with the exploitation of the granted rights must also be licensed to the producer.

- *Other rights* are subject to negotiation but frequently granted to the producer, such as the right to make derivative works (such as television shows, radio plays, sequels, remakes, video games, plays, and novelizations of up to 7,500 words for the purpose of advertising, publicity, and exploitation of the motion picture).

Copyright

This clause governs the mechanics of ownership and transfer of the screenplay, motion picture, and certain other aspects of the literary property's copyright.

- Unlike the screenplay option/purchase agreement, for an adaptation the entire copyright is usually not transferred. For instance, if you are acquiring the rights to turn a novel into a movie, you may only be acquiring the television and motion picture rights for one film.

- It is critical that the producer perform a copyright search with the U.S. Copyright Office to ensure that the acquired property is not owned by anybody other than the owner(s) or that it is not in the public domain. (See "Copyright Searches and Permissions," p. 132.)

- The literary property's copyright information should be listed in the agreement, including the property's title, registration number, and year of publication.

- The producer typically acquires the rights granted in perpetuity (forever). (But see Appendix A, "Termination of Transfer," p. 350.)

- The owner must promise to execute any additional documentation necessary to transfer the copyright to the production company.

DEV.

Reserved Rights

Reserved rights specify which rights the owner retains. These are the rights the producer does *not* get. The rights the owner keeps are the subject of negotiation.

Often, the owner keeps:

- *Book rights* (the right to make an author-written sequel).
- *Radio rights.*
- *Comic book rights.*
- *Stage rights.*
- The producer may ask for a *holdback period* for the reserved rights (often five to seven years). This means that for the holdback period, the owner *cannot* exploit those reserved rights that are subject to the holdback.
- Even though the rights are reserved by the owner, the producer will often ask for the *right of first negotiation/right of last refusal* for any sale or exploitation of the rights.

Right to Make Changes

The producer must have the unfettered right to adapt the literary property into a script and then into a motion picture as she sees fit. If the property is well known, however, there may be some restrictions on what changes the producer can and cannot make. For example, if the producer were acquiring the right to make another James Bond movie, she couldn't rewrite the Bond character so that he came from Bangladesh and not Britain.

Payment

This is where the purchase price is specified. Different rights (theatrical, television, etc.) are compensated at different rates.

- It is advisable to negotiate a *floor* (a minimum) and a *ceiling* (a maximum) to any monies being paid to the owner on a royalty basis.
- If the contract is not under the jurisdiction of the WGA, the purchase price is not regulated by the WGA MBA and will be what the parties themselves agree on, taking into consideration the nature of the literary work and the media in which it will be exploited.
- Rights transfer should be conditional on payment of the purchase price.
- Payment is usually due on the earlier of the exercise of the option or the first day of principal photography.

Rights Reversion

Often the owner will negotiate a return of the rights granted if they are not used within a certain period of time. The owner will usually want the rights to revert back to himself if the film has not begun principal photography within five years from the date of the assignment of rights.

Right of First Negotiation/Right of Last Refusal

If the owner wants to sell or otherwise exploit any of the reserved rights, the producer often negotiates a right of first negotiation as well as a right of last refusal. (See Appendix C, "Right of First Negotiation," p. 389; "Right of Last Refusal," p. 389.)

Representations and Warranties

These are the promises the owner is making to the producer and are coupled with an indemnification clause. The owner must promise that:

- He or she is the sole owner of the literary property and nothing in the script infringes the rights of anybody else.
- Copyright registration is up to date and accurate.
- No other motion picture, dramatic, or other version of the script has been made or authorized.
- None of the granted rights are or have ever been granted to anyone else.

- By selling the literary property the owner will not be violating any third-party rights.
- The owner will not impair, encumber, or otherwise do anything to interfere with the granted rights.

In addition, the owner should indemnify the producer for breaches of representations and warranties, misrepresentations, or damages resulting from the owner's breach of contract.

Credit

How the owner and producer determine credit obligations will be determined by the WGA MBA if the owner is a union member and the producer is a signatory.

The producer should include a clause disclaiming liability for inadvertently making a mistake with the owner's credit. Typically, the remedy for credit error is a promise from the producer to correct the credits in future copies of the film.

No Obligation to Produce

While the producer has the right to produce the film using the literary property, he needs to be sure that he is not obligated to produce the film.

DEV.

Publicity

The producer needs to be able to exploit the owner's name, likeness, biography, and so forth in connection with the marketing of the film. Conversely, the producer will want to prohibit the owner from releasing any publicity about the motion picture without the producer's approval.

Remedies

The owner should waive any claim to injunctive relief arising out of a breach of the contract. Depending on the advice of counsel, producers may want any dispute to be settled through binding arbitration rather than through the courts.

◆◆◆◆◆

Law: The Right Rights

One of the biggest business issues involved in literary acquisition agreements is making sure that you have *all* the rights you need to fully exploit the motion picture that you intend to create. You have to be extremely cautious and understand which rights are available, which rights are reserved by the owner, and which rights have been granted by the owner to other rights holders.

Remember, a producer typically acquires the following rights with regard to a particular literary property:

- The right to make motion pictures based on the property, in all media throughout the universe in perpetuity (obviously, the most critical right).

- The right to promote, publicize, advertise, distribute, and otherwise exploit any version of the literary property the producer is allowed to make.

- The right to make television programs based on the property and/or to televise the film.

- The right to create and market merchandise based on the film adaptation of the property.

THE ADVENTURES OF MAGGOT MAN

Penelope Producer wants make a movie of her favorite comic book series, *The Adventures of Maggot Man*. She first contacts the comic book's publishing company, Carrion Publishing, Inc., and learns that they own all the rights (the copyrights, trademarks, and all other intellectual property rights) to the comic book series. In this regard, Penelope has been lucky; although it is often standard practice for the comic book publishing company to own the IP rights to its characters, this is not always the case.

Carrion Publishing, Inc., agrees to sell her the motion picture rights. If Penelope does not have the money to purchase these rights outright, she may structure the deal as an option/purchase.

While she is negotiating the agreement, she discovers that although the motion picture rights are available, the television rights are not—they've recently been sold to a Japanese anime company. Furthermore, Carrion Publishing, Inc., is steadfast in retaining ownership of all publishing, video game, and merchandising rights. As a result, they will completely own all the revenue streams from action figures or future comic books.

This leaves Penelope with only the motion picture rights, significantly hampering her ability to fully exploit the property. Without the additional revenue streams of television, merchandising, and publishing, Penelope will be limited to monies from theatrical motion picture distribution in the sale of DVDs and video cassettes. What looked like a good deal may now have to be reconsidered.

The Right Rights Holders

Prior to any literary acquisition deal, the producer must research and investigate the ownership of the copyright and other intellectual property rights to the literary property in question. (See "Copyright Searches and Permissions," p. 132.)

If any part of the literary property was created by writers or artists other than the owner, the owner's contracts with those artists and writers must be reviewed to ensure that the work was created as a work made for hire or that those rights were effectively assigned to the owner. (See "Work Made for Hire," p. 344.) If the owner can't prove his chain of title, the producer must demand that the owner obtain a written assignment of the writer's and artist's copyrights in the literary work prior to the deal moving forward. Problems here *could be fatal* to the producer's ability to own the copyright to the motion picture.

Step by Step: Screenplay Adaptations

Once the producer has decided to adapt the particular literary property, he or she should take the following steps, similar to those of a screenplay acquisition:

1. Identify the owner of the literary property. For novels, comic books, and other text-based works, the publishing company is the best place to start to get this information.

DEV.

2. Cross-check the owner information with the search of the copyright office records. (See "Copyright Searches and Permissions," p. 132.)

3. Telephone or write the owner and discuss the possibility of acquiring the motion picture rights. Follow up your discussion with a certified letter that restates the main points of your conversation with the owner.

4. Assuming that you reach agreement on the main deal points, commission a copyright search report.

5. Negotiate and draft the literary property acquisition agreement. If your copyright search report turns up any other owners, this situation must be addressed before the contract is signed. If there are other owners, you must have their written approval to acquire the rights from them.

6. Execute the contract.

7. The owner should also execute a short form copyright assignment, which the producer should record in the copyright office. (See "Copyright Recordation, Assignments, and Transfers," p. 139.)

8. The producer should also prepare and have the author or owner execute a certificate of authorship. (See "Certificate of Authorship," p. 142.)

LIFE STORY RIGHTS

If the movie or project you're planning to shoot is based on someone's life story, you should obtain that person's *life story rights* through a *life rights consent agreement*.

Although no one has the exclusive right to tell his or her own life story, there is a veritable catalog of claims that a subject can file against the filmmaker who shoots an unauthorized biography, unflattering documentary, or fictionalized account of him or her. The frustrating thing is that film subjects who sue often lose their lawsuits, largely due to the protections afforded filmmakers by the First Amendment. That being said, the subjects can, and do, sue. The purpose of a life rights consent agreement is to get the subject's permission up front and to avoid lawsuits altogether.

Filmmakers need to be especially cautious when portraying subjects in a false light, attacking their reputations, or creating the appearance that the subjects have endorsed the movie when they haven't. Lawsuits stemming from these claims are not always won by the filmmakers. Furthermore, filmmakers should never feature a person in a television commercial or other advertising without their express written permission.

DEV.

What Are Life Story Rights?

Actually, the term *life story rights* is a bit of a misnomer. In reality, what you will be acquiring is a collection of rights and releases from liability. Typically, a life rights consent agreement grants to the filmmaker the following rights:

- The right to portray a particular person's life in whole or in part
- The right to fictionalize or modify that person's life story
- The right (and sometimes the obligation) to use pseudonyms for people and places portrayed in the life story
- The copyright to or license to use any accounts of that person's life story (this may be limited by preexisting literary works, such as biographies, based on the life story)

In addition to the grant of rights, the life rights consent agreement should also include clauses, called *releases and waivers*, that say that the person granting the life rights (the *grantor*) will not sue the filmmaker for any of the following:

- Libel and defamation. (See p. 359.)
- Invasion of privacy. (See p. 230.)
- Infringement of the right of publicity. (See p. 356.)
- Copyright infringement. (See p. 353.)
- Trademark infringement. (See p. 136.)
- Intentional and negligent infliction of emotional distress.
- Any other claim arising from the granted rights.

In addition to the previously listed causes of action, plaintiffs who have sued motion picture companies over life story issues have asserted claims for false advertising, false endorsement, commercial disparagement, and unjust enrichment. This is why it is critical for the producer to secure the release of "any claim or cause of action whatsoever arising from the use of the granted rights or portrayal of my likeness or life story."

Although it is true that the First Amendment may provide a solid foundation for defending against many of these claims, the point is to avoid the lawsuit altogether. Furthermore, your E&O insurance policy will probably demand a signed life rights consent agreement.

KRUSHER KRABB: ARMED AND DANGEROUS

Pedro the Producer wants to shoot a biography of wrestling superstar Krusher Krabb, the only one-armed professional wrestler ever to be inducted into the Schenectady Wrestling Hall of Fame. Pedro first approaches Krusher for his life story rights but is turned down. He goes ahead with the movie anyway, excited to tell Krusher's uplifting triumph-over-adversity story. Trying to make his biography as compelling as possible, he decides to fictionalize a portion of Krusher's story.

In real life, Krusher lost his arm in a car accident; in Pedro's version, however, Krusher's limb is devoured by an alligator during a wrestling match at a gator farm. Because Krusher's 40-year marriage to his high school sweetheart is motion-picture monotony, Pedro creates a scene in which Krusher has an illicit affair with his trainer's wife—an event that never happened in real life.

Eager to contrast Krusher at his physical peak with the withered old man whom he has become, Pedro secretly photographs Krusher at home, struggling to bathe himself.

After screening the rough cut for his film for several licensing agents, Pedro strikes a deal with a toy manufacturing company to produce Krusher action figures.

Needless to say, Krusher is livid. He can sue Pedro for invasion of privacy (both false light and intrusion upon seclusion), libel, false endorsement, and misappropriation of the right of publicity.

DEV.

What's Allowed in One State May Not Be Allowed in Another

What makes this area particularly tricky is that most of the rights involved are governed by state laws. And to make things even more complex, the laws differ from state to state. For instance, some states recognize a right of publicity; others don't.

To be on the safe side, you should obtain the broadest possible set of rights and releases from all people whose stories are depicted recognizably in the film.

It's CYA time here. If you don't, you could expose yourself to liability if you distribute your film in a state that gives the grantor rights that you have not received permission to use. For instance, depending on the state, if the subject is dead, certain rights may survive death. Therefore the estate of the deceased may have to be negotiated with.

EVEN THE DEAD MAY HAVE RIGHTS

Even though someone may be dead, his or her right of publicity may live on! The duration of rights of publicity varies from state to state. In New York it dies with you; in California, it lasts for 70 years after your death. When planning on telling a story about a dead person, filmmakers should seek permission from the *estate* of the deceased.

WHAT IS AN ESTATE?

An estate is not just a house in the country. The term also describes the property, assets, and rights left behind by a dead person. Rights of publicity, copyrights, and other intellectual property rights can be held by an estate. The person who manages the estate is the *executor* or an *administrator*.

Example: In New York, Felicity Filmmaker shoots and broadcasts a television commercial in which Elvis Presley literally rises from the grave to endorse Rockin' Rippled Pork Rinds: "They're so good I just had to come back for more!" Felicity knows that in New York the right of publicity dies with you. She has even put a disclaimer on the commercial saying that the product is not endorsed by Elvis Presley™ Enterprises, in the hopes that this will defeat any trademark infringement lawsuits. Her client loves the commercial so much that it broadcasts the spot in California, which does allow the right of publicity to survive death. Elvis Presley™ Enterprises successfully sues Felicity in California.

If the consent cannot be obtained, the filmmaker must try to fictionalize that person's life story. Here the producer must use extreme caution—the life story must be so modified that the subject must not be recognizable. This, of course, may leave the producer with a very different story from the one she had started out to tell.

THE BOTTOM LINE: If you are filming someone's life story, have them sign a life rights consent agreement, change the events in the movie so that the story is no longer recognizable as theirs, or write the character out of the film altogether.

GOALS AND DEALS

For definitions and explanations of common contract clauses, see Appendix C, "The Clause Companion," p. 375.

- The filmmaker must make sure to negotiate and execute a life rights consent agreement with the appropriate party. Usually this is the person whose story the filmmaker wants to portray. However, there are some notable exceptions:

  - If the subject of the story is dead, you might need to get the consent of his or her estate.

  - Minors and legally incapacitated individuals will probably require the consent and signatures of their guardians.

- The filmmaker should get a life rights consent and release from every person who is portrayed in the film. In the Krusher Krabb example, this would mean getting releases from the wrestler's wife, his manager, and other real-life people who will be a part of the movie.

- If the motion picture is based on a preexisting literary work (e.g., a biography), the filmmaker may need to negotiate for the motion picture rights with the holder of the copyright of that book. (See "Screenplay Adaptations," p. 117.) Additionally, the filmmaker must verify that the book's copyright owner has already obtained a life rights consent from the subject and that such consent can be assigned to the filmmaker.

DEV.

MAJOR DEAL POINTS: LIFE RIGHTS CONSENT AND RELEASE

The Parties

- *Producer.* It is critical that the producer negotiate the life rights consent *before* any other steps are taken on the film. If the producer waits until after the film is shot, the grantor can effectively hold the production hostage by refusing to sign the agreement unless a much higher price is paid. The producer should try to pay a flat fee to the grantor for the rights and releases contained in the agreement and should be very careful about giving any sort of approval over the story to the grantor.

- *Grantor.* The grantor is the person granting the life story rights in the *subject's* life. The grantor could be the same person as the subject of the biography; however, the grantor could also be the subject's parent, if the subject is a minor; her estate, if she's dead; or the business that owns the subject's life story rights. The grantor may want to consider whether he or she plans to turn the life story into a literary work, such as a book, separate and aside from the motion picture. If so, the right to authorize a book about the subject will have to be excluded from the grant of rights to the producer, because the producer will most likely want all the rights to a grantor's life story.

Rights Granted

This section spells out the specific rights granted to the producer (also referred to as *assigned rights*).

- The producer will want the broadest grant of rights possible:
  - The right to portray the subject's life in whole, or in part
  - The right to fictionalize or modify the subject's life story
  - The right (and sometimes the obligation) to use pseudonyms for people and places portrayed in the subject's life story
  - The copyright and concept rights to any accounts of the subject's life story (this of course may be limited by any preexisting literary works based on the life story)
  - Any other rights necessary to exploit the subject's life story
- *Scope.* As a starting point for the negotiation, the producer should attempt to secure the rights throughout the universe, in perpetuity, in all media, whether now known or hereafter discovered, all methods of advertising, and merchandising.
- At a minimum, the producer needs *motion picture and television rights*. The producer needs to make sure that these rights extend to all media in which that motion picture or program will be exploited, such as theatrical release, television, video, DVD, online media, and "any exhibition medium, now known or hereinafter developed."

Reserved Rights

Reserved rights specify which rights the owner retains. These are the rights the producer does *not* get. As mentioned earlier, the producer should attempt to limit the reserved rights. However, the grantor may want to reserve the right to make a literary work, such as an autobiography, based on the subject's life story.

Releases

The producer should secure the following *releases* from the grantor. In other words, the subject is giving up the right to sue for any of the following:

- Libel and defamation
- Invasion of privacy
- Intentional and negligent infliction of emotional distress
- Misappropriation of right of publicity
- Copyright infringement
- Trademark infringement

- False endorsement
- Any other claim arising from the granted rights

Right to Make Changes

The producer should retain the unfettered right to change, modify, fictionalize, add, edit, rearrange, or otherwise add to or detract from the subject's life story—without the approval of the grantor. Obviously, this may be a hard sell given that most people want some control over how their own story is told. The producer should be wary about giving any control greater than a "consultation" right (which just means that the producer must consult with the grantor but does not have to incorporate the grantor's suggestions).

Representations and Warranties

The grantor must promise that he or she has the sole authority to grant the rights and releases in the agreement. The grantor must indemnify the producer, and anyone the producer has assigned the rights to, for a breach of that promise. As seen in other contracts, such representations and warranties often include promises that:

DEV.

- The life story is true and accurate.
- The grantor is the sole owner of the life story, and nothing in the story infringes the rights of anyone else.
- Copyright registration in any literary property based on the life story is up to date and accurate.
- No other motion picture, dramatic, or other version of the life story has been made or authorized.
- None of the granted rights are or have ever been granted to anyone else.
- By selling the life story, the grantor will not be violating any third-party rights.
- The grantor will not impair, encumber, or otherwise do anything to interfere with the granted rights.
- The grantor should indemnify the producer for breaches of representations and warranties, misrepresentations, or damages resulting from the grantor's breach of contract.

Payment

Grantors are typically paid a flat fee for life story rights. The amount is largely based on how central the character is to the story. Fees may range from a few hundred dollars for a character who is ancillary to the story to thousands of dollars for a main or otherwise integral character. A famous personality or celebrity, especially one who has benefited from the commercial exploitation of his or her personality, will command a much higher price than someone who has not.

No Obligation to Produce

Although the producer has the right to produce the film about or featuring the subject, the producer is not obligated to produce the film.

Remedies

The grantor should waive any claim to injunctive relief arising out of a breach of the contract. Additionally, in all events the grantor should be prohibited from rescinding the contract and recapturing the granted rights.

Credit

- In addition to the person whose life story is being depicted, the movie should also credit the author of any source material (such as an autobiographical book) used to make the film that was based on the life story.
- The credit roll should contain a disclaimer, such as: "Certain characters, events, and dialogue in the motion picture in the film were created for the purpose of fictionalization."

DEV.

Business Issues

- You have better negotiating leverage if you secure the subject's life rights prior to production. The best practice is to secure the rights prior to writing a screenplay.
- Check your E&O insurance policy: when portraying actual people, a life rights consent and release is *almost always required* by distributors and by E&O insurance companies.

Step by Step: Life Story Rights

1. Make sure you get a life rights consent and release from *everybody* whose lives will be portrayed in your movie.
2. If someone does not consent, try to write them out of the movie or change their character so substantially that they are not recognizable.
3. Include a disclaimer at the end of the motion picture. (See "Copyright Notice and Disclaimer," p. 285.)

10

CHAIN OF TITLE: THE CARE AND FEEDING OF YOUR COPYRIGHT

WHAT IS A CHAIN OF TITLE?

It's not enough to have a great screenplay. You also have to protect it by safeguarding its copyright. To care for your copyright, you must register it with the U.S. Copyright Office, always display the proper copyright notice on all copies of the script and prints of the film, and maintain a clean *chain of title*.

DEV.

The chain of title is the unbroken record of ownership of the copyright and other legal rights to the film property. You will need to prove the film's chain of title to distributors, financiers, unions, insurers, and a variety of other parties during the course of the life of a film.

The following are key components in establishing and maintaining a clean chain of title for film property:

- Investigating the copyright to all source material used to make the script. (See "Copyright Searches and Permissions," p. 132.)
- Commissioning a screenplay clearance report to detect potential copyright ownership conflicts and problems. (See "Screenplay Clearance Report," p. 135.)
- Properly drafting and executing contracts which transfer copyright and other IP rights from the writer, screenwriter, or literary property owner to the production company.
- Registering the copyright in the script. (See "Copyright Registration," p. 136.)
- Obtaining a certificate of authorship from the writer. (See "Certificate of Authorship," p. 142.)
- Recording all copyright transfers and assignments with the U.S. Copyright Office. (See "Copyright Recordation, Assignments, and Transfers," p. 139.)

TIP: **Time is of the essence here. Do these steps before you go into production!**

COPYRIGHT SEARCHES AND PERMISSIONS

Frequently producers will need to find out copyright information concerning a particular work. For instance, you might want to make a movie from somebody's copyrighted novel or use a copyrighted sculpture as art direction for a scene. Or you might need to provide an insurer, financier, or distributor with a copyright search report. In short, at some point (hopefully, early on) the producer or one of his staff will need to conduct or commission a copyright search. The process of researching a copyright and getting permission from the copyright's owners is called *clearing a copyright*.

Copyright searches are an art form all to themselves. All too often, an author's contact information is difficult to find and may require a good deal of diligent investigative work. Remember, just because you can't find out who the author is doesn't mean that you're off the hook and that you are excused from getting permission to use the work. Unknown authors still have rights, and you don't want to get the author's contact information for the first time from her lawyer's cease-and-desist letter. (See "Cease-and-Desist Letters and Lawsuits," p. 46.)

To clear a copyright:

1. The producer needs to establish whether the particular work is still protected by copyright
2. If it is, the producer needs to get the contact information for that work's copyright owner so that he can attempt to negotiate a license to use that work.

There are four basic methods for researching the copyright to a work:

1. You can perform the research yourself.
2. You can hire a lawyer to perform the search.
3. You can commission the Copyright Office to perform a search.
4. You can use a professional copyright research company.

Often, your investigation will involve all these methods.

DEV.

> **PUBLIC DOMAIN IN THE UNITED STATES MAY NOT BE PUBLIC DOMAIN IN OTHER COUNTRIES**
>
> If a work is *not* protected by copyright it is in the *public domain*. This means that it can be used by anybody without seeking permission from the original author.
>
> However, a work may be in the public domain in the United States yet still be protected by copyright law in other countries. This is because each country has its own laws regarding the scope and duration of copyright protection. Accordingly, a film that

> **PUBLIC DOMAIN IN THE UNITED STATES MAY NOT BE PUBLIC DOMAIN IN OTHER COUNTRIES (cont.)**
>
> incorporates an unauthorized work that is in the public domain in the United States but is still protected in another country may be considered an infringing work when it is distributed in that country without the permission of the copyright owner.
>
> For more information on the public domain, see Appendix A, "Public Domain," p. 332.

Step By Step: Copyright Searches and Permissions

At some point in the filmmaking process you will need to get permission to use somebody else's copyrighted work in your film. Unfortunately, finding a copyright owner can often be tricky. Here are some tips to help you locate a copyright owner and seek permission to use their work:

1. Get basic information about the work. To begin, you will need to get some fundamental information about the work itself:

   - *The year of publication.* If this is a book, this information will be found as part of the copyright notice. For example, "*Eight-Track Tape: a Herald of the Future* © 1975 Myopic Publishing, Inc.," means that this book was published in 1975. (See "Copyright Notice," p. 139.) Remember, if it is a work originally created and published in the United States before 1923, it is probably in the public domain and you will not need permission from the author. (See "Copyright Duration," p. 351.)

   - *Author and publisher information.* For a book, this information will also be included next to, or as part of, the copyright notice. For sound recordings the copyright symbol is Ⓟ. The Copyright Office offers this advice: "Examine the disk, tape cartridge, or cassette in which the recorded sound is fixed, or the album cover, sleeve, or container in which the recording is sold."

2. Check out the Copyright Office website. For works registered or renewed since 1978, search the Copyright Office website for free at www.copyright.gov/records/.

3. Pay the Copyright Office to search for you. If you can't find the information you need or if the work was registered prior to 1978, you might want to commission a search by the Copyright Office itself.[1] The Copyright Office charges an hourly rate and will provide you with an estimate of how long the search will take before it starts. You should be prepared to give the following information to the Copyright Office researchers:

   - The title of the work, with any possible variants
   - The names of the authors, including possible pseudonyms

DEV.

- The name of the probable copyright owner, which may be that of the publisher or that of the producer
- The approximate year when the work was published or registered
- The type of work involved (book, play, musical composition, sound recording, photograph, etc.)
- For a work originally published as a part of a periodical or collection, the title of that publication and any other information, such as the volume or issue number, to help identify it
- The registration number or any other copyright data[2]

4. Hire a professional search company. If all else fails, you can hire a professional copyright research company such as Thomson-Thomson to conduct a full copyright search report. See http://compumark.thomson.com/do/US_copyright_search. This may be the most expensive option, but given the fact that these companies search additional databases to the ones used by the Copyright Office, it is probably the most thorough option.

5. Use your production attorney to help you locate and secure permissions from the right parties.

DEV.

6. Get permission *in writing* to use the work. Once you've identified the copyright owner, get permission to use the copyrighted work with a written copyright license signed by the rights holder.

- For literary works. (See "Literary Property Acquisition Agreement," p. 117.)
- For painting and sculptures. (See "Artwork License," p. 248.)
- For music. (See "Music License Agreement," p. 267.)
- For film clips. (See "Film Clip License Agreement," p. 281.)

RESEARCHING COPYRIGHTS

Copyright Office circular #22 provides information on how to research the status of the copyrighted work. For more information, see www.copyright.gov/circs/circ22.pdf.

To commission a search by the Copyright Office, contact them at Library of Congress:

Copyright Office-RRC
101 Independence Avenue SE
Washington, DC 20559-6306
Phone: (202) 707-6850 (M–F, 8:30–5:00 eastern time)
Fax: (202) 252-3485
E-mail: copysearch@loc.gov

Screenplay Clearance Report

Prior to production, you should have your entertainment attorney prepare a screenplay clearance report. Essentially, this report details potential legal problem areas in the screenplay. The report should combine the efforts of a copyright records search to identify conflicting copyright ownership and infringement issues with a comprehensive legal analysis to identify other intellectual property, defamation, and liability issues.

The report should alert you to the following legal issues, if present:

- *Libel and defamation.* (See "Libel and Defamation," p. 359.) Documentaries need to be particularly aware of libel and defamation claims. Any material that could affect somebody's reputation should be scrutinized carefully. If the person being discussed or depicted is not a public figure such as a politician, extreme care should be used to ensure that all portrayals and discussions about that person are accurate and truthful. Ideally, anyone discussed or portrayed in the film should give his or her written consent. If you have E&O insurance, your insurance carrier will probably require written consent for all depicted individuals.

- *Invasion of privacy.* (See "Violation of Privacy Rights," p. 356.) Does your film discuss private facts about people's lives? Remember, here the inquiry is focused on whether your script is prying into someone's personal life in an overly intrusive manner. For fictional films and programs, you should check all character names; you're better off having a character name that nobody in the real world shares or, conversely, that many people share. A character name shared by only a few people could help support an argument that your film is referring to that real individual, which is a prerequisite for a defamation or invasion-of-privacy lawsuit. For instance, from a legal perspective, John Smith and Xerxes Vander-Flärpenboot would be good legal choices for character names. The former name is common, the latter name unique.

DEV.

- *Copyright.* (See "What Is a Copyright Infringement," p. 353.) Your attorney should flag any instances of copyright infringement. This is a two-part inquiry, which scrutinizes any copyrighted works referenced in the screenplay as well as the copyright to any works on which the screenplay is based.

- *Referenced copyright.* The first part of the inquiry focuses on any third-party copyrighted material directly referenced in the screenplay, such as song lyrics sung by a character or a scene in which two characters watch a copyrighted movie. In other words, references in the screenplay itself to other copyrighted works will need to be cleared and licensed. If these works cannot be cleared, they should be changed to noncopyrighted works or works commissioned by the production company as works for hire. If neither clearing the copyright nor changing the work is possible, the copyrighted work should be omitted from the film.

- *Underlying copyright and chain of title.* The second part of the inquiry analyzes the copyright in the screenplay itself, as distinguished from any copyrighted works *referenced* in the screenplay. Here the attorney will try to make sure that the structure, plot, scenes, characters, and dialogue originated with the screenwriter. If these elements are taken from another copyrighted work (e.g., a graphic novel, play, or book), the attorney will need to verify that the screenwriter had the right to create a derivative work based on that source and that the screenwriter has validly transferred that right to the production company. (See "Screenplay Adaptations," p. 117.) If the screenplay was written by two or more authors, the attorney should verify that all authors have conveyed their copyright interests to the production company. (See Appendix A, "Joint Authors and Joint Works," p. 341.)

- *Trademark infringement, tarnishment, and false endorsement.* In addition to ensuring that the screenplay doesn't depict any copyrighted works without permission, the production attorney should review all script references to trademarked products and services. Like copyrights, unlicensed trademark use should be avoided. The attorney should be on the lookout for any use of trademarks or a celebrity's image:

  - That might cast that trademarked product or service in a negative light, or

  - That implies that the owners of the trademark endorsed the film (see "Trademarks on the Set," p. 250; also "False Endorsement," p. 250)

- *Potential legal problems in production.* The attorney should also bring to bear her general legal knowledge. If a scene involves extensive pyrotechnics, the attorney should make note that special permits will probably be needed. If the movie involves extensive use of child actors, the attorney should note that special child labor laws may restrict the shooting schedule. This portion of the review is often done in conjunction with script breakdown.

- *Conflicts with talent agreements.* Talent agreements often impose restrictions on the way an actor may be photographed. If partial nudity is required, make sure that there is a nudity rider in that actor's contract. For child actors, make sure that the parents give their signed consent to allow children to appear in scenes dealing with adult situations.

- *Conflicts with production services agreements.* If your company has been hired to make a program for a network or cablecaster (see "Production Services Agreement," p. 149), you need to make sure that nothing in your script violates that company's standards and practices guidelines. Furthermore, if you are planning on featuring specific products in your script, you will need to run that list of manufacturers by the network's marketing division to make sure that there are no conflicts with the network's current advertisers.

The screenplay clearance report should be completed well before shooting takes place, to give the production company enough time to secure the proper permissions or to make creative changes as needed.

COPYRIGHT REGISTRATION

Registration is the process of filing your copyright information with the government. You should register the copyright to both your script and to your motion picture. You can hire a service to register the copyright for you or you can do it yourself. You register a copyright by depositing a copy of your work with the U.S. Copyright Office. Registration consists of filling out and submitting an online copyright registration form along with a sample of the work you're registering as well as the correct registration fee.

COPYRIGHT CONCEPTS

- *Work.* Under copyright law, the term *work* is used to describe scripts, movies, musical compositions, and any other copyrightable form of artistic expression. On the copyright registration form, the word *work* is used quite frequently to refer to the underlying copyrightable portion.

- *Publication.* "Publication of a motion picture takes place when one or more copies are distributed to the public by sale, rental, lease or lending, or when an offering is made to distribute copies to a group of persons (wholesalers, retailers, broadcasters, motion picture distributors, and the like) for purposes of further distribution or public performance."[3] For more, see Appendix A, "Copyright Law," p. 331.

DEV.

Why Register the Work?

Although registration is no longer a requirement of copyright protection, it does provide the following benefits:

- Registration is usually required by distribution companies, E&O companies, and other third parties who may have an interest in maintaining and protecting the film property.

- Registration establishes a public record of the copyright claim.

- Before an infringement suit may be filed in court, registration is necessary for works of U.S. origin.

- If registration is made before or within five years of publication, courts will start with the presumption that the copyright is valid and that all the facts stated in the certificate are correct.

- If registration is made within three months after publication of the work or prior to an infringement of the work, statutory damages and attorney's fees will be available to the copyright owner in court actions. Otherwise, only an award of actual damages and profits is available to the copyright owner. (See "Copyright Infringement," p. 353.)

- Registration allows the owner of the copyright to record the registration with the U.S. Customs Service for protection against the importation of infringing copies.

DEPOSIT YOUR WORK–IT'S THE LAW!

Even if you don't want to *register* the copyright, it is a legal require-ment that all copyrightable published works be *deposited* with the Copyright Office within three months of publication.[4] Failure to do so may expose you to a fine of $250 for each work, plus the retail price of the copies. And if you've repeatedly or intentionally refused to deposit the copies, an additional fine of $2,500 may be assessed against you.

This deposit requirement is fulfilled if the works are registered with the Copyright Office, so you might as well register the work while you're at it.

Online Copyright Registration

The Copyright Office has made registration easier than ever by moving it online. Although you can still print out a paper form (Form CO), fill it in, and mail it to the Copyright Office, it's so much easier to do everything from your browser, from filling in the form to uploading the video files and paying with a credit card. To register a motion picture, visit the website of the U.S. Copyright Office at www.copyright.gov.

For a detailed, step-by-step explanation of how to register your copyright using the Copyright Office's online registration, see *The Pocket Lawyer for Filmmakers* website. 💻 www.thepocketlawyerforfilm.com

What You Submit

To register the copyright to your script or movie, submit the following to the Copyright Office:

1. A completed application form (preferably completed online).
2. A "best-edition" nonreturnable copy of your work. A best edition is the version that is the cleanest, most legible, and most complete.
   - For films:
   - For *unpublished* films, one copy of the motion picture, which can be uploaded digitally, size permitting.
   - For *published* films, two best edition copies of the movie, which must be sent in physically.
   - For screenplays, submit a copy of the script.
   - Check with the Copyright Office as to the particular format you are submitting.
3. A description of the work itself—for example, a shooting script or synopsis of the film.
4. A $35 payment, if registering online.

The Copyright Office accepts the deposit of movies and scripts in the following formats:

Screenplay:	Printed script
Film:	Preprint material with special arrangement
	35-mm positive prints
	16-mm positive prints
Video:	Betacam SP
	Digital Beta (Digibeta)
	DVD
	VHS cassette

For more information, see Copyright Office Circular 7B at www.copyright.gov/circs/circ07b.pdf.

You should receive a certificate of registration within a few months (sometimes as many as six months) after sending in your materials. No matter how long the Copyright Office takes to register your copyright, the date of registration will be the date on which the Copyright Office receives all your materials.

THE COPYRIGHT NOTICE

DEV.

Although it is no longer a requirement for copyright protection, it is advisable to include a copyright notice on all your copyrighted work. The proper format for the notice is ©, "Copyright," or "Copr.," followed by the year in which the work was first published, followed by the name of the copyright owner.

Example: *Wombats in Love II: A Womb with a View* © 2010 Zeus Pictures, Inc.

For motion picture or video, the copyright notice should be placed in one or more of the following places[5]:

• With or near the title
• With the cast, credits, and similar information
• At or immediately following the beginning of the work
• At or immediately preceding the end of the work

For the screenplay, it is customary to display the copyright notice prominently on the cover of the script.

For more information about copyright notice, see U.S. Copyright Office Circular 3, "Copyright Notice," at www.copyright.gov/circs/circ03.pdf.

COPYRIGHT RECORDATION, ASSIGNMENTS, AND TRANSFERS

Assignments and Transfers

Any contract or other document that transfers copyright ownership may be recorded at the Copyright Office. In other words, you should record writing agreements, options, literary property purchase agreements, copyright assignments, and contracts containing copyright assignment or licenses clauses. In fact, the Copyright Office will record any document "pertaining to a copyright."

Why Record?

Recording a contract or other document pertaining to copyright ownership has several effects:

- It establishes a public record of ownership by giving the world *constructive notice* of the new owner. Constructive notice means that once the copyright in a work is registered, everyone is presumed to know the ownership and other registration information on file with the Copyright Office—even if they have not, in fact, actually looked up the registration records.
- It determines *priority* of conflicting transfers (see following).
- It is necessary to prove a chain of title required by distributors, insurers, and other third parties.

DEV. Conflicting Transfers

It might be surprising to learn, but you could lose a copyright transferred to you if you don't record the transfer in time! If you fail to record the transferred copyright and the original copyright owner transfers that same copyright to a third party who then records that second transfer, you could lose the copyright.[6]

BURNT BY *TOAST*

Wanda Writer has written a screenplay. Eager to strike a deal, she transfers the rights in her screenplay, *The Exciting World of Toast,* to Fly by Night Productions on July 1, 2012.

A week after Wanda signed the purchase agreement with Fly by Night Productions, Major Studio, Inc., approaches her to acquire the rights in her screenplay. Realizing that she has a much better deal with Major Studio, Inc., Wanda decides to transfer the rights to *The Exciting World of Toast* to Major Studio, Inc., even though she had assigned the same rights to Fly by Night Productions a week earlier. Major Studio, Inc., is unaware of the deal between Fly by Night Productions and Wanda. She signs a purchase agreement with Major Studio on July 15, 2012.

- If Fly by Night Productions records the assignment of copyright with the Copyright Office within one month after Wanda transfers her copyright to it (i.e., by August 1, 2012), Fly by Night Productions will own the rights to the screenplay.

BURNT BY *TOAST* (cont.)

- However, if Fly by Night Productions *does not record* the assignment of copyright by August 1, 2012, and Major Studio records its assignment of copyright first (for instance, on August 10), Major Studio will own the copyright to the screenplay, regardless of whether Fly by Night Productions records its assignment of copyright on August 11.

No matter which production company gets the copyright to the script, the other (losing) production company cannot recover the screenplay copyright unless the winner is willing to sign it over.

Does the losing company have any cause for action? Yes, a breach-of-contract lawsuit against Wanda Writer. (See Appendix B, "Breach of Contract," p. 371.)

Short-Form Copyright Assignment

Keep in mind that recorded documents become publicly available, so any terms in a contract that is recorded will become known to anyone who views the recorded document. If you record the entire contract that contains the assignment clause, the entire world will also be able to read the contract clauses containing compensation, contact information, and other paragraphs that the parties might not want the public to access. For this reason short-form assignments and transfers are often used, rather than the longer contracts that justify the transfer.

DEV.

Short-form assignments contain the minimum amount of information needed to effectuate the transfer of copyright. They are often executed concurrently with the longer contract that details the deal terms under which the assignment occurs (for instance, a literary acquisition agreement).

SAMPLE SHORT-FORM COPYRIGHT ASSIGNMENT

Date: _____

For one dollar in hand and other good and valuable consideration, the receipt and sufficiency of which is hereby acknowledged by all parties, the undersigned _____ (Assignor) does hereby assign and convey to _____ (Assignee), its successors, assigns, and licensees, the copyright to that [*motion picture, video, screenplay, etc.*] (the "Work"), currently titled: "_____," and registered with the United States Copyright Office Registration #_____. This assignment is perpetual in duration and applies to all derivative works of the Work and all copyrightable components which have comprised the Work.

Agreed to and Accepted by:

Assignee: _____ Assignor: _____

How to Record a Document

The Copyright Office does not determine the form of the documents to be recorded, so virtually any contract, from screenplay options to distribution agreements to director's services contracts, may be recorded.

A few basic requirements must be met. The document to be recorded must:

1. Have original signatures of the parties who signed it (or proper certification of photocopy)
2. Be complete by its own terms
3. Be legible
4. Be accompanied by the correct fee, which is $105 for one title[7]

COPYRIGHT CONCEPTS

The document must be *complete by its own terms*. That is, a document that contains a reference to any schedule, appendix, exhibit, addendum, or other material as being attached or made a part of it is recordable only if the attachment is also submitted for recordation with the document.[8]

For example, if you state in the assignment that the assignment is "subject to the terms and conditions of that option agreement entered into between the parties on December 3, 2009..." that option agreement had better be attached, or the assignment would be unrecordable.

See Copyright Circular 12 on the U.S. Copyright website for more information at www.copyright.gov/circs/circ12.pdf.

CERTIFICATE OF AUTHORSHIP

A *certificate of authorship* is a key document in the chain of title of a motion picture. This is a notarized statement by the writer identifying the author of the script. In the case of a work made for hire, the script's author is considered to be the production company. A certificate should be executed by all the script's authors.

THE CERTIFICATE OF AUTHORSHIP

"I, [writer's name] certify that I have written the attached screenplay as a work made for hire for *[production company's name]*, pursuant to that writer's services agreement, dated _____, between me and the aforementioned production company. Accordingly, I understand and agree that the production company shall be considered the author of the attached screenplay. If a court of competent jurisdiction determines that the screenplay was not created as a work made for hire, I hereby assign all copyright, title, and interest to that screenplay to the production company with full rights to assign said copyright in whatsoever manner the production company chooses. I waive any right to *"droit moral,"* or other moral right, now known, or hereafter enacted.

I understand and agree that as full owner of the copyright to the screenplay, the production company and its assigns, may make any modification or change whatsoever to the screenplay or its derivative works.

I represent and warrant that nothing in the screenplay infringes upon any rights of third parties; the screenplay contains no defamatory material and does not infringe the privacy rights of any parties. All of the material not original with me which was used to create the screenplay was either provided to me by the production company or was in the public domain. I have the full right and power to execute this document, and nothing in the screenplay, or my services in connection with the creation of the screenplay does, or shall infringe the rights of a third party."

DEV.

Keep Your Records Clean

All the documents that affect your chain of title should be kept in a separate, well-organized binder. Presenting a financier, network, distribution company, insurer, or other coproduction company with an easy-to-follow, comprehensive file goes a long way toward establishing your credibility as a trustworthy and reliable filmmaker.

5

PRE-PRODUCTION

Once you've figured out which movie you're going to make and you've acquired all the rights to that film property, it's almost time to start staffing up and getting ready for the production. But first…

PRODUCTION SERVICES AGREEMENTS

If another company wants to hire your production company to produce a film or television show, you will first need to negotiate a *production services agreement* with them. (See "Production Services Agreement," p. 149.) This agreement lays out the budget and scope of the project, determines how your company will be paid, and dictates the precise technical and legal compliance standards of the program. The agreement may even dictate who you need to hire to write, direct, or star in your project.

PRODUCT PLACEMENT

You might want to save money on props and set decoration by having manufacturers and advertisers supply you with their products in exchange for your promise to include their goods, trademarks, and/or services in your film. On bigger-budget films, movies with well-known actors, and programs with the potential to reach large audiences, manufacturers may also pay you a fee to feature their wares onscreen. (See "Product Placement," p. 157.) The time to start this process is in pre-production, before the cameras start rolling.

PRE-PROD.

Now it's time to cast actors, sign up a director (if it's not going to be you), and hire your crew.

HIRING CAST AND CREW

Hiring and managing employees and independent contractors is one of the trickier legal areas a filmmaker must face. This is because a whole host of laws apply to the employer/employee relationship. For instance:

- *Services contracts.* A *services contract* between the production company and the worker will govern the relationship of the parties and control issues such as the worker's duties, the worker's salary, the film credit the worker expects to receive, benefits for the worker (if any), and so on. Don't forget, a worker can be an employee or independent contractor, and the worker may have her own loan-out company, which is also a party to the services agreement. (See "Loan-Out Company," p. 42.)

- *Union collective bargaining agreements.* If the worker is a member of an entertainment union, such as SAG, WGA, or IATSE, and the production company is a signatory of that union, the working relationship is governed by the rules of that entertainment union. That union's collective bargaining agreement will win out over any conflicting provisions in the services contract.

- *Federal and state labor and employment laws.* To complicate matters further, federal and state labor and employment laws will also trump the services agreement and impose limits and requirements on how a production company employer must deal with its employees.

Hiring Employees: Layers of Law

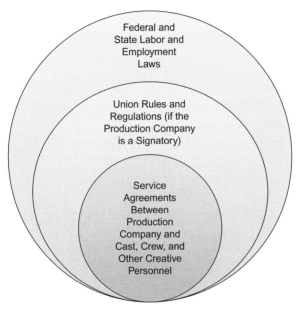

This section of the book provides information on:

- Negotiating a production services agreement, which is used when another company is hiring your production company to create a film, webisode, or television program for them. (See "Production Services Agreement," p. 149.)

- Negotiating a product placement agreement when you want to feature a product in your film and be compensated for it. (See "Product Placement Agreement," p. 157.)

- A brief overview of employment and labor law. (See "Federal and State Labor and Employment Law," p. 147; for more detail on these issues, see Appendix D, "A Filmmaker's Guide to Labor and Employment Law," p. 393.)

- How to hire a producer. (See "Producer's Services Agreement," p. 171.)

- How to hire a director. (See "Director's Services Agreement," p. 183.)

- How to hire a crew member. (See "Crew Services Agreement," p. 195.)

- How to hire an actor. (See "Performer's Services Agreement," p. 212.)

- Dealing with the Screen Actor's Guild. (See "The Screen Actor's Guild," p. 205.)

- Getting a script to an actor and dealing with the agent. (See "How to Get a Script to a SAG Actor," p. 222.)

THE PRODUCTION SERVICES AGREEMENT

Let's turn to television and webisodes for a moment. Sometimes you're not making a program on your own dime, but instead someone is hiring your production company to produce a program for them. It could be a webisode for a television network's website, a reality series for a basic cable channel, or a documentary commissioned by a premium cable network. However, one basic fact never changes: The larger media company is paying your smaller production company to shoot and deliver to them a program according to their detailed specifications. The *production services agreement* between the larger media company and your smaller production company controls both how the program will be produced and the technical and legal standards that govern its production.

NETWORKS, STUDIOS, TELEVISION MEDIA COMPANIES, AND OTHER BEASTS OF THE FIELD

In this day and age of global production, there are many kinds of entities that produce programming: television media companies, production arms of a distribution companies, broadcast divisions of a motion picture companies, and so on. The lines between them are blurry and getting blurrier. For the sake of clarity in this chapter, I'll refer to the larger television media company that is commissioning a program from your production company as "the network."

PRE-PROD.

GETTING A NETWORK INTERESTED IN YOUR PROJECT

As a general rule, a network will only commission programming from a smaller production company if:

- You or your company has a track record in producing such programming
- You've worked with the network or one of its executives before
- You have the exclusive rights to a key program element, such as life rights to the subject of a docu-drama

   Example: Your company, Pleonasm Pictures, has an exclusive option on the life story rights of octogenarian demolition derby driver Maude "The Marauder."

You pitch the Carnage Network on your idea of a one-hour documentary on the fender-bending grandma. Although the network might be able to do an unauthorized documentary on Maude "The Marauder," it really wants her cooperation for the interview segments in the one-hour documentary. Because it wants her, the network must deal with your company to get her participation.

Once you have the network's attention, you have to go in and pitch your program idea. Bringing a short trailer to the pitch meeting can help showcase both your concept as well as your ability to execute the program. Before you go in to pitch your idea, make sure you understand how to protect your rights. (See "Idea Rights," p. 77.) If the network likes your idea, thinks it can market or exhibit it, and thinks that your company can competently produce it, it is time to negotiate the production services agreement.

MAJOR DEAL POINTS: THE PRODUCTION SERVICES AGREEMENT

The Parties

The network may hire your production company directly to produce the program, or it might contract with a larger production company to supervise your company's production.

If you haven't done so already, you should form a limited liability entity, like an LLC or a corporation, and have your company (rather than you personally) be a party to the production services agreement. That way if something goes wrong during the production and the network sues, it is your company's assets that will be on the line rather than your personal assets. (See "Setting Up the Production Company," p. 35.)

Engagement/Production Services

This paragraph outlines the specific duties required of the production company in producing the program. It typically contains:

- *The tentative title, subject matter, running time, and delivery date of the program.* Often, this section will reference a treatment or script that the production company has pitched to the network.

- *A reference to an attached schedule, budget, and production technical and legal specifications of the program.*

- *A key person clause* designating you or one of your production company's employees as the executive producer in charge of the production. (See "Clause Companion: Key Person Clause," p. 379.) Note that this is usually a material provision. In other words, it is critical that this key person act as executive producer; no substitutions allowed! If they quit the project you could find yourself in breach of contract. That's why you should make sure the key person is someone you know that you can rely on, such as someone you've worked with before. If you are working on other projects in addition to the one that is the subject of the production services agreement, make sure to stipulate that you may continue to work on those "outside projects" as long as it does not materially interfere with the work you're doing on the project covered by the production services agreement.

Rights

If the network is paying for the production, they will want ownership of the copyright and other intellectual property rights in the program. In the agreement there will typically be a work-for-hire or rights assignment from your company to the network. (See Appendix C, "Rights Granted," p. 381.) If you own the underlying rights on which the program will be based (see "Getting a Network Interested," earlier in this chapter), try to negotiate a grant only of the rights necessary to make the program at hand without giving away all rights to the property. In other words, if you are producing a one-hour documentary for basic cable, try to retain the theatrical film rights. However, be prepared for the network to laugh politely at this request and say "no."

Payment Schedule/Acquisition Price

This is the total production budget you will be given to make the program. If the network is paying for the entire production, your company will likely be offered a fixed budget to produce the program, out of which you will need to pay your own production company its fee. That may be the only money your company makes from the program, so make sure to protect your *production company fee* in the budget; many is the production company that ate into its own fee to pay for one more "perfect shot" that wasn't properly budgeted for.

PRE-
PROD.

This is because the production company is responsible for all overages. In other words, if you run over budget, your production company must fund the difference. To counterbalance this risk, producers try to negotiate a provision allowing their companies to keep any monies left over (called *underages*) if they bring in the project under budget. Another variation is to split underages 50/50 with the network. You should be careful here; you don't want to give the impression that you will short-change the production in order to keep any underages.

- Often the largest payment, frequently as much as one half the budget or more, will be payable on execution of the agreement.

- The next payment, often a quarter of the budget, will be payable on delivery of the rough cut and production insurance binder. (See "Insurance Coverage," p. 49.)

- The final payment to your company will be withheld until the approval of all *deliverables, including* the *legal deliverables*. (See "Delivery Requirements," below.)

In addition to the fixed compensation of your production company fee, try to negotiate a contingent compensation provision if you have the leverage. For instance:

- If you are producing a one-hour documentary for a network, try to negotiate a residuals clause. For example, you may ask for your production company to receive a percentage of every home video (DVD, Blu-Ray) sale.
- If you are producing a webisode series, try to negotiate a percentage of the advertising revenue received from online ads posted on the same webpage as the webisode.

Production Specifications

Often included as a separate schedule, this list of production requirements is what your production company must strictly adhere to in preparing the program. It includes sections on approvals, required elements, and legal and technical deliverables. It may also include a statement that the production must not be subject to any entertainment guild or union. Conversely, if it is a union production, the production specifications will often state which union contract should govern the production.

Right of First Refusal

Suppose you suspect that the one-off production or webisode you've been hired to shoot may be a *backdoor pilot*—a way for the network to test the waters to see if there is enough audience interest in the show for them to sink more money into an actual series. If you have the leverage, ask for a right of first negotiation for your company to produce any future productions derived from the production that you're currently shooting. (See Appendix C, "Right of First Negotiation," p. 389.)

BACK-DOOR PILOTS

Variety defines a backdoor pilot as a "pilot episode filmed as a standalone movie, so it can be broadcast if it is not picked up as a series."[1]

Approvals/Required Elements

Part of the production specs, this section will detail those elements over which the network will reserve the right of prior approval. It should also list the network executive in charge of giving that final approval (usually it's the network's executive producer or the executive in charge of production). *Be very careful here*: If the contract requires you to get network approval over an element, such as the choice of talent, you must make sure to get that approval prior to hiring that performer! Failure to do so may result in your having to buy that rejected performer out of his contract later *and* having to pay for the approved performer.

Networks will often require clearances or permissions for and reserve approval rights over the following:

- Above-the-line and below-the-line personnel. This is typically coupled with a requirement that all talent and above-the-line personnel grant the rights to use their names, likenesses, and biographies for marketing and promotional purposes for the program.

- All story outlines, treatments, scripts, and other materials.

- Photographs, titles, music, rough cut, final cut, and all credit obligations.

- Composer and music licensing agreements. Usually included is a minimum term for which licensed music must be acquired, as well as a list of media and territories for which the music must be licensed. Typically the network requires a perpetual license throughout the universe, which is much more expensive than a license that is of limited duration and location. (See "Music Licensing," p. 263.)

- Any product placement agreements. Be sure to budget extra time for this; product placement agreements will almost always have to be cleared by the ad sales department of the television company to avoid sponsor conflicts.

  Example: If the Buds n' Suds beer company has bought air time to run its commercials during the broadcast of your cooking program, it may get upset and cancel future ad buys if your cooking show spends too much time singing the praises of another brand of beer.

- Any trademarks, copyrights, or other intellectual property-protected materials shown in the program, no matter how briefly.

- Permissions from all persons shown on camera.

With regard to permissions and clearances, it is important to keep in mind the difference between permissions *required by law* and those *required by your contract*.

  Example: You may have filmed some people walking in the background on a city street as part of your B-roll footage. Generally, people do not have a right of privacy over noncommercial uses of their images filmed while they are on a public street. As a result, you may not be *legally* required[2] to get a release from people incidentally shown on camera walking down the sidewalk, as long as you're careful not to defame them or use footage of them for commercial purposes. (See "Depiction Releases," p. 229.)

However, your production services agreement will almost certainly have a *contractual* requirement that you obtain a written release from every person photographed and shown in the program. From a practical standpoint, this can be unwieldy.

The solution? Get your production attorney involved. Have her put a call into the legal affairs attorney or the executive in charge of production at the network and negotiate a waiver of your appearance release requirement for a particular sequence. Failure to do so may result in you being noncompliant with your legal deliverable requirements and could delay your final payment.

PRE-
PROD.

Delivery Requirements

Be prepared to receive to a rather lengthy schedule of technical and legal delivery requirements that you must adhere to in creating your show. The *deliverables* are the finished program and other materials that the production company must deliver to the network to satisfy its producing obligations on the program; in a nutshell, it's the program, its components, and the contracts, releases, waivers, and other paperwork that give you the rights to the program. The list can be exhaustive and includes both technical deliverables (program masters, photographs, cue sheets, etc.) and legal materials (contracts, insurance binders, clearances, etc.).

This section specifies:

- **Technical deliverables:**

  - The length of the program, including where the commercial breaks must occur (this is called the network "clock").

  - Specific media on which program, program elements, and sound track must be delivered.

  - Soundtrack mixing requirements and cue sheets. Take this one seriously! Often when a show fails the network's quality control review, it is because of problems with the audio specs. Hold your audio studio contractually accountable for delivering the soundtrack in compliance with the network's requirements (which you will need to give your audio studio, of course).

  - Specifications for promotional and marketing materials for the show. *Note:* Because networks advertise a program in advance of its broadcast, photos, video clips, and other program promotional materials usually must be delivered to the network earlier than the program itself. Be sure to stick closely to the exact technical specifications demanded by the television company. That being said, there may be a lot of boilerplate language here, requiring you to deliver such outdated items as 35-mm slides when a hi-res JPEG might just as easily do the trick. Be sure to look for, point out, and change any antiquated delivery requirements before you sign the contract.

- **Legal deliverables:**

  - You will have to deliver a legal binder containing all your talent and crew contracts, releases, permissions, and credit requirements.

  - The program must be compliant with the network's *standards and practices* policies. Standards and Practices is the network department responsible for evaluating program content for obscenity, violence, and legal vulnerability. Unfortunately, many media companies fail to maintain written standards and practices policies, which can make it very hard for you to know what you're agreeing to under this clause. Try to obtain specifics; failing that, build in a notice-and-cure period where you have a chance to try to fix any problems before the network can declare that you are in breach contract for failing to comply with its policies. (See Appendix C, "Default and Cure," p. 384.)

- Publicity restrictions and requirements. The production company is typically restrained from issuing any publicity without the prior written approval of the network. This means no posting about the project on Facebook!

It bears repeating: If you don't deliver everything as required by this section, your final payment will be withheld!

Representations and Warranties

The representations and warranties are statements of fact and promises that one party makes to another with the intention that the other party will rely on them. (See Appendix C, "Representations and Warranties," p. 381.) Representations and warranties are usually coupled with an indemnification clause requiring a party who has misrepresented something in the contract to pay the other party's damages that stem from that misrepresentation. Your company will be required to represent and warrant that:

- It has all the rights it is granting, and it will not infringe on any other rights holder in the making of the production.

- There is no libelous, defamatory, or obscene material in the program.

- It will be responsible for all royalties and reuse payments.

- It has not exhibited the program anywhere else (including festivals), and its first exhibition on the television company's channel is the program's premiere.

- There has been "no payola." Pursuant to federal regulations, the production company has not accepted any money, services, or other compensation in exchange for advertising goods or services in the program (unless it has prior approval from the network and the program discloses the sponsorship in the end credits).

PRE-
PROD.

Of course, your production services agreement will also contain other standard contract clauses such as such as notice, arbitration, jurisdiction, *force majeure*, etc.

PRACTICE TIPS

- *Alert the network to problems early on.* During the production, if you feel that you will have difficulty meeting a particular requirement, let the network know *as soon as possible.* You may be pleasantly surprised to find out how reasonable they can be. After all, they want to make the program, too. Remember, the production services agreement can be amended and changed many times during the course of creating your program. However, if you wait until delivering your program to let them know that, for example, you didn't get all the required clearances, your final payment will be withheld, and you may be faced with a breach-of-contract suit.

- *Best of knowledge and belief.* Try to modify the representations and warranties concerning intellectual property clearances so that they are to "the best of production company's knowledge and belief." Presumably, you do not have the resources to ensure that the wall poster in the background of an interview scene is in the public domain throughout the world, or that the tastefully nude sculpture in front of the interview subject does not violate obscenity laws in Dubai. Accordingly, try to convince the network that while you will make a diligent effort to clear all materials, any promises as to whether or not they violate the laws of another country are only "to the best of your knowledge and belief."

- Try to limit your indemnification to payment of legal costs after any case has been lost and appeals exhausted. In other words, try to make sure you don't have to pay to defend bogus lawsuits. Make sure there is reciprocal indemnification!

- Build in a cure period for those breaches that can be cured.

- Whenever possible, try to avoid absolute obligations ("producer shall …") and replace them with good-faith obligations ("producer shall use reasonable business efforts to …").

PRODUCT PLACEMENT

Product placements can be a valuable source of production funding. Whether it's a sports car driven by a cinematic secret agent or the soda guzzled by television's latest "tween" idol, product placement plays an increasingly important role in the funding of television programs and motion pictures.

> **WHAT IS PRODUCT PLACEMENT?**
>
> *Product placement* is the intentional inclusion of a brand name or product in a movie or television program for the purpose of increasing brand awareness.
>
> **Example:** Pierre the Producer is raising money for his film *The Girl with the Killer Knees.* He makes a deal with the Rubber Hose Stocking Company to include their stockings in a pivotal scene in the movie. In exchange for the company's logo to be featured prominently in the scene, the Rubber Hose Company provides a crate of stockings and pays $25,000 to Pierre's Production Company. The stocking package's inclusion in the film is a *product placement.*

PRE-PROD.

PRODUCT PLACEMENT AGREEMENT

Let's turn first to the basics of a product placement deal.

The Parties

- *Production company.* The production company wants (1) to save money on props by getting products given to them by manufacturers, (2) to receive money from manufacturers for including those products in the film, and (3) to retain the greatest amount of creative control over how, and whether, those products appear in the final edit.

- *Manufacturer/advertiser.* The manufacturer or advertiser wants to be sure the production company will (1) feature its products in the film, (2) do so in a manner that is consistent with the product's typical use, and (3) do so in a way that makes the product look attractive to potential consumers.

Placement Defined

Right off the bat it's important to define what exactly is meant by *placement*. Will any depiction of the product satisfy the obligation? Must the product be featured in the scene, or is a brief glimpse in the background enough to satisfy the placement requirements? Producers may further want to limit the obligation to depict the product by medium and geographic territory (e.g., the product is only required to be shown on theatrically distributed versions of the movie in North America). The reason for this is that television broadcasters, in-flight movie regulations, and the laws of other countries may result in the distributor or exhibitor of the film editing out particular scenes, including those in which the product has been placed.

Payment

Is there a monetary payment or simply a donation of goods for use by the filmmakers? If inexpensive goods are being donated and there is no payment to the filmmaker, the filmmakers should be wary of agreeing to any absolute obligations to feature the products; a "good-faith attempt to depict the products" may be sufficient. After all, why tie your hands in production and the editing room for a crate of free soda?

If payment is being made in addition to the product being supplied, the fees can range from the tens of thousands to hundreds of thousands, depending on the extent to which the product is used in the film and the potential drawing power of the film itself.

The filmmaker may want the manufacturer to feature the film within a coordinated marketing campaign (think *E. T.* and Reese's Pieces). Of course, any marketing campaign featuring the film or characters from the film should also meet with the approval of the studio producing the film. Furthermore, if the film's performers will be featured in any commercial tie in, they will need to have given their prior written permission (see below).

Failure to Place Products

What happens when the filmmaker fails to include the product in the film? Must the production company return any monies it has received from the manufacturer? The more money that the production company was paid, the more likely the answer to this question will be "yes."

In addition to repayment, another solution to the problem of the omitted product placement is for the production company to offer a "redo" and feature the manufacturer's product in another program or motion picture. This is more common in a television series, where production companies produce more than one episode of a program.

PRE-PROD.

Approvals/Manner of Depiction

The manufacturer wants to make sure that the product is shown in a flattering light. The producer, on the other hand, wants to make sure that she has as broad creative control as possible concerning the depiction of the product. Understandably, creative control over a product's depiction is a highly negotiated area. This clause should spell out exactly how the product will be depicted in the picture. It's typical to reference a particular scene in the script, which should be attached as an exhibit to the agreement.

Manufacturers will often insist that their products not be featured in a manner that is inconsistent with the products' ordinary use, which begs the question: What happens when the director shows the product in a way that is objectionable to the manufacturer? Is the fee reduced? Does the matter go to binding arbitration? Does the manufacturer get to veto the product's inclusion in the film after the scene is shot? Producers are strongly cautioned to avoid giving manufacturers this sort of veto power (unless they want to shoot two versions of each scene, one with a product and one without).

TIP: A producer who wants to avoid overreaching control by the manufacturer may want to point out to them that the more control a manufacturer has, the more likely the film may be seen as an advertisement. If the film is an advertisement, it may be subject to increased regulations by the Federal Trade Commission (FTC) and the Federal Communications Commission (FCC) (if broadcast on television), such as stricter disclosure standards and manufacturer liability for inaccuracies in the way the product is described or represented.

PRE-
PROD.

License of Intellectual Property Rights

To depict a brand, you need a license of that brand's intellectual property rights. This clause grants a nonexclusive license to the production company for the depiction of the trademark, trade dress, copyrights, and any other intellectual property rights in the brand that are necessary to effectuate the product placement.

The manufacturer should also be required to supply all necessary branding artwork, graphics files, mock-ups, etc.; *don't recreate a branded product or logo yourself!* If your art department makes a mistake in creating a mock-up of the product placement brand (wrong color label ... oops!), you may be forced to pull that shot from the film.

If possible, the producer should secure a waiver from the manufacturer of any claims of trademark and copyright infringement, vicarious infringement, trademark dilution, and trademark tarnishment if the brand is depicted in the film consistent with the product placement agreement and the annexed script.

Representation and Warranty and Indemnity

The manufacturer will need to promise that it has the power to enter into the agreement and that it owns all the intellectual property rights (copyrights, trademarks, trade dress and other rights in and to the products).

The producer will need to promise that the picture does not infringe any copyright, trademark, or other third-party right and that the producer has the authority to enter into this agreement.

Always coupled with the representations and warranties is an indemnification. Typically this is a reciprocal indemnification. Many times, however, manufacturers want to be indemnified for any harm arising out of the production company's use of its product.

Insurance

The manufacturer will require that the production company name it as an additional insured in its general liability policy. Furthermore, the manufacturer may also require the production company to maintain certain policy limits and to insure high-ticket items such as vehicles.

Restricted Uses

Particularly with respect to potentially dangerous products, such as handguns and automobiles, the manufacturer may want to include a clause that requires that the producer only use the product in a very limited and specific manner and only with a licensed professional operating the product.

Publicity; Use of Performers

Manufacturers will often want to use, for their own advertising purposes, photographs, video footage, and other publicity materials featuring the film's performers using the products. Producers need to be aware that this will often raise issues with the performers themselves. Although most performers' services agreements have clauses allowing the producers to use an actor's likeness for publicity and promotion, that clause is typically restricted for publicity and promotion of the movie itself, not for unrelated products. Prior to agreeing to a manufacturer's use of publicity stills for its own advertising campaigns, a producer may need to negotiate with the particular actor or require that the manufacturer obtain the actor's permission directly. Typically, this involves paying the actor an additional fee for use of his likeness.

> **Example:** Rex Raptor appears in a new action film, *Dino-mite*, which features a number of motorcycle chase sequences. Harley-Davidson, Inc., which lent several bikes for the film shoot, wants to use footage from the film in a

new television commercial. Even though Rex has signed a performer's services agreement (see p. 212) for his role in the film, Harley-Davidson must still have his permission to use any film clip with him in it in their commercial. Of course, if Rex's performers services agreement contained a provision allowing the production company to license *Dino-mite* film footage for commercial use unrelated to advertisements for the film itself, Harley-Davidson would only need to seek permission from the film company for the use of the footage.

Loss and Damage of Product

For consumables and inexpensive goods, manufacturers typically allow the producers to keep the products (although producers will have to pay any taxes on these). For more expensive products, such as automobiles, planes, expensive jewelry, etc., the production company typically assumes the risk of loss and responsibility for maintaining the products in good working order. In addition, the production company may be restricted in the manner in which it maintains or services the product (automobiles may be repaired only by authorized dealers, etc.)

Credit

This clause details how the manufacturer will be listed in the film's credits and should make clear that the production company has complete discretion over the look of the credits. As is true for all credit provisions, the production company should insert a clause in the contract that says that "inadvertent failure to accord the contracting party credit shall not be actionable." This clause should also require the injured party to waive the right to injunctive relief, leaving an obligation on the production company's part to correct the problem on all future prints as the only remedy for the production company's credit mistakes. The clause should further state that a mistake of this nature is not a breach of the product placement agreement.

PRE-
PROD.

Remedies

The right to injunctive relief should be waived by the manufacturer. Furthermore, no breach of the agreement by the production company should entitle the manufacturer to recapture any rights that he may have granted the production company.

LEGISLATIVE RESTRICTIONS ON PRODUCT PLACEMENT AND ENDORSEMENTS

Both the FTC and the FCC play active roles in determining what producers must do when they decide to take money in exchange for including an advertiser's product in their program or film. The FTC rules apply to all endorsements and advertising, including television, movies, and the Internet. The FCC rules, in addition, apply to broadcast mediums, such as television and radio.

Furthermore, infomercial producers and viral marketers need to be very aware of the changes in the laws governing endorsements. A *product endorsement* is an advertising message or testimonial that consumers are likely to believe reflects the opinions, beliefs, findings, or experience of someone other than the advertiser. Whether it's a celebrity describing the benefits of a golf club on a talk show or a lab-coat-wearing doctor touting the latest vitamin drink, federal laws govern the amount of disclosure that must be given consumers about such testimonials.

CONTRACTUAL RESTRICTIONS ON PRODUCT PLACEMENT AND ENDORSEMENTS

As my father is fond of saying: "There is the law, and then there's real life." In other words, even if you comply with the letter of the law, there may be contractual and other forces that govern how, or if, you can place a product in your film or television program or show endorsements and testimonials. These forces include:

- *Standards and practices.* Networks and most cablecasters have a department that sets the standards for what can be shown on that particular broadcaster's network, usually referred to as *standards and practices*. Before producing any content for a network or cablecaster that has product placements or endorsements, be sure to check with this department to make sure that you comply with that particular network's regulations.

- *Conflicts between paid advertisers and product placement integrators.* Television networks make money by selling airtime to advertisers. This can create conflicts when a producer includes product placement for one branded product inside a program whose commercial airtime has been purchased by an advertiser of a competing brand. Producers are advised to clear any prospective product placements with the network sales department prior to accepting a product placement.

- *Talent veto.* Directors and actors, especially A-list talent, may refuse to work with product placement on principle. Furthermore, even those actors who agreed to work with placed products may demand additional fees on the grounds that they are appearing in a television commercial as well as television program or motion picture.

TIPS

- Before you take money from a sponsor, manufacturer, or advertiser in exchange for including that company's products in your program or film, you should discuss that placement with an experienced media lawyer.

PRE-
PROD.

- A bit of a reality check is in order: If your film does not feature a "bankable" star (many indie films don't), you will probably not receive paid product placements and may be lucky to receive free goods. Still, it doesn't hurt to contact a variety of companies, a press kit for your film at the ready, and see if anyone bites. One of the first film jobs I had in Hollywood involved my securing product placement goods for an indie film. It worked: We ended up with crates of blenders, beer, and powdered soup mix!

- Filmmakers often work with product placement agencies to help them match their productions with companies seeking to place their products in films. A great resource to help filmmakers find the right product placement agency is the Entertainment Resources and Marketing Association (ERMA): 3401 Winona Avenue, Burbank, CA 91504, Phone: (818) 525-1600, www.erma.org.

PRE-
PROD.

HIRING CAST AND CREW

FEDERAL AND STATE LABOR AND EMPLOYMENT LAWS: AN OVERVIEW

During pre-production you will be hiring your cast and crew. This means that in addition to the service contracts you negotiate with them, you also *must* comply with state and federal employment laws.

Federal and state employment and labor laws govern discrimination, wages, workplace safety, child labor, and workers' compensation/disability/unemployment insurance. Under these laws, an *employee* may be treated differently by the law than an *independent contractor*. These issues and more must be addressed during pre-production or the production may face delay, fines, or state and private legal action. An employer/producer must comply with these laws or show exemption from them, but she may not ignore them. Before you staff up or cast your film, bring in your attorney and accountant to advise you.

DON'T DISCRIMINATE

Discrimination in the workplace is strictly prohibited. If you use a worker's race, color, sex, age, disability, religion, or national origin as a basis on which to hire, fire, or demote someone, you are in violation of federal and state laws. If you harass someone because of those attributes, you are violating the law. Some states also prohibit discrimination based on actual or perceived sexual orientation and against persons with AIDS.[1] In many areas of labor and employment law, state law may demand more of the employer than the federal law's protections and requirements.

INDEPENDENT CONTRACTOR OR EMPLOYEE?

Generally, an independent contractor and an employee are viewed differently by federal and state laws. Independent contractors, for example, do not have the same benefits as employees. However, the distinction between the two types of workers is not always a bright line, and courts and state agencies look at many factors when determining who is an employee or independent contractor.

There's no doubt about it—if the person you hire is an employee rather than an independent contractor, there's more law you need to pay attention to. How you hire and fire employees, the way you treat withholding taxes, and how much or how little you can pay employees are just some of the issues governed by federal and state employment law.

Unfortunately, simply writing the words *independent contractor* in your contracts will not change somebody from employee to independent contractor.[2] It's not always obvious which category a worker falls into. For instance, under California law any time you sign someone to a work-for-hire agreement, they are considered an employee and you must provide them with workers' compensation insurance.[3] Failure to insure them subjects your company to serious fines and possible criminal misdemeanor charges.[4]

Fortunately, most states employ a multifactor test to determine a worker's status. These tests look at a number of aspects of the working relationship to determine how independent the worker is. The worker who has more control over his own hours and manner in which the job is performed is more likely be classified as an independent contractor. However, even if the production company does not directly supervise all the work details, the worker may still be classified as an employee and not an independent contractor if:

- "The production company retains pervasive control over the operation as a whole,
- The worker's duties are an integral part of the operation, and
- The nature of the work makes detailed control unnecessary."[5]

As is, even issuing a worker an IRS Form 1099 rather than a W-2 does not automatically change an employee into an independent contractor.[6]

If the work relationship is an employer/employee relationship, the production company is considered the employer, and a movie set or location is the workplace.

For more on the distinction between independent contractors and employees, see Appendix D, "Employee or Independent Contractor?" p. 393.

WORKING WITH MINORS

As a rule, hiring and employing a child or minor is more regulated by federal and state law than hiring and employing an adult.

- Many states require an employer or production company to obtain special permits to employ children, and each child is required to obtain a permit to work.
- Children may also be restricted in the number of working hours according to their age.
- Some states, like New York and California, require that a portion of the child's income be deposited in a trust for the benefit of the child until he or she is 18 years old.

- Special state-regulated teachers may be required to be on set to help minors meet their educational requirements during a shoot.

A producer should consider whether an actual minor, someone under the age of 18, is required when an adult who can "play younger" would suffice.

For more on independent contractors, minors, and other employment laws, see Appendix D, "A Filmmaker's Guide to Labor and Employment Law," p. 393.

UNIONS

In addition to labor and employment laws, production companies may need to concern themselves with union laws and regulations. Many professionals in the entertainment industry are members of a union such as the Screen Actors Guild (SAG), the Writers Guild of America (WGA), the American Federation of Television and Radio Artists (AFTRA), or the International Alliance of Theatrical Stage Employees (IATSE). When you work with these unions, your contracts will need to comply with the applicable union's collective bargaining agreements and master bargaining agreements. These master contracts contain minimum salary, health and welfare contribution rates, grievance procedures, and regulations on how the member must be credited in the film. Employers/production companies are encouraged to seek guidance from the union signatory office of the union with jurisdiction over their type of production.

This book is written with the independent filmmaker in mind. Although it is true that the most experienced members of the film industry are members of an entertainment union, the typical independent filmmaker tends to avoid dealing with unions because of the perceived headache of paperwork, rules, and compliance that accompanies every union-regulated film production. I do want to make a plea for "going union" when you can, not because I'm getting a kickback from the unions but because I believe you get what you pay for. Your film will look better when it is shot by a professional camera operator rather than a film student. That being said, I also understand that given the availability of cheap, passionate film students, many independent filmmakers will still choose to work with a nonunion crew.

PRE-
PROD.

There is one union, however, that you should consider working with, even if you decide to avoid all the others: the Screen Actors Guild. This is because casting a recognized "name" actor increases the likelihood that your film will be picked up by a distributor. (See "The Screen Actors Guild," p. 205.)

SERVICES AGREEMENTS

In addition to contracts with the unions, a production company must also concern itself with its own contracts between itself and its workers (cast, crew, director, producer, etc.). The *services agreement* is the contract between the production company and the employee or independent contractor it's hiring. The terms of these contacts control the working relationship—except when they are superseded by union bargaining agreements or state and federal employment laws.

Negotiate your services agreements early in the pre-production stage. If a potential cast member knows your back is against the wall and you have to cast somebody for next week's shoot, you will have lost a good deal of leverage.

CHECKLIST: ELEMENTS OF A SERVICES AGREEMENT

In general, cast and crew services contracts will have clauses that deal with the following essential issues, many of which are defined in Appendix C, "The Clause Companion," p. 375:

- Duties of both the production company and the employee or independent contractor
- Payment: amount, frequency, kind (fixed, contingent, deferred, bonus)
- Per diem
- Term of service; days expected to work/be available
- Travel and accommodations
- Exclusivity
- Releases: right of publicity, defamation
- Work-for-hire/assignment of intellectual property rights
- Union/nonunion status; if union, which union contract governs the agreement
- Screen credit and other billing provisions
- Force majeure
- Suspension/termination
- Approvals (if any) and their limitations
- Limits on employee/independent contractor remedies, such as a "no injunction" provision, arbitration, duty to cure credit errors only on future prints, etc.
- Likeness and biography approvals
- Notice and cure
- Confidentiality and publicity restrictions
- Representations and warranties that employee/independent contractor is free to enter into the contract and will not infringe any third-party IP rights
- Restriction on the employee's/independent contractor's ability to hire others

- Net profit definition and accounting rights (if the employee/independent contractor is a profit participant)
- Permission to pay monies to an agent/manager
- Permission to withhold taxes
- Permission to take out insurance covering the employee/independent contractor
- Choice of law
- Merger and integration
- Inducement

THE CONTRACT RIDER

A *rider* is a document attached to a contract, supplementing or amending it. Sometimes amending documents are labeled *exhibits*, but the meaning and effect are the same. In service contracts, riders can be used to list the duties an employee must perform or equipment the employee is supplying or to change an already existing contract by replacing preexisting language with newer, mutually agreed terms and conditions.

PRE-
PROD.

14

THE PRODUCER'S SERVICES AGREEMENT

This book assumes that most people reading it will be the executive producers for their own independent films. However, there are different kinds of producers on a film—some of whom you may need to hire.

- An *executive producer* is at the top of the food chain. He is usually in charge of finding financing for the picture and making the top-level management decisions, such as which director or lead actor to hire. The executive producer often ends up with an ownership position in the film property.

- A *producer* supervises and controls the film project. She manages the project from the early stages of development and stays with the project until it is in the can. Her duties range from hiring the cast and crew to overseeing the technical, logistical, and financial aspects of the production. If the executive producer is like a chairman of the board, the producer is like the CEO.

- A *line producer* is the day-to-day logistical manager on the film. He will hire the crew, organize and coordinate between the production office and the set, and handle the purse strings during production. Because line producers generally do not share in any ownership of the film property, filmmakers may be better off negotiating a deal with them that more closely resembles a crew services agreement. (See "Crew Services Agreement," p. 195.)

- An *associate producer* can mean anything and in fact is often a "giveaway title" handed out to entice name actors and financiers to sweeten the deal. Like a line producer, an associate producer usually does not own part of the film property, so a crew services agreement might be a better template to start the negotiation process. (See "Crew Services Agreement," p. 195.)

PRE-PROD.

Furthermore, to get the project off the ground, a filmmaker might want to partner with other producers, such as a production company with studio facilities, a group of financiers, or a more experienced film producer. Accordingly, even on an independent film, a filmmaker may need to negotiate a *producer's services agreement* with a third party (not to be confused with a *production services agreement*, which is used when a network hires a production company to produce a show; see "Production Services Agreements," p. 149).

GOALS AND DEALS

For definitions and explanations of common contract clauses, see Appendix C, "The Clause Companion," p. 375.

Generally speaking, a producer who contracts with another independent producer or independent production company will obtain a better position with respect to issues such as intellectual property rights, creative approval, net profit definitions, credit, and so forth than she would receive if she were to contract with a larger film studio or network. Of course, the downside of working outside the studio system is that the film may have a harder time finding financing in the beginning or finding distribution when it is complete.

MAJOR DEAL POINTS: PRODUCER'S SERVICES AGREEMENT

The producer's services agreement is used to hire a producer. With slight modifications it can be used for line producers, producers, and executive producers.

Note: Most of the agreements in this book are written from the producer or production company's point of view. The deal points for the following producer's services agreement are given from the point of view of a production company that wants to hire a producer.

The Parties

- *Production company.* The production company will want to hire a producer while still maintaining final control over the rights, creative elements, and other management issues. The production company needs to be sure that the producer will deliver on time, on budget, and to spec. The production company also needs to be able to shift risk of loss and legal liability to the producer if the producer fails to meet those obligations. Because negotiating is a large part of what producers do, a production company negotiating with a producer may find it one of the more intense negotiations of the shoot. Producers come in all shapes and sizes, from independent producers to other production companies offering technical services in exchange for a producing credit and a chance to add to their reels, résumés, and IMDB profiles; both the compensation as well as the engagement provisions need to be tailored to each situation.

- *Producer.* As the top level of management in the film's production, producers need to be sure they have all the funds and resources available to make the film that they are hired to make. It is not unusual for a producer to ask to verify production funding prior to executing his contract. Especially on independent features, a producer may ask that his salary be set aside in an escrow fund.

Is the producer working under a loan-out company? If so, the contract needs to be drafted accordingly. For instance, you will need to include clauses for *inducement* and *further assurances.* (See "Loan-Out Companies," p. 42.)

Conditions Precedent

Because engaging a producer's services is often contingent on the project having financing, a production company will often want to make its obligations under the producer's services agreement contingent on certain conditions. In other words, if all the *conditions precedent* are not met, neither party is obligated to the other under the contract. (See Appendix C, "Conditions Precedent," p. 377.) Typical conditions precedent include:

- The receipt of a fully executed agreement from the producer
- The receipt of financing from a particular entity
- The engagement of a particular actor or director
- A performer successfully passing a drug test prior to principal photography
- Securing all the distribution agreements; this may not be necessary in the case of an independent film, where a distribution deal is often secured after the film is shot

Engagement

- Describe the particular services the producer is obligated to perform for the production company. This paragraph should be written broadly, as in the following: "Producer agrees to perform all services as are customarily rendered by producers on a feature-length theatrical motion picture [or television program, webisode, etc.], additional services as specified in any rider attached hereto, and any other reasonable services which may be required by the production company during the term of the Agreement."

    PRE-PROD.

- A list, called a *rider*, should be attached at the end of the contract. This rider catalogs the producer's job duties.

- This provision also contains the *term* of the agreement. The term provides the time periods during which the producer is obligated to provide his services to the production company.

- Producers with enough leverage may try to negotiate a "pay or play" deal, in which they are paid regardless of whether the production company actually makes the film. (See Appendix C, "Pay or Play," p. 380.)

- The production company should also state that the producer's services are "unique" and the loss of such services cannot be fully compensated by monetary damages. This may entitle the production company to injunctive relief against the producer, preventing her from working on another film, should the producer harm the production by quitting midstream.

- Producers may want to negotiate the ability to work on their own projects concurrently with your film. This may be fine if it's writing another screenplay at night, but it could be problematic if it involves a producer shooting footage for his own film while on lunch break during your film's production. Be sure to limit the producer's ability to work on his own matters during the term of his agreement with your production company by requiring that any such "personal work" shall not in any way conflict or interfere with his producing duties under his contract to you.

Exclusivity

Often, the producer's services are *nonexclusive* during development, pre-production, and post-production and *exclusive* during principal photography. However, depending on the needs of the film, the production company may need the producer to be either exclusive or first-priority during pre-production and post-production as well.

Option on Future Services

If the film is successful, the production company may want the option to hire the same producer again at a rate they lock in now. Similar in concept to optioning a screenplay, this clause is an option for the producer's future services. The producer will usually require any future service obligations to be subject to her "professional availability." (See Appendix C, "Option on Future Services," p. 380.)

Costs and Expenses

Producers should be reimbursed by the production company for all out-of-pocket expenses relating to the motion picture. However, to protect the production company, repayment of producer's expenses over a certain amount (e.g., $100) should require the production company's prior written approval.

Travel and Accommodations

Travel, accommodations, and *per diem* expenses should be negotiated and agreed on in advance.

Compensation

- Like other above-the-line personnel, producers are often compensated in a variety of ways: fixed, deferred, and contingent compensation. Bonuses are sometimes given on independent films.

- Additionally, the producer's fee is often paid out in stages. (This differs from an actor's fee or a below-the-line crew member's fee, which is typically paid out on a weekly basis). If not paid weekly, producers often get paid as follows: first, on the completion of financing of the picture; second, on start of principal photography; third, on wrap of principal photography; and fourth, on completion of the picture or completion of all the producer's services under the contract.

- The producer should agree to allow the production company to withhold taxes or other deductions required by law from the producer's fee.

Fixed Compensation: The Producer's Fee

The producer's fee is usually considered *fixed compensation*. In other words, it is payable regardless of whether the film makes money. One method of calculating a producer's fee is to compute the fee as a percentage of the production budget. From 2% to 4% is customary.

Profit Participation

A producer may receive anywhere between 5% and 10% of the Film's Net Profits. (See "Net Profits," p. 379.)

Compensation: Deferred

By definition, deferred compensation is not guaranteed. Accordingly, if a large percentage of a producer's fee is deferred, that producer may feel entitled to a higher overall salary to offset the risk of not recouping her fee. (See Appendix C, "Deferred Compensation," p. 377.)

PRE-
PROD.

Accounting

If the producer is a net-profit participant or will receive any form of deferred or contingent compensation, this paragraph will delineate how often the producer may expect to receive accounting statements. This is coupled with the right to audit the production company, usually no more frequently than once a year.

Credit

For all above-the-line contracts, position in the credits is a heavily negotiated deal point. Producers and executive producers may expect to receive credits on a separate card.

Other issues include:

- Whether the producer's individual production company logos must also be shown in the credit roll.
- Whether the production company is obligated to include the producer's credit in paid advertising and promotional materials.

- This clause may also specify the order in which the credit must appear and how large the credit must be in relation to the other credits.

As is true for all credit provisions, the production company should insert a clause in the contract saying that "inadvertent failure to accord the contracting party credit shall not be actionable." This clause should also require the injured party to waive the right to injunctive relief, leaving an obligation on the production company's part to correct the problem on all future prints as the *only* remedy for the production company's credit mistakes. The clause should further state that a mistake of this nature is *not* a breach of the producer's services agreement. The clause should make clear that the production company has complete discretion over the look of the credits.

Rights

The assignment of rights/work-made-for-hire provision is another standard clause in all motion picture or service contracts. In this paragraph the producer must agree that all rights, proceeds, and results of his creative efforts are to be treated as a work made for hire. Any remaining rights not captured by the production company as a result of the work-made-for-hire clause should be assigned by the producer to the production company under the agreement. (See "Work Made for Hire," p. 344.)

Project Requirements

PRE-
PROD.

This section delineates the scope of the film or program itself and what the producer is responsible for delivering. It includes specifics on:

- The project's running time
- The project's rating (if applicable)
- Deliverables (format, media, etc.)
- The legal deliverables for which the producer is responsible

This is such a critical provision of the contract that production companies should insist on "strict performance" and "time is of the essence" with respect to a producer's meeting the project requirements and deliverables deadlines. Producers, on the other hand, may want to qualify this paragraph by making their compliance "to the best of the producer's ability" and making deadlines "on or about" a certain date.

Publicity

The production company will want to control the publicity for the motion picture and thus require the right to use the producer's name and likeness in any publicity, promotion, or marketing of the motion picture.

TIP: **Although it may be an unspoken "standard practice," if you are a producer make sure to insert language in the agreement allowing you to include footage of the film in your reel or on your website, subject to the production company's approval. You should also require the production company to list you as producer on IMDB.com.**

Confidentiality

Usually coupled with publicity provision are confidentiality obligations. Production companies need be able to restrain the producer from issuing publicity statements about the motion picture without the production company's prior written consent. Producers take note: This means no blogging, Tweeting, Facebooking, etc., unless the production company approves it in advance.

If you are a producer:

- Carefully review the production company's definition of "confidential material" to make sure you understand what you can and cannot discuss.

- The production company may require that the producer ensures that all cast and crew sign NDAs. (See "Nondisclosure Agreements," p. 77.) Make sure to do so, but be careful about any language that requires that you indemnify the production company for breach of confidentiality by cast and crew.

- Put a time limit on this provision. Remember, lots of films never get finished, let alone distributed. You want to be sure you can talk about your project at some point!

PRE-
PROD.

Pay or Play

The production company and the producer should agree that there is no obligation on the part of the production company to produce and distribute the film (called a *no obligation* clause, naturally). The producer, however, may want the production company to pay her producer's fee regardless of whether the film is actually produced. If the production company agrees to this clause, the producer's compensation is *pay or play*. The pay-or-play clause obligates the production company to pay the producer a certain sum regardless of whether her services are actually used. Alternately, the production company might counter a producer's pay-or-play request with a "kill fee." (See Appendix C, "Pay or Play," p. 380; "Kill Fee," p. 379.)

Representations and Warranties

The producer is typically required to represent and warrant that he is under no other obligations that would prevent him from performing his obligations under this contract.

Indemnification

A production company will typically require to be indemnified (to have their losses paid) by producers for damages arising from:

- IP infringement lawsuits stemming from the results and proceeds of producer's service
- Breaches of contract by the producer
- Conflicting contractual obligations of producer
- Falsehoods in the representations and warranties made by the producer

> **Example:** In her producer's services agreement for *Green, Black, and Blue: Ultimate Vegan Martial Artists*, Fatima Filmmaker indemnifies her employer Potto Productions that the material she produces (her "results and proceeds") are original with her. However, she includes a clip of an old Jolly Green Giant commercial in the title credits and fails to get permission from the clip's owner, Giant Food Company. The Cable Channel, which broadcasts the show, and Potto Productions are both sued by the Green Giant Food Company for copyright and trademark infringement, false endorsement, and a host of other claims. Because of the indemnification clause, Fatima must pay the legal defense costs of both Potto Productions and the Cable Channel.

Final Say/Production Company Controls

This clause states bluntly that the production company has the final say with regard to creative, financial, artistic, managerial, and other matters on the motion picture. It should also list the production company executive in charge of giving that final say (usually the executive producer or the executive in charge of production).

This section may also detail those elements over which a production company will reserve the right for prior approval. Producers be very careful here! If the contract requires you to get production company approval over an element, such as the choice of talent, make sure to get that approval prior to hiring that performer! Failure to do so may result in having to pay for the damage, such as having to butt that rejected performer out of his contract and pay for the other "approved" performer.

Suspension/Termination

- This paragraph lays out the mechanism for resolving disputes. It typically describes events that would constitute *force majeure* (acts of God) and sets a time limit for how long a producer's services may be suspended before the services are considered terminated.
- The production company should retain the right to terminate the producer's services for any reason whatsoever, provided the production company pays the producer's fee up to the date of termination.

Assignment

The production company always needs the right to assign the contract and the rights, results, and proceeds created under it. The producer should never have the right to assign or delegate her duties under the contract.

Remedies

As with all motion picture services agreements, the right to injunctive relief should be waived by the producer. Furthermore, no breach of the agreement by the production company should entitle the producer to recapture any rights that he may have granted the production company. When well drafted, this clause should leave the producer only with a right to recover money, if anything at all, from the breaching production company. You will also want to address such issues as whether to solve problems through arbitration or courts of law. (See Appendix C, "Arbitration," p. 383.) And while you're at it, just where will any adjudication or arbitration take place? (See Appendix C, "Choice of Law: Forum," p. 384.)

Further Documents

Here the producer should be obligated to execute any other documents necessary to further the intent of the contract. Examples include copyright assignment forms, workers' compensation claim forms, and so forth.

PRE-
PROD.

Inducement (If Dealing with a Loan-Out Company)

If the producer is working under a loan-out company, it is the loan-out company that will be a party to the contract. Furthermore, the contract should contain an inducement and further assurances clause. (See "Loan-Out Companies," p. 42.) If the production company is financing the film with production incentives like tax credits, you may need to include a provision in the agreement that:

1. Requires the loan-out company to register to do business and file a return in the production state

2. Gives your production company the power of attorney to register the loan-out company to do business in the production state if the loan-out company fails to do so within a certain period of time (see "Production Incentives: Eligibility Requirements," p. 64)

Right of First Negotiation

The producer may want a right of first negotiation/first refusal for any sequels or derivative works arising out of the motion picture. Other variations of this clause include the right of last refusal. This is only given if the producer has a track record or has the leverage of being the initial rights holder.

Festivals and Premieres

The producer may want accommodations, tickets, and transportation to premieres of the motion picture and festivals that feature the film. However, the production company may get more bang for its buck by paying the costs of any of the film's well-known lead actors to attend these events than it does when it picks up the producer's tab. Accordingly, the production company may want to sharply define the festivals and premieres for which it will foot the producer's bill.

LAW

Producers, like other employees, will be protected by federal and state labor laws. However, the producer may be treated as an independent contractor if she is working through her own company, such as a loan-out company. (See "Loan-Out Companies," p. 42.)

(See "Loan-Out Companies," p. 42.)

PRE-PROD.

BUSINESS ISSUES

Try to Cap the Producer's Fixed Compensation Fee

Production companies may want to cap the maximum fee a producer is entitled to. For instance, if a low-budget film shooting on a budget of $500,000 has agreed to pay its producer 2% of the budget, the producer is entitled to $10,000. However, if the production company is able to secure several well-known actors, raising the budget to $5 million, the producer would be entitled to a fee of $100,000. Understandably, the production company may not want hand over $100,000 to a relatively unknown producer simply because the film has had the good fortune of attracting name talent. Accordingly, the production company may want to cap the producer's fee at a specific sum, say $50,000, regardless of how high the budget goes. This cap is often referred to as a *ceiling*.

The producer, however, may make the counterargument that attracting name performers and other personnel may be due to his efforts as a producer and, thus, he should be entitled to a fee based purely on the percentage alone, without a cap. In fact, the producer may want to guard against the possibility of the production budget diminishing by negotiating a *floor* for himself. A floor is a fixed sum that sets the lower limit of the producer's fee.

Without a floor, in the previous example, if the producer's fee is 2% and the production budget suddenly drops to $250,000, the producer would be entitled to only a $5,000 producer's fee. The producer should try to guard against this contingency by negotiating a floor of, say, $8,000 as a producer's fee. If the production company agrees, the producer knows that no matter how low the production budget drops, he will receive a fee of at least $8,000.

Net Profits

Like all profit participant contracts, the producer's services agreement should contain a rider that defines the Film's Net Profits. (See "Net Profits," p. 379.)

STEP BY STEP: HIRING A PRODUCER

From the production company's point of view:

1. Try to select a producer with experience in film contract negotiation. However, the more experienced the producer is, the more you will have to pay her.

2. Make sure everyone understands exactly what *duties* are expected of the producer. Will the producer negotiate contracts? Select and hire crew? Organize the shoot? Depending on the size of the production, the producer's role may be spread among several crew members. Make sure to define the producer's specific duties in the producer's services agreement.

3. Define what is expected of the producer during each phase of production. Does the production company need the producer full time during pre-production? Will the producer manage the post-production process? How active a role will the producer play during the hunt for a distributor? All these issues should be defined in the producer's services agreement.

PRE-
PROD.

4. Define what rights to the film property the producer will receive. Normally no one except the production company should receive rights to the film property (although many people may receive royalties from the exploitation of the film property). However, a producer who initially owns the film may want to retain an ownership position in the copyright to the film. If this is the case, make sure the production company retains the sole authority to decide how and when the film property is exploited.

5. Negotiate, draft, and execute the producer's services agreement.

6. During pre-production, make sure one production company executive is responsible for supervising the producer. Keep in mind that in this scenario it is the production company that is the boss.

15

THE DIRECTOR'S SERVICES AGREEMENT

Like professional actors, professional directors have their own union, the Directors Guild of America (DGA; www.DGA.org). According to the DGA, "The Director's function is to contribute to all of the creative elements of a film and to participate in molding and integrating them into one cohesive dramatic and aesthetic whole."[1]

Although many independent films are made with nonunion directors, the DGA's definition of a director is instructional in that it outlines the expectation of every director—that is, to be involved in all of the creative aspects of a film's production. Not surprisingly, many of the battles fought between directors and the production companies that hire them involve issues of creative control.

Keep in mind that like the other services agreements discussed in this book, federal and state labor and employment laws will trump any contract provision to the contrary.

GOALS AND DEALS

For definitions and explanations of common contract clauses, see Appendix C, "The Clause Companion," p. 375.

The *director's services agreement* is used to engage the services of a director for a production company. In many respects, it is similar to another above-the-line agreement, the producer's services agreement, so many of these clauses may look familiar. The director's services agreement, however, has a number of clauses that specify how creative approval is handled, delivery requirements for the film, and the director's obligations regarding reshoots and other post-production tasks.

Assistant and second-unit directors are often not profit participants, and a production company may base their contracts on a *crew services agreement*. (See "Crew Services Agreement," p. 195.)

Because many, if not most, independent films are shot by nonunion directors, the following are deal points for a non-DGA contract.

MAJOR DEAL POINTS: DIRECTOR'S SERVICES AGREEMENT

The Parties

- *Production company.* The production company wants to hire a passionate, creative, and responsible director. Its primary concern is making sure that the director can perform creatively while making sure that the film is made on time and on budget. Consequently, the contract provisions of critical importance to the production company are those that control the production company's ability to oversee the director.

- *Director.* The director wants to be sure the production company will not run out of money before the film is made. Like the producer, the director may require that the funding for the film and his salary be placed in an escrow account. The director might fight the hardest for creative control, wanting input over the script rewrites and casting and crew hiring decisions and demanding the chance to control the editing process and to direct reshoots.

Here, as in other services agreements, the production company must be aware of exactly whom they are contracting with. Is it a loan-out company or individual? If it is a loan-out, you will need to include clauses for inducement and further assurances. (See "Loan-Out Companies," p. 42.)

PRE-
PROD.

Conditions Precedent

Because engaging a director's services is often contingent on the project having financing, a production company will often want to make its obligations under the director's services agreement contingent on certain conditions. In other words, if all the conditions precedent are *not* met, neither party is obligated to the other under the contract. The following conditions are often included:

- The receipt of a fully executed agreement from the director
- The receipt of financing from a particular entity
- Securing all the distribution agreements
- The engagement of a particular actor

Engagement

- This paragraph lays out the particular services the director is obligated to perform for the production company. It is usually drafted fairly broadly, such as: "Director agrees to perform all services as are customarily rendered by directors on a feature-length theatrical motion picture, plus additional services as specified in any rider attached hereto." Any additional services that the director is required to perform should be attached to the agreement in a separate rider.

- The production company should also recite that the director's services are "unique" and the loss of such services cannot be fully compensated by monetary damages. This may entitle the production company to injunctive relief against the director, should the director harm the production by quitting midstream.

- This provision also contains the term of the agreement: the time periods during which the director is obligated to provide his services to the production company. The term is critical because the director needs to know when she is free to enter into other contracts with other production companies. The director will want to know the start date of the production. If the start date cannot be determined at the time the contract is executed, the production company may want to include a range during which it can designate a start date.

Exclusivity

On independent films, the director wears many hats, ranging from writing to casting and directing to editing. Exclusivity as well as the director's duties and obligations need to be sharply defined.

- *Writing and development services.* The director usually works hand in hand with the writer to prepare the script for production. Although the director's services are typically nonexclusive during this period, scripts in need of substantial rewrites may need the director's services on an exclusive basis.

- *Casting and location scouting.* Like writing services, the director's casting and location scouting services tend to be on a nonexclusive basis. Keep in mind that "nonexclusive" does not mean that the director can cancel appointments at will. If the director has committed to a casting session on a particular day, he is obligated to make that session.

PRE-
PROD.

- *Principal photography.* Obviously, the director's services must be exclusive during principal photography. It is often a good practice to have the director's services on an exclusive basis prior to the start of principal photography. For complex projects, such as feature films, this period of exclusivity can be as long as 12 weeks in advance of the start of production.

- *Post-production.* The production company should secure the director's services on an exclusive basis during post-production, reshoots, automated dialogue replacement (ADR), and editing. If that's not possible, the director should, at a minimum, be on a first-call basis.

Because post-production invariably takes longer than anybody thinks it's going to, it is in the director's best interest to negotiate his termination-of-services date; this is the date beyond which he is no longer obligated to provide services on a first-call or exclusive basis to the production company. Conversely, the production company will want to make sure that it has enough padding in the schedule to ensure that overages in post-production will not find the film without a director.

Creative Controls

- *Final say/production company controls.* This clause states bluntly that the production company has the final say with regard to creative, financial, artistic, managerial, and other matters with regard to the motion picture.

- *Designated decision maker.* Because of the perennial argument over creative control between directors and the producers who hire them, it is often wise to expressly state in the contract which production company executive the director must answer to. The easiest method for resolving creative control issues is to designate a particular production company executive (e.g., the executive producer) as the person with the final say over any particular creative decision. However, many directors balk at the idea of the production company being a backseat director. If the director has sufficient leverage, he may negotiate one of several kinds of provisions that govern the resolution of creative conflicts. (See Appendix C, "Approval," p. 375.)

Additional Engagement Points

- *Television cover shots.* Despite the fact that the producer is the top manager on a production, on set the director, quite literally, calls the shots. As a result, the production company may want to include a television cover shot clause that protects the company's interest in receiving a commercially viable film when the director's services are completed. The television cover shots clause requires the director to shoot additional shots of scenes that might be too sexual, violent, or otherwise inappropriate for television viewing. When the motion picture is aired over network television, the cover shots will take the place of the more graphic shots shown in the theatrically distributed version. Sometimes directors are averse to providing television cover shots, feeling that they damage the integrity of their work. However, because the production company's primary interest is in receiving revenue from as many different sources as possible, television cover shots are a necessity when it comes to sanitizing a PG-13, R, NC-17, or unrated film for network television.

- *Perquisites.* On studio films, directors get an office and administrative help. On low-budget films this is infrequent at best. However, if such facilities are readily available, providing them to a director who has had to work at a reduced fee might be an acceptable concession on the part of the production company.

Costs and Expenses/Hiring Others

Directors should be reimbursed by the production company for all out-of-pocket expenses relating to the motion picture. However, to protect the production company, repayment of director's expenses over a certain amount (e.g., $100) should require the production company's prior written approval.

The director should also be prohibited from hiring others without the prior written approval of the production company.

Travel and Accommodations

Travel, accommodations, and *per diem* expenses should be negotiated and agreed on in advance.

Compensation

- The structure of a director's compensation provision is similar in many respects to a producer's compensation. Both have fixed, contingent, deferred, and bonus provision possibilities.
- The director should agree to allow the production company to withhold taxes or other deductions required by law from the director's fee.

Fixed Compensation: Director's Fee

- Fixed compensation is compensation that is due and payable regardless of how well the film does in the box office. In short, it is the guaranteed money a director can expect.
- One common practice among independent filmmakers is to structure the director's fee as a flat fee; this means that despite overtime or other overages, the director's fixed compensation will not increase. In other words, if the film shoots for 45 days as opposed to 40, the director's compensation will remain the same.

PRE-PROD.

- The amount the director is paid varies considerably and is largely dependent on the film's budget. However, given the fact that many independent films are directed by the people who write them or who are also the principal investors, many independent film directors create films for little or no fixed compensation, trading the certainty of a fixed paycheck for a larger portion of the back end or a larger deferred compensation package. (See Appendix C, "Compensation," p. 376.)
- A director who is not a rights holder will be less comfortable accepting a reduced fee. Production companies need to keep in mind that a director's responsibilities start well before the production starts filming and end only when the picture is delivered. As a result, a director may spend the major portion of the year working on one particular film, leaving little time available to search for other paying work. Seen in this light, a fee of $75,000 is not unreasonable.
- Fixed compensation fees are often paid in stages, similar to producer's and writer's fees. The stages can be as frequently or infrequently as the production company and the director agree. Some common payment stages include:
  - Approval of the budget

- Weekly payments starting several weeks prior to the start of principal photography
- Payments made weekly during the course of principal photography
- A payment made when the director's cut is delivered
- A final payment of the fixed compensation fee when the answer print is completed

Keep in mind that these are all flexible stages, and the amounts paid during each stage can be the subject of negotiation.

Profit Participation

- A director may also receive a portion of the Film's Net Profits, typically 5%. On independent films that percentage might be higher, depending on several factors such as whether the director is the rights holder, the amount of the director's salary that has been deferred, and the number of additional services other than directing that the director has had to perform.
- For profit participants, such as a director, the net profit definition is usually included in the contracts of all contingent compensation participants. (See "Net Profits," p. 379.)

Deferred Compensation

Many independent films will attempt to save money for the production by deferring a portion of a director's compensation. Deferred compensation is paid out when the production company receives proceeds from the exploitation of the film. Since the film might not make any money, there is no guarantee that any or all of the deferred compensation will be paid. Accordingly, if a large percentage of a director's fee is deferred, the director may feel entitled to a higher overall salary to offset the risk of not recouping her fee. (See Appendix C, "Deferred Compensation," p. 377.)

Accounting

If the director is a net–profit participant or will receive any form of deferred or contingent compensation, this paragraph will delineate how often the director may expect to receive accounting statements. This is coupled with the right to audit the production company, usually no more frequently than once a year.

Credit

- For all above-the-line contracts, position in the credits is a heavily negotiated deal point. Directors and executive producers may expect to receive credits on a separate card and a listing on IMDB.com as the film's director.

- Even though the production company might not be a signatory to the DGA MBA, director's contracts often contain a billing provision that guarantees the director a "directed by" credit if a similarly situated director would receive the same credit on a production governed by the DGA MBA. The more heavily negotiated provisions of this clause include how large the director's credit is in relation to the title of the movie and whether the director's credit is required to appear on all paid advertising and promotional materials.

- As is true for all credit provisions, the production company should insert a clause in the contract that says that "inadvertent failure to accord the contracting party credit shall not be actionable." This clause should also require the injured party to waive the right to injunctive relief, leaving an obligation on the production company's part to correct the problem on all future prints as the only remedy for the production company's credit mistakes. The clause should further state that a mistake of this nature is not a breach of the director's services agreement.

- The clause should make clear that the production company has complete discretion over the look of the credits.

Rights

The assignment of a rights/work-made-for-hire provision is another standard clause in all motion picture or service contracts. In this paragraph, the director must agree that all rights, proceeds, and results of his creative efforts are to be treated as a work made for hire. Any remaining rights that are not captured by the production company as a result of the work-made-for-hire clause should be assigned by the director to the production company under the agreement. (See "Work Made for Hire," p. 382.)

PRE-
PROD.

Approval

- The production company should try to retain final approval over all creative elements. The director may balk at this. If so, one of the approval mechanisms discussed in Appendix C, "The Clause Companion," may be used. (See Appendix C, "Approval," p. 375.) In no case should the director be allowed unfettered creative control without some budgetary oversight from the production company.

- The production company should designate particular persons (e.g., the producer and the executive producer) who are the sole representatives responsible for authorizing approval on behalf of the production company.

Publicity

The production company will want to control the publicity for the motion picture and thus be able to restrain the director from issuing publicity statements about the motion picture without the production company's prior written consent.

The production company will also require the right to use the director's name and likeness in any publicity, promotion, or marketing of the motion picture. Make sure to include language that allows the director's image to be used in the "making of" documentary that seems to appear on every DVD.

Pay or Play

- The production company and the director should agree that there is no obligation on the part of the production company to produce and distribute the film. The director, however, may want the production company to pay his director's fee regardless of whether the film is actually produced.

- If such a pay-or-play clause is inserted, the production company will need some protection as well. The clause should be drafted so that the production company is not obligated to pay the director the entire fixed compensation if the director cannot work on the film as a result of his own incapacity or unwillingness. In addition to the fixed compensation being pay or play, a concern is whether the contingent compensation is also pay or play. One way of handling this is to state that if the DGA would have awarded the director a "directed by" credit on the picture, the director's contingent compensation is considered vested and therefore due him, even though the director may no longer be associated with the project.

Reshoots, ADR, and Post-Production Services

- In life two things are certain: death and taxes. If you're a filmmaker, two more categories get added to this list: reshoots and ADR. This clause ensures that the director will still perform services for ADR, reshoots, and other post-production services not directly related to the editing of the film. If these services are required after the term of the contract has expired, the director is usually obligated to provide those services as long as she is not contractually obligated to provide services to another party at that time. If she is, the director should be obligated to provide those services at her first availability thereafter.

- For post-production, the director may be compensated at a daily rate based on a formula derived from her weekly rate. Alternatively, and this is often the case on independent feature films, the director may not be paid at all for these additional post-production services. Either way, this clause should address whether compensation is due.

Performance and Delivery Standards

This clause details the delivery standards for the picture and controls such issues as:

- The picture's rating (for instance, "The picture shall receive no greater than a PG-13 rating as that rating is accorded by the Motion Picture Association of America")

- Duration of the film
- Delivery date
- Delivery materials, also known as deliverables (for instance, the film shall be delivered on high-definition masters or super-16 film stock)
- The requirement for TV cover shots
- The need for the director to stay within budget

Representations and Warranties

- The director is typically required to represent and warrant that he is under no other obligations that would prevent him from performing his duties under this contract. This clause typically contains an indemnity provision that obligates the director to indemnify the production company for any breaches of the representations and warranties or other breaches of the agreement.

- The director should also warrant that any material that he contributes to the production—writing, gags, *mise-en-scène,* and other creative elements—is original with him. This shifts liability to the director if the production company is sued as a result of the director adding unlicensed, copyright-protected material to the film.

Suspension/Termination

- This paragraph outlines the mechanism for resolving disputes. It typically describes events that would constitute *force majeure* (acts of God) and sets a time limit for how long a director's services may be suspended before the services are considered terminated.

PRE-PROD.

- The production company should retain the right to terminate the director's services for any reason whatsoever, provided that the production company pays the director's fee up to the date of termination.

Assignment

The production company always needs the right to assign the contract and the rights, results, and proceeds created under it. The director should never have the right to assign and delegate his duties under the contract.

Remedies

Like all motion picture services agreements, the right to injunctive relief should be waived by the director. Furthermore, no breach of the agreement by the production company should entitle the director to recapture any rights that he may have granted the production company. Well drafted, this clause should leave the director only with a right to recover money, if anything at all, from the breaching production company. You will also want to address such issues as whether to solve problems through arbitration or courts of law. (See Appendix C, "Arbitration," p. 383.) And while you're at it, just where will any adjudication or arbitration take place? (See Appendix C, "Choice of Law: Forum," p. 384.)

Further Documents

Here the director should be obligated to execute any other documents necessary to further the intent of the contract. Examples include copyright assignment forms, workers' compensation claim forms, and the like.

Inducement (if Dealing with a Loan-Out Company)

If the director is working under a loan-out company, it is the loan-out company that will be a party to the contract. Furthermore, the contract should contain an inducement and further assurances clause. (See "Loan-Out Companies," p. 42.) If the production company is financing the film with production incentives such as tax credits, you may need to include a provision in the agreement:

1. Requiring the loan-out company to register to do business and file a return in the production state, and

2. Giving your production company the power of attorney to register the loan-out company to do business in the production state, if the loan-out company fails to do so within a certain period of time. (See "Production Incentives: Eligibility Requirements," p. 64.)

Right of First Negotiation

The director might want a right of first negotiation to direct any sequels or derivative works based on the motion picture. Other variations of this clause include the right of last refusal. This is only given if the director has a track record or has the leverage of being the initial rights holder. (See Appendix C, "Right of First Negotiation," p. 389.)

Festivals and Premieres

The director may want accommodations, tickets, and transportation to premieres of the motion picture and to festivals that feature the film. If granted, the production company may want to sharply define the festivals and premieres for which it will foot the director's bill.

LAW

Directors, like other employees, will be protected by federal and state labor laws. However, your director may be treated as an independent contractor if he is working through his own company, such as a loan-out company.

BUSINESS ISSUES

- *Perks.* As part of the director's perks, it is typical to give her copies of the finished film on DVD or videocassette and to allow the director the right to incorporate portions of the film into her reel.

- *Net profits.* Like all profit participant contracts, the director's services agreement should contain a rider that defines how the production company defines the Film's Net Profits. (See "Net Profits," p. 379.)

STEP BY STEP: HIRING A DIRECTOR

1. Review the director's reel and résumé. Double-check the director's credits with the Internet Movie Database at www.imdb.com.

2. When interviewing the director, find out what experience he has had with other production companies. Try to get a sense of how the director dealt with creative control issues with those companies.

3. Ask the director to provide production company references. When you contact her references, ask whether the director's films were delivered on budget and whether there were any creative control issues.

4. Negotiate and execute the director's services agreement.

PRE-
PROD.

16

CREW SERVICES AGREEMENT

In contrast to the above-the-line contracts, below-the-line contracts tend not to be as heavily negotiated. Accordingly, many production companies tend to work with deal memos rather than long form contracts when hiring crew members. This approach has the advantage of simplicity—a fill-in-the-blank approach favored by time-strapped producers.

The downside is that many deals are not as "one size fits all" as producers would like to believe. For instance, a cinematographer who is hired on the condition that he comes with his own camera requires additional provisions in his contract concerning insurance and equipment damage, as opposed to a gaffer who will be working with the equipment supplied him by the production company. The best way to deal with these contracts is to handle them the same way all your contracts should be handled: by sending them to the production attorney for their review prior to execution.

UNION OR NONUNION CREW?

As mentioned before, many indie films are shot with nonunion crews. However, shooting with a union crew has its advantages. For instance, a union crew member is likely to be more experienced than her nonunion counterpart. The decision to work with a union crew member is similar to the decision of whether to work with a union actor: If you want a cinematographer whose work is known in the film industry, you will probably have to "go union" and become a signatory to that cinematographer's union.

The two main theatrical unions for crew members are:

- *IATSE.* The International Alliance of Theatrical Stage Employees, Moving Picture Technicians, Artists and Allied Crafts of the United States, Its Territories and Canada (www.iatse-intl.org). This union represents nearly everyone who is not an actor, director, or choreographer. This includes wardrobe, camera operators, sound recordists, gaffers, grips, carpenters, and so forth.

- *NABET-CWA.* The National Association of Broadcast Employees and Technicians-Communications Workers of America (www.nabetcwa.org). It represents crew members working in broadcasting, distributing, telecasting, recording, cable, video, sound recording, and related industries.

> The downside of working with a union crew is that the production company has another set of rules and regulations to adhere to the union rules themselves; and in contrast to the world of studio film-making, many indie directors act as their own cinematographers, making the decision to take the film union a murkier one. Unlike name actors, who are always union members, having a union gaffer associated with the film will not increase your chances of landing a distributor except insofar as your film is better lit as a result of that union member's expertise. With the exception of cinematographers, union crew members are, by and large, not considered marketable elements, notwithstanding the fact that they undoubtedly contribute to the overall professional look of the film.

TIP: **It is important to note that just because you are working with SAG actors, you are not required to work with a union crew. However, union or not, you are still required to comply with federal and state labor laws.**

GOALS AND DEALS

For definitions and explanations of common contract clauses, see Appendix C, "The Clause Companion," p. 375.

PRE-
PROD.

Crew services agreements tend to be shorter than above-the-line agreements. They often contain only two parts:

1. *A "fill-in-the-blanks" deal memo,* often a single sheet, that details the deal points of that particular crew member's deal: salary, position in the crew, contact information, other terms

2. *A longer "standard terms" rider* that provides the (usually) nonnegotiated terms and conditions of the contract; this rider is used for every crew member contract

Because many independent films are shot with a nonunion crew, the following deal points are for a nonunion contract.

MAJOR DEAL POINTS: CREW'S SERVICES AGREEMENT

The Parties

- *Production company.* Because the production company will be hiring many crew members, it wants a contract it can use over and over with a minimum amount of redrafting and negotiation. If you need a crew member to perform duties additional to those customarily performed by such a person, make sure to detail the exact services the crew member will be providing.

Example: If you just write "camera operator," most crew members would not assume that the job also includes picking up the rest of the crew in the production van every morning.

- *Crew.* Crew members will want definitive work and pay schedules. If they are to supply their own equipment (e.g., cameras, trucks, lighting), they will want a rental fee in addition to their services fee, and they will want their equipment to be protected by the production company's insurance policy.

Here, as in other services agreements, the production company must be aware of exactly whom it is contracting with. Is it a loan-out company or an individual? The drafting of the contract, and whether an inducement and further assurances are required, will be affected by each consideration. (See "Loan-Out Companies," p. 42.) Most crew members are hired as individuals, although cinematographers and other crew members who supply their own equipment often work though loan-out companies.

Legally, the safest route is to treat the crew member as an employee rather than an independent contractor. However, if you are dealing with a loan-out company, you are probably dealing with an independent contractor rather than an employee. (See Appendix D, "Employee or Independent Contractor?," p. 393.)

Make sure to get full contact information, including Social Security numbers for individuals and federal ID numbers for companies. These will be necessary for handling payroll and other taxes. Also include contact information for the crew member's attorney or agent if she has one.

PRE-
PROD.

Engagement

- This paragraph describes the particular services that the crew member is obligated to perform for the production company. The clause is usually drafted fairly broadly, as in the following: "Crew member agrees to perform all services as are customarily rendered by [insert position, e.g., "grips," "gaffers," etc.] on a feature-length theatrical motion picture, plus additional services as specified in any rider attached hereto."

- Any additional services that the crew member is required to perform should be attached to the agreement in a separate rider. You may need the crew member to pick up equipment and drop it off again when the shoot wraps. You may also need the crew member to be responsible for purchasing materials necessary to do his job. For example, you may need the gaffer to be responsible for buying lighting gels and tape; an art director may be needed to pick up building supplies and props; and so on. All of this detail should be included in the rider.

- This provision also contains the *term* of the agreement: the time periods during which the crew member is obligated to provide his services to the production company. If the start date cannot be determined at the time the contract is executed, the production company may want to include a range during which they can designate a start date.

- The production company should also state that the crew member's services are "unique and the loss of such services cannot be fully compensated by monetary damages." This may entitle the production company to injunctive relief against the crew member, preventing her from working on another film, should the crew member harm the production by quitting midstream.

Exclusivity

Often, the crew member's services are nonexclusive during development, pre-production, and post-production and exclusive during principal photography. However, depending on the needs of the film, the production company may need the crew member to be either exclusive or first priority during pre-production and post-production as well. A crew member whose daily services were required during pre-production or post-production should probably be exclusive for these periods as well.

Costs and Expenses

Crew members should be reimbursed by the production company for all out-of-pocket expenses relating to the motion picture. However, to protect the production company, repayment of crew member's expenses over a certain amount (e.g., $100) should require the production company's prior written approval. The crew member should also be prohibited from hiring others without the prior written approval of the production company.

CREW MEMBER GEAR

If the crew member is supplying his own equipment (camera rigs, lighting, etc.), the contract should state that the crew member is solely responsible for the upkeep, maintenance, and safety of his own gear. The production company should check with its insurance company to determine to what extent the crew member's equipment is covered under the production company's policies.

Travel and Accommodations

Travel, accommodations, and *per diem* expenses should be negotiated and agreed on in advance.

Compensation

- Typically, crew members receive only fixed or deferred compensation, or some combination of the two kinds of compensation, but not a portion of the Film's Net Profits. (See Appendix C, "Compensation," p. 376.)

- There is typically no guarantee that all the deferred compensation will be paid out to the crew member, because the film may not make any money at all. Accordingly, if a large percentage of a crew member's fee is deferred, that crew member may feel entitled to a higher overall salary to offset the risk of not recouping his fee. (See Appendix C, "Deferred Compensation," p. 377.)
- The crew member should agree to allow the production company to withhold taxes or other deductions required by federal and state laws from the crew member's fee.

Credit

- As is true for all credit provisions, the production company should insert a clause in the contract that says that "inadvertent failure to accord the contracting party credit shall not be actionable." This clause should also require the injured party to waive the right to injunctive relief, leaving an obligation on the production company's part to correct the problem on all future prints and copies as the only remedy for the production company's credit mistakes. The clause should further state that a mistake of this nature is not a breach of the crew member services agreement. The clause should make clear that the production company has complete discretion over the look of the credits.
- Crew members typically want their credits listed on IMDB.com.

Rights

PRE-PROD.

The assignment of the rights/work-made-for-hire provision is another standard clause in all motion picture or service contracts. In this paragraph the crew member must agree that all rights, proceeds, and results of her creative efforts are to be treated as a work made for hire. Any remaining rights which are not captured by the production company as a result of the work-made-for-hire clause should be assigned by the crew member to the production company under the agreement. (See "Work Made for Hire," p. 382.)

Publicity

The production company will want to control the publicity for the motion picture and thus be able to restrain the crew member from issuing publicity statements about the motion picture without the production company's prior written consent. The production company will also require the right to use the crew member's name and likeness in any publicity, promotion, or marketing of the motion picture. Make sure to include language that allows the crew member's image to be used in the "making of" documentary that seems to appear on every DVD.

Representations and Warranties

- The crew member is typically required to represent and warrant that he is under no other obligations that would prevent him from performing his duties under this contract. This clause typically contains an indemnity provision that obligates the crew member to indemnify the production company for any breaches of the representations and warranties or other breaches of the agreement.

- The crew member should also warrant that any material that she contributes to the production—writing, props, scenery, wardrobe, gags, *mise-en-scène,* and other creative elements—is original with her. This shifts liability to the crew member if the production company is sued as a result of the crew member adding unlicensed copyright-protected material to the film.

Suspension/Termination

- This paragraph lays out the mechanism for resolving disputes. It typically describes events that would constitute *force majeure* (acts of God) and sets a time limit for how long a crew member's services may be suspended before the services are considered terminated.

- The production company should retain the right to terminate the crew member's services for any reason whatsoever, provided that the production company pays the crew member's fee up to the date of termination.

Assignment

The production company always has the right to assign the contract and the rights, results, and proceeds created under it. The crew member should never have the right to assign or delegate his duties under the contract.

Remedies

Like all motion picture services agreements, the right to injunctive relief should be waived by the crew member. Furthermore, no breach of the agreement by the production company should entitle the crew member to recapture any rights that he may have granted the production company. When well drafted, this clause should leave the crew member only with a right to recover money, if anything at all, from the breaching production company. You will also want to address such issues as whether to solve problems through arbitration or courts of law. (See Appendix C, "Arbitration," p. 383.) And while you're at it, just where will any adjudication or arbitration take place? (See Appendix C, "Choice of Law: Forum," p. 384.)

Further Documents

Here the crew member should be obligated to execute any other documents necessary to further the intent of the contract. Examples include copyright assignment forms, workers' compensation claim forms, and so forth.

Inducement (if Dealing with a Loan-Out Company)

If the crew member is working under a loan-out company, it is the loan-out company that will be a party to the contract. Furthermore, the contract should contain an inducement and further assurances clause. (See "Loan-Out Companies," p. 42.) If the production company is financing the film with production incentives like tax credits, you may need to include a provision in the agreement:

1. Requiring the loan-out company to register to do business and file a return in the production state, and

2. Giving your production company the power of attorney to register the loan-out company to do business in the production state if the loan-out company fails to do so within a certain period of time. (See "Production Incentives: Eligibility Requirements," p. 64.)

◆◆◆◆◆

LAW

- Crew members, like other workers, will be protected by federal and state labor laws. However, the crew members may be treated as independent contractors if they are working through their own companies, such as a loan-out company. (See Appendix D, "A Filmmaker's Guide to Labor and Employment Law," p. 393; "Federal and State Labor and Employment Law: An Overview," p. 165.)

- If you are certain that the crew member is an independent contractor and not an employee, you should include a clause in the crew services agreement stating that the parties understand that the crew member shall be treated as an independent contractor. However, keep in mind that a court will look at the actual work relationship to determine the crew member's status rather than determining status based solely on what the parties agreed in the contract.

PRE-
PROD.

BUSINESS ISSUES

As part of the crew member's perks, it is typical to give her copies of the finished film on DVD or videocassette and to allow her the right to incorporate portions of the film into her reel.

17

PERFORMERS

The choice of performers is critical to a film's success. The majority of the time, the lead performers are the single most important elements in making your film. Actors' performances breathe life into a film, and their fame gives a film its marketing power.

An actor's creative contributions begin before he is even cast. Watching performers audition can expose the weaknesses in a role and underscores the need for a script rewrite. Often a performer's audition will shed new light on a role and bring out its nuances, allowing the director to see the role in a different light and again underscoring the need for a rewrite. Casting directors are often a great investment and can help you get access to performers you might not otherwise be able to reach.

Because performers realize the power they have over a film project, negotiating the performer's services agreement can be a nail-biting experience. Virtually every recognizable performer has a team of agents, managers, and attorneys ready to protect the actor's interests and negotiate the best deal they can for their client. Negotiating the actor's contracts is one area in which you may want to lean heavily on your entertainment attorney or an experienced executive producer.

The *performer's services agreement* is the contract between the production company and the performer.

PRE-
PROD.

- If the production company wants to use actors to secure film financing but is not yet ready to bind them to a full performer's services agreement, it will need to use a letter of intent. (See "Letters of Intent," p. 203.)

- If the production company wants to hire well-known actors, it will also need to deal with the Screen Actors Guild (SAG) and comply with Guild rules. (See "SAG," p. 205.)

- If your production company is using non-SAG actors only, you can skip the SAG section and jump right into the performer's services agreement deal points. (See "Major Deal Points: Performer's Services Agreement," p. 213.)

LETTERS OF INTENT

Hands down, the thing that is most likely to get your film sold is having a known actor or actress as your lead. Your brother—your film's major investor—may be a wonderful actor, but unless he has had a recurring role in a television series or at least a supporting role in a feature film, he will not help you sell your movie.

Sure, there are exceptions to this rule; for instance, the three lead actors in the movie *The Blair Witch Project* did not have substantial television and film credits prior to being cast in that film.[1] However, this is a rare occurrence in a film that makes money. Remember, the first audience you will need to sell your film to is the distribution company. For them to feel confident enough to put their resources behind the marketing and selling of your film, they need to believe there is a reasonable chance for a return on their investment. Putting the name and picture of a known actor or actress in a film's advertising and on its DVD case increases the likelihood that the film will be sold.

However, as one might guess, the more well-known a performer is, the more "bankable" she is and the less likely she is to obligate herself to a film that has no financing. In fact, as a practical matter, most theatrical agents will want to know whether or not the film is financed prior to showing your script to their clients.

However, assuming that you can get a known actor to read your script and like it, how do you get her to agree to be in a film that doesn't have financing? As you can see, it's "chicken-and-egg time" (or "Catch-22," depending on where you fall on the avian reproductive-military logic scale of metaphor preferences). (See "How to Get a Script to a SAG Actor," p. 222.)

One potential solution is to get the performer to agree to let you use her name to secure financing for the film without obligating her to shoot your film if you can't raise the money. This is where a *letter of intent* (LOI) comes in handy. An LOI is a letter from the performer that shows her interest in appearing in your film and includes some of the main deal points to be agreed on. Like many entertainment industry contracts, letters of intent come in many different "flavors," some more binding than others. Many LOIs are just "agreements to agree," which is not the same thing as a legally enforceable contract.

Some financiers, especially those used to the seat-of-the-pants world of independent low-budget filmmaking, will accept a letter of intent that states little more than the fact that the actor has read the script, likes it, and is interested in portraying a specific role once contingent on:

1. Financing being secured
2. The performer's availability
3. Material contract terms being negotiated and agreed on in a performer's agreement. (See "Performer's Services Agreement," p. 212.)

Such letters of intent are far cry from a binding contract that obligates the actor to perform in your film. However, such an LOI from a bankable performer may be enough to convince your financiers that that performer is interested enough to be in your film if the investors will just put the money behind it.

SHORT-FORM PERFORMER'S LETTER OF INTENT

[PERFORMER'S AGENT'S CONTACT INFORMATION]

[PERFORMER'S NAME]

[DATE]

Thank you so much for your interest in our film, tentatively titled [INSERT NAME OF FILM] (the "Film"). As we've discussed, this letter serves to confirm that your client [INSERT PERFORMER'S NAME] has reviewed our script, is familiar with the Film project, and is interested in performing in the Film in the role of [INSERT PERFORMER'S ROLE], subject to [INSERT PERFORMER'S NAME]'s professional availability and an agreement between all parties on financial and other material terms.

[INSERT PERFORMER'S NAME] hereby grants to the producers of the Film the right to use this letter of intent in seeking financing for the Film, and the right to use [INSERT PERFORMER'S NAME] name and likeness for project development purposes in conjunction with the Film, for a period not to exceed [ONE YEAR] from the date of this letter.

If this letter reflects your and your client's understanding, please have your client sign below, and return an original signed copy to me.

We look forward to the possibility of working together on [INSERT NAME OF FILM].

Best regards,

_____

[PRODUCER'S SIGNATURE]

_____

[PERFORMER'S NAME]

PRE-
PROD.

It is important to note that the more money that is being raised and the more sophisticated the financier, the less likely it will be that a nonbinding short-form LOI alone will satisfy the financier's requirements.

THE SCREEN ACTORS GUILD (SAG)

If you want to work with a professional actor, you will also need to work and comply with the rules of the Screen Actors Guild (SAG).

What Is SAG?

The Screen Actors Guild (SAG) is a labor union for professional film and television actors. Production companies that want to work with actors who are SAG members must become *signatories* of the SAG Codified Basic Agreement (Basic Agreement). This means that the production companies must sign a contract with SAG in which they agree to abide by SAG's rules and regulations with respect to the SAG actors they employ.

Among other things, the basic agreement dictates the minimum requirements for:

- An actor's payment and other forms of compensation
- The hours the actor is required to work
- Pension and health contributions
- Overtime
- Consecutive employment
- Working conditions

SAG Contracts Trump Production Company Contracts

Once a production company is a SAG signatory, the SAG Basic Agreement, like other union agreements, will overrule any contrary provisions in the contract between the production company and an actor.

PRE-
PROD.

> **Example:** Electric Space Pickle Productions, LLC, has just become a SAG signatory and is producing a low-budget film for $500,000. Due to its budget, the film will be produced under SAG's Modified Low-Budget Agreement, which requires that actors be paid a minimum of $933 a week. Because the producers want to pour most of the funds into special effects, everybody has agreed to take a salary cut. The production company drafts Actor's Services Contracts giving the SAG actors only $100 per week, which the actors gladly sign. Unfortunately for the production company, the SAG Modified Low-Budget Agreement trumps the production company's contracts. Therefore, even though the actors agreed to $100 a week, they must still be paid the $933 a week specified in the SAG agreement.

A Low-Budget Contract for Every Film

SAG has made an effort to accommodate filmmakers of all budgetary levels. Whether you're making a $1,000 short film, a $2.5 million low-budget film, or something in between, SAG has a contract for you.

In general, the lower your budget, the less you have to pay your SAG actor. However, there are restrictions on how your film may be exhibited, depending on the level of contract you've used to engage your actors. If a film is distributed in a manner that exceeds the SAG contract limitations, the filmmakers may have to pay additional fees.

The following list highlights a few major deal points of SAG's contracts for low-budget independent filmmakers. Filmmakers are advised to request both more detailed summaries as well as the contracts themselves from the Screen Actors Guild.

The SAG low-budget contracts change from time to time. As this book is being written, the following are the current low-budget SAG contracts available to independent producers who are shooting their films entirely within the United States:

1. Student film contract. This contract is only for students who are currently enrolled in film school:

   - *Budget limitations.* The film must be made for $35,000 or less.
   - *Running time.* The film may not exceed 35 minutes in length.
   - *Production.* The film may not exceed a maximum of 20 shooting days.
   - *Exhibition limitations.* Student film festival; in-classroom exhibition; one week in a paying movie house to qualify for Academy Award nomination.
   - *Actors' salaries.* Salaries and other monies may be deferred pending any sale, distribution, or release of project.

2. Short film agreement:

   - *Budget limitations.* The film must be made for less than $50,000.
   - *Running time.* The film may not exceed 35 minutes in length.
   - *Exhibition limitations.* Although this film may generally not be distributed commercially, it can be exhibited:
     - In film festivals
     - In a paying movie theater for a limited time to qualify for award consideration for the Academy of Motion Picture Arts and Sciences
     - In front of industry members to showcase a producer's talents
     - For limited distribution on public access television
   - *Actors' salaries.* SAG principals must be paid at least $100 a day, but the salaries are deferred. Certain fees and expenses may not be deferred:
     - *Consecutive employment.* No consecutive employment (except on overnight locations)
     - *Professional status.* Both professional and nonprofessional performers can be used.
     - *Shoot days.* May not exceed 30 days of principal photography.

PRE-PROD.

- *Exclusions:*
  - Demos for funding
  - Music videos
  - Animated films

See "Short Film Contract" at www.sagindie.org/docs/sag-short-film-agreement-sample2009.pdf.

3. Ultra-low-budget agreement:

- *Budget limitations.* The film must be made for less than $200,000.
- *Running time.* The running time may exceed 35 minutes.
- *Exhibition limitations.* The film may be distributed theatrically without additional compensation to performers; however, if the film is distributed to television or video, the actors must be paid residuals.
- *Residuals.* The residual percentage is paid to SAG, which allocates money to the SAG actors who appeared in the film. The current residual percentage that must be paid to SAG is 3.6% of the distributor's gross receipts for television and cable and 4.5% of the first million for videocassettes and DVDs, and 5.4% thereafter. (See "The Money Pipeline," p. 291.) For Internet distribution, performers must be paid 3.6% of any license fee received by producers for such Internet distribution.
- *Actors' salaries.* $100 a day (not deferred) plus pension and health contributions.
- *Consecutive employment.* No consecutive employment (except on overnight locations).
- *Professional status.* Both professional and nonprofessional performers can be used.
- *Exclusions:*
  - Demos for funding
  - Music videos
  - Animated films

See "Ultra-Low Budget Contract" at www.sagindie.org/docs/sag-ultralowbudget-sample2009.pdf.

4. Modified low-budget agreement:

- *Budget limitations.* This film must be made for less than $625,000.
- *Exhibition limitations.* Within three years from the completion of principal photography, the film must have an initial theatrical release prior to any other releases (free television, cable, video, etc.). Any nontheatrical release occurring prior to the theatrical release will cause the performer's salaries to be *upgraded* to the much higher level of the basic agreement terms, including consecutive employment. However, if, after three years, the film has not

been distributed theatrically, the film may then be distributed in other media without incurring step-up payments to low-budget or television agreement rates. For Internet distribution, performers must be paid 3.6% of any license fee received by producers for such Internet distribution.

- *Actor's salaries.* $268 a day/$933 dollars a week plus pension and health contributions.
- *Running time.* Must be at least 80 minutes and filmed entirely within the United States.
- *Exclusions:*
  - Animated films
- *Consecutive employment.* Consecutive employment can be waived (except on overnight locations).

See "Modified Low-Budget Contract" at www.sagindie.org/docs/sag-modified-lowbudget-2005_6-09_39-th.pdf.

5. Low-budget agreement:
   - *Budget limitations.* This film must be made for less than $2,500,000.
   - *Exhibition limitations.* Within three years from the completion of principal photography, the film must have an initial theatrical release prior to any other releases (free television, cable, video, etc.). Any nontheatrical release occurring prior to the theatrical release will cause the performer's salaries to be *upgraded* to the much higher level of the basic agreement terms, including consecutive employment. However if, after three years, the film has not been distributed theatrically, the film may then be distributed in other media without incurring step-up payments to low-budget or television agreement rates.
   - *Residuals.* No residuals for theatrical exhibition; however, if the film is distributed to television or video, actors must be paid residuals as outlined earlier.
   - *Background actors.* Within certain geographic zones, notably New York, Los Angeles, and other major U.S. metropolitan cities, the production company is required to hire 30 SAG background actors prior to hiring any other non-SAG background actors. Rates for background actors start at $122 a day.
   - *Actor's salaries.* $504 a day/$1,752 a week plus pension and health contributions. For Internet distribution, performers must be paid 3.6% of any license fee received by producers for such Internet distribution.
   - *Running time.* Must be at least 80 minutes and filmed entirely within the United States.
   - *Exclusions*:
     - Animated films
   - *Consecutive employment.* Consecutive employment can be waived (except on overnight locations).

PRE-PROD.

See "Low Budget Contract" at www.sagindie.org/docs/sag-modifiedlowbudget-2005_6-09_39-th.pdf or www.sagindie.org/docs/sag-lowbudget-2005_rev6-09-41.pdf.

For more info on SAG low-budget contracts, see www.sagindie.org/resources/contracts/.

SAG TERMS DEFINED

Consecutive Employment

The SAG MBA requires that producers pay actors for *consecutive employment*. This means that actors must be compensated for days in between those days when they were directly involved in the shoot.

Example: If an actor is supposed to work on Tuesday and Thursday, you must pay him or her for Wednesday as well. However, all the low-budget SAG agreements have done away with this rule. As a result, if an actor is working under a low-budget agreement and it is scheduled for Tuesday and Thursday, these are the only two days for which he gets paid—unless, of course, the producer has agreed to pay consecutive employment in the performer's services agreement. *Remember, SAG only sets the minimum requirements for an actor's services agreement and does not prohibit actors or their representatives from negotiating better deals than those required by the union.*

Residuals

Residuals are additional payments required to be paid to union performers when the film is licensed in ancillary markets such as broadcast television, cable, and home video. When the production company becomes a SAG signatory, it agrees to make residual payments for the film's actors and to ensure that the film's distributors sign an *assumption agreement*. The assumption agreement is a contract with the distributor (or a clause in the distribution agreement itself) in which the distributor agrees to pay the residuals directly to SAG.

Example: Pariah Pictures has shot its film *The Adventures of Millard Fillmore* under the SAG ultra-low-budget agreement. The film is shown on television and 3.6% of the distributor's gross receipts are owed to the SAG actors. Because of Pariah Pictures' assumption agreement with Dusty Distribution, Inc., Dusty pays 3.6% of its gross receipts to SAG, which disburses the monies directly to the actors.

Becoming a Signatory

To become a signatory with SAG, you will need to provide them with a good deal of legal documentation—much of which, if you've been following along in this book, you should have by now. SAG requires that you submit the following forms *at least one month prior* to working with SAG actors. You will need to start the process by downloading, filling out, and submitting to SAG a *preliminary theatrical information sheet,* available on its website at www.sagindie.org/resources/contract-downloads/.

Once the information sheet has been reviewed, you will be assigned a SAG representative, who will be your contact with the Guild.

For SAG to approve your production company's eligibility to work with its members, you must also give the union the following:

1. A copy of the completed copyright registration form. (See "Copyright Registration," p. 136.)

2. A copy of the U.S. Copyright Office receipt, which shows that the office has received the completed form.

3. All chain-of-title documents relating to the copyright in the screenplay and the picture. (See "Chain of Title," p. 131.)

4. A copy of the script.

5. A copy of the shooting schedule.

6. A detailed film budget.

7. Financial structure documents. These are the legal documents pertaining to the formation of your business. Examples include partnership agreements, articles of incorporation, articles of organization and operating agreements, business certificates, and fictitious name statements. (See "Setting Up the Production Company," p. 35.)

8. Financial assurances. SAG may also require assurances that your production company has the money it needs to make the film. SAG may require:

   a. A security deposit.

   b. A first-position *security interest* in the film. A security interest is similar to a mortgage on a house: If you default in your mortgage payments, the bank can sell your house to repay your loan. With SAG's security interest, if you default on your payment obligations to the SAG actors, SAG can seize your film and sell it to pay your debts to your actors.

PRE-
PROD.

Remember: SAG Sets the *Minimum* Contract Requirements Only

- If the production company is a SAG signatory and is using SAG actors, the terms of the union's contracts will set the *lower* threshold of elements such as compensation, working conditions, and the like. Actors and their agents, of course, will try to negotiate higher salaries than those required under these union contracts.

- *Be careful here!* It is easy for budgets to spiral out of control when it comes to an actor's compensation.

  - On one hand, a name actor is, without a doubt, the most important element in selling a motion picture to a distribution company and therefore is worth the time and expense it takes to negotiate a deal with which all parties feel comfortable.

  - On the other hand, if you have several name actors of approximately the same industry recognition value, you simply cannot increase the salary of one without dealing with the demands of the others. This is why low-budget films featuring a cast of several name performers frequently pay only the SAG minimum and not a penny more. Remember, despite your best efforts, you will not be able to keep salaries a secret. Do not pay one actor more than another similarly situated actor unless you want a disgruntled performer on your hands. (See Appendix C, "Favored Nations," p. 378.)

SAG Cautionary Notes

- Remember: a production company that is a signatory with SAG is *required* to abide by all of SAG's rules. Anything in your contracts contrary to SAG's agreements will be superseded by SAG's agreements.

- SAG requires production companies to post a bond to secure the actors' payroll (which can be up to 40% of the budgeted payroll).

- Once the company is a signatory and is working with SAG actors, you may be limited in your ability to use nonunion actors. If you're shooting a film under the student, short, or ultra-low-budget contracts, you may use both SAG and non-SAG actors. However, if you are shooting under the modified low-budget and low-budget agreements, all your actors may need to be SAG members or become members shortly after being hired.

For more information on SAG contracts and policies for independent producers, see www.sagindie.org.

TIP: Start your SAG signatory application processes as early as possible. You need to be a signatory before you can sign a SAG actor to a deal.

THE PERFORMER'S SERVICES AGREEMENT

Goals and Deals

For definitions and explanations of common contract clauses, see Appendix C, "The Clause Companion," p. 375.

Very often a *performer's services agreement* will come in two parts: a brief (two pages or so) *deal memo* coupled with a much longer "Terms and Conditions" section.

The deal memo proper contains key compensation and engagement terms applicable to that particular actor's deal. The "Terms and Conditions" section is designed to apply to the deals of *all* the actors in the film.

MAJOR DEAL POINTS: PERFORMER'S SERVICES AGREEMENT

The Parties

- *Production company.* Most independent producers do not have much money; therefore the most important thing a low-budget producer can offer a professional actor is a great role in a great script in a great movie that will receive distribution. Other ways that you can entice an actor to be in your film without breaking your bank include:
  - Offering him a higher salary but making most of it deferred compensation.
  - Offering him an "associate producer" credit.
  - Offering those perks and amenities you may be able to acquire through your contacts. For instance, if your family owns a car rental business, offer him the free rental car during the duration of the shoot.

- Make sure to get the proper spelling of the performer's professional and legal names, her contact information, and the both the performer's Social Security number and her company's federal tax ID number, if she has a loan-out company. (See "Loan-Out Companies," p. 42.) Get contact information for the performer's attorney or agent, if the actor has one.

- *Actor.* Because independent producers are often untried in the film industry, actors are very wary of committing to a role if they see any signs that the film is not fully financed. In addition, because their image is so important to actors, they will:
  - Seek to limit the ways in which their likeness can be merchandised without their consent.
  - Seek approval over publicity shots and nonphotographic likenesses, such as poster art.

Engagement

- *Services.* These should be described as "all services as are customarily rendered by actors on a feature-length theatrical motion picture, including appearing in any 'making-of' or 'behind-the-scenes' documentaries, plus additional services as specified in any rider attached hereto." If this is a nonunion shoot requiring everybody, even actors, to perform more than just the customary duties of their job, these additional services should be spelled out in a detailed rider attached to the contract. For actors on a nonunion shoot, this might include transporting

PRE-
PROD.

themselves and other actors to the set, selecting and purchasing their own wardrobe, and so forth.

- If this is a union agreement, this paragraph should specify under which union contract the services are being rendered to the production company (e.g., SAG's modified low-budget agreement).

- *Location.* The location of all principal photography is usually specified. This is important, especially for SAG agreements, which have different rules regarding consecutive employment, travel, and other accommodations, based on the particular geographic zone in which the shoot occurs.

- *Unique services.* The production company may want to say that "the performer's services are of a unique nature, the loss of which cannot be fully compensated by monetary damages." If the performer breaches the contract with the production company, then starts work for a third party, the producer can use the "unique services" language and try to get an injunction preventing the performer from working for the third party. Unfortunately, an injunction can't compel a performer or other employee to work with your production company. It can only prevent them from working with another party during the term of your performer's services agreement with that actor.

Availability Dates

This section details all the dates for which an actor must be available to the production company; this includes pre-production, production, post-production, and publicity and promotional activities.

- *Define the start date.* This is the first day for which the actor will get paid.

- *Preproduction.* This is the number of days or dates for which the actor must be available for wardrobe fitting, rehearsal, makeup, and so on. These dates are typically nonconsecutive and often are nonexclusive to the production company. If the pre-production dates are to be nonexclusive, the production company should require that they have first priority on the actor's time for those dates.

- *Production.* These are the dates for which the actor must be available to the production for shooting. It is typical to list all consecutive days and weeks of employment and to make an actor's services exclusive to the production company on those days or weeks on which the actor is performing in the movie.

- *Post-production.* Number of days or dates for which the actor must be available for looping, reshoots, etc.

  - *Reshoot tip.* Often dates for post-production activities have not yet been scheduled when the actor's agreement is being negotiated and signed. In those instances, it is common practice to put the number of days, rather than the date, for which an actor must be available for these activities. Keep in mind, however, that when a specific date is not negotiated, performers usually condition their availability to the production company on whether they have prior contractual commitments that keep them from performing for the production company on a particular date. If this is the case, contract language should specify that it is the actor's obligation to provide services at the earliest possible date thereafter.

- *Publicity.* Number of days or dates for which the actor must be available for photo sessions, interviews, and other publicity or promotional activities.
- *Free days.* Days beyond the production dates for which the performer will be available for reshoots and the like. Compensation should be negotiated for these days as well.

Compensation

- *Fixed compensation.* This is the rate at which the actor will be paid regardless of whether the movie makes money. It is typically coupled with the pay-or-play provision, which requires the production company to pay the actor even if the actor's services are not used. If you are a SAG signatory company working with SAG actors, the particular SAG contract under which your production is being shot will dictate the minimum amount you can pay your performers.

- *Contingent compensation:*

  - *Deferred compensation.* SAG agreements impact whether or not an actor can defer his salary. (See Appendix C, "Deferred Compensation," p. 377.)

  - *Profit participation.* An actor might get a portion of the Film's Net Profits. For longer contracts, the Film's Net Profit definition is often included in the contracts of all contingent compensation participants. (See "Net Profits," p. 379.)

  - *Reuse/residuals.* These are fees payable to a performer when the motion picture is televised, broadcast, or the like. Union contracts will set the minimum rate for these as well. On a nonunion production, companies often have the actors waive these fees.

  - *Favored nations.* Most principal cast members will insist on favored-nations treatment for their compensation and any definition affecting compensation. (See Appendix C, "Favored Nations," p. 378.)

- *Merchandising.* Although the right to manufacture merchandise from an actor's likeness is typically granted to the production company, the performer will want to receive a portion of the proceeds from the merchandise. One formula is to grant the performer 5% of whatever the producer receives from the license of merchandising rights. This fee should be reduced if other actors share the same merchandise property. For example, for a T-shirt deal that features a picture of several cast members, the percentage each actor receives should be reduced according to the number of actors featured on the shirt, so that they all share in the 5%.

- *Agent fee.* Actors and agents will often try to negotiate to have the production company, rather than the actor, pay the agent's 10% commission. If this is agreed to, producers need to understand that this effectively means a 10% increase in

PRE-
PROD.

compensation to be paid to the actor, as well as a 10% increase in compensation for any other actors who have a favored-nations provision regarding compensation perks.

- *Pay the agency.* Agents usually require that their actor clients have their salaries paid directly to the agency. The agency then takes its commission and passes the remainder on to the actor. If this is the arrangement for your performer, the performer's services agreement must contain a clause giving the production company the right to pay the salary to the agency as opposed to the actor.

Perquisites

Perks are fringe benefits not counted as part of the salary.

- *Per diem.* This is a daily allowance that is supposed to compensate the actor for meals, incidental transportation, and other expenses the performer incurs as a result of being away from home. Be wary of agents here—especially when an actor has agreed to work below his quote, an agent may attempt to recapture money for the actor by increasing the actor's *per diem.*

Credit

- It should come as no surprise that credit is one of the more hotly negotiated provisions of the contract. In addition to the position that the credit occupies with respect to the other actors' credits, other negotiable credit terms are whether the credit must appear in all paid advertising, posters, publicity, and so forth.

- It is common for lead actors to negotiate a favored-nations clause with respect to the size and placement of their credit.

- As with all credit provisions, the producer should contract for as much discretion as possible in creating the look of the credits and any other matter with respect to the credits for which the performer has not been given approval rights.

- As is true for all credit provisions, the production company should insert a clause in the contract that says that "inadvertent failure to accord the contracting party credit shall not be actionable." This clause should also require the injured party to waive the right to injunctive relief, leaving an obligation on the production company's part to correct the problem on all future prints as the only remedy for the production company's credit mistakes. The clause should further state that a mistake of this nature is not a breach of the performer's services agreement.

Rights Granted; Results and Proceeds

This section lays out the specific rights granted ("assigned") to the producer. This should always be structured as a work-made-for-hire provision. That way, initial ownership by the production company in the performer's work on the film is automatic. (See Appendix A, "Work Made for Hire," p. 344.)

- Make sure to define the film as including behind-the-scenes footage.
- The producer needs the broadest grant of rights possible:
  - The copyright in the performer's work on the film.
  - A waiver of *moral rights* and *droit moral*. (See Appendix A, "Moral Rights," p. 366.)
  - A grant of the right of publicity to exploit the actor's likeness for merchandising and other tie-ups. (See Appendix A, "Right of Publicity," p. 354.)
  - The right to use doubles for the performer and to dub the performer's voice.
  - The production company needs the perpetual right to be able to use the actor's name and likeness in connection with the publicity and promotion of the film.

Approval

Principal performers often require certain approval rights over elements of the film's promotion, merchandise, and publicity, such as poster images or publicity stills, used to promote the film.

- The production company should never give absolute approval rights to the performer; instead, the performer should be obligated to approve no less than 50% of all the images submitted to him for approval (and perhaps 75% if the performer is in the picture with somebody else).
- This stipulation should be coupled with a time limit within which the performer must approve or reject the stills or likenesses. If the performer does not reject the likenesses within such time period, the clause should state that the production company may assume that the performer's approval has been granted.

PRE-
PROD.

Right to Withhold

The production company needs the right to withhold monies for tax purposes as well as to pay a performer's agents and managers directly.

No Obligation to Produce

Although the production company has the right to produce the film, it needs to be sure that it is not *obligated* to produce the film.

Suspension and Termination Rights

It's no secret that sometimes actors can go off the deep end during a production. This clause allows the production company to terminate its relationship with the performer, subject only to payment of monies earned to date, if certain triggering events occur.

Reasons to suspend/terminate often include:

- A performer who is either unable or unwilling to show up for production
- A drastic change in that performer's appearance
- Unprofessional or illegal behavior
- *Force majeure* (act of God)

This paragraph typically gives the producer the right to suspend or terminate the performer's contract at the discretion of the producer. If the contract is *terminated,* it means that neither the producer nor the performer have further obligations with respect to the other. If the contract is *suspended,* the performer is put on hold until the performer corrects the problem. During the suspension period, the performer may not work for other people.

Representations and Warranties; Indemnification

The performer typically promises the production company that:

- She is free to enter into this contract with the production company and that she has no prior commitments or legal obligations that would prevent her from performing her duties under the contract.
- Any material that she contributes is original with her (e.g., lines of dialogue that she improvises in the film are original with her).
- She has no health conditions that would undermine her ability to perform her services. The performer should also grant the production company the right to take out insurance on the performer, naming the production company as a beneficiary.
- The performer should indemnify the production company for breach of these warranties.

Remedies

The performer should waive any claim to injunctive relief arising out of the production company's breach of the contract. Additionally, in all events the performer should be prohibited from rescinding the contract and recapturing any of the granted rights.

Publicity

- The producer needs to be able to exploit the performer's name, likeness, biography, and so forth in connection with the marketing of the film.
- Conversely, the producer will want to prohibit the performer from releasing any publicity about the motion picture without the producer's approval.

Accounting

If the performer is a net-profit participant or will receive any form of deferred or contingent compensation, this paragraph will delineate how often the performer may expect to receive accounting statements. This is coupled with the right to audit the production company, usually no more frequently than once a year.

Assignment

The production company needs the right to assign this contract and all the rights under it. At the same time, the production company needs to prohibit the performer from being able to assign the contract.

Inducement

If the actor is providing services on behalf of a loan-out company, it is the loan-out company that will be a party to the contract. Furthermore, the contract should contain an inducement and further assurances clause. (See "Loan-Out Companies," p. 42.) If the production company is financing the film with production incentives such as tax credits, you may need to include a provision in the agreement:

1. Requiring the loan-out company to register to do business and file a return in the production state, and

2. Giving your production company the power of attorney to register the loan-out company to do business in the production state if the loan-out company fails to do so within a certain period of time. (See "Production Incentives: Eligibility Requirements," p. 64.)

◆◆◆◆◆

LAW

Like all services contracts, the actor/production company's relationship is also controlled by federal and state employment and labor laws.

In working with any children for any length of time, child labor laws must be complied with. (See Appendix D, "Child Labor Laws," p. 400; "Working with Minors," p. 166.)

SAG Compliance

Delegate to a member of the producer's team the task of making sure the production company is complying with all SAG's rules and regulations. This "SAG compliance producer" should pay special attention to rules regarding:

• Payment
• Working conditions for the performers

- Minors
- Work schedule and overtime
- Meals
- Transportation
- Nudity
- Exhibition restrictions
- Any other item required under the contract with SAG

Regarding nudity, if you are a SAG signatory you must let actors know when the role requires nudity. Additionally, you must let them know before they audition for the role. All performers who appear in nude scenes must agree in writing to do so, usually as part of the actor's services agreement. The right to use a double in place of the actor must also be agreed to in writing beforehand. In shooting nude scenes, it is critical that the set be closed to all nonessential personnel.

PRODUCER'S TIP: When shooting a nude scene, the key is to make the performers feel as comfortable as possible. Make sure the temperature is warm enough for the actors to feel comfortable in the buff. This may mean space heaters and a sweaty crew, but the actor's performances will be the better for it. See that blankets and robes are always handy. Talk to the crew beforehand to make sure that there are absolutely no off-color or bawdy remarks. Not only should the crew be on its best behavior, it should be as silent as possible. The more crew members blend into the background, keeping chatter to a minimum, the less vulnerable and exposed the actors will feel. Above all, the only people who should be on the set are those necessary for taking the shot. There should be nobody standing around who does not have a job to do—absolutely no gawkers and no still photographs without the prior written permission of the actors. Unless you want to lose an actor's trust and have SAG come down on you hard, avoid turning your set into a peep show.

PRE-PROD.

BUSINESS ISSUES

Perks

Perks are fringe benefits not counted as part of salary. What you gain in keeping down an actor's compensation you may lose when it comes to negotiating the perquisites. It is not uncommon for an actor to agree to defer a good portion of his salary while steadfastly insisting on first-class airfare and five-star hotel accommodations.

Frequently requested perks include the following:

- *Per diem*
- First-class airfare

- Five-star hotel accommodations
- Flying the actor's family to the shooting location and providing them with accommodations
- An on-set nanny for the actor's child
- Invitations to, airfare to, and accommodations at film festivals
- A dressing room
- The right to keep wardrobe
- Video copies of the finished film

Although you may be tempted to give these perks to your lead actor, keep in mind that if you do, you may be obligated to provide the same perks to any other actor with a favored-nations clause regarding perks. (See Appendix C, "Favored Nations," p. 378.)

Option on Future Services

If the production company is making a television series or a movie with sequel potential, it may want to obtain an *option* on the performer's future services. (See Appendix C, "Option on Future Services," p. 380.) Performers, on the other hand, might not want an option on their future acting services; they want the greatest freedom possible, especially the right to renegotiate their quotes with the production company.

PRE-
PROD.

Net Profits Definition

If the actor is a profit participant, the performer's services agreement should contain a rider defining how the production company will compute the Film's Net Profits. (See "Net Profits," p. 379.)

The Morals Clause

In the days of the Hollywood studio system, performer's contracts often included a paragraph called the *morals clause*. This clause attempted to regulate the actors' behavior on and off set during filming. It prohibited the performer from:

- Engaging in acts of moral turpitude
- Committing illegal acts
- Performing acts that would bring them disrespect, disrepute, scorn, contempt, or ridicule from the public

Failure to abide by the morals clause in their contracts would cost performers their jobs and, during the anti-Communist scare of the early 1950s, their careers. Today, however, the morals clause tends to be the first thing an actor's representative will strike from a contract. A filmmaker's best bet is to include in the suspension and termination rights clause the right for the production company to suspend the actor's services on a particular film for specific acts, such as breaking the law or being intoxicated.

HOW TO GET A SCRIPT TO A SAG ACTOR

Find the Actor's Agent

The best way to locate a particular SAG actor is through her agent. If an actor is represented by an agent, pitch the project first to the agent; never talk business directly with the actor. Agents are very protective of their actors. Nothing gets under an agent's skin more than feeling like a production company is going behind his back and negotiating directly with the performer.

But how do you find out which actor is represented by which agent? If you're working with a casting director, don't worry about it—that's part of her job. But if you're trying to get a script to an actor by yourself, here again SAG comes to the rescue. The SAG "Actors to Locate" service provides contact information for SAG members' agents. Simply dial the toll-free number and get agent information on up to three SAG actors per phone call.

You can reach the Screen Actors Guild "Actors to Locate" service by calling (800) 503–6737.

Pitch the Movie to the Agent

Once you've located the agent, your next step is to figure out how to best pitch the project to him. If the agent thinks the project is a good fit for the actor, he will then set up a meeting or rehearsal with that performer.

Some points to consider in constructing your pitch to the agent:

• First and foremost, trot out your strongest elements first. Is your screenplay based on a well-known book? Has the writer or the director ever won an award for his work? Are other well-known actors already attached to the project?

• Actors are always looking for good scripts, especially those with complex lead characters. Movie actors often get typecast; this is especially true for television actors. You could make headway in attaching a known actor to your movie by offering her a chance to play against type.

• Actors are always eager to work with other well-known actors they have not worked with before. Once you've secured your first actor, others may be easier to entice.

- When television programs wrap their production each year, the actors go on hiatus. Many of them spend this time acting in independent film projects. Try to schedule your production accordingly. It also helps if you're shooting your film someplace an actor might enjoy; the Adirondack Mountains in the autumn coupled with an offer to fly out your lead actor's family may be just the thing to clinch the deal.

- It can be extremely helpful to have your script submitted by your casting agent or your attorney.

> *CAUTION!* I have never found the "sympathy pitch" to be very successful. Don't try to win over an agent by explaining to them that without their client you can't make the movie. It's a bad ploy because (1) it shows that you're desperate, which completely destroys your leverage if and when it comes time to negotiate with the agent, and (2) it destroys any credibility you might have built up with the agent. No agent will want to attach their client to a production unless they know that the production will be made or, at the very least, that the client will be paid in full.

Casting Directors Hiring an experienced casting director might seem like a luxury on a low-budget independent film. However, it can mean the difference between hiring a known actor and casting a lead whose only experience is community theater. Casting directors add credibility to a project; it signals to the actor's agent that you are professional. *It cannot be stressed strongly enough: until you have built a reputation in the film industry, you'll have to constantly fight against the presumption that you will not be able to get a professional film in the can.* Casting directors go a long way toward alleviating an agent's concerns about your inexperience. Casting directors also free up the producer and director, requiring their presence only at the final stages of the auditions.

You can locate casting directors by contacting the Casting Society of America: www.castingsociety.com.

Auditions You should be aware that the more famous an actor is, the less likely she will want to audition for you. They might meet with you to discuss the script; but they might not even do that until they are actually *offered* the role in your film. One possibly apocryphal story illustrates this point: When multiple-Oscar® winner Shelley Winters was being considered for a certain movie role, she was asked to audition for the part. She sat down with the producer, looked him in the eye, pulled out her Oscars, and plopped the statuettes on the table between them saying, "Audition? Some people think I can act."

PRE-
PROD.

Negotiating the Deal

Once you've gotten an actor's attention, it's time to negotiate the deal. Here again is where casting agents can come in handy: they will be familiar with the actor's current *quote* (the salary range the actor has received for his last few films).

You will want to have an experienced negotiator help you with this part. The negotiator who is experienced in performer's services agreements can help you navigate the rough waters of actors' agents and managers. Here are a few tips:

- *Show restraint.* It is far too easy to "give away the farm" during your first few negotiations. For instance, one clause most agents will insist on for a principal actor is a favored-nations clause. As mentioned earlier, a favored-nations clause obligates the producer to ensure that no one has a better deal than that actor. Favored-nations clauses typically come into play when it comes to compensation and credit provisions. If you grant a favored-nations clause to a supporting actor with regard to his compensation, you will have to pay him the same rate that you pay your principal actors.

- *Be wary of the "two bites of the apple" ploy.* You negotiate with an actor's agent, giving ground to close the deal. Just when you think you're done, the agent shifts you over to another agent or the attorney for the agency to continue the negotiations. This is often a business necessity from the agency's point of view. After all, the agent may have painted the deal in large brushstrokes, and it's the agency's attorney's job to provide the fine details. There is a danger for the production company, however, that goes beyond mere exhaustion. Sometimes the second agent or attorney will try to backpedal, removing some of the deal points the first agent conceded to while leaving your concessions on the table. To counter this tactic, point out that the deal points were already agreed to and they form the basis for concessions on your part. If they can backpedal, so can you.

- *Walk-away point.* Before you start the negotiation process, make sure you have a walk-away threshold with regard to compensation. This is the point at which you will walk away from the deal, no matter how much you love the actor, because you simply can't afford to hire him. Make sure that this figure includes all the fixed costs, perks, and other expenses associated with hiring that particular actor. *It cannot be stressed strongly enough:* It is very important to leave the bargaining table if the deal exceeds your walk-away threshold.

  For one, the other side may be seeing how far they can push. When you walk away, that sets your limits. They may respond by lowering their quote to keep the deal. Be flexible; there may be some in-kind services and perks you can give them that won't break your bank but may enable you to trade them against higher fixed compensation costs.

  If you continue to hash out a deal with a performer once he has exceeded your threshold, you may not have enough resources to pay other necessary performers.

- *Start early.* Make sure to start your negotiations early so that your back is not up against a wall. It will absolutely destroy any leverage you have if a performer's agent realizes that you don't have time to look for another performer should this deal fall through.

STEP BY STEP: HIRING ACTORS

- Decide on union or nonunion performers. If you decide to shoot a union production, you need to become a signatory. (See "Becoming a Signatory," p. 211.)

- SAG regulations and labor laws must be complied with. Assign a producer, ideally two producers, the task of ensuring that the production company complies with SAG and labor laws both on the set as well as off. (See "SAG," p. 205; "Labor and Employment Laws," p. 393.)

- Engage a casting agent to help select performers and provide initial contact with agents.

- If you are not using a casting director, locate the performer's agent and deal with him or her first. Do not initiate contact with a represented actor directly.

- When negotiating the deal with the actor's representative, make sure to have a walk-away threshold. (See "Negotiating the Deal," p. 224.)

- If you are dealing with child actors, you may need to get their contracts approved by the appropriate state court so that they cannot disaffirm their contracts. Additionally, you may need to set up a trust fund for the child's salary, in accordance with that state's version of the Coogan laws. (See Appendix D, "Child Labor Laws," p. 400.)

PRE-
PROD.

6

PRODUCTION

QUIET ON THE SET!

Okay, now it's almost time to roll camera. But wait! There are still some legal issues you will have to take care of first. Ideally, many of these issues will be addressed during pre-production rather than waiting for the first day of principal photography.

This section will help you:

- Identify when you need a release from an extra. (See "Depiction Releases," p. 229.)
- Recognize trespass and other potential property claims. (See "Why You Need a Location Release," p. 235.)
- Negotiate a location agreement. (See "Major Deal Points: Location Agreement," p. 239.)
- Know when you need a shooting permit. (See "Shooting Permits," p. 237.)
- Keep your art direction from infringing somebody's copyrights. (See "On-Set IP Infringement," p. 243.)
- Understand the fair use of copyrights. (See "Fair Use of a Copyright," p. 245; Appendix A, "Fair Use," p. 335.)
- Negotiate an artwork license. (See "Artwork License," p. 248.)
- Learn about problems relating to shooting trademarks. (See "Trademarks on the Set," p. 250.)
- Negotiate a trademark license. (See "Trademark Clearance Letter," p. 254.)

STAGES OF PHOTOGRAPHY

- *Principal photography* is what most people think of when they think of a film shoot. It is the time when the cameras roll, capturing the filmed dialogue sequences. It is the heart of the shoot itself.

- *Second-unit photography,* by contrast, consists of that photography done by a second camera crew that films scenes that do not include the main performers. Examples of second unit photography include establishing shots, backgrounds, crowd scenes, and footage for computer animation.

- *Pick-up shots* are shots or scenes shot after the completion of principal photography. The need for a pick-up shot is established when a scene couldn't be shot during principal photography—for instance, due to bad weather or, as is often the case, when the director is in the editing room, cursing at himself for not having the *one* shot he needs to make the sequence or movie perfect....

18

EXTRAS AND DEPICTION RELEASES

Extras and background performers are almost always needed in feature films to provide a sense of reality. In fact, one of the marks of an amateur film is seeing actors performing in empty streets. Even worse are scenes in which actors perform in crowded streets while pedestrians steal glances at the camera, wondering what's going on.

To avoid these problems, you will want to hire *extras*, also known as *background performers*. If you are a SAG signatory, you will have to comply with the SAG background performer rules that govern your particular contract. (See "SAG," p. 205.)

Whether you are a guerrilla filmmaker filming your actors in a crowded city street or an independent producer who films all her scenes on a locked-down, tightly controlled set, you will need to worry about securing releases for your extras.

THE BOTTOM LINE: As a general rule, if a person is identifiable in a scene, you need to worry about depiction releases.

DEPICTION RELEASES

Although there is generally a very limited right to privacy on public streets, there are several legal claims producers need to concern themselves with, namely misappropriation of the right of publicity, defamation, and invasion of privacy.

- *Right of publicity.* The right of publicity protects a person's rights to commercial exploitation of his or her likeness (e.g., voice, image, catchphrases). This generally isn't an issue in feature films, but producers shooting television commercials—a form of commercial exploitation—will require signed releases. (See Appendix A, "Right of Publicity," p. 354.)

- *Defamation.* Defamation and libel suits arise when a person who is distinguishable on camera claims that he was portrayed in a false manner harmful to his reputation. (See Appendix A, "Libel and Defamation," p. 359.)

    Example: Even newsmakers are not exempt from defamation lawsuits. In a news story on prostitution, ABC News producers shot footage featuring close-ups of a black woman walking down the street as the voice-over commented on the number of black prostitutes who cruise for white johns. The woman featured was not a prostitute but an ordinary pedestrian, unaware that she was being photographed for the story. When she sued for defamation, the court held that she had made a case for defamation.[1]

- *Invasion of privacy.* "Hidden camera" documentaries need to be especially cautious here. While you may have a First Amendment right to photograph somebody, you generally don't have the right to intrude where a person has a reasonable expectation of privacy or to expose his private affairs in a way that is objectionable to a reasonable person. (See Appendix A, "Violation of Privacy Rights," p. 356.)

A depiction release is the best solution to these situations. In fact, such a release is often required by errors and omissions (E&O) insurance carriers.

Note: In keeping with industry practice, the following depiction release is structured as though the person being filmed were writing a letter to the producer. It uses the pronouns *I* for the person being filmed and *you* for the producer.

DEPICTION RELEASE

For the sum of $_____[*the producer should pay someone something—i.e., $5.00*] and other good and valuable consideration received, and as full and complete payment for all rights and releases granted hereunder, I hereby grant to_____PRODUCTION COMPANY, LLC (hereinafter "Producer" or "you" or "your"), and its assigns and licenses the ownership and any and all rights to use any and all of the depictions you have taken of me, including photographs, voice recordings, video footage, film footage, likenesses, sobriquets, contained in any interviews, performances, "behind the scenes" footage, or any other recording of me, whether that depiction is recorded in film, video, audio, or still photography, or any other medium, now known or hereafter developed (the Depiction).

I give up any and all rights to the Depiction and assign them to you. These rights include, but are not limited to, copyright, trademark, rights of publicity, rights of privacy, and moral rights. You may copyright the Depiction in your name. You may use my name in connection with the Depiction.

I hereby waive, release, and discharge any claims I may have for libel, defamation, misappropriation of right of publicity, invasion of privacy, intentional or negligent infliction of emotional distress, or any other claim I may have resulting from your use of the Depiction.

The rights I grant to you in the Depiction are perpetual and irrevocable and may be transferred by you to any other party at your discretion. Coupled with your ownership of the Depiction, I grant you the rights to sell, display, perform, distribute, publish, republish, commercially exploit, use in advertising, promotion, and to create derivative works from the Depiction and any work which embodies it.

You have complete discretion to edit or otherwise modify any work in which the Depiction appears and to use the Depiction in any manner or for any purpose whatsoever without any further remuneration to me.

DEPICTION RELEASE (cont.)

I shall indemnify you and hold you harmless from any claims or actions arising from any misrepresentations I have made in this release. I hereby release you, your agents, and your assigns from any claims resulting from any injuries I may sustain while my Depiction is being taken.

You are not obligated to use the Depiction or to exploit any of the rights I have granted. All rights conveyed inure to the benefit of you and your assigns.

I am of full legal age and capacity and fully understand the rights I am assigning or waiving. I am freely and voluntarily entering into this Agreement, and have read and understood each and every provision, as set forth herein. I agree that any interpretation of this Agreement shall not be construed against a party by virtue of its having drafted the terms and conditions hereunder. This is the entire agreement between me and the Producer. In entering into this agreement, I have not relied on any statements by the Producer or anyone else regarding the nature of the film, its content, or how I will ultimately be depicted.

This release shall be interpreted according to the laws of the State of [insert your state here].

Name and Contact information: [insert the contact information of the person being filmed]

Signature_____

[The person being filmed should sign the release]

Depiction Release: Child

PROD.

For a child, the depiction release will require the signature of a parent or legal guardian. Additionally, the parent should agree as follows.

"Parent/Guardian acknowledges that he/she has read, understood, and agrees to all of the terms, conditions, grants, and waivers contained in the release. Parent/Guardian understands that the production company is relying on the rights and releases conveyed under this document, the loss of which by the production company cannot readily be compensated through the awarding of monetary damages. The Parent/Guardian represents, warrants, and guarantees that neither they, nor the child, will disaffirm this release any time, whether as a minor or as an adult."

Under the law, minors may be able to *disaffirm* a contract, that is, to void their obligations under a contract. Although the preceding parent/guardian clause may not provide iron-clad protection against the release being disaffirmed by the child, it should obligate the parent/guardian to avoid encouraging or helping the child disaffirm the release. To provide greater protection against a minor being able to disaffirm any production contract, you should have that contract ratified by a court. (See Appendix D, "Child Labor Laws," p. 400.)

Notice Release

What if you're filming in a crowded restaurant, concert hall, or other large public venue and obtaining signed releases from all the potential background performers is not possible? You may want to post a sign, known as a *notice release*. Although this might not be as effective as a signed release, it could afford some protection.

A notice release should be posted outside the entrance to the location and contain the following information.

ATTENTION

You are about to enter an area in which [*name of production company*] is filming a motion picture [*or television program, video, etc.*]. Accordingly, your voice and/or likeness may be captured on film. By entering this area you are consenting to be filmed by us. Furthermore, you agree that we shall own in perpetuity and without reservation any and all rights to the footage shot here today. We may use this footage for any purpose whatsoever, including, but not limited to, theatrical, television, promotional, and advertising use without any further compensation to you. Furthermore, you waive any claims you may have arising out of or use of this footage, or any depictions of you contained within. You understand that we are relying on your consent to these terms.

If You Do Not Agree To These Terms, Please Do Not Enter.

If you do not agree to these terms you may proceed to:

[*Provide alternate directions for those who wish to enter the venue but not be photographed. For example, those who do not consent should be directed to another area of a stadium where the cameras will not be focused.*]

PROD.

TIP: **Signs like this one should be posted near all entrances! Shoot some footage of the crowd walking past the sign to establish that the sign has been posted in an open and obvious position. Try to get footage of people reading the sign as they enter.**

CAUTION: NO FRAUD OR MISREPRESENTATIONS ALLOWED!

Many courts will try to view the depiction release in a light most favorable to the person whose depiction you are using. If your subject can persuasively argue that he was misled as to how you would use the footage or that you have defrauded him into signing the release, the court may void your release. If you are planning to use the depiction in a way that a subject might object to, make sure to include language in the release that describes that use.

> *Example:* "Production Company may use your depiction in any manner, including as a background in a violent satanic music video."

THE *BORAT* DEFENSE

The producers of the movie *Borat* were sued (several different times, actually) by the unwitting subjects of the mockumentary. In one case, Michael Psenicska, a driving instructor from Maryland, had agreed to give a driving lesson to Sacha Baron Cohen, aka fake Kazakhstani journalist Borat, for what Mr. Psenicska thought was a "documentary about the integration of foreign people into the American way of life."

Mr. Psenicska signed a depiction release and was promptly subjected to a hair-raising car ride by Borat, in which the actor cursed at other drivers and pretended to drive drunk. When the film was released, Mr. Psenicska sued[2] for fraud, unjust enrichment, and infliction of emotional distress. At the heart of his complaint was that the depiction release was invalid because he had been told that this was a documentary and not a parody; in short, he contended, he was *defrauded* into signing the release because he relied on the producers statements regarding the kind of film it was.

The Court thought otherwise, pointing to specific language in the depiction release that disclaimed reliance on "any promises or statements made by anyone about the nature of the Film or the identity of any other Participants or persons involved in the Film." Nor did the release contain any written statements that the film was in fact a documentary about a foreigner's travels in the United States.

The Court held that where a plaintiff "has in the plainest language announced and stipulated that it is not relying on any representations as to the very matter as to which it now claims it was defrauded," the disclaimer "destroys the allegations in plaintiff's complaint that the agreement was executed in reliance upon these contrary oral representations."

Sacha Baron Cohen won the lawsuit. As Borat might say: *"Very nice!"*

BOTTOM LINE: Always include language in your depiction release that specifically states that the subject is not relying on any statements or representations by the film crew on the nature of the film or how he or she will be depicted.

PROD.

Filming People without Their Permission

If you film, photograph, or record, or otherwise depict people without their permission, you could be opening up yourself or the production company to lawsuits. Review the situations that follow to determine how vulnerable you are.

Possible Claims — **Typical Defenses**

You are using someone's image or likeness for commercial or advertising purpose.
Possible claim: Infringement of Right of Publicity (see "Right of Publicity," p. 354)
- Noncommercial use (media, film, news)
- De Minimis use
- Incidental use

You are using someone's name or likeness which they also use as a trademark.
Possible claim: Trademark Infringement, False Endorsement, Tarnishment (see "Trademarks on the Set," p. 250)
- Fair use
- Informational use
- Criticism
- Incidental use
- Parody

Your false portrayal of the subject might damage the subject's reputation.
Possible claim: Defamation (see "Defamation," p. 359)
- Truth
- Opinion
- "Actual malice" required for public figures
- Privilege
- "Gross Irresponsibility" for matters of public concern

You disclose embarrassing personal facts about the subject.
Possible claim: Public Disclosure of Private Facts (see "Public Disclosure of Private Facts," p. 357)
- Public interest
- Nonintrusion
- Facts in public record

You false portrayal of the subject causes him or her mental distress and indignity.
Possible claim: False Light (see "False Light," p. 358)
- "Actual Malice" required for public figures
- Portrayal not offensive person

You filmed or recorded the subject where they had a reasonable expectation of privacy.
Possible claim: Intrusion Upon Seclusion (see "Intrusion Upon Seclusion," p. 357)
- Filmed in public place
- Filming not intrusive to reasonable person

You used footage or recordings of a subject that you didn't create.
Possible claim: Copyright Infringement (see "Copyright Infringement," p. 353)
- Fair use
- De Minimis
- Parody
- Criticism

19

LOCATIONS

WHERE ARE YOU SHOOTING?

Once you've scouted and chosen your locations, you need to ensure that you have the legal right to shoot there. If you are shooting on public property, you may need a *shooting permit*. If you are shooting on private property, you should have a *location release*. Depending on the location, you may also need a shooting permit to shoot on private property.

Special locations, such as military bases, federal buildings, airports, and cruise ships, will probably require more than just the simple permit issued by a city.

WHY YOU NEED A LOCATION RELEASE

If you shoot on somebody's private property without his or her permission, you may expose your production to criminal penalties and civil liability for *trespass, trespass to chattels, invasion of privacy,* and *nuisance*. A location release is a contract between you and the property owner or other authorized party that gives you the right to enter that property and shoot your film. In addition to preventing lawsuits, a location release is also an enforceable contract that gives you a right to shoot in a location at a particular time. Nothing is worse than showing up to a location with a cast and crew only to find that the owner has now changed his mind about allowing you to shoot on his property.

PROD.

If you shoot on someone's property without a location release, you could be sued for the following:

- Trespass to land
- Trespass to chattels
- Invasion of privacy
- Nuisance

Trespass to Land

Most people know that if you enter the property of another person without permission, you are trespassing. However, you don't need to set foot on somebody's property to be liable for trespassing; any physical intrusion on the land of another will do. This means that if you place your light stand on somebody's property, park a truck in his driveway, or plug a cord into her electrical outlet, you are trespassing unless you have that person's permission to do so.

Trespassing also occurs when your rights to be on somebody's property have expired. So, if you have a location release that allows you to shoot in a warehouse on Saturday, you'll technically be trespassing if you or your equipment are still there on Sunday. This is why you want to leave ample room in your location releases to allow you to leave equipment that needs to be set up or wrapped out.

Watch out for the following:

- You don't even need to touch the land to commit trespass! A boom microphone or crane that never touches the ground but that nonetheless crosses a property line would expose you to a claim of trespass.

- The fact that you didn't know the property was owned by somebody else will not relieve you from liability. Mistake is no defense to a claim of trespass; if you intended to enter the property, you're trespassing unless you have the owner's permission.

- Just because a shop or restaurant is open to the public does not mean it is public property for the purposes of filmmaking. The business has opened its doors and granted an implied license for customers to enter the property for purposes of shopping, not for the purposes of production companies who want to shoot a film there. You'll still need to secure the store's permission to shoot your film on the premises.

Trespass to Chattels

Chattel is the legal term for physical property, as distinguished from *real property,* the legal term for land and the houses on it. *Trespass to chattels* occurs when you interfere with somebody's right of possession to their physical property. For instance, if you interfere with somebody's car, bicycle, television set, computer, and so forth, you may be liable for trespass to chattels. The point here is that a gaffer who, without the owner's permission, clamps a light to the roof of a parked car, scratching the paint, is exposing the production to liability for trespass to chattels.

To claim trespass to chattels, the plaintiff has to establish that you interfered with the property owner's right of possession and you caused some sort of damage. However, depriving the owner of use in the chattel may amount to sufficient damage. So, in the case of the car, because the gaffer rigged the light to the top of the car, the owner could not use the car until the light was removed, and thus his or her ownership rights have been violated and trespass to chattels has probably occurred.

Privacy Law

Photographing people on private property when they have a reasonable expectation of privacy may violate their rights. For a detailed discussion of privacy rights, see Appendix A, "Violation of Privacy Rights" (p. 356).

Nuisance

A nuisance results when a filmmaker creates a substantial, unreasonable interference with the *use* and *enjoyment* of somebody's private property. Nuisance very often comes into play when a filmmaker shoots in a residential neighborhood in the middle of the night. The production company's bright lights, smoke machines, generators, and loudspeakers may create a nuisance. Note that if you are planning to use equipment like this, a location release for the particular lot on which you're filming might not be enough. You might need to secure the permission of the neighbors as well.

GETTING PERMISSION TO USE A LOCATION

Shooting Permits

A shooting permit is permission from the city or municipality to shoot on public or private property within that jurisdiction. Many filmmakers believe that they only need to worry about shooting permits if they are filming on public property, such as streets or parks. In actuality, some jurisdictions require filmmakers to secure permits and pay filing fees even if they plan only to shoot on private property within the municipality!

The key is to check with the city clerk's office in the city or municipality in which you will be shooting several weeks prior to the shoot. Expect to pay a fee for a shooting permit. Some cities charge upward of $500 a day!

Shooting Permit Requirements

Although the requirements for issuing a shooting permit differ from city to city, filmmakers are often required to provide some or all of the following:

PROD.

- *A completed application.* This must be signed by an authorized representative of the production company.

- *A certificate of insurance.* You will probably be required to add the municipality as an additional insured on your policy. An additional insured, you may remember, is a person, company, or municipality whose interests will also be protected by your insurance policy. In the case of shooting permits, the city will be added as an additional insured to your general liability policy so that if it is sued by someone injured by your film production, the city will be covered by your insurance policy. (See "Insurance," p. 49.)

- *Fees.* Remember, film shoots are a source of revenue for many municipalities; therefore, expect to pay for the right to film within a municipality's borders. Common fees include:
  - *Application fee.* A nonrefundable fee for processing the application.
  - *Filming fee.* A daily or weekly fee for the right to film within the municipality.

- *Bond check*. This is sort of like a security deposit on an apartment; it is money the city can use if you damage its property. Assuming you haven't caused any damage or caused the city other expenses, your check should be returned several weeks after filming is completed.
- *Garbage removal fees.*
- *Fees to hire off-duty police officers.*
- *Letters of intent and notification* to be distributed to the neighbors near the filming location.
- *Notarized letter of indemnification* stating that your production company will indemnify and otherwise hold harmless the municipality for any damages to property or injuries incurred by your production company.
- *Parking list*. A list of all the trucks, generators, vans, crew cars, and any other mobile equipment to be parked on the city streets.
- *Shooting schedule.*

WARNING: **If you do not obtain a permit and choose instead to shoot guerrilla style, you may be looking at substantial penalties, both civil and criminal, as well as jail time, depending on the jurisdiction.**

Local Rules

In addition to securing a permit for a shoot, municipalities may also have special rules that apply to the film shoot itself. You can find this out from the office that issues the permit. Such rules typically govern:

- "Blackout hours"—times when no shooting may take place
- You may not be able to park catering trucks or "honey wagons" (portable bathrooms) near restaurants
- Noise
- The requirement of having local police on the set
- Garbage and waste
- Lighting (you may need to provide blackout material for residents' windows when doing a night shoot)
- Treatment of electrical cables
- Treatment of pedestrians and local traffic
- Truck height and weight limits for streets and bridges

THE LOCATION AGREEMENT

For definitions and explanations of common contract clauses, see Appendix C, "The Clause Companion," p. 375.

A *location agreement* is a contract that grants the production company the permission to shoot on *private* property.

PROD.

For the contract to be valid, the production company needs the signature of the property owner or the owner's authorized representative. In securing permission to shoot in a commercial establishment, make sure to get the permission of the owner or supervising manager. A clerk, waiter, or other nonmanagerial employee usually does not have the power to sign contracts for a company or property owner. In fact, many businesses do not even allow their managers to enter into contracts on behalf of the company. The safest route is to secure the permission of both the owner of the building and the owner of the business.

MAJOR DEAL POINTS: LOCATION AGREEMENT

Parties

- *Production company.* The production company wants to be able to shoot unhindered in a particular location. It will need time to load and set up equipment, the right and the time for the art directors to change the location, and time to remove equipment and to restore the property to its original state.

- *Grantor.* The person or company granting the rights in the location release is called the *grantor.* It is usually the property or business owner. Make sure to get the full legal name of the grantor if it is a business. Do not assume that the manager of a business has the power to grant the location release.

Right to Depict Location

- The grantor must grant the production company the right to depict the location in the motion picture and in stills, audio, video, and nonphotographic licenses, in "any and all media whether now known or hereafter developed, for any purpose whatsoever."

- For commercial establishments, these rights must include the right to depict any trademarks or *trade dress* owned or licensed by the business that occupies the location. Trade dress is a particular and distinctive way a store is decorated, when such decoration functions as a trademark.

The grantor must also grant the following rights:

- The right to alter the appearance of the location (any physical alterations should be subject to the filmmaker's obligation to return the property to its original condition on completion of the shooting)

- The right to juxtapose scenes filmed in other locations with the location that is subject to the release so as to create the appearance of a seamless whole

- The right to use the name of the location

- The right to bring personnel and equipment onto the location and to leave the equipment there

PROD.

- The grantor must agree that the production company is not obligated to use any of the footage in the final film, nor will the production company be obligated to depict the location in any particular matter

Right of Access to Location

This is the paragraph that protects filmmakers against trespass charges. Filmmakers must be careful to specify not only the days and hours on which they want to film but also the amount of time and start and stop dates needed for loading and setting up equipment and set dressing and wrapping out the same.

Releases

- The grantor must release the production company and its employees from any claims of libel, invasion of privacy, trespass, trademark and trade dress infringement, copyright infringement, nuisance, trespass to chattels, right of publicity, or violation of any other right that may be implicated in the normal course of filming on location.
- The grantor must agree to waive any equitable relief, such as injunctions, against the production company and look solely to monetary damages for any remedy.

Period During Which Location Access Is Granted

- It is often helpful to avoid being too specific as to the timeframe for equipment removal. The filmmakers should use the phrase "on or about [*time frame*]" to give them the flexibility to be a little late or a little early.
  - Write something like: "The production company will use reasonable efforts to remove all of its equipment from the Property on or about 9:00 A.M., Friday the 13th, 2011."
  - If, instead, you write: "The production company will remove all its equipment from the Property at 9:00 A.M., Friday the 13th, 2011," the production assistant who shows up to remove the equipment at 9:15, 15 minutes late, may be denied access, and the presence of your equipment on the property may expose your production company to a claim of trespass.
  - Include a statement that should the timeframes change, the terms of the location agreement shall apply to the new times as well.

Payment Terms

- This is usually structured as a flat one-time fee.
- Include a statement that the grantor did not pay the production company any fee to be featured in the film. This is often referred to as a *no kickbacks provision*.

PROD.

Indemnification

- The production company should indemnify the grantor against damage or lawsuits that arise out of the production company's use of the location (except for breaches of the grantor's warranties).
- The grantor should indemnify the production company against the grantor's breaches of the warranty of authority. A *warranty of authority* is a promise by the grantor that he has the power to grant the location release. If the person granting the location release does not, in fact, have the power to grant the release, this clause holds that false grantor accountable for any of the production company's losses that result from the grantor's misrepresentations of his authority to grant the release.

Insurance

Grantors typically require that they be named as an additional insured on the production company's insurance policy.

Credit Provisions

The grantor's credit preferences should be indicated; however, any credit should be at the production company's sole discretion. Producer should include a clause disclaiming liability for inadvertently making a mistake with the grantor's credit and preventing the grantor from seeking an injunction.

Remedies

The grantor should waive any claim to injunctive relief arising out of either a breach of the contract or destruction of his property. Depending on the advice of counsel, producers may want any dispute to be settled through binding arbitration rather than through the courts.

PROD.

TIPS

- The property owner is first and foremost worried about having the property damaged and having his business disrupted; as a result, the production company should be prepared to do a lot of hand-holding with the property owner, constantly providing reassurances that nothing will go wrong.
- The production company should arrange the shoot so as to minimize the amount of interference the shoot will cause to the owner's business or life.

If the location is a private home, the production company may have to pay for the family to stay in a nice hotel for several days.

- The property owner should be added as an additional insured to the production company's insurance policies. Even though your insurance company should pay claims stemming from location damage, it doesn't hurt to have some petty cash on hand to pay the grantor for minor damages.

- When shooting exteriors, it is often helpful to have some petty cash on hand to pay people to be quiet. Knowing how disruptive noise can be to a film shoot, some unscrupulously opportunistic people will actually stand on public property and yell, mow their lawns, or otherwise try to throw off a shoot in the hopes of getting some hush money. Unfortunately, it's often quicker to hand them a couple of bucks than to try to charge them with being a public nuisance.

PROD.

20

WHAT'S ON THE SET?

ON-SET IP INFRINGEMENT

When the director yells "Action!," what the camera captures can spark lawsuits. All it takes is one suddenly inspired art director to place an uncleared Warhol print on the wall of the hero's apartment or the Coca-Cola® logo on the mirror the drug-addicted villain uses to cut his cocaine. Unless the producer has the permission of all the respective copyright and trademark owners, photography can lead to infringement.

Copyrighted materials appear everywhere: posters, sculptures, product labels, makeup designs, even the tinny music playing over the radio held by an extra. All these materials should be *cleared* for use. Indeed, copyright is the bane of the conscientious art director. Don't fall into the trap of thinking that just because you have a valid location release from a homeowner that you also have the right to photograph any of the copyrighted materials in his or her home. The homeowner may no more have the right to authorize the photography of the Warhol print than the art director does.

BE CAREFUL THAT YOUR INSPIRATION IS NOT INFRINGEMENT

In a scene in the film *12 Monkeys*, Bruce Willis's character spends a few minutes being interrogated while being restrained in a futuristic chair. The design of the chair was inspired by a drawing of a chair, titled *Neomechanical Tower (Upper) Chamber*, by the artist Lebbeus Woods. The film's director, Terry Gilliam, discussed the drawing with his production designer, and the film's chair was constructed without Mr. Wood's permission being obtained.

When Mr. Woods sued,[1] the court found that substantial portions of his drawing were copied; in other words, unless the copying was excused, it would constitute infringement. Universal tried to argue that because the chair appeared in less than five minutes of the 130-minute film, the copying was *de minimis*—in other words, insignificant. (See Appendix A, "*De Minimis* Taking," p. 339.) The court disagreed with Universal and granted Mr. Woods motion for a preliminary injunction enjoining Universal from "distributing, exhibiting, performing or copying those portions of the motion picture entitled *12 Monkeys* which reproduce his copyrighted drawing, or any portion of it." The movie company settled the suit and paid a license fee to Mr. Woods.[2]

PROD.

Filmmakers must worry about more than artwork on the set. Trademarks can also cause problems. It's a sign of the breadth of the global economy that some trademarks, such as Coca-Cola® or the Nike "swoosh," are among the most recognized symbols in the world. With a trademark's fame comes tremendous legal power to control its use. Unauthorized trademark use can often bring the unwelcome attention of the trademark owner's lawyer—especially when the trademarked goods are shown in a bad light. Famous trademarks may be *tarnished* if they are placed in a vulgar or slanderous context, and the trademark owner can sue. (See "Trademarks on the Set," p. 250.)

CLEARANCES

Clearance is the process of:

1. Determining which trademarks and copyright-protected artwork and music used in a film require the rights owner's permission before it can be used, and then

2. Obtaining permission to use that trademark or copyright.

When a film or video is "cleared," all the necessary intellectual property (IP) rights associated with the film or video–the copyrights, trademarks, and rights of publicity–have been granted. Consequently, the film or video work may be distributed and shown to the public without undue fear of costly IP infringement suits. However, clearances can be time-consuming. IP law controls virtually every aspect of a film–the soundtrack, the screenplay, an actor's appearance, a corporate logo, stock footage–everything. The best tactic is to know what clearances are needed before production starts and to work with a staff trained in securing the proper permissions. (See "Copyright Searches and Permissions," p. 132; Appendix A, "A Filmmaker's Guide to Intellectual Property Law," p. 327.)

PROD.

Caution: Artwork and Logos Ahead

The following items can cause problems if featured in a scene without first clearing their trademarks and copyrights:

- Paintings
- Posters
- Sculptures and sculptural reproductions
- Books and magazines
- Product labels
- T-shirt logos and designs
- Dolls, action figures, and other toys
- Location background music

- Halloween masks
- Television or video clips that play over an on-screen television
- Video games
- Street performances
- Billboards
- Storefront signs
- Trademarks used in a manner that tarnishes their image

COPYRIGHTS ON THE SET

Watch out for props and set dressing. Remember, mere ownership of a particular copy of a work of art does not give you any copyright rights to it. Even though you bought a poster, sculpture, painting, prop, and so forth, you still need to get the permission of the owner of the copyright to use that item.

If you are unable to get permission to use a particular piece of art, you may be better off removing it from the scene. If that's not possible, make sure, at a minimum, that the artwork is not featured in the scene, and if it's depicted at all, such depiction should be fleeting and incidental.

Of course, you may be able to defend a copyright infringement lawsuit on the grounds that your use constituted *fair use* under copyright law. However, as a practical matter, relying on fair use is probably a pretty bad idea. People assert a fair use defense after they've already been sued and have had to pay a lawyer to defend them. That being said, what exactly is fair use of a copyright?

Fair Use of a Copyright

PROD.

Fair use is a defense to copyright infringement. It allows the taking of some part of a copyrighted work without the need to secure the author's permission. Examples of fair use include news reporting, criticism, comment, teaching (including multiple copies for classroom use), parody, scholarship, or research.

In general, a court is more likely to find fair use when the use has been *transformative*. To determine whether the use is transformative, the court will ask: Does this new work add anything to the original or recast it in a different light? Or, instead, does it merely copy and compete in the same marketplace as the original?

How Do Courts Decide If a Use Is Fair Use?

The federal copyright statute[3] says that courts must give weight to the following four factors in determining fair use under copyright law:

1. "The purpose and character of the use, including whether such use is of a commercial nature or is for nonprofit educational purposes;

2. The nature of the copyrighted work;

3. The amount and substantiality of the portion used in relation to the copy-righted work as a whole; and

4. The effect of the use upon the potential market for or value of the copyrighted work."

Unfortunately for the producer, it is up to the court to decide—after the fact—whether the taking was excused because of the fair use doctrine. This means that the filmmaker has already been dragged into court by the copyright holder, something clearances are designed to avoid altogether.

Documentary filmmakers may have a bit of an advantage over narrative filmmakers when it comes to fair use. In general, a copyrighted work that just happens to appear fleetingly in the background of a scene in a documentary should not cause infringement.

> *Example:* Penelope Producer is shooting an interview with Dr. Matheus Liebeenhög, world's foremost authority on dryer lint, for her documentary *Dust Bunnies and Their Furry Friends.* On a side table behind the good doctor is a small copyrighted sculpture, which is partially obscured by his elbow. If she were sued for infringement by the sculpture's copyright owner, a court would probably side with Penelope. Note, however, that Penelope could still be sued for infringement. The better practice would be to move the sculpture.

One helpful resource for evaluating whether your use of an unlicensed copy-righted work in a documentary is fair use is the *Documentary Filmmakers' Statement of Best Practices in Fair Use,* created by American University's Center for Social Media (AUCSM). You can find the report at www.centerforsocialmedia.org/resources/publications/statement_of_best_practices_in_fair_use/. The University also has a report specifically to help you with fair use in online media: www.centerforsocialmedia.org/files/pdf/online_best_practices_in_fair_use.pdf. AUCSM has also created a helpful website to help artists negotiate the often rough waters of fair use: www.centerforsocialmedia.org/resources/fair_use/.

For more on copyright and fair use, including some helpful examples, see Appendix A, "Fair Use," p. 335.

Architectural Copyright

Architecture is a special case under copyright law. Even though architecture is protected by copyright, an exception to the law allows you to photograph buildings that are located in or visible from a public place without first securing the permission of the copyright owner.[4] However, there is an exception to this exception... stay with me here... special local and state rules may protect local landmark buildings, requiring you to obtain permission.[5] If you routinely shoot in a particular geographic area, it might be helpful for your attorney to compile a list of any local, state, or historic landmarks that your camera crew should avoid.

Fair Use in Copyright

Fair use is a defense to copyright infringement. It allows the taking of some part of the copyrighted work without the need to first secure the author's permission. *Caution: only a court can tell you (after you've been sued) whether your unpermitted use was fair use.* When you defend a copyright infringement lawsuit with a fair use defense, the court will analyze what you did by asking the following four questions and balancing the answers.

What did you do with the copyrighted work you took?	
For fair use	**Against fair use**
✔ You made a documentary or news program ✔ You used it for education ✔ You used it for parody or social criticism ✔ You substantially transformed the original work	✘ You made a TV commercial ✘ You used it to replace work you could have made yourself ✘ You featured the work in a narrative film that did not parody or comment upon the work you took

What kind of copyrighted work did you take?	
For fair use	**Against fair use**
✔ News ✔ A compilation of facts or data ✔ A scholarly to technical work	✘ The work was fiction, narrative film, or an expressive work ✘ Copyrighted paintings, sculptures, graphic arts ✘ Copyrighted stories, poems, novels ✘ Copyrighted musical compositions or recordings

How much of the copyrighted work did you take? How important was the portion you took to the rest of the work?	
For fair use	**Against fair use**
✔ You took a small portion ✔ Your use was fleeting or incidental ✔ The portion you took was not critical to the overall meaning of the copyrighted work	✘ You took a large portion of the work ✘ You used the work in your film for a substantial amount of time ✘ You took the "heart" of the copyrighted work ✘ You featured the copyrighted work prominently in a scene

How did your taking affect the value or market for the work?	
For fair use	**Against fair use**
✔ The work has limited economic value ✔ The work is not usually licensed or resold ✔ You used it for parody or social criticism ✔ Your work does not directly compete with the work you took	✘ The original work's owner lost potential or actual licensing revenue ✘ Your infringing work directly competes with the original work

Other factors
Acting in good faith. Give proper attribution; make sure to display the copyright notice of any work you take. Keep in mind, however, that giving proper attribution will not automatically entitle you to fair use. The court still must ensure that the answers to the preceding questions favor you as well. *Transformative use.* A court will be more likely to consider your use fair use if you can show that you "transformed" the copyrighted work you took. A transformative use is one that adds something new to the original work, recasts it in a different light, giving it a new meaning or message.

PROD.

The Artwork License

If you really need to include a particular work of art in your film and you can't hire an art director to create a satisfactory original work as a work made for hire, try obtaining an *artwork license*. This license grants the production company the right to use the art in all versions of the motion picture.

For definitions and explanations of common contract clauses, see Appendix C, "The Clause Companion," p. 375.

MAJOR DEAL POINTS: ARTWORK LICENSE

The Parties

- *Production company.* The production company wants to be able to use a work of art in its motion picture.

- *Grantor.* The person or company that owns the rights to the artwork. It could be the artist, the artist's estate, or any party to whom the artist has assigned the copyright to the art. If the artist is well known, the production company will probably not be able to get the right to reproduce and sell the art itself, apart from its depiction in the motion picture.

REPRESENTATIONS AND WARRANTIES: AUTHORIZED PERSON

PROD.

In addition to the usual representations and warranties, the grantor, in this case the copyright holder, must represent and warrant that he is either the legal owner of the copyright to the artwork or someone with the power to authorize licenses of the work (such as an attorney for the legal department of a corporation that owns the work).

Title and Description of Film

Provide the title of the film, but make sure it is described as "tentatively titled."

Description of the Artwork

The artwork itself must be described. Be careful here. There are often several versions of a piece of art. The production company will only have permission to use those versions specifically listed in the artwork license agreement.

Grant of Rights

This section lays out the grant of rights from the grantor to the producer. The grantor must license the following rights to the production company:

- The right to use the artwork in the motion picture, in whatever forms that motion picture takes (i.e., film, video, DVD, streaming, etc.). This is usually phrased as "in any and all media, whether now known or hereafter devised."
- The right to make copies of the film containing the artwork.
- The right to exploit and distribute that film any way the producer sees fit.
- The right to use the artwork in advertising promotional materials.
- All rights should be of perpetual duration and irrevocable.
- The rights are usually nonexclusive, meaning that other production companies can license the same artwork for their films. If the producer requires the rights to be exclusive, the licensing fee will be much greater.

Compensation

- A licensing fee should be negotiated, and some amount, even if it's only a few dollars, should be paid. Nonexclusive licenses are cheaper than exclusive licenses.
- The producer should try to negotiate the license fee as a one-time flat fee, with no residuals or other contingent payments to be paid.

Credit and Copyright

- The manner in which the copyright owner and artist is credited should be specified. The production company often retains the right not to credit the artwork owner at all. In addition to credit, the production company may be obligated to place the owner's copyright notice and information in the credits.

PROD.

- As with all credit provisions, the producer should contract for as much discretion as possible in creating the look of the credits and any other matter with respect to the credits for which the copyright owner has not been given approval rights.
- As is true for all credit provisions, the production company should insert a clause in the contract that says that "inadvertent failure to accord the contracting party credit shall not be actionable." This clause should also require the injured party to waive the right to injunctive relief, leaving an obligation on the production company's part to correct the problem on all future prints as the *only* remedy for the production company's credit mistakes. The clause should further state that a mistake of this nature is *not* a breach of the artwork license agreement.

Waivers

- The grantor must waive any right to inspect the film or approve of the matter in which the artwork is depicted.

- The grantor must waive any copyright claim to the film itself.

- The grantor must waive any and all moral rights, rights under the Visual Artists Rights Act, trademark rights, or other related rights with respect to the artwork's use in the film.

Remedies

The artist should waive any claim to injunctive relief arising out of a breach of the contract. Depending on the advice of counsel, producers may want any dispute to be settled through binding arbitration rather than through the courts.

TRADEMARKS ON THE SET

When most people think of a trademark, they think of logos for products (Coke®, Nike®, McDonalds®) or services (Club Med®, SuperCuts®, Amazon.com®). This is fairly accurate, since trademarks and service marks are used: (1) to identify and distinguish a trademark owner's goods and services from those sold by others; and (2) to identify for consumers the source of those goods and services.

Trademarks are found on product labels, billboards, and clothing insignias. But trademarks can also be sounds, such as the NBC three-tone network chime. Trademark rights can also protect a particular and distinctive way a store is decorated, called *trade dress* (think the design of every Starbucks® or McDonald's® you've ever visited).

In general, there are broader fair use and free speech rights concerning trademarks than there are for copyrights. The essence of trademark infringement is that the consumer *might be confused* as to the source of the goods or service being marked.

> **Example:** If you sell a bag of nacho cheese chips and call it "Dolitos," the Frito-Lay company, makers of Doritos® brand tortilla chips, will probably win if they sue you for trademark infringement. Your brand name is confusingly similar to theirs, and consumers may be confused as to just who is manufacturing the bag of chips in their powdered-cheese-stained hands.

False Endorsement

Filmmakers get into trouble when it appears as though a trademark owner or celebrity endorsed, approved, or sponsored the film, a claim known as *false endorsement*.[6]

PROD.

Example: In the Steve Martin/Eddie Murphy film *Bowfinger*, Martin's character, Bowfinger, secretly follows and films a famous actor, Ramsey, played by Murphy. Bowfinger makes a film by editing together the surreptitiously obtained shots of Ramsey, along with shots starring an actor who looks like Ramsey. The result is *Chubby Rain,* a movie in which Ramsey appears to have starred. If this had been real life and not "reel" life, Ramsey could sue Bowfinger for *false endorsement* (as well as invasion of privacy and a few other claims) because *Chubby Rain* creates the illusion that Ramsey intentionally starred in the film and, therefore, endorsed it.

Filmmakers who feature celebrity "look-alikes" in their work should display a prominent disclaimer that boldly and explicitly states that the actual celebrity did not endorse the film or the products and services being advertised.[7] Even the unlicensed use of a celebrity's *voice* can raise the issue of false endorsement, as the makers of the video game "Madden 06" found out when they used the voice of football announcer John Facenda in their game without first securing his permission.[8]

Using the name of a real person in a film's title is generally permitted as long as there is an artistic relationship between the movie's content and the film's title.[9] The title, however should not be explicitly misleading.

Example: A Fellini film about two aging dancers, nicknamed *Fred and Ginger* after famous hoofers Fred Astaire and Ginger Rogers, did not falsely imply that Ginger Rogers had endorsed the film.[10]

Be very careful if you are using a celebrity impersonator in a commercial or other advertisement! As one court reasoned: "a celebrity whose endorsement of a product is implied through the imitation of a distinctive attribute of the celebrity's identity has standing to sue for false endorsement."[11]

NAKED EXCEPT FOR A LAWSUIT

Times Square in New York features neon lights, Broadway shows, and a nude singing cowboy. He's naked except for a hat, boots, underwear, strategically placed guitar… and a trademark registration for the same. The Naked Cowboy®, aka performer Robert Burck, a famous New York City street performer, sued candymaker Mars, Inc., for misappropriation of his right of publicity (in New York, a privacy law claim) and trademark infringement. The candymaker and its advertising agency had created an advertising campaign featuring a blue M&M candy dressed up as the Naked Cowboy, placing the ads on electronic billboards in Times Square and inside its Times Square candy store. Burck sued and Mars, Inc., filed a motion to dismiss the suit.

Burck lost on his right of publicity claim. Even though the New York statutes make it a misdemeanor to use "for advertising purposes, or for the purposes of trade, the name, portrait or picture of any living person without having first obtained the written consent of such person,"[12] the court held that the scantily clad blue M&M was

PROD.

NAKED EXCEPT FOR A LAWSUIT (cont.)

neither a portrait nor recognizable likeness of Burck. Furthermore, it pointed out, "merely evoking certain aspects of another's character or role" does not violate New York's right of privacy law.[13] In "look-alike" cases, the Court reasoned, although "any recognizable likeness, not just an actual photograph, may qualify as a 'portrait or picture,' that likeness must be a 'close and purposeful resemblance to reality' of the actual person."

Although the right of publicity claim fizzled, the court allowed Burck to continue with a *false endorsement* claim, appropriate when a person (or company) falsely implies the endorsement of a product or service by a person.[14]

To prove a false endorsement claim,[15] you have to show that the defendant (1) in commerce, (2) made a false or misleading representation of fact, (3) in connection with goods or services, (4) that is likely to cause consumer confusion as to the origin, sponsorship, or approval of the goods or services.[16]

Even though Mars, Inc., asserted a parody defense, the court ruled that whether the "naked" M&M was a protected parody was a question for a later proceeding. M&Ms may melt in the mouth, but this false endorsement claim survived a motion to dismiss.

Informational Use of a Trademark Is Permitted

If you are using a trademark to describe or depict the goods or services of the trademark owner, generally your use is *informational* and you don't need permission from the trademark owner.[17]

PROD.

> *Example:* Max Mogul is shooting a documentary about soft drinks and wants to feature a montage of the changing shape of the Coca-Cola bottle throughout the 20th century. Even though both the name Coca-Cola® and the shape of the bottle itself are registered trademarks of the Coca-Cola Company, it is unlikely that Max needs to seek the company's permission, since his use is informational.

Courts understand that: "[T]he appearance of products bearing well-known trademarks in cinema and television is a common phenomenon."[18] However, note again that it is a court that will make this determination—after the trademark owner has sued you and brought you into court.

Tarnishment

Unlicensed use of famous trademarks can get filmmakers into trouble when the trademark is depicted in a vulgar or disparaging context. In such an instance, the trademark owners can sue for *tarnishment*. To be tarnished, a trademark must be both famous and cast in an unflattering or unseemly light. One such case arose when the Dallas Cowboys Cheerleaders successfully sued the makers of the adult film *Debbie Does Dallas* for using the cheerleaders' trademarked uniforms in the context of a pornographic movie.

However, not every negative reference to a trademarked good must be cleared by the good's manufacturer. Trademark law must yield to the First Amendment, and thus using trademarks to convey information, news, or for comparative advertising is usually permitted. For example, the makers of Caterpillar® brand bulldozers sued Disney when their machines appeared in the film *George of the Jungle 2* and were described as "deleterious dozers" and "maniacal machinery."[19] The court sided with Disney, and the case settled. The point here for independent filmmakers to remember is not just that Disney won but that they got sued in the first place.

Parody

Parody is another defense to the claim of trademark infringement, false endorsement, and tarnishment. To be successful, a parody by its very nature must conjure up the appearance of the original trademark. The key here is to:

- Avoid confusing that audience. Make the parody different enough so that an average person would know that it is not looking at the trademark itself.

- Use the parody to poke fun of the original trademark rather than just using it for humorous effect.

PROD.

SPA'AM: A TRADEMARK PARODY IN ACTION

Jim Henson Productions successfully asserted a parody defense when they were sued for trademark infringement by Hormel Foods over a character from *Muppet Treasure Island*. Henson created a wild boar character named "Spa'am," and was promptly sued by Hormel, makers of SPAM® brand luncheon meat.

The court pointed out that a successful parody must evoke the original to be effective: "A parody must convey two simultaneous—and contradictory—messages: that it is the original, but also that it is not the original and is instead a parody. To the extent that it does only the former but not the latter, it is not only a poor parody but also vulnerable under the trademark law." As the court stated: "No one likes to be the butt of a joke, not even a trademark. But the requirement of trademark law is that a likely confusion of source, sponsorship or affiliation must be proven, which is not the same thing as a 'right' not to be made fun of."[20]

Keep in mind that just because you might have the fair use right to use a trademark, many trademark designs are also protected by copyright, and you might not necessarily have the right to use the copyrighted material that embodies that trademark.

> *Example:* Spider-Man is protected by both trademark and copyright. You might have the right to use the Spider-Man trademark in a documentary on comic books, but you would not automatically have the right to reproduce pages from an entire comic book in your film, since these are also protected by copyright.

Trademark Clearance Letter

If you plan on featuring a trademark or logo prominently within a scene, the best practice is to get permission from the trademark owners. The best way to do that is with a *trademark clearance letter.*

It is common practice to first contact the trademark's owners and to explain your needs. You might need to send them your script or the scene from the film that contains their mark. Once the trademark's owners have agreed to let you use their trademark in your film, follow up your telephone conversation or e-mail with a letter of agreement. This very simple release is often drafted in the form of a letter *from* the trademark owner *to* the production company granting the nonexclusive right to use the trademark in the film.

PROD.

TRADEMARK CLEARANCE LETTER

Dear [*Production Company Name*]:

We, [*Trademark Owner Name*], are the owners of the trademark(s) [list the trademarks; you may need to attach them to the letter. If they are federally registered trademarks, include the registration numbers as well] (the "Trademarks"). You have requested our permission to include the trademarks in your feature film, currently titled [*insert movie title*] (the "Film").

For good and valuable consideration, the sufficiency of which is hereby acknowledged, we hereby grant you the irrevocable, perpetual, nonexclusive rights to use the Trademark(s) in any manner you so choose, in your sole discretion in connection with the Film. These rights include, but are not limited to, the right to photograph, videotape, create film depictions of, refer to in dialogue, and to otherwise use the Trademark(s) in your Film, in any advertising, promotional, and marketing materials related to the Film, in any and all media, manner of exhibition, reproduction, transmission, or display now known or hereafter invented in perpetuity throughout the universe. The rights granted herein are fully assignable and transferable to your licensees, assigns, and successors.

TRADEMARK CLEARANCE LETTER (cont.)

We hereby warrant and represent that we are the owners of the above-referenced Trademark(s) and that we have the power to grant the license in rights herein. We agree to indemnify you for any breach of these representations or warranties and against all claims, expenses, damages, arising from our breach of this agreement.

Sincerely,_____

[*Trademark Owner*]

Ways to Avoid Infringement on the Set

Get Permission.

- Contact the owner of the artwork in question and negotiate a license to use the work. (See Artwork License, p. 248.) If you are planning to feature a trademark prominently, try to get the trademark owners' written permission. (*See* Trademark Clearance Letter, p. 254.)

Prop Rental Houses.

- One way to make sure that your props have been cleared is to rent them from the prop rental house. Most prop rental houses rent items that have already been cleared for use. Make sure, however, that your contract with the rental house stipulates that they have represented and warranted that the props to rent have been cleared for motion picture use. (*See* Appendix C: Representations and Warranties, p. 381.)

Commission.

- If a particular piece of art is going to be crucial to your film, you may want to commission the artwork from an artist. Make sure that you have a written contract with the artist that grants you the copyright in the work as a work made for hire. (*See* Work Made for Hire, p. 344.)

Public Domain Work.

- Artwork in which the copyright has expired is always a safe bet. (*See* Appendix A: Copyright Duration, p. 351.) Artwork and imagery that is prepared by the federal government is also in the public domain. (*See* Appendix A: Public Domain, p. 332.)

No Trademark Tarnishment.

- Don't show trademarks in a scandalous manner. (*See* Tarnishment, p. 252.)

No False Endorsement.

- Don't imply the trademark owner or the celebrity endorsed or sponsored the film when they haven't. (*See* False Endorsement, p. 250.)

Fair Use.

- Although fair use can be a valid defense to copyright infringement (*see* Fair Use, p. 335), it is never wise to rely on fair-use principles for protection. Remember, it is up to a court to decide whether your unpermitted use is "fair use." In short, fair use should be your last defense.

PROD.

Likelihood of Fair Use

The more the following factors are present, the more likely it will be for court to find "fair use":

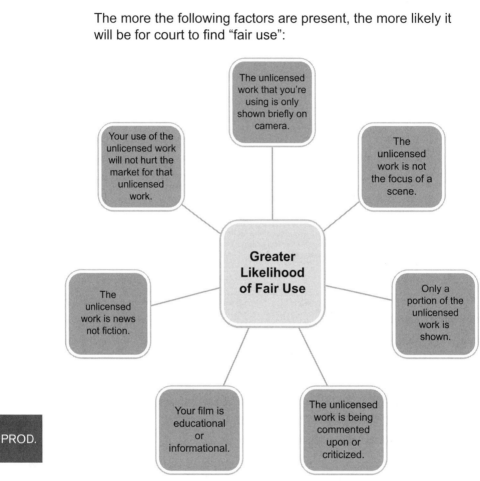

PROD.

E&O AND OTHER CONTRACTUAL OBLIGATIONS

If you have errors and omissions (E&O) insurance, make sure that you comply with their policy regarding artwork and other clearances. Remember: You need this insurance, and the surest way to get a claim denied by an insurance company is to fail to comply with the policy requirements.

If your policy states that you must get a release for all identifiable trademarks, *you need to do so,* regardless of the fact that your use may be informational, and thus, not infringing.

Similarly, if you are under a production services agreement to deliver a film or television program to a broadcaster, studio, or other commissioning party, you will be bound by those contractual obligations as well. (See "Production Services Agreements," p. 149.) It is standard practice for studios and broadcasters to require filmmakers to clear *all* copyright- and trademark-protected materials.

From the point of view of maintaining an effective E&O policy or production services agreement, whether you would ultimately win an infringement suit may be beside the point. If the policy or contract says you need a clearance, you need a clearance. (See "Insurance," p. 49.)

PROD.

POST-PRODUCTION

IT'S IN THE CAN

It is said that a film is made three times: once when it is written, once when it is shot, and once when it is edited.

If a producer runs into legal problems during principal photography, it is usually as a result of the frenzied pace of production. By contrast, legal problems that arise during post-production usually occur as a result of fatigue. Exhausted after a shoot, producers are still hard at work trying to schedule reshoots, secure music licenses, and line up distribution companies to view screener tapes. Furthermore, money is usually tight during post-production, and producers often find themselves having to secure additional funds to complete a film.

The most important thing a producer can do is to slow down and make sure that all the legal issues are being dealt with. Above all, don't abandon your lawyer at this point!

Some of the legal issues a producer will encounter during post-production include:

- Hiring an editor, post-production artists, and technicians. (See "Post-Production Staff," p. 261.)

- Understanding special issues relating to music copyright. (See "Music Copyright," p. 263.)

- Licensing a prerecorded song. (See "Using Prerecorded Music," p. 263.)

- Rerecording a song. (See "Rerecording an Existing Song," p. 266.)

- Commissioning music. (See "Commissioned Music," p. 271.)

- Using stock footage. (See "Stock Footage Companies," p. 280.)

- Obtaining film clips from a movie studio. (See "Movie Studio Footage," p. 280.)

TIP: **It is often extremely helpful to hire a post-production manager to help deal with many of these issues. (See "Crew Services Agreement," p. 195.)**

POST.

21

POST-PRODUCTION STAFF

During post-production you will be working with an entirely new crew: editors, composers, special effects artists, graphic artists, Foley artists, sound engineers, and laboratory technicians, just to name a few.

Some of these artists will be hired directly by the production company, but some will be providing services while in the employ of either their own or other companies.

HIRING POST-PRODUCTION ARTISTS AND TECHNICIANS DIRECTLY

If you are hiring these artists directly or through their loan-out companies, you can create an agreement using the crew member deal points shown earlier in this book. (See "Crew Services Agreements," p. 195.) For composers, you'll want to use a separate agreement based on the deal points as outlined later in this section. (See "Commissioned Music," p. 271.)

As always, if the production company is employing these artists, you need to comply with all labor and employment laws. (See Appendix D, "A Filmmaker's Guide to Labor and Employment Law," p. 393.)

ARTISTS AND TECHNICIANS PROVIDED BY POST-PRODUCTION FACILITIES

POST.

If you are using an editor, engineer, animator, or other artist provided by a post-production facility, you may be presented with one of their "standard contracts." Read it before you sign it! At a *minimum,* these production facilities contracts *must* contain the following provisions:

- *Work for hire/assignment of rights.* The artist and the company he works for must agree that the copyrights and other rights to the artist's contributions shall be entirely owned by the production company. *The contract must contain a work-made-for-hire/assignment clause!* Remember: For copyrights to transfer from nonemployees to the production company, you must have a written agreement stating that the work is a work made for hire—and that agreement must be signed by the contractor. (See "Work Made for Hire," p. 344.)

- *Representations and warranties/indemnity.* The artist and the company he works for must agree that all contributions by the artist will originate with the artist or are in the public domain. This should be coupled with an indemnity provision creating an obligation for the artist's company to indemnify the production company for any breaches of the representations and warranties or other breaches of the agreement. This shifts liability to the artist's company if the production company is sued as a result of the artist adding uncleared copyright-protected material to the film. (See Appendix C, "Representations and Warranties," p. 381; "Indemnification," p. 386.)

Remember: If the contract does not have these clauses, you might not be protected—and you might not have the rights you need to distribute your film!

CAUTION!

- *Assignment of copyright.* Some post-production companies, especially startups, have been known to bury within their contracts copyright assignment clauses that assign a portion of the film's copyright to the post-production company! Although it is not unusual for a post-production company to provide services to a production company in exchange for a portion of the film's revenues, the ownership of the copyright should remain with the production company.

- *Liens.* Many post-production contracts contain clauses allowing the post-production house to have a *lien* on the film and other materials used in post-production. A lien is a creditor's interest in property, like a security interest, similar to a mortgage on a house: If you fail to pay your mortgage payments, the bank can seize your house and sell it to pay the debt that is owed. If a post-production company has a lien on your film, it can seize your film and sell it to pay any debts you owe it. Try to negotiate a waiver of the lien in exchange for the production company providing the post-production company with a cash security deposit.

POST.

MUSIC

In general, there are three ways music is acquired for film:

• Preexisting musical recordings are licensed for use in the picture
• A preexisting musical composition is rerecorded and used in the picture
• Music is composed especially for the picture

Many films use a combination of these three methods.

MUSIC LICENSING

Using Prerecorded Music

Music licensing is one of the trickiest areas of entertainment law. For prerecorded songs, the work of seeking permissions is doubled. This is because there are actually *two* kinds of copyrights to every piece of recorded music, and licenses need to be obtained from each copyright owner. You need to secure the permissions from:

• The party who owns the copyright to the *musical composition*
• The party who owns the rights to the *recording* of the composition that you plan to use

Music Copyright

The two copyrights contained in every piece of recorded music are (1) a copyright in the *musical composition* and (2) a separate copyright in the *recording* itself.

• A copyright in the musical composition.
  • The musical composition, also referred to as the *musical work* under copyright law, is the combination of music and lyrics (if there are any). The copyright protects those notes and words that you would see transcribed into sheet music.
  • This musical composition copyright is typically owned by one or more music publishing companies or the music publishing company and the songwriter.

Example: The song composition "Lump," written by the band The Presidents of the United States of America, is owned, respectively, by David M. Dederer Publishing, EMI April Music Inc., Flying Rabbi, Raw Poo Music, and Universal Polygram International.

- A copyright in the recording itself.
  - The sound recording of a musical composition is protected by its own copyright, usually owned by the record company. You can find this information by looking at the copyright owner information contained in the phonographic copyright notice—the "P in a circle."

Example: The recording of the song "Lump" used in the music video of the same name is owned by Sony Music Entertainment, Inc.

Rights Required and the Licenses That Grant Them

To use a piece of prerecorded music in your film, you will need several different kinds of rights, and consequently, you will need to negotiate and acquire several different types of licenses that grant you those rights. The licenses you need are the following:

1. *Synchronization license.* A synchronization license is needed from the *music publisher.* This license allows the producer to use the musical composition in an audiovisual work.

2. *Master use license.* A master use license is needed from the *recording company.* This license allows the producer to use the particular recording in the film.

3. *Performance license.* A performance license is needed from the *publishing company.* This license allows the producer to show the film containing the composition to the public via broadcast, cable, and satellite television. If the film will be transmitted digitally over the Internet, a performance license may be needed from the *recording company* as well.

   - In the United States, you do not need a performance license to show your film in movie theaters. Furthermore, most television entities have blanket licenses, which cover the performance rights of songs. Despite this, you should still secure performance rights for your film because your film may be distributed internationally, and performance rights requirements differ from country to country. Furthermore, you may show your film in other public venues that do not have blanket license agreements (trade shows, business conventions, in-store advertisements, etc.).

4. *Videogram license.* A videogram license is needed from the *music publisher.* This license allows the producer to make and sell videotape and DVD copies of the film that contains the publisher's composition.

Locating the Correct Music Publisher for a Particular Song

To find the music publisher of a particular song, conduct a search with the *performance rights societies.*

Performance rights societies are organizations that monitor music use on radio, on TV, and in nightclubs. They collect royalties for public performances from these entities to pay to the music publishers (not to the record companies). The main performing rights societies are:

- The American Society of Composers, Artists, and Publishers (ASCAP; www.ascap.com)
- Broadcast Music, Inc. (BMI; www.bmi.com)
- SESAC (www.sesac.com)

What Music Rights do you Need for a Pre-Recorded Song?

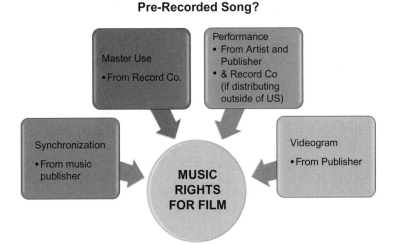

When a performing rights society collects money for a certain song, it pays half the money to the writers of that song and half the money to the song's publishers. These royalty payments are referred to as the *writer's share* and the *publisher's share,* respectively.

MUSIC LICENSING IN ACTION

Fred wants to use a song in his film *Life Sucks,* written by Greg Grubb and published by Dirtz Publishing, LLC, an ASCAP-affiliated publishing company. The recording of the song that Fred wants to use is by The Grubz, off of their 1994 album, *Eat the Dirt.* The record company that owns the copyright to this song's recording is Dark Dayz Records, Inc.

Fred knows he will want to sell DVDs of his film after it has been shown in theaters.

Fred will need:

1. A *synchronization license* from the music publisher, Dirtz Publishing, LLC, which allows the producer to use the musical composition in an audiovisual work

MUSIC LICENSING IN ACTION (cont.)

2. A *master use license* from the recording company, Dark Dayz Records, Inc., which allows the producer to use the particular Grubz recording in the film

3. A *performance license* from both the publishing company, Dirtz Publishing, LLC, and the record company, Dark Dayz Records, Inc., if the film will be shown in public, over the Internet, or theatrically outside the United States

4. A *videogram license* from the publishing company, Dirtz Publishing, LLC, which allows the producer to make and sell video copies of the film that contains the publisher's composition

THE BOTTOM LINE: There are two copyrights in every musical recording. To be able to put one prerecorded song on your film's soundtrack, you must secure several types of licenses from several different parties.

Rerecording an Existing Song

Instead of licensing a preexisting recording of a song, filmmakers often choose to have an existing song composition rerecorded. This can save money by eliminating licensing fees to the record company.

It does not, however, eliminate licensing fees to the publishing company, and it adds the cost of rerecording the song (musicians, technicians, studio time, etc.) to the budget. Furthermore, if musicians are hired to rerecord the song, the producer must take care to engage them under contracts stating that the work they do is a work made for hire. You might want to add up all the costs of rerecording a song and compare them to the cost of licensing a song before you decide to go one way or the other.

For rerecorded songs, the producer will still have to get permission from the music publishing company and will still need to negotiate and obtain the following:

POST.

- A synchronization license
- A performance license
- A videogram license

CAUTION! IMITATION IS THE SINCEREST FORM OF INFRINGEMENT

Sound-alike recordings. Suppose you want to use a popular song in your movie, but you don't want to pay for the rights to use the recording. You decide to rerecord the song, and you tell your singer to sound as much like the original singer as possible. Believe it or not, this can land you in legal hot water. Sound-alike recordings may violate a singer's right of publicity and give rise to claims of false endorsement.

CAUTION! IMITATION IS THE SINCEREST FORM
OF INFRINGEMENT (cont.)

Example: Singer Tom Waits successfully sued the Frito-Lay company when it broadcast a commercial jingle for its SalsaRio Doritos corn chips that featured a sound-alike singer—a performer who had spent years imitating Wait's distinctive gravelly voice in a cover band.[1] (See "Right of Publicity," p. 354, and "False Endorsement," p. 250.)

Sampling. For those who want to create their own compositions by sampling (taking snippets of other people's recordings): Think twice before sampling without a license. One court recently indicated that even small musical samples (three notes long!) needed to be cleared. According to this court, sampling was per se (automatic) infringement—and that the *de minimis* exception to copyright infringement did not apply to sampling. (See Appendix A, "*De Minimis* Taking," p. 339.) As the court put it: "Get a license or do not sample."[2]

GOALS AND DEALS

You will need to deal with several parties in securing the rights to a piece of music. Each music licensing agreement should be drafted differently, depending on which rights are being licensed and from whom. For prerecorded songs, you will be approaching both the music publishers and the record companies. If you plan on recording your own version of a song, you only need to approach the music publisher.

Most licensors have their own standard agreements that they prefer to use. Remember, just because something is a "standard agreement" doesn't mean that it is not negotiable.

Before negotiating the rights to a licensing agreement, keep in mind your exact needs. If you are releasing your movie straight to video, you probably do not need to pay for theatrical release rights; if you're shooting a television commercial that has a shelf life of one year, you probably do not need to pay for the music rights in perpetuity. The less you need, the less it will cost you.

For definitions and explanations of common contract clauses, *see* Appendix C, "The Clause Companion," p. 375.

POST.

MAJOR DEAL POINTS: MUSIC LICENSING
AGREEMENT

The Parties

- *Production company.* The work of the production company is doubled and it may need to negotiate and execute two separate license agreements from two or more parties. Make sure you are asking the correct party for the correct license.

- *Music publisher.* You will always need to secure the license to use the musical composition from the publisher. In one contract from the publisher, obtain the following licenses: synchronization, performance, and videogram licenses.
- *Record company.* If you need to use a particular recording of a musical composition, you will need to negotiate with the record company for the following licenses: master use and international performance licenses.

Grant of License(s)

- Unless you have a pressing reason that your film should be the only one entitled to use the song, all you need is a nonexclusive license.
- The *synchronization license*, obtained from the publisher, is the right to use the composition in synchronization or in time-relation with the motion picture in all its forms.
- The *performance license*, obtained from the publisher, is the right to publicly perform the composition in relation to the motion picture in all its forms.
- The *master use license*, obtained from the record company, is the right to use a particular recording of the composition in relation to the motion picture in all its forms.
- The *videogram license*, obtained from the publisher, is the right to reproduce in video form and sell the composition as matched to the motion picture in all its forms.

Term

For feature films you should almost always have a perpetual licensing term.

Territory

- For feature films, try to define the territory as "the world" or "the universe."
- For television commercials, you may be able to reduce the cost of the license fee by restricting the territory to domestic television.

Media

- When negotiating the language of the license, try to define your motion picture as broadly as possible—for instance: "The Motion Picture, in all its forms, in every media now known or hereafter invented."
- Even for feature films, make sure your licenses cover all television distribution media (broadcast, cable, satellite, in-flight movie, closed-circuit, video cassettes, and DVD).

POST.

- Try to include Internet distribution in your definition of television, although many licensors will want to treat this as a separate medium.

License Fee

- Be aware that music licensing can be very expensive. It is not unusual for popular recorded songs to be licensed for tens of thousands of dollars.

- Try to negotiate a flat fee and avoid having to pay any royalties or other contingent compensation.

- If the Screen Actors Guild (SAG), American Federation of Musicians (AFM), or the American Federation of Television and Radio Artists (AFTRA) has jurisdiction over the movie, reuse payments may have to be made to the musicians and vocalists on the recording.

Modifications to the Composition/Recording

- If you intend to modify or change the composition or recording, you must have the rights holder's permission to do so.

- At the very least, you will need the rights to edit the recording or the composition for time—shortening or lengthening it to fit your shots.

Representations and Warranties

- The licensor must represent and warrant that it is the sole holder of the rights being licensed and/or have the power to enter into this agreement on behalf of the sole rights owners.

- The licensor must indemnify the producer for any breach of the representations and warranties.

Credit

- As is true for all credit provisions, the production company should insert a clause in the contract that says that "inadvertent failure to accord the contracting party credit shall not be actionable." This clause should also require the injured party to waive the right to injunctive relief, leaving an obligation on the production company's part to correct the problem on all future prints as the only remedy for the production company's credit mistakes. The clause should further state that a mistake of this nature is not a breach of the agreement.

- The clause should make clear that the production company has complete discretion over the look of the credits.

STEP BY STEP: PRERECORDED MUSIC LICENSING

1. Find out who the rights holders are.
   - The CD label will probably list both the record company and the publishing company.
   - For more detailed contact information on the music publisher, use one of the performance rights societies' databases. ASCAP's "ACE" title search feature is very helpful for locating music publishers. See www.ascap.com/ace.
2. Once you've located the correct music publisher and the record company, review their websites and look for information on their licensing department. Very often your preliminary questions about who to contact, what kinds of rights they can grant, how long the licensing process takes, and so on are answered on the website.
3. Contact the rights holders. Prior to writing a letter, it is often preferable to put in a preliminary phone call to the licensing department to explain your needs.
   - Be prepared to tell them how the song will be used. For instance, they might want to know what scene the music will accompany and the duration of the song in the movie.
   - If you license any other songs for your movie, you may want to let the rights holder know. It shows that you have been trusted by other licensors.
   - Negotiate the deal points discussed previously.
   - Offer to provide a licensing agreement in letter form, drawn up for their signature. However, be prepared for them to send you their "standard contract."
4. Send the person you spoke to a letter restating the deal terms that you've discussed. If the licensing manager has agreed to your providing the agreement, your letter can be drafted as a contract, with the signature block for all parties at the bottom.

Securing music licenses takes a lot of work. If you have the budget, consider working with an attorney who handles music licensing or a music permissions and licensing service. For a fee, these services will investigate the availability of your chosen music and negotiate the appropriate licenses.

POST.

STOCK AND ROYALTY-FREE MUSIC

Rather than dealing with the headache and cost of licensing music from publishers and recording companies, many producers choose to purchase stock and royalty-free music. Although technically the producers are still licensing this music, the procedure is far less involved.

Stock and royalty-free music is music designed especially to be used in connection with audiovisual programs. Most stock music companies also license sound effects. Many companies offer a one-time fee purchase whereby a producer pays for a particular track one time and then can use it in perpetuity. Usually these companies have websites that allow you to demo certain tracks and buy them over the Internet. For background tracks, the variety and volume of available royalty-free music makes this a very attractive option for producers on a budget.

A new development in the area of music scoring marries the advantages of royalty-free music with the customization of a personal composer. A handful of emerging software packages create soundtracks that are customized to your movie. These programs work in conjunction with your computer video editing program. Some even analyze the duration of your video track and create a piece of music tailored to your film. Licensing is usually a one-time fee, but producers will need to make sure that they are paying for the *commercial* license if they plan on selling the film that contains the royalty-free music.

TIP: **With royalty-free music, licensing costs are usually handled as a one-time fee. However, producers will need to make sure that they are paying for the *commercial* license if they plan on selling the film that contains the royalty-free music.**

COMMISSIONED MUSIC

Sometimes a filmmaker needs a soundtrack or song composed especially for her movie. In other words, she needs to commission some music from a composer.

Independent producers typically work with composers who own their own recording studios. Thanks to the proliferation of computer-based music composition, recording, and editing software, finding a composer with a studio should not be that hard. From a legal perspective, a composer/studio owner makes things easy as well: instead of dealing with two contracts—one for a composer's services, the other for studio facilities—you can handle the issues in a single contract.

POST.

THE AMERICAN FEDERATION OF MUSICIANS (AFM)

Just like cast and crew, musicians have their own union: the American Federation of Musicians (AFM; www.AFM.org). Just like SAG members, musicians belonging to AFM can only work for companies that comply with their union's guidelines. If you are not willing to deal with the regulations, rights, and residuals terms of AFM, you must make sure that your contract with your composer specifically states that the production company is *not a signatory* to any AFM agreements and will not be obligated under the terms of the AFM contracts. As extra protection, the composer agreement should limit the composer's ability to hire musicians without the production company's prior written approval.

For definitions and explanations of common contract clauses, see Appendix C, "The Clause Companion," p. 375.

MAJOR DEAL POINTS: COMPOSER'S SERVICES AGREEMENT

If you are hiring a composer with his or her own equipment and recording studio, you will need to negotiate a *composer's services agreement*.

In working with the composer, the ownership of the rights to the soundtrack is a key issue. Producers should structure the deal as a work made for hire, with rights to both the recording and to the composition vesting initially in the production company. This will avoid issues of controlling the exploitation of the publisher's share of the copyright. It is almost always better to pay a little bit more money to the composer in exchange for ownership of all of the rights.

The Parties

- *Production company.* The production company is seeking an all-in-one composer/ recording studio. In addition to the actual physical recorded soundtrack master, the production company should try to obtain all the copyrights to the materials produced by the composer.

  Here, as in other services agreements, the production company must be aware of exactly whom they are contracting with. Is it a loan-out company or an individual? The drafting of the contract, and whether an inducement and further assurances are required, will be affected by each consideration. (See "Loan-Out Companies," p. 42.) Along with the contact information, remember to get Social Security numbers for individuals and federal ID numbers for companies. These will be necessary in handling payroll and other taxes.

- *Composer.* The composer might want to retain a copyright interest in the composition. Keep in mind that it is fairly standard for production companies to require the entire copyright interest be assigned to them.

  However, if the composer is allowed to retain any copyright interests, the production company should negotiate—up front—the royalty fees for future licenses. These license royalty fees, such as synchronization, mechanical, performance licenses, are typically split 50/50 with the other copyright owner of the composition—in this case, the production company. Additionally, the composer will want royalties from record sales and music publishing.

Engagement/Services

- This paragraph describes the particular services the composer is obligated to perform for the production company. It is usually drafted fairly broadly, such as: "Composer shall write, score, compose, conduct, record, produce, mix, complete and deliver to the Producer the final instrumental Composition and Master for and to the feature film tentatively titled *[name of picture],* for use in the Motion Picture, as hereafter defined."

- The term "Master" should be defined as the recording of the soundtrack.

- The term "Composition" should be defined as the written musical work and accompanying lyrics (if any) for the soundtrack.

- The composer should be obligated to comply with all the directions and reasonable requests of the director.

- Composers with their own studios are often hired as independent contractors rather than employees. If you are certain that the composer is an independent contractor and not an employee, you should include a clause in the contract stating that the parties understand that the composer shall be treated as an independent contractor. However, keep in mind that in determining whether a composer is an employee or an independent contractor, both the courts and the IRS will focus on the actual work relationship rather than what the parties agreed in the contract. (See "Labor and Employment Law," p. 393.)

Term

- The *term* should be defined as starting on commencement of the composer's services, which is usually a predetermined date, such as the date of contract execution. The term continues until the composer's services are completed to the production company's satisfaction.

- The composer will want to know when he or she can start scoring the picture. The date the film is delivered to the composer for scoring is called the *start date*. If the start date cannot be determined at the time the contract is executed, the production company should include a range during which they can designate a start date.

Deliverables

- The exact form, media, and format of the finished soundtrack should be specified and defined as the *deliverables*.

- The *delivery date* (as distinguished from the term) is the date that the deliverables are due.

- Payment of any final fees should be conditioned on the production company's acceptance and approval of the deliverables. However, mere receipt of the deliverables should not count as "acceptance"; only a written notice that the deliverables have been accepted and approved by the production company should suffice.

Approval

- The production company needs to build in approval stages, allowing them to periodically review and approve the composer's work.

- All approval over the deliverables, the composition, and the master should rest entirely with the production company. Furthermore, payment should be contingent on approval of each stage by the production company.

Nonunion Status

If the production company is not an AFM or other music union signatory, it should state that in the contract and require that none of the recordings be made under union contracts.

Costs and Expenses

Who pays for the tape stock, studio musician fees, and equipment rentals? If these costs are not figured into a flat fee for the composer, they need to be itemized here. Costs should be capped, and any expenses over a certain amount should require prior written authorization from the production company.

Composer's Equipment

If the composer is supplying his own equipment (computer, microphones, mixers, musical instruments, etc.), the contract should state that the composer is solely responsible for the upkeep, maintenance, and safety of his own gear. This provision notwithstanding, the production company should check with its insurance company to determine to what extent it is covered for damage to composer equipment.

Compensation

- On independent films, composers are typically paid a flat fee. Like directors and producers, composers are often paid in several stages: commencement, production company's review of sound track, and on approval and acceptance following delivery of the soundtrack.

POST.

- If the composer retains a copyright interest, you will have to include provisions for how royalties and residuals will be computed and paid to the composer. As mentioned earlier, it is in the production company's best interests to take the entire copyright for itself.

Credit

- As is true for all credit provisions, the production company should insert a clause in the contract that says that "inadvertent failure to accord the contracting party credit shall not be actionable." This clause should also require the injured party to waive the right to injunctive relief, leaving an obligation on the production company's part to correct the problem on all future prints as the *only* remedy for the production company's credit mistakes. The clause should further state that a mistake of this nature is *not* a breach of the composer's services agreement.

- The clause should make clear that the production company has complete discretion over the look of the credits.

Rights

- The production company should hire the composer on a work-made-for-hire basis. A well-written assignment of rights/work-for-hire provision is another standard clause in all motion picture or service contracts. In this paragraph the composer must agree that all rights, proceeds, and results of his creative efforts in both the composition and the master are agreed to be treated as a work made for hire. Any remaining rights that are not captured by the production company as a result of the work-made-for-hire clause should be assigned by the composer to the production company under the agreement. (See "Work Made for Hire," p. 344.)

- All transferred rights should be perpetual in duration and irrevocable and survive any termination of the agreement.

- If the composer is allowed to retain any portion of the copyright, the production company may want these reserved rights to be subject to a holdback provision. This would require the composer to refrain from exploiting his reserved rights for a period of time. (See Appendix C, "Holdback Provisions," p. 379.)

Publicity

The production company will want to control the publicity for the motion picture and thus be able to restrain the composer from issuing publicity statements about the motion picture without the production company's prior written consent. The production company will also require the right to use the composer's name and likeness in any publicity, promotion, or marketing of the motion picture. Make sure to include language that allows the composer's image to be used in the "making of" documentary.

POST.

Hiring Others/Purchases

If the production company authorizes the composer to hire other musicians or singers, these other artists must also be bound by written and signed contracts stating that their contributions are works made for hire, similar to the provision in the composer's agreement. The production company should either provide these contracts or, if the composer is supplying the contracts, the production company attorney should review them prior to their execution.

Representations and Warranties

- The composer must promise that she is under no other obligations that would prevent her from performing her obligations under this contract. This clause typically contains an indemnity provision that obligates the composer to hold harmless and indemnify the production company for any breaches of the representations and warranties or other breaches of the agreement. (See "Indemnification," p. 386.)

- The composer must also warrant that any material that she contributes to the production—samples, melodies, harmonies, and so forth—are original with the composer or are in the public domain. This shifts liability to the composer if the production company is sued as a result of the composer adding uncleared copyright-protected material to the film.

Errors and Omissions (E&O) Insurance

You should check your E&O policy to determine whether there are any special requirements for composers and add your composer as an additional insured. (See "Insurance," p. 49.)

Assignment

The production company always has the right to assign the contract and the rights, results, and proceeds created under it. The composer *never* has the rights to assign and delegate her duties under the contract.

Remedies

- Like all motion picture services agreements, the right to injunctive relief should be waived by the composer.

- Furthermore, no breach of the agreement by the production company should entitle the composer to recapture any rights that he may have granted the production company. Well drafted, this clause should leave the composer only with a right to recover money, if anything at all, from the production company.

Further Documents

Here the composer should be obligated to execute any other documents necessary to further the intent of the contract. Examples include copyright assignment forms, workers' compensation claim forms, certificates of authorship, and so forth.

INDUCEMENT (IF DEALING WITH A LOAN-OUT COMPANY)

If the composer is working under a loan-out company, it is the loan-out company that will be a party to the contract. Furthermore, the contract should contain an inducement and further assurances clause. (See "Inducement," p. 277.)

◆◆◆◆◆

LAW

- Composers may be treated as independent contractors if they are working through their own company, such as a loan-out company. (See Appendix D, "A Filmmaker's Guide to Labor and Employment Law," p. 393; "Federal and State Labor and Employment Laws," p. 165.)

- You should have the composer complete a certificate of authorship (COA), similar to the one completed by a screenwriter. (See "Certificate of Authorship," p. 142.)

- *Fair use* (see "Fair Use," p. 335). Don't forget, fair use applies to musical copyrights as well. *Expelled* was a feature documentary that addressed the debate between proponents of intelligent design and the scientific theory of evolution. Its filmmakers included a sequence contrasting marching soldiers and other symbols of dictatorship with a 15-second sound recording of John Lennon singing: "Nothing to kill or die for/And no religion too," from his most famous song, "Imagine." The intended effect was to show "the naïveté of John Lennon's views on a world without religion."[3] The film's producers used the music clip without permission from the song's owners. When Mr. Lennon's widow, Yoko Ono, and other owners of his song sued for copyright infringement, the filmmakers defended, in part, on the grounds that their criticism of the Lennon song and the fact that they used so little of it should be excused as fair use. The court agreed with the defendants:

POST.

Defendants' use of "Imagine" is transformative because their purpose is to criticize the song's message. Moreover, the amount and substantiality of the portion used is reasonable in light of defendants' purpose. Although "Imagine," as a creative work, is at the core of copyright protection, and defendants' use of the song is at least partially commercial in nature, [finding fair use is likely] given that defendants' use is transformative.[4]

Business Issues

- If the composer, in addition to composing the soundtrack, is also creating and recording it, the technological specifications should be decided in advance. The format and delivery date of the soundtrack materials should also be determined in advance.

- If the composer is working with other musicians, they should be under contracts either provided or reviewed by the production company's attorneys. Remember, if the production company is not working under a musician's union contract, it will need to make sure that the musicians the composer uses are not members of that union.

FILM CLIPS AND STOCK FOOTAGE

Using clips from other movies is a common practice. For instance:

- Documentarians may want to use a film clip from an old movie to illustrate a particular time period or natural phenomenon.

- For establishing shots, filmmakers may find it cheaper to use another film's footage of the Eiffel Tower rather than fly to Paris to shoot it themselves (although going to France would be more fun).

- A scene in which characters watch television or a movie will require the filmmakers to either use clips or create the onscreen programming themselves.

Depending on the kind of footage a filmmaker needs, there are three categories of sources filmmakers tend to turn to:

- A stock footage company
- A studio or other rights holder of a film
- The National Archives

Filmmakers should first identify the length and type of clip they need and then contact the appropriate party to obtain permission to use it.

OWNING A COPY OF THE FILM IS NOT THE SAME AS OWNING THE COPYRIGHT TO THE FILM

POST.

Filmmakers must keep in mind that, just like music, copyright-protected film clips must be licensed before they can be incorporated into a movie. The mere ownership of a *copy* of a movie does not grant any rights to the *copyright* of that movie. If you own a DVD, you merely have the right to watch that film. You do not have the right to create another movie with it.

We've seen how relying on fair use is problematic. (See "On-Set IP Infringement," p. 243; Appendix A, "Fair Use," p. 335.) The solution? Our old friend the license agreement. (See "Film Clip License," p. 281.)

STOCK FOOTAGE COMPANIES

Stock footage companies are in the business of licensing clips to production companies. In addition to providing the right licenses and footage, they will also help you search for a good clip for your production. Their fees are based on:

- The length of the clip
- The filmmaker's final exhibition and distribution media
- The duration of the license
- The geographic territories in which the film that incorporates their clips will be shown

Note: Laboratory fees and duplication costs are often additional.

These companies will supply their own license agreements and are generally reluctant to change them. When you license stock footage, make sure that the stock footage company is representing and warranting that it has all the rights needed to enable it to license the clip to you. (See Appendix C, "Representations and Warranties," p. 381.) Further, make sure that you're being indemnified by them for any breach of these representations and warranties. (See Appendix C, "Indemnification," p. 386.) Fortunately, most reputable stock footage houses have made sure that their clips have been cleared for stock footage use.

MOVIE STUDIO FOOTAGE

Unlike stock footage houses, movie studios might not be as amenable to licensing clips of their films to independent producers. Furthermore, the studio might not have all the rights you need to license. For instance, if the film was based on a preexisting literary property, such as a stage play, novel, or comic book, the studio might have obtained the rights to exploit that literary property within that motion picture only. In other words, it might not have the right to license clips from that movie for use as stock footage.

If any professional actors appear in the footage, you should contact SAG or AFTRA to determine whether residual payments need to be paid to the performers. The production company might also need to secure the written permission of recognizable performers who appear in the film. (See "Right of Publicity," p. 354.)

POST.

BE WARY OF "QUITCLAIM" LICENSES

A *quitclaim* is a statement by the studio that it is not promising to the filmmaker that it has all the rights to convey. All that is being granted to the filmmaker are any rights that the studio has, along with the promise that the studio won't sue for copyright

> **BE WARY OF "QUITCLAIM" LICENSES (cont.)**
>
> infringement if the clip is used according to the film-clip licensing agreement. In other words, it is expressly *not* promising that the filmmaker won't be sued by any other rights holder who may have a legal stake in the footage.
>
> **Example:** Frodo Filmmaker licenses the rights to a film clip from *Bayonne or Bust* from Big Studio, Inc., under a quitclaim license agreement. Frodo uses the footage in his film and is promptly sued by Paola Playwright, the owner of the play on which the movie *Bayonne or Bust* was based. Paola's contract with Big Studio specified that clips from the movie version of her film could not be relicensed for inclusion in another film. Because Frodo's license came with a quitclaim, Frodo can't sue the Big Studio, Inc., for a breach of a representation.

For definitions and explanations of common contract clauses, see Appendix C, "The Clause Companion," p. 375.

MAJOR DEAL POINTS: THE FILM CLIP LICENSE AGREEMENT

The rights holder, typically a studio, will issue a nonexclusive license to the filmmaker for the rights to use a particular film clip in the filmmaker's movie.

The Parties

- *Production company.* The production company should seek the broadest possible grant of rights in perpetuity. Additionally, the production company should ask for assurances from the studio/rights holder that all of the rights needed to use the clip are being granted.

- *Studio/rights holder.* The studio or rights holder may attempt to limit its liability by *quitclaiming* any warranties (see earlier). It may also require certain restrictions over the way the film clip is used.

POST.

Grant of License/Rights

- The license will almost always be nonexclusive.
- As is true for any license, the *territory, duration, media,* and *fee* will be specified, as will a description of the particular clip. The fee should be a one-time flat fee. These requirements are often detailed in a separate exhibit or rider.

- The studio/rights holder may also require the filmmaker to provide a script and assurances that the clip will be used only in the manner depicted by the screenplay. Because the studio/rights holder may be bound by its own contractual restrictions regarding the footage, it may specify that the clip may not be used in commercials, may not be used in a derogatory manner, and that the filmmaker may not edit or change the clip in any way other than editing it for time.

- The studio/rights holder will explicitly reserve for itself any rights not granted under the agreement. This means that the filmmaker may not reuse the clip for other purposes, such as inclusion in a sequel.

Copy of Finished Film

The studio/rights holder will often require the filmmaker to send it a copy of the filmmaker's finished film.

Representations and Warranties

The filmmaker should seek representations and warranties from the studio/rights holder that all rights in the clip have been cleared. Conversely, the studio/rights holder may want to quitclaim any rights.

Guild Payments, Permissions, and Music Licenses

- As a condition for the grant, the studio/rights holder may require the filmmaker to obtain permissions from performers, directors, writers, and music rights holders whose work appears in the film clip. The filmmaker may be required to pay any union-mandated residuals to musicians and performers—even if the filmmaker is not a union signatory. (See "SAG," p. 205.)

- The studio/rights holder will usually require copies of these permissions to be delivered to it.

POST. Credit

- As is true for all credit provisions, the production company should try to insert a clause in the contract that says that "inadvertent failure to accord the contracting party credit shall not be actionable." This clause should also require the injured party to waive the right to injunctive relief, leaving an obligation on the production company's part to correct the problem on all future prints as the *only* remedy for the production company's credit mistakes. The clause should further state that a mistake of this nature is *not* a breach of the agreement.

- The studio/rights holder may not agree to letting the production company have complete discretion over how the clip is credited. Be prepared to give a little on the wording of your credit clause.

Copyright Notice

The studio/rights holder will require that its copyright notice be placed on the film. This does not transfer the copyright in the filmmaker's work, but it will serve to protect the copyright in the clip itself, reserving it for the studio/rights holder.

Remedies

- The studio/rights holder may insist on an equitable relief clause, giving it the right to seek an injunction against the filmmaker for breaches of the license agreement. (See Appendix C, "No Injunction," p. 387.) The filmmaker, on the other hand, should try to eliminate any equitable remedies, leaving the studio/rights holder's only remedy the right to sue for money damages.

- The studio/rights holder will probably want an automatic termination provision, which cancels the license for any breach of the agreement. The filmmaker, on the other hand, should attempt to negotiate a cure provision, creating a mechanism for remedying any default before it becomes a breach of the agreement.

THE NATIONAL ARCHIVES

The National Archives in Washington, D.C., has a huge selection of public domain footage produced by the U.S. government. This material is copyright-free, does not require a license agreement, and can be obtained for little more than the cost of laboratory and other duplication fees.

For details on how to obtain copies of public domain films from the National Archives, see www.archives.gov/research/formats/film-sound-video.html.

STEP BY STEP: FILM CLIPS

1. Locate the copyright holder of the film clip you want to use. (See "Copyright Searches and Permissions," p. 132.)
2. Contact the copyright holder and negotiate a film clip license agreement.
3. Secure the necessary permissions from the other rights holders (performers, directors, musicians, etc.) included in the clip.
4. Provide copies of these permissions to the film clip's copyright holder.
5. When you edit the clip into your film, make sure that you are using it in a manner consistent with the license you have been granted.
6. In your credit roll, make sure that the copyright holder's credit provisions are strictly adhered to.
7. When you distribute, exhibit, and/or broadcast your film, make sure it is consistent with the license provisions in the film clip license agreement.

POST.

CREDITS AND COPYRIGHT NOTICE

CAUTION! Be very careful here! Make sure to check your credit roll to ensure that it conforms to the credit clauses in all your contracts. If you have used union writers, actors, or crew, make sure that your credits conform to any union requirements.

- Double-check the credit clauses in every agreement, especially:
  - Performers, above- and below-the-line crew agreements
  - Trademark and copyright licenses
  - Music licenses
  - Location releases
  - Special effects and other post-production agreements
  - Distribution agreements
- If you are a WGA signatory company working with a WGA writer, you will need to submit your proposed writing credits to the WGA for approval. (See "WGA Credits," p. 98.)
- Keep in mind that you may have "favored nations" credit obligations, such as making sure that one actor's name is displayed as big as or as prominently as another actor's. (See "Favored Nations," p. 378.)
- Make sure that your advertising and promotional material also complies with these requirements.

COPYRIGHT NOTICE AND DISCLAIMER

POST.

In addition, your credits should always feature a copyright notice and disclaimer that says something similar to this:

Copyright © [YEAR] [NAME OF PRODUCTION COMPANY]. All Rights Reserved. This motion picture is protected under the laws of the United States and other countries. Any unauthorized duplication, distribution, or exhibition is strictly prohibited and may result in both civil and criminal penalties. The persons, characters, and events depicted in this film are fictitious. Any similarity to actual persons, living or dead, is purely coincidental.

DISTRIBUTION

SELLING YOUR FILM

Distribution is the act of licensing the film to exhibitors, broadcasters, and other parties in exchange for a fee or participation in the film's revenues. Distribution is the Holy Grail for filmmakers; without distribution, a film will not make money. Of course, even with a distribution deal, a film might not make money, but if the distributor does its job, at least the film will be seen by prospective licensees and buyers. These licensees and buyers range from theatrical exhibitors and network television broadcasters and cable casters to airlines and military bases and retail stores that rent or sell DVDs.

Unfortunately, not all good films are picked up by distribution companies. When that happens, the filmmaker has to switch hats and become her own distributor. Such "DIY" distributors may pay theaters to show their films, put them online with iTunes or Netflix, and sell DVDs direct from Amazon.com or the production company's website.

This section will explore:

- The role of a distribution company. (See "What Distributors Do," p. 289.)

- How the money gets from the audience's pocket into yours. (See "The Money Pipeline," p. 291.)

- Common varieties of traditional distribution deals. (See "Types of Traditional Distribution Deals," p. 290.)

- How to negotiate a distribution deal. (See "Distribution Rights Acquisition Agreement," p. 295.)

- How to put your film in a theater without a distributor. (See "DIY Distribution," p. 307.)

- How to sell your DVDs without a distributor. (See "DIY DVD Distribution," p. 314.)

- How to get your film on iTunes or Netflix without a distributor. (See "DIY Online Distribution," p. 317.)

- How to make money from putting your film on YouTube. (See "YouTube," p. 320.)

DISTR.

25

TRADITIONAL DISTRIBUTION

WHAT DISTRIBUTORS DO

Distributors "exploit" a film in a variety of markets. Depending on the deal the production company negotiates, the distributor, or its agents—called *subdistributors*—may license the film for exhibition, broadcast, or sale in the following markets:

- Theatrical: movie theaters
- Free television: broadcast television, as opposed to cable
- Pay television: cable, satellite, pay-per-view, on-demand
- Home video: sales of the film via DVD or videocassette
- Commercial video: distribution of DVD or videocassettes for public exhibition
- Internet: distribution and exhibition via streaming and/or downloaded video
- Airline: in-flight movies
- Ships: public exhibition aboard ships
- Hotel/hospitality: hotel and motel closed-circuit television
- Nontheatrical: distribution via cable, closed circuit, or satellite for school exhibition
- Military: exhibition on military bases

In addition to these exhibition media, the filmmaker may grant the distributor the power to license and exploit the film rights in other nonfilm exhibition markets, such as:

- Television series rights
- Sequels
- Merchandising: toys, clothing, games, etc.
- Legitimate theater: plays and musicals
- Records
- Books and comic books

NOTE: Most filmmakers try to hold on to these rights and exploit the rights themselves or through a licensing agent.

DISTR.

TYPES OF TRADITIONAL DISTRIBUTION DEALS

There are several common types of traditional distribution deals (DIY distribution is discussed in the next chapter):

- *Production-financing/distribution agreement* (also known as a *PF/D agreement)*. Here a distributor with a studio division (or a production studio with a distribution division) is the primary source of production funding. The distributor/studio usually steps in after the producer has presented it with an already developed and packaged project. Because the distributor/studio company is putting up the lion's share of the funds, it usually retains a strong ownership position in the film.

- *Negative pickup agreement*. This is similar to the PF/D agreement in that the distributor's money is enabling the production to be funded; however, in this scenario the distributor does not advance the money. Instead, the distributor agrees to pay the production costs and expenses if the film meets certain delivery requirements. This contractual guarantee from the distributor is used by the producer to secure a loan from a bank or group of investors. The downside, of course, is that the producer cannot turn to the distribution company as a source of funding. That being said, sometimes a distribution company may provide post-production funding for a film while maintaining, substantially, a distribution rights acquisition deal structure.

- *Distribution rights acquisition agreement*. In this scenario, the producer comes to the distributor with an already finished film and the distributor advances the money to market, distribute, and exploit the film. The distribution rights acquisition agreement is, hands down, the most common type of deal available to independent producers without a prior track record; the distributor is not being asked to fund the film, merely to distribute it. Because the distributor's risk is lower than it would be under a negative pickup or PF/D deal (see earlier point), a distributor may be more likely to give a new producer a chance. After all, the distributor can take a look at the film itself to see whether it is marketable.

There are three ways a producer is typically paid under the distribution rights acquisition agreement. The payment model the producer ends up with is a subject of negotiation with the distributor:

1. *Royalty deal*. The distributor absorbs all marketing, promotion, distribution expenses, and any advances paid to the producer; it then pays the producer a royalty. For example, if the distributor is only acquiring DVD rights, it would pay the producer a royalty on the wholesale price (perhaps 15–25%) of each DVD it sells to the retailer or video rental company. This deal can benefit the producer if the costs to bring the film to market are high because a producer receives some money regardless of the distributor's expenses; the downside is that if the film is an indie success, the producer is still only getting a 25% royalty.

2. *50/50 Net deal*. The distributor receives money from the film's exploitation; deducts any advances paid to the producer, marketing, promotion, and

distribution expenses; and splits the rest with the producer 50/50. With this deal the filmmaker gets more money if the film is a hit—50% of the proceeds after expenses. The flip side is that distributor's expenses can take a big bite out of the proceeds of a film with lackluster sales.

3. *Distribution fee.* Here the distributor receives money from the film's exploitation, deducts a distribution fee (perhaps 35%), then deducts any advances paid to the producer, marketing, promotion, and distribution expenses. The remainder is given to the producer. For details on this popular financial model, see "How Does the Money Get from a Movie Theater to the Producer?" p. 292.

THE MONEY PIPELINE

DISTRIBUTION FINANCIAL TERMS

- *Distributor's gross rentals.* The money received by the distributor for renting the film to theatrical exhibitors for movie house exhibition.

- *Distributor's gross receipts/distributor revenue.* Collectively, all the monies the distributor receives, through film rentals, television licensing, DVD sales, and any other income stream related to the film property.

- *Distributor's fee/distribution fee.* The fee a distributor charges for its services. This is typically a percentage of the distributor's gross receipts, before expenses are deducted.

- *Distribution expenses.* Costs a distributor incurs for distributing the film property. It typically includes marketing, prints, advertising, promotional, and other costs.

- *Subdistributor fee.* A fee charged by a subdistributor hired by the main distributor to exploit the film property, usually in foreign markets.

- *Prints and ads (P&A).* The costs of printing copies of the film (but not DVD) to distribute to the exhibitors plus the costs of advertising the film.

- *Film's Net Profits/producer's gross.* The monies remaining after the distributor has taken its fee and has been repaid its expenses. This money is then paid directly to the production company and is usually the level from which the investors and net profit participants draw their payments. (See also "Net Profits," p. 379.)

- *Negative cost.* The cost of actually getting the finished film in the can (but not the advertising, prints, or marketing expenses).

DISTR.

> **DISTRIBUTION FINANCIAL TERMS (cont.)**
>
> - *Production company's net profits.* Any money that is left over from the Film's Net Profits after the production company has paid investors and net profit participants, deferred salaries, costs of producing and promotion the film, and other costs of doing business.

HOW DOES THE MONEY GET FROM A MOVIE THEATER TO THE PRODUCER?

Let's say that a distributor wants to put your movie in theaters. How does the money from ticket sales get from the audience's wallets into yours? As you may imagine, it all depends on the kind of deal that you've been offered. So let's assume that you have a theatrical distribution rights acquisition deal in which the distributor is taking a fee (see earlier discussion) and let's follow the money.

Movie Audience

1. *Moviegoer* pays for ticket. A theater's ticket sales from a particular movie are its *box office receipts*; the total ticket sales of a movie become the *box office gross*.

Movie Theater (Exhibitor) Takes Its Cut

2. *Exhibitors* (movie theaters) first deduct an agreed on amount, called the *house nut*, from their box office receipts to cover their overhead. The balance after the house nut is deducted is called the *exhibitor's net*. During the first week or two of the movie's run, the distributor may get as much as 90% of the exhibitor's net. Each successive week of the movie's run, the distributor's share is reduced and the exhibitor's share is increased. Over the run of the film, the distributor may receive between 25–65% of the exhibitor's net, with the average being close to 43%. The distributor's share of the exhibitor's net is called the *distributor's rentals*. It is important to note that any money from concessions—candy, popcorn, soda—is kept by the exhibitor and not shared with the distributor.

The monies actually given to the distributor may be lower than the contractually obligated amount due to *settlement transactions*, which are negotiated reductions in the monies paid to the distributor. Settlement transaction are based on a number of factors, including the film's box office performance, how many other films by the distributor are being shown by that exhibitor, and cooperative advertising obligations between the exhibitor and the distributor.

Distributor Takes Its Cut

3. The money that the distributor receives from the exhibitors is called the *gross rentals.* This sum, plus other sums from the exploitation of other rights (television, video, cable, etc.) granted under the distribution contract, make up the *distributor's gross receipts.*

4. The distributor may exclude from its definition of gross receipts items such as advances to the producer and monies not collected (*distributor exclusions*). The gross receipts minus the exclusions become the *distributor's adjusted gross receipts* (although the distributor may still call it the *distributor's gross receipts*).

5. The distributor takes its *distribution fee,* typically between 20% and 40% of the *distributor's adjusted gross receipts.*

6. *Subdistribution fees* are then deducted, especially in foreign markets. *Watch out here*—make sure that your distribution company doesn't charge you for its full distribution fee in a market where you are paying a subdistribution fee.

7. *Distributor's expenses* are then deducted, such as the following:
   - *Direct distribution expenses.* All costs associated with the advertising, exploitation, marketing, and distribution of the film. Some of the biggest expenses are:
     - Prints
     - Advertising and publicity
     - Any money advanced by the distributor to pay for the deliverables

   CAUTION! **The distributor may try to include expenses for overhead. Overhead is the distributor's cost of doing business not directly attributable to your film, such as rent, insurance, salaries, and so on.**

8. *Union residuals* are paid if the distributor has signed an assumption agreement. *Note:* If the production company is a Screen Actors Guild (SAG) signatory, it must have the distribution company sign an *assumption agreement.* (See "Assumption Agreement," p. 304.)

9. *Other costs.* Depending on the deal, other costs will be deducted at different stages:
   - Taxes
   - Interest
   - Collection costs
   - Distributers may also want to deduct anticipated expenses. Try to cap this or eliminate it altogether.

DISTR.

Production Company Is Paid

10. *Remainder* is passed on to the production company, along with the remainder from the other revenue streams from all distributors and licensees, and becomes the *producer's gross,* aka the *Film's Net Profits.* (See "Net Profits," p. 379.)

Theatrical Distribution Money Pipeline

MOVIE AUDIENCE

- Moviegoer pays for ticket.
- Ticket sales from theater are Box *Office Receipts.*
- The total ticket sales of a movie are the *Box Office Gross.*

DISTRIBUTOR TAKES ITS CUT

- Distributor's Gross Receipts. All of the money the distributor receives from the exploitation of the film in all of its formats.
- Distributor's subracts from its Gross Receipts any *Distributor Exclusions.* The total becomes the *Distributor's Adjusted Gross Receipts.*
- Distributor's deducts its Distribution Fee (in a fee model).
- Distributor's then deducts Expenses, e.g.:
  - Sub-distribution Fees
  - Prints
  - Advertising and publicity
  - Any money advanced by the distributor to pay for the deliverables
  - Union residuals (i.e. SAG television residuals)
  - Taxes
  - Interest
  - Collection costs

MOVIE THEATER (EXHIBITOR) TAKES ITS CUT

- Exhibitors (movie theaters)
  - First deduct *"house nut"*
  - Balance after the house nut is deducted is called the *exhibitor's net.*
  - All money from sale of concessions- candy, popcorn, soda, etc. is kept by the exhibitor.
- Distributor's Gross Receipts may be further reduced by Settlement Transactions

PRODUTION COMPANY IS PAID

- Remainder is passed on to the production company, along with the remainder from the other revenue streams from all distributors and licensees, and becomes the *Producer's Gross a.k.a* the *Film's Net Profits.*

PRODUTION COMPANY PAYS:

- Residuals, (Unless they have been paid by the distributor).
- The Negative Cost of the Film (i.e. the costs of producing the film).
- Investors are repaid a return on their investments, plus interest.
- Production Company's Profit Participants are paid (e.g. writers, actors, director, etc.).
- Deferred Salaries
- Overhead and other Costs of Doing Business.
- Any monies remaining become *The Production Company's Net Profits.*

Production Company Pays

DISTR.

11. The order in which the production company pays the following is up to negotiation with the profit participants.

- The production company may have to pay *residuals* as per its union agreements (unless they have been paid by the distributor).

- The *negative cost* of the film (i.e., the costs of producing the film).

- Investors are repaid a *return* on their investments, plus interest.

- Production company's *profit participants* (e.g. writers, actors, director, etc.) are paid. (See "Net Profits," p. 379.)
- *Deferred salaries*. (See Appendix C, "Deferred Compensation," p. 377.)
- *Overhead* and other costs of doing business.
- Any monies remaining become the *production company's net profits*.

Keep in mind that this revenue map only emphasizes monies coming in from one distributor's theatrical exploitation. Ideally, the production company will have additional revenues from other markets, such as home video, television broadcast, merchandising, and the like.

DISTRIBUTION RIGHTS ACQUISITION AGREEMENT (DISTRIBUTOR'S FEE DEAL)

Goals and Deals

The distribution agreement may be the single most important document to a producer trying to make money from his film. This is the document that controls how the film makes money.

The distribution agreement controls the grant of the distribution right and specifies the places, duration, and scope of this copyright license. The agreement's terms control:

- When, where, and for how long a distributor has the license to distribute
- How and when a producer gets paid
- What rights the producer can still license to others

For definitions and explanations of common contract clauses, see Appendix C, "The Clause Companion," p. 375.

MAJOR DEAL POINTS: DISTRIBUTION AGREEMENT

DISTR.

The distribution agreement is the contract governing the relationship between the distributor, who exploits the film, and the production company, which created the film. The following pages outline a distribution agreement where the distributor is taking a *fee*. (See "Types of Traditional Distribution Deals," p. 290.)

The Parties

- *Production company.* The production company is seeking a distributor with the ability to license the film effectively in certain territories. All distributors have their strengths and weaknesses: for instance, many distributors are better at exploiting domestic rights than international rights. It may be in a producer's best interest to split the rights among several distributors, each exploiting the property in its own individual territory.

- *Distributor.* The distributor, on the other hand, will probably want to acquire as many rights as it can from the production company. After all, it figures that if it doesn't have the contacts to distribute the property in one market, it can always bring in a subdistributor who can. Additionally, the distributor may be able to offset losses from one market against gains in another, a practice known as *cross-collateralization*.

Rights Granted

- This clause defines specific rights being granted to the distributor. It typically grants the right to distribute, exhibit, market, exploit, advertise, publicize, and manufacture copies of the film.

- Also included here are media and markets with respect to which the distributor can distribute the film:
  - Theatrical
  - Free television
  - Pay television
  - VOD and PPV
  - Home video
  - Commercial video
  - Internet
  - Airline
  - Ship
  - Hotel/hospitality
  - Scholastic
  - Military
  - Any additional markets to which the producer agrees

- The distributor needs the right to create trailers, commercials, and other promotional materials.

- The distributor needs the right to edit the film to meet with the censorship laws of a particular country or to dub the film into another language. However, any editing rights provision should be carefully worded to avoid giving the distributor any right to edit the picture solely for creative reasons.

DISTR.

Reserved Rights

The rights not granted to the distributor should be reserved to the producer. Such rights often include:

- Print publication
- Merchandising
- Radio and stage

Exclusivity

- The distributor will insist on being the exclusive distributor of the film with respect to the rights granted within the specified territories for the specified term.
- Sometimes Internet, VOD, PPV, streaming video, and similar distribution methods will be granted on a nonexclusive basis.

Term

- The *term* is the length of time that the distributor will have the rights granted to it.
- Distributors will want a "perpetual" term. However, it is to the production company's advantage to avoid having the film locked up with a distributor that might not be performing well. The production company should try to obtain a limited initial term of two to three years, during which time the distributor must meet certain financial thresholds in terms of gross receipts from the exploitation of the film. If these thresholds are not met, the production company should be given the right to cancel the contract. If the threshold is met, the distributor should be given an option to renew the distribution contract for a longer period of time—for instance, 10 years.
- *Be careful of rights being granted beyond the term of the distribution agreement.* For instance, if the distributor has the power to subdistribute and sell the rights, the filmmaker can be bound by a contract that exceeds the term of the original distribution agreement. This happens if, toward the end of the term of the distribution contract with the production company, the distributor enters into an agreement with a subdistributor. This new subdistributor agreement might have a new term that extends beyond the term of the original agreement between the distributor and the production company.
- Production companies may want to limit the ability of the distributor to enter into an agreement like this by capping the term of such a subdistribution agreement so that it cannot extend more than five to seven years beyond the term of the original agreement between the production company and the distributor.

DISTR.

Territories

- The *territory* is the geographic area within which the distributor may exploit the film.

- It is not uncommon for one distributor to handle domestic distribution and another to handle international distribution (called a *split rights deal*). Split rights deals actually help producers; splitting up the territories prevents a single distributor from cross-collateralizing between a poorly performing domestic market and a lucrative foreign market. Even distributors who insist on capturing both domestic and international distribution rights usually work with subdistributors who distribute the film in other markets.

- Producers should try to set territorial minimums for the distributor. The effect of these minimums are to require the distributor to seek a producer's written approval prior to accepting a deal that would bring in less than the agreed-on territorial minimum.

Advertising and Promotion

- If pushed, distributors may agree to consult with the production company regarding key art in the ad campaign and marketing strategy for the film, but they will usually insist on having final approval.

- The production company should reserve the right to approve (rather than consult on) the performers' bios, performer's pictures, and appearance of the credits in all paid ads. Remember—the production company may have obligated itself to the performers and above-the-line personnel with regard to photo, likeness, and credit considerations.

Allocation of Proceeds

- This paragraph can be lengthy; it sets out who and what gets paid before the producer receives her share. (See "The Money Pipeline," p. 291.)

- Typically, the *gross receipts* represent all the monies taken by the distributor for the exploitation of a particular film.

- The distributor then computes its *distribution fee* based on a percentage of the distributor's adjusted gross receipts. This fee typically ranges from 20% to 40%.

- After the distributor computes its fee, it recoups its marketing and promotional expenses, advances to the producer, and interest. (See the following section, "Distributor's Recoupable Expenses.") The producer should insist on a fairly detailed list of recoupable expenses, coupled with financial caps on certain expenses.

- The remaining money then becomes the *producer's gross*, which, from the investor's and net profit participant's point of view, is the *Film's Net Profits*.

Distributor's Recoupable Expenses

These are the expenses the distributor is allowed to recoup prior to distributing the producer's gross. Typical recoupable expenses include:

- Advertising and promotional expenses, such as preparing posters, trailers, one-sheets, commercials, and so forth
- Expenses for taking the film to film markets for its first year
- Prints, DVDs, and other manufacturing expenses directly related to producing copies of the film

Be *very* careful here! When structuring the deal:

- Provide a minimum and maximum the distributor can spend on ads and promotions.
- Make sure to cap the distributor's expenses for going to markets so that your film does not end up paying for more than its fair share of the distributor's market costs.
- Limit all the distributor's expenses to actual, verifiable "out-of-pocket" expenses.

Advance

The filmmaker should push very hard for any advance; this may be the only money a production company actually sees. As a result, the production company should be wary of giving away any rights without first receiving a nonrefundable advance from the distributor.

Distributor's Right to Package Film Property

- The distribution company will probably want the right to package the film with other films, thus offering a sort of bulk discount to a broadcaster or cablecaster. The production company should try to make sure that in a package sale, the distributor can license the film for no less than a prespecified minimum.
- Make sure that in any package deal the amount of money allocated to your film is specified in writing and is computed according to a reasonable formula.

DISTR.

Credit

- The distributor will negotiate the language and placement of its own credit.
- The distributor must be obligated to adhere to all credit provisions in the producer's contract with third parties, such as actors, directors, musicians, and so forth.

Default

- Prior to termination, the injured party is usually obligated to serve notice of default to the defaulting party, giving the defaulting party a reasonable time with which to cure the problem (e.g., 30 days).
- The production company should insist that if the distributor defaults on the contract and does not cure the default, the contract may be terminated by the production company and all rights under the contract will then revert back to the production company. The production company would then be free to seek out another distributor.

Notice

This paragraph is fairly straightforward and lists the parties and representatives, such as attorneys and agents, to whom notice must be delivered.

Audit Rights

- The audit is typically conducted at the production company's or its profit participants' expense unless the audit uncovers a discrepancy of 5% or more, in which case the distribution company or its profit participants should have to pay for the audit.
- The production company usually only has the right to audit once a year and may be required to give 30 days' notice of an audit.

Production Company's Representations and Warranties

The production company usually promises that:

- The production company owns a valid copyright to the film and that nothing in the film infringes any intellectual property or other rights of third parties.
- The production company will safeguard its copyrights and other rights needed to exploit and license the film property.
- The production company is responsible for and has secured all rights, licenses, and permissions to any music contained in the film property. The distributor will make it the production company's obligation to pay any music-licensing royalties and other fees.
- The film has not been previously distributed or exhibited in the territory, with the exception of film festivals.
- The production company will promise to pay for all production costs, including deferred payments, residuals, and royalties.

DISTR.

- The production company is under no other obligations that would prevent it from performing its obligations under this contract.

- This clause typically contains an indemnity provision that obligates the production company to indemnify the distribution company for any breaches of the representations and warranties or other breaches of the agreement. (See Appendix C, "The Clause Companion: Indemnification," p. 386.)

The Distribution Company's Representations and Warranties

The distribution company should promise that:

- It is not on the verge of bankruptcy and can pay all its bills.

- There are no lawsuits or pending claims that would interfere with the distribution company distributing the film property and performing its duties under the contract.

- All work done on the marketing and advertising campaign will be done as a work made for hire.

- Because the distributor is able to recoup the costs of producing these materials, the production company should try to negotiate a provision that states the marketing and ad materials become the property of the production company at the expiration of the term of the distribution agreement.

- That it will comply with all credit, likeness approval, photographic, and biographic obligations for which the production is obligated, provided that the production company has provided the distribution company with copies of those provisions.

- The distribution company will use its best efforts to exploit, promote, and distribute the film property.

- This paragraph should contain an indemnity provision that obligates the distribution company to indemnify the production company for any breaches of the representations and warranties or other breaches of the agreement.

Deliverables

- The exact date of delivery of the film and other materials to the distribution company is the *delivery date*.

DISTR.

- The *deliverables* are the film and other materials that the production company must deliver to the distributor. The list can be exhaustive and includes both physical and legal materials. Make sure there's enough money in the budget to pay for all the deliverables the distribution company will require.

- The deliverables usually are separated into two categories:
  - *Physical deliverables.* These are items related to the manufacture of copies of the film and its publicity and exploitation. The distributor will need all the elements to make copies of the film, television commercials, trailers, posters, censored versions of the film, and so forth. Such physical deliverables often include:
    - The completed film's negative
    - The film soundtrack, with dialogue on a separate track from the other audio
    - Music and effects track
    - Access to the original film negative
    - Interpositive and internegative prints
    - Videotape masters
    - DVD master and DVD authoring files. *Note:* It is becoming more and more common that distribution companies are authoring DVDs themselves; as a result, you might not be asked for these materials
    - Photographs
    - Music cue sheets
    - Title sheets
    - Medium-specific copies, including versions for broadcast television and in-flight movies
    - Copies of the film's script
  - *Legal and business deliverables.* These are items that prove the producer has both the ownership of the film and the rights necessary to exploit it. Legal and business deliverables often include:
    - Copyright title search reports
    - All cast and crew contracts
    - Separate credit requirements
    - All copyright and trademark licenses and clearances
    - Laboratory access letters
    - All publicity restrictions
    - Music licenses and composer agreements
    - Copyright chain of title materials
    - E&O policy listing the distributor as an additional insured

Assignment

The production company must always have the right to assign the proceeds it receives from the distributor. The distributor should not be able to assign the contract without the production company's prior written permission.

Errors and Omissions (E&O) Insurance

If the production company has E&O insurance, the distribution company will want to be added as an additional insured.

◆◆◆◆◆

LAW: COPYRIGHT ISSUES

The distributor might want to investigate your film's chain of title pretty thoroughly. Be prepared to supply the following:

- All contracts pertaining to the film property. These include screenplay agreements, literary rights acquisition agreements, life rights consents, and assignments of all the copyrights in and to the film property to the production company. (See "The Film Property," p. 24.)

- All service contracts of creative personnel, especially performers, writers, directors, and musicians. The key here is that all these contracts should contain adequate work-made-for-hire provisions. (See "Work Made for Hire," p. 344.) In addition to copyright, these contracts should also grant to the production company all the other necessary rights, such as rights of publicity, waiver of defamation claims, and so forth, needed to exploit the film.

- Proof of copyright registrations and recordation of assignments. (See "Copyright Registration," p. 136.)

- Credits will be checked to make sure that they comply with the production company's contractual obligations.

- Financing documents and documents creating a security interest in the film.

Under copyright law, the owner of a copyrighted work has the exclusive right to distribute that work.[1] Without a copyright license from the film's owner, distribution of the film is copyright infringement. In the distribution agreement, the copyright owner grants to the distributor the exclusive right to distribute and exploit the film. Because a distribution agreement is a document that "pertains to a copyright," it may be registered with the U.S. Copyright Office. (See Copyright Recordation, Assignments and Transfers," p. 139.) Recording all transfers and licenses of copyright ownership preserves a clean chain of title. (See "Chain of Title," p. 131; Copyright Circular 12 on the U.S. Copyright website for more information: www.copyright.gov/circs/circ12.pdf.)

DISTR.

Lab Access Letter

The distributor will also require permission from the production company to deal directly with the film laboratory or video duplication house responsible for producing copies of the film. This is usually done in the form of a *laboratory access letter*

> **CAUTION!** THIS IS WHY YOU NEED CLEARANCES
>
> A distributor needs to know that it has very little chance of being sued when it sells the film to exhibitors and broadcasters. Accordingly, permissions and clearances are a central component of the producer/distributor agreement. As part of every distribution contract, the producer must represent and warrant to the distributor that all the intellectual property (IP) rights in the film or video have been cleared and that there are no pending or anticipated legal claims created by the film or video. (See "Copyright Searches and Permissions," p. 132.) The producer also indemnifies the distributor for any misrepresentations of the representations and warranties. (See Appendix C, "Indemnification", p. 386; Representations and Warranties," p. 381.)
>
> As a result, if the distributor is sued for IP infringement, the distributor now has the right to look to the producer of the allegedly infringing film or video to cover any money damages and costs that arise from such lawsuits.
>
> *Example:* One scene in Max Mogul's film was shot inside a museum's sculpture garden. Unfortunately, Max never secured copyright licenses to photograph all the sculptures. Now both he and his distributor are hit with a copyright infringement lawsuit from an irate artist. Because of his distribution contract, Max must cover *both* his own and the distributor's legal costs of defending against the suit.

in which the production company grants to the distributor the right to access the copies and to order more on account.

Assumption Agreement

If your production company is a SAG signatory (see "SAG," p. 205), you are required by the terms of your signatory agreement to ensure that a distributor sign an *assumption agreement*. In this agreement the distributor assumes the obligations of paying performer residuals directly to SAG. A signed copy of the assumption agreement must then be delivered to SAG.

DISTR.

BUSINESS ISSUES: DISTRIBUTOR'S EXPENSES

Because distributors may deduct their expenses prior to paying the production company, the expenses that a distributor may be allowed to deduct should be carefully defined. Care should be taken to expressly limit the distribution company's ability to include any overhead within the recoupable expenses. When negotiating with the distributor, you should argue that because the distributor is taking a distribution fee, it is from that fee the distributor should pay for its ordinary costs of doing business. Only verifiable out-of-pocket expenses should be deducted.

Reread Your Talent Agreements

Before the film is publicized, exploited, or distributed, it pays to read your talent agreements. (See "Performer's Services Agreement," p. 212.) Double-check your agreements for:

- *Any publicity restrictions or likeness approvals* you may have given to the talent. Movie posters can create big problems if they are created without attention to a performer's likeness approval clause.

- *Credit and billing obligations.* Find out which performer's names must appear in paid advertising, how large the names need to be, in what order they must appear, and so on.

- *Publicity obligations.* Work with performer's agents in arranging screening and publicity events.

Film's Net Profits

The producer's gross receipts from the distributor may be the same thing as the Film's Net Profits as far as your investors and net profit participants are concerned. When you negotiate an investor's or net profit participant's contract, be sure to define the Film's Net Profits as monies actually received from the distributor(s) for the exploitation of the film, pursuant to the distribution agreement with the respective distributors. It follows then that investors and net profit participants might want to include clauses in their contracts allowing them to examine the distributor's accounting records for the film.

TIPS FOR ATTRACTING A DISTRIBUTOR

Getting a distributor interested in your project can be a difficult task. You know that your horror movie is a thrilling and original cinematic *tour de force,* but how do you convince a distributor who has seen 20 other slasher movies that week alone? Here are a few tips:

DISTR.

- *Marketable elements.* As we've already seen, the single most attractive element to a distributor is your choice of cast. (See "SAG," p. 205.) It's unfortunate but true: A well-known actor in a mediocre film will attract more distributors than an unknown actor in a good film. If you're reading this section before you've cast and shot your film (and kudos to you for planning ahead), try to hire recognized actors. If you've already shot your film with unknown actors and are struggling to land a distributor, try submitting the film to film festivals or working with a producer's representative.

- *Film festivals.* When you win a film festival, distributors will tend to come to you. Some festivals will only consider films that have not been screened at other festivals, so your first task should be to develop a strategy for which film festivals you submit your film to. Winning at Sundance is obviously more prestigious than winning at the Podunk film festival. IMDB.com has a helpful list of film festivals, organized by month, at www.imdb.com/festivals/. Make sure to budget for the festival entry fees, travel, and accommodations.

- *Producer's representative.* A producer's representative is like an agent for a film. For a fee, the producer's rep will try to place the film with a distribution company. The rep will find and negotiate the distribution agreement, leaving with the producer the final decision over whether to accept the deal with the distribution company. As payment, the producer's rep often takes 15% of what the producer makes on the film (including 15% of any advances). In addition to fees, the producer's rep will also require the producer to reimburse him for the costs and expenses of attracting the distributor. A few notes of caution:

    - Make sure any fees paid to the producer's rep are calculated based on the producer's share of the film's proceeds rather than from the distributor's share. After all, the only money you truly have control over is the producer's share. (See "Distribution Financial Terms," p. 291.)

    - Negotiate a cap over the producer's reps expenses.

    - Never give the rep the final say over whether to accept a particular distributor's deal—always keep that right for yourself.

DISTR.

26

DIY DISTRIBUTION

You've tried landing a distributor, but you just keep striking out—*or* perhaps you like the idea of distributing your own film and having a shot at keeping most of the money it makes. Either way, you've made the decision to go it alone and to self-distribute your film (a process often called do–it–yourself or *DIY distribution*).

Some of the more common ways in which producers self-distribute their films include these:

- **Theatrical distribution:**
  - Working with a film booker
  - Booking the film theater by theater, without a booking agent
  - "Four Walling" (aka rent–a–theater distribution)
- **DVD distribution:**
  - Selling the film from your website and working with a fulfillment company or fulfilling orders yourself
  - Selling your film via duplication on demand, such as CreateSpace
- **Online distribution:**
  - iTunes
  - Amazon video on demand
  - Netflix
  - YouTube
  - Mobile phones

A LAST RESORT

Before you decide to self-distribute your film, you need to stop and consider the impact of DIY distribution on your ability to attract conventional distributors. Many DIY distribution platforms require you to give up rights (such as streaming video) that would otherwise be exploited by a conventional distributor. Furthermore, just the process of making your film available to a nonpaying audience, say, through YouTube, could dilute the market sufficiently that a distributor will later turn down your otherwise worthy film. The bottom line: Be sure you've exhausted all your conventional distribution options before you turn to DIY distribution.

YOUR DIY PLAN

The first step in DIY distribution should be to hammer out a distribution strategy that takes into account the following:

- *Timing and exclusivity.* When will your film will be released, and on what platforms? Some exhibitors require exclusivity in a particular medium or market or require the producer to "hold back" licensing similar rights for a period of time. For example, some online distributors require you to sign with them exclusively; as a result, as long as they distribute your film, you may be prohibited from self-distributing it—for example, on Amazon.com. Before you grant anyone exclusivity over your film rights, a good practice is to create a two- to three-year release schedule detailing when and in what media you plan to release your film.

- *Marketing and advertising.* How will you attract audience members to your rented theater or drive traffic to your website? What will your movie poster look like? Is your DVD case eye-catching enough? With "old-school" film distribution, it is the distributors who have to worry about these issues. They engage PR and marketing firms, create trailers, place ads in newspapers, and build banner ads for Facebook. Now it's on you, buddy, and not only is it expensive (see the next bullet), but generating a professional-looking marketing campaign often requires as much time, effort, and *money* as making the film itself. You have to create a consistent look, feel, and quality for your packaging, marketing, and advertising materials, and that often requires you to hire professionals, such as Adobe Flash animators, graphic artists, and PR companies, just to name a few. Make sure that you have written contracts with all service providers and that any creative work they do is owned by you pursuant to a valid work-for-hire agreement. (See "Work for Hire," p. 344.)

- *Budget.* How much will it cost? From the bandwidth fee charged by your website host to the costs of renting a movie theater, DIY distribution costs money. Of course, you could put your project on YouTube or Facebook for free and try to seek ad revenue, but it can be hard to generate the number of "eyeballs"—that is, viewers—you'd need to make money with that kind of distribution model. Usually, if you want to make money on your films, you have to charge the audience, and that means spending money to press DVDs, print fliers, rent theaters, advertise in newspapers, and do the numerous other things required to prompt an audience to part with their cash so they can watch your film. For instance, some distribution methods, such as booking a theater, may require you to spend at least a contractually specified minimum amount on advertising your film. A budget helps you anticipate costs and lets you make informed decisions, such as whether to chose between a Google ad buy and a case of promotional bobblehead dolls of your movie's main character.

- *Net profits.* Don't forget that you may have to account to investors and other net profit participants. (See "Net Profits," p. 379.) If you are DIY distributing, you must keep meticulous records of all income and expenses related to your film's marketing, promotion, distribution, and exploitation. Remember, if an investor doesn't get paid what they are due, *you* are the distribution company that will be sued.

PACKAGING AND PROMOTIONAL MATERIALS

You will need several kinds of packaging and promotional materials, regardless of the form of DIY distribution you decide on. Be sure to create different versions—web browser thumbnail icons, DVD covers, movie lobby cards, posters, and so on. They should all feature a title, image, and design that will be picked up in all your marketing materials.

- If you are working with a graphic artist, make sure that the artist signs a work-for-hire agreement.

- Make sure that all graphic elements used in your packaging have been cleared. (See "Clearances," p. 244.)

- For DVDs and Blu-Ray discs, you will need a Universal Product Code (UPC) bar code if you plan to place the film with retailers. UPCs help both you and retailers track the sales of your film. You can purchase a UPC from GS1 US: www.gs1us.org.

DIY THEATRICAL DISTRIBUTION

Although it can be the most expensive form of DIY distribution, there is nothing like sitting down in that red cushioned seat, bucket of popcorn on your lap, and watching your film flicker to life on the silver screen. *Now* it's a movie! But theatrical distribution has additional benefits beyond greasy popcorn and self-gratification:

- It is required to be considered for Academy Awards nomination. For instance, "To be eligible for 83rd Academy Awards consideration, a documentary feature must complete *both* a seven-day commercial run in a theater in Los Angeles County, *and* a seven-day commercial run in a theater in the Borough of Manhattan during the eligibility period."[1]

- When you exhibit your film in a major city, you are more likely to interest other theaters in showing your film and DVD distributors in selling it.

- A film with a theatrical run (not just a premiere) is eligible to be included in the Internet Movie Database (IMDB.com).

There are generally two ways a DIY distributed film makes it to a theater: via a *film booker* or via the filmmaker herself.

- *Film bookers (aka movie booking agents).* Although they are technically agents, film bookers can be thought of as theatrical distributors for hire. You pay them a monthly fee (or a fee based on theaters booked) and they try to interest theaters in showing your film. Bookers can be expensive, with fees of thousands of dollars per month. Their contracts often require the filmmaker to utilize their services for a contractually specified minimum number of months. However, bookers have solid relationships with theaters and theater chains and can often

DISTR.

place films when a filmmaker has struck out. Keep in mind that, like theatrical agents, bookers serve a "gatekeeper" function and often have to be convinced that your film will bring in an audience before they will work with you.

When the theater is interested in your film, the film booker negotiates the *theatrical exhibition agreement* with that theater, hopefully trying to get you the highest percentage of the box office revenue she can. The film booker negotiates the *commitment*—the number of weeks the theater is obligated to show your film. Theaters often require the option of extending the commitment of a film that performs well and the ability to cancel a run due to poor performance; a skilled film booker will know how to negotiate and set limits to both of these options. Finally, once the film is booked and the contract negotiated, the booker oversees the task of getting the physical film into theaters for exhibition.

- *Self-booking.* If you can't afford a booker, you may try to keep the DIY theme going and book theaters by yourself. Without connections from a distributor, sales agent, or booker, this can be difficult, although it helps if your film has won awards at film festivals, is about an extremely topical subject, or features a well-known actor.

Basically, there are two kinds of deals you can expect to work out with an interested theater:

- *Percentage of the box office.* This is the deal you probably want: The theater pays you a percentage of the ticket sales (usually between 25% and 65%) for your film during its run. If you're a filmmaker who has yet to establish a core following, be prepared for the theater to ask for a *minimum guarantee* against your percentage. In other words, if your film does not make at least the minimum guaranteed amount from ticket sales, you are responsible for paying the minimum amount to the theater.

    Example: Drago's new film, *The Way of the Wimpy Warrior,* has been booked for a one-week run at Spooler Cinema. The theatrical exhibition agreement specifies a minimum guarantee against the box office of $7,000. Unfortunately, the film's lackluster performance has generated only $6,500 in box office receipts by the end of the week. Instead of making money from the run, Drago now owes the theater $500 ($7,000 − $6,500 = $500)!

    You will also have some expenses: generally, theaters will require the distribution company (you, in this scenario) to spend at least a contractually specified amount of money on local adverting (print ads, television commercials, radio spots). Additionally, they may require that you hire a PR firm to help bring your film to the attention of film reviewers.

- *Four wall.* Also known as "rent-a-theater" distribution, because you do just that: You rent the four walls of the theater and pretty much everything between them. For one fee you hire the theater, the projectionist, the ticket taker, and so on. Unlike a percentage of the box office deal, you get to keep all the ticket sales (and you can charge as much as you want for those tickets). The catch is that you need to pay the rental fee for showing your film, and that fee can range from $10,000 to $20,000 per week in larger metropolitan areas.

Example: Drago decides to gamble with *The Way of the Wimpy Warrior* by placing it in a major metropolitan theater under a "four wall" agreement. Now he's paying the theater up front—$10,000 for the week. To maximize his chances for success, he's done a lot of advanced advertising and promotion, secured a favorable review in a local paper, and given his cast and crew enough time to send e-mail blasts to all their friends and family. His promotion has paid off: The film pulls in a lucky $13,000. Unlike last time, now he gets to keep all this money. Drago has made $3,000 ($13,000 − $10,000 = $3,000). Even better, the theater management is so impressed with the movie's success that they decide to book it for the next three weeks under a percentage of the box office agreement.

THE FOUR-WALL AGREEMENT

Parties

The company that owns the movie theater will be one party to the contract. The producer or the production company will be the other.

Engagement

This section lays out the fact that the relationship is a "four-wall" relationship (in other words, you're renting the theater). It also specifies the specific dates on which the movie will be shown. A typical movie run is one week; make sure to specify how many times that film must be run within a week. Also include the minimum number of runs per day your movie must have. Typically, you will get to specify the movie times when your movie will be shown. You may also want to specify the format (35 mm, 16 mm, DVD, etc.) in which the film is to be shown, as well as the particular screening room, if the movie theater houses more than one.

Services

Be as detailed as you can about the specific services the theater will provide you, including the provision of managers, ushers, cashiers, cleaning crew, and, of course, the projectionist. The exhibitor should also agree to set your film up for advanced ticket purchases through MovieFone. If you plan to do a Q&A session afterward, you should specify that the theater will remain open during that time.

Four-Wall Fee

DISTR.

This is the amount of money that you will have to pay the theater. Make sure you understand all of the costs involved. Typically the theater sets the rental fee, which includes the staff salaries, cleanup fees, utilities, and so on. In other words, you should be paying a flat fee for the week that your film is shown there. Confirm that no concession stand costs are being charged to you, since the typical four-wall arrangement allows the theater to keep all the money made on concessions.

Box-Office Receipts/Income

This section specifies that you get to keep all the money from your movie's ticket sales (aka box office receipts). *Be careful here:* If the movie theater includes a provision in which they take a portion of the box-office proceeds, then it is not a four-wall agreement but rather a very bad percentage of the box-office deal. Be sure to include a deadline by which you must receive the box-office proceeds. Many theaters ask producers to wait 30 days before they get the money from the ticket sales. Try to negotiate immediate and complete payment upon conclusion of the movie's run; that way when the film leaves, so do you and your money. Ask for an accounting provision to be included in the contract as well so that you can double-check that the theater has given you all the money that you are due. (See Appendix C, "Audit and Accounting Provision," p. 383.)

Publicity and Advertising

The theater should agree to place your movie posters and lobby cards (which you will need to supply) in its theater, place your movie title on the marquee, and run your movie's ad in the entertainment section of the local newspaper, along with the other movies it's showing. You should also try to get the theater to agree to show your movie trailer before its other films in advance of your movie's exhibition dates.

Shipping Costs

The producer always pays for the costs of shipping the film to and from the theater.

Rights and Permissions

The producer grants the theater the right to exhibit the film during the engagement period as well as the rights to advertise and promote the film in the theater's newspaper advertisements.

Representations and Warranties

DISTR.

The producer typically promises that the film is a certain running time, that nothing in the film will infringe any rights, is obscene, or libelous, and that the filmmaker has secured all rights and permissions necessary for the theater to exhibit the film. The theater company should promise that the theater will be clean and operable and complies with all safety codes. (See Appendix C, "Representations and Warranties," p. 381.) Both sides should indemnify each other for any damages they cause to each other. (See Appendix C, "Indemnification," p. 386.)

FOUR-WALL CASE STUDY: QUAD CINEMA, NEW YORK CITY

Some theaters specialize in four-walling a producer's film. One such well-known theater is New York's Quad Cinema, which has catered to independent, foreign, and documentary films since 1972. Whereas many, if not most, independently owned and operated theaters will four-wall a producer's film, the Quad realizes that a theatrical release is just one part of the producer's DIY distribution strategy. To help such filmmakers, the Quad offers a new media-friendly four-wall package that includes:

- Showing the producer's film for a weeklong run, five showings a day, complete with press screenings
- Helping the filmmaker get on Amazon.com and Netflix
- Setting the filmmaker up with his own online e-store to sell the film
- Submitting the filmmaker's film to IMDB.com
- Including the film in the theater's Friday *New York Times* advertisement
- Inviting *The New York Times* film critic to the screening
- Assisting the filmmaker with placing Google ads for the film

See www.quadcinemafourwall.com for more details.

Producers should always try to get a distributor first; four-walling is a last resort. That being said, when you do four-wall with us, your film is treated like a big studio picture and the public never needs to know that you have a four-wall deal.

–Elliott Kanbar, owner of the Quad Cinema

Four-Wall Tips and Tricks

- Use a well-established theater. Part of what will draw your crowd is the reputation of the movie house.
- Know what film formats the theater supports. The last thing you need is to lose a day of your movie's run while they transfer your film into another format they support … and charge you for the transfer.
- Make sure you are aware of all the costs. When you're four-walling, you shouldn't have to pay additional fees for a projectionist, ticket seller, or usher. These should all be included.
- Four-walling a film used to be the sign of a potentially bad film—the rationale being that if a film couldn't attract a distributor, it wouldn't attract an audience. This perception has started to change: As more and more people are making movies, the sheer number of films on the market means that many good films aren't able to attract theatrical distributors. Although four-walling your film no longer has the stigma it once did, it's usually not something you want to advertise.

DISTR.

The public doesn't need to know that you are renting the theater; they just need to know what your film is about and when they can see it.

- If you are going to incur the expense of four-walling, you must put in the money to promote it. What good is having a rented theater if you can't fill the seats with interested patrons? One of the most important things you can do is get your film reviewed. Hold a press screening early or send a screener DVD or hyperlink to local film critics, along with a press kit.

DIY DVD DISTRIBUTION

People still love DVDs and Blu-Ray discs; they're physical icons, standing as a testament to our viewing habits, shelved in that great tabernacle of televised entertainment: the video library. With theatrically distributed films, DVD distribution gives the filmmaker the opportunity to sell his film to the same audience twice. For a DIY distributing filmmaker, the DVD may be the first or primary method of distribution.

For DIYs, the two main methods of creating and distributing DVDs are working with a fulfillment company or working with a *duplication on-demand* service. Both services require the filmmaker to supply the DVD video master and the artwork for the DVD case. Of course, you could duplicate the film yourself, but if you're lucky and your film sells, this can become very time consuming.

Fulfillment Companies

As a producer, you need to concentrate on selling your film, not on duplicating DVDs every single time somebody wants to buy a copy. That's where *fulfillment companies* come in handy. These businesses will make copies of your DVDs, package them, and ship them directly to your customers. When somebody orders your movie from your website, the fulfillment company receives the customer's information and takes care of getting a copy of your movie to the customer.

Thanks in part to the growth of the independent film industry, there are fulfillment companies to fit every producer's needs. Some companies require that a minimum number of DVDs be purchased; some are willing to duplicate your DVD on demand. As one might guess, producers who pay for DVD duplication in bulk (several hundred copies at a time) typically pay less per DVD than producers who work with a service that will duplicate one DVD on demand each time a customer orders.

- When you're looking into fulfillment companies, make sure to identify the per-unit cost of your DVDs.

- Double-check the customer service policies. If the customer has a problem, how can they handle it? The last thing you want is to play middleman between a customer and the fulfillment company.

- Will your fulfillment company help you put together the e-commerce back end (payment functions, inventory tracker, shipping management, etc.) of the website from which you will be selling your film?

• Make sure no rights are transferred from you to the fulfillment house. Remember, although they are putting your movie in the hands of customers, they are not film distributors. All you should be giving them is money, not any rights in your film.

REPLICATION VS. DUPLICATION

Broadly speaking, there are two ways in which copies of your DVD can be made: *duplication* and *replication*. Duplication is what most people are familiar with: You duplicate a DVD every time you burn information onto a blank DVD using your computer. Replication, by contrast, requires a special glass mold being made, and your DVD must be physically created from that. In the short run, duplication is quicker, but in the long run the cost per unit of replicated DVDs is cheaper.

DVD Duplication on Demand: Amazon.com

One of the quickest ways to get your DVD into the marketplace is by using Amazon.com's CreateSpace service. Once a producer has set up an account with CreateSpace,[2] the film can be licensed for on-demand exhibition or sold as a duplication-on-demand DVD.

The advantage for the producer is that she does not have to pay to duplicate and store multiple copies of her movie. Each time the movie is ordered from Amazon.com or her website, a fresh copy is created, complete with slipcase, and is delivered to the purchaser. Furthermore, setup is easy; a producer just sends in the artwork and her DVD, and CreateSpace does the rest. Producers can opt to also have their movies available as *Download to Own* and *Download to Rent* selections (movies downloaded "to Rent" expire after a certain number of viewings; "to Own" movies do not).

For a filmmaker who is out of options, this might not be a bad deal. That being said, there are a few drawbacks to distributing in this way:

• Unlike working with a film distribution company, the producer has to do all his own marketing, advertising, and promotion.

• There is no negotiating the contract.

• Amazon.com takes a fairly large percentage of the royalties—up to 45%.

But of course, there is a tremendous upside:

• You're selling your DVDs (or downloads) through a retail outlet that is recognized worldwide.

• Your film can be listed on IMDB.com, which is critical for enhancing your reputation as a filmmaker.

DISTR.

- The Amazon agreement is nonexclusive, so you can continue to distribute your film through other channels.
- There are no membership or setup fees. CreateSpace gives you a UPC barcode if you don't already have one.

For the authors and musicians in the crowd, CreateSpace also allows you to publish books and music.

Making Money with CreateSpace

There are two ways to make money using the CreateSpace service: You can sell through Amazon.com and/or you can sell through a CreateSpace eStore. Regardless of where you sell, there is a fixed per DVD cost of $4.95 as of the time of this writing.[3]

In addition to the fixed costs, producers also pay a royalty to Amazon and CreateSpace; this royalty varies, depending on which service the producers are using. As mentioned, Amazon.com takes a fairly large percentage of the royalties—45% on top of the per-unit cost of each DVD. By contrast, theatrical distribution companies typically take between 20% and 40% as a distribution fee, and they promote and market your film, which Amazon.com does not.

However, for those DVDs that you sell through your own CreateSpace eStore, you only pay a 15% royalty, as opposed to the Amazon.com royalty of 45%.

EXAMPLE: LOVE YURTS

Phoebe Producer is ready to distribute her film *Love Yurts*, a six-hour black-and-white documentary on the history and construction of yurts, complete with Mongolian subtitles. For some reason no film distributor wants to carry it, so Phoebe has decided to self-distribute through Amazon.com. She decides to sell her film for $20, and wants to know how much she will make from each sale.

When someone buys her DVD on Amazon.com, CreateSpace first deducts $4.95 from her $20, leaving an adjusted gross price of $15.05. Next, Amazon.com deducts its 45% royalty (*remember, this is 45% of the $20, not 45% of the adjusted gross!*), which equals $9; $15.05 minus $9 leaves $6.05 for Phoebe.

If she sold the same DVD through a CreateSpace eStore, CreateSpace would first deduct $4.95 from her $20, again leaving an adjusted gross price of $15.05. Of this, CreateSpace takes a 15% royalty (*also from the $20, not from the adjusted gross*), which equals $3. So, $15.05 minus $3 leaves $12.05 for Phoebe.

The CreateSpace Contract

Even though you will not be able to negotiate the contract with CreateSpace, it is important to understand that the contract between you and CreateSpace requires you to:

- Be responsible for all third-party payments (license fees, residuals, royalties, etc.).[4]

- Indemnify them and their affiliates for any breach by you of the agreement. (See Appendix C, "Indemnification," p. 386.)

- Represent and warrant that you have all the rights required to distribute your film. (See Appendix C, "Representations and Warranties," p. 381.)

- Represent and warrant that your film is "not defamatory, libelous, obscene, or otherwise illegal, does not invade any right of privacy, and does not infringe upon any Intellectual Property Right or right of publicity of any person or entity, and any recipe, formula, or instruction contained in the Content is accurate and is not injurious to the user."[5]

  - *Note:* Since you are not saying this is "to the best of your knowledge," you are promising that your film doesn't contain anything that's obscene or illegal in any part of the world where your video could be purchased on Amazon.com. Depending on your content, that could be a tall order indeed!

  - You are also promising that your video content will not injure users. Producers of exercise or how-to sports videos want to use extreme caution here.

DIY ONLINE DISTRIBUTION

You might want to cut out the DVDs altogether and distribute your movie as a digital download. Two of the most popular online video sites are iTunes and Netflix. However, as of this writing, iTunes and Netflix won't take your film—that is, not directly. These services have become so popular, and so inundated with independent films, that both sites require films be submitted via a *content aggregator*. Content aggregators are companies that act as both sales agents and content gatekeepers for larger distribution outlets.

Here's how that works: You submit your film to a content aggregator. Then, for a fee, the aggregator submits your film to iTunes.

CONTENT AGGREGATOR

A content aggregator is a distributor and/or exhibitor who specializes in new media technologies such as streaming video, VOD, pay-per-view, and mobile downloads. The aggregator gathers media content, such as your film, and offers it for sale or license through a variety of exhibition platforms. Some aggregators are also exhibitors; some merely distribute to exhibitors. Aggregators usually

DISTR.

CONTENT AGGREGATOR (cont.)

have relationships with popular online video portals, such as iTunes and Netflix, and may be the only way to get your film on such sites. As a result, working with an aggregator is like working with a distributor in that the relationship requires the filmmaker to pay careful attention to the exclusive rights she is granting, in what markets, and for how long.

Some content aggregators work for a percentage of your film's licensing fees; some companies, such as Distribber (www.distribber.com), charge a flat fee to submit your film to iTunes and Netflix and let you keep all the licensing fees.

THE CONTENT AGGREGATOR DEAL

FEE

Is the aggregator paid a flat fee or a portion of your film's licensing proceeds? If it's a flat fee, make sure that a majority or all of it is refundable if the aggregator cannot place your film on iTunes or Netflix. If the aggregator is paid from your film's proceeds, make sure the payment only comes from those companies or territories that the aggregator actually licensed. In other words, the aggregator should not be entitled to a portion of your theatrical box-office receipts. Make sure you understand all the additional costs and expenses the aggregator plans to charge. For instance, some aggregators charge a setup fee to convert your film into the proper format for online distribution.

GRANT OF RIGHTS/TERRITORIES

The only rights that you should grant to the aggregator are:

- The rights to distribute your film on iTunes and Netflix and to other video-on-demand services on which you and the aggregator agree.

- The right to advertise and promote your video to potential exhibitors, as noted previously.

RESERVATION OF RIGHTS

You should reserve the right to distribute your film in *all* other media and manners. Unless a content aggregator has strong relationships with merchandisers, you should not give it the right to enter into merchandising deals on your behalf. You may also want to reserve the right to distribute the film yourself—for instance on your own website or through Amazon.com (see earlier discussion).

TERM

When starting off with a content aggregator, try to limit the term to one year or 18 months. You might want to place further restrictions by requiring that they

DISTR.

secure a deal with iTunes or Netflix within the first six months; if they don't, the contract becomes voidable by you.

POWER OF ATTORNEY

A content aggregator will ask for the authority to negotiate and enter into agreements with distributors/exhibitors on your behalf. Producers who have some familiarity with licensing their films should require prior approval over the deals the aggregator negotiates.

EXCLUSIVITY

Be prepared for the aggregator to require that it be the exclusive online distributor for your film. If you are paying the aggregator a flat fee, it is acting more like a service provider than a distributor, and you might not want to give it such exclusivity. Aggregators working on a percentage of the license fee basis are taking a greater risk and thus have a better argument for being your exclusive online distributor. However, if you grant exclusivity, you might want to include some restrictions, such as the following:

- Limiting the duration of the exclusive relationship.
- Limiting the media or outlets over which the aggregator has exclusivity. For instance, you might grant the aggregator the right to be the exclusive distributor with respect to iTunes and Netflix, but you retain the right to sell downloads of your movie from Amazon.com.
- Requiring certain benchmarks to be achieved prior to exclusivity kicking in. For instance, the content aggregator must place your film with iTunes and Netflix to get exclusivity over your film's distribution on either site.

NO ASSIGNMENT

You want to make sure you know who has the rights to license your film and that they will be in business to do so; accordingly, you should limit the aggregator's ability to assign the rights to distribute your film to third parties. After all, mayflies live longer than some online businesses.

ACCOUNTING

The aggregator should be required to send you periodic accounting statements as well as grant you access to its books for an audit no less frequently than once per year.

DISTR.

REPRESENTATIONS AND WARRANTIES/ INDEMNIFICATION

If you've been following the discussions in this book since the beginning of your project, you should be familiar with this clause. In short, you're promising that you have all the rights required for the film to be distributed without anyone having to worry that they will be sued for copyright infringement, defamation, trademark tarnishment, or the like. Furthermore, you're promising to pay the aggregators' and the exhibitors' damages should they get sued because of your film's content. (See Appendix C, "Representations and Warranties," p. 381; "Indemnification," p. 386.)

YOUTUBE

Nothing beats YouTube.com when it comes to the ease of getting your film on the web. And because YouTube is the Internet's number-one video site,[6] you have the potential for getting your work seen by a *lot* of eyeballs.

Sounds great, but how do you make money from a site that's virtually free to anyone who wants to watch? Here are a few ways you can do that:

- *Become a YouTube partner.*[7] Anybody with a webcam can, and does, upload video to YouTube. Only a select few, however, can become a YouTube partner; membership is completely at YouTube's discretion and is generally reserved for the big studios, networks, and the like as well as those posters whose videos generate hundreds of thousands of views. YouTube partners enjoy a number of benefits, including:
  - Sharing in ad revenue from ads posted next to or overlaid on partner videos.
  - Deriving revenue from posting their own ads.
  - Being able to charge fees for their videos as on-demand rentals. As of this writing, YouTube has started a video-on-demand program allowing YouTube partners to post video content for on-demand rentals. The good news is that YouTube is already the market leader in video; the bad news is that it is very choosey in terms of who it allows to charge rental fees. Time will tell if YouTube's rental market opens up to more content providers. For more information, see www.youtube.com/t/youtube_rentals.
- *Drive traffic to your e-store site.* YouTube members are allowed to use YouTube to "to promote [their] business or artistic enterprise."[8] Create your own YouTube "channel" and post trailers and teasers for your film on YouTube, featuring a link to your e-store website at the end of the clip. Viewers who follow the link to your website are presented with options on how to buy or view your film.
- *Embed and host advertising.* You can also embed your YouTube clips on your site and partner with Google's AdSense,[9] a program that allows you to post ads from Google and get revenue each time a visitor to your site clicks through to the ad's website. Make sure that you understand and comply with the AdSense rules, such as:
  - You can't encourage viewers to click the ads.
  - You cannot feature content or link to sites that are violent, pornographic, excessively profane, or promoting illegal behavior or racial intolerance.

- All intellectual property on your website must be cleared.
- You must adhere to Google's webmaster guidelines on content, quality, video program policies,[10] and technical specifications.

YouTube Tips

- Remember, even though you might not charge a fee to show your film on YouTube, you can still be sued and found liable for infringement if you include somebody else's copyrighted material in your video. (See "Clearances," p. 244.)
- If DIY distribution is a last resort, YouTube is the *last* last resort. In general, you shouldn't give away your film. Trailers and teasers are fine; so is an episode or two of a webisode—but when you get down to it, aggregators and distributors might not want to pick up your film if it has been given away for free. The good news is that this situation could be changing: The success of the originally free webisodes series *Dr. Horrible's Sing-Along-Blog*[11] translated into sales when the same webisodes were pressed onto DVD and sold. However, that particular webisode series was extremely popular and featured an A-list actor and director. Don't count on selling your once free-of-charge online video unless it has gone so viral that it has become an entertainment epidemic.

DIY DISTRIBUTION: THE BOTTOM LINE

Remember: You are now doing the work of the distributor, which means that you must:

- Double-check all your clearances.
- Prepare advertising, promotional, and marketing materials.

Create a distribution schedule, budget, and plan of attack *before* you start spending your hard-earned cash.

DISTR.

9

CONCLUSION

If you find daunting the prospect of dealing with so many legal issues, take heart. You can do this.

Having worked with many different kinds of artists in my law practice, it has been my experience that producers, more than any other type of artist, tend to grasp legal concepts the most quickly. Perhaps it's because in many ways a producer's job and a lawyer's job are similar: Both involve negotiating, lining up alternatives, creating contingency plans, and making the best of emergency situations.

If you can juggle the logistics of producing, you can manage all the law you need to keep your film in the clear. The trick is to realize that legal and business decisions are every bit as important to the success of your movie as the decisions you make regarding your script, camera angles, performances, and editing choices.

Remember—this book is not intended to replace a lawyer. However, it is designed to help you reduce your legal costs by giving you much of the information you need to make informed decisions about the legal aspects of your production. After all, the less time your attorney has to spend teaching you the law, the more time she can spend drafting contracts and negotiating on your behalf.

So get yourself a good attorney, put this book in your bike messenger bag, and go make a great movie!

FINAL TIPS

To protect a film's assets, a filmmaker should:

- Establish a tight working relationship between your staff and a production attorney and accountant.
- Make sure your contracts protect your IP.
- Register and maintain your copyrights.
- Get permission to use any IP that is not yours.
- Keep a well-organized production book containing all the project's contracts and clearances.
- Maintain an E&O insurance policy.
- Try to secure a distributor before you decide to distribute by yourself.
- When in doubt, seek permission!

LAW LIBRARY: APPENDICES A–E

THE LAW LIBRARY

The remainder of this book contains your very own portable law library. Here you will find material that fleshes out and supplements the topics presented in the main part of the book.

The library is composed of five sections:

- Appendix A, "A Filmmaker's Guide to Intellectual Property Law" (p. 327). Learn more about copyright, rights of publicity, defamation, privacy law, and moral rights.
- Appendix B, "A Filmmaker's Guide to Contract Law" (p. 367). Learn more about contract law basics, contract formation, types of contracts, breach of contact.
- Appendix C, "The Clause Companion" (p. 375). Learn more about typical contract clauses found in most film and video contracts.
- Appendix D, "A Filmmaker's Guide to Labor and Employment Law" (p. 393). Learn more about independent contractors and employees, legal requirements for employers, dealing with child labor laws particular to the film industry.
- Appendix E, "State Film Commission Offices" (p. 404). Learn where to find production and tax credit information for each state.

A FILMMAKER'S GUIDE TO INTELLECTUAL PROPERTY LAW

This appendix provides you with a general background on the areas of intellectual property law that most impact the filmmaking process. Here you will find resources to help your understanding of the following topics:

- Copyright law (p. 328)
  - What is a copyright? (p. 328)
  - Copyright rights (p. 309)
  - Copyright terminology (p. 330)
  - What is not protectable under U.S. copyright law? (p. 332)
  - Fair use (p. 335)
  - Copyright ownership (p. 340)
  - Work made for hire (p. 344)
  - Copyright duration (p. 351)
  - Copyright infringement (p. 353)
- Right of publicity (p. 354)
  - What is the right of publicity? (p. 354)
  - First Amendment and the right of publicity (p. 355)
  - Tests to determine infringement of the right of publicity (p. 356)
- Violation of privacy rights (p. 356)
  - Intrusion upon seclusion (p. 357)
  - Public disclosure of private facts (p. 357)
  - False light (p. 358)
- Libel and defamation (p. 359)
  - Defamation defined (p. 359)
  - Public figures (p. 361)
  - Defenses to defamation (p. 362)
- Moral rights (p. 366)

Note: Trademark issues are discussed in "Trademarks on the Set," p. 250.

A FEW WORDS OF CAUTION

This section is not intended to be an exhaustive treatment of intellectual property (IP) law. It is intended to highlight the areas of IP law most important to filmmakers. Copyright, trademark, rights of publicity, and idea protection laws are examined from the viewpoint of how they impact the filmmaker's ability to make and protect his or her movie:

- *Limited scope.* The areas of IP law that don't directly apply to the filmmaking process, such as patent, trade secret, and trademark registration, are not examined.

- *Limited jurisdiction. Only U.S. laws are discussed in this book.* It is critical to keep in mind, especially when dealing with intellectual property, that the laws of other countries may differ significantly from those of the United States. Accordingly, a film that does not violate anybody's rights in the United States may violate somebody's rights in a foreign country! To help guard against this, make sure that your contracts are drafted to include the broadest possible grant of rights to the filmmaker.

Before distributing a film outside the United States, it is good practice to have your film viewed and your agreements analyzed by an attorney who is familiar with *international* intellectual property laws.

COPYRIGHT LAW

WHAT IS A COPYRIGHT?

Copyright is actually a collection of legal rights, all of which protect "original works of authorship fixed in a tangible medium of expression."[1]

Copyright can protect:

- Literary works such as screenplays, novels, magazine articles, and poems
- Motion pictures, television shows, and other audiovisual works
- Musical works, including any accompanying words
- Dramatic works such as plays, including any accompanying music
- Pantomimes and choreographic works
- Pictorial, graphic, and sculptural works
- Sound recordings
- Architectural works
- Other works of original authorship

IP

Copyright is one of the easiest forms of intellectual property protection to obtain: Simply create an original work of authorship, write it down or record it in some way, and you automatically have a copyright in that work. Only a minimum amount of creativity is required in obtaining a copyright. You don't even have to fill out a form or put a "C" in a circle to get copyright protection, *but you will get more legal protections if you do.* (See "Copyright Registration," p. 136.)

> *Example:* You write a screenplay. If you've written it yourself and haven't based it on anybody else's work, it's original to you. Because you've written it down (or saved it to your hard drive), you've recorded it. Smile—you've automatically been granted a copyright in your work, without having to do anything else.

Copyright in Selection and Arrangement

When we think of what can be copyrighted, we often think of types of expression, such as paintings, sculptures, films, or screenplays. In addition to these works, a *particularly creative arrangement or selection of materials may also be copyrighted,* despite the fact that what is arranged or selected may be in the public domain. (See "Public Domain," p. 332.) Examples include:

- A collage made from scraps of 19th-century advertisements
- A creative sequence of yoga poses
- A selection of words—for example, "terms of venery" in James Lipton's work *An Exaltation of Larks*

It is important to note that since it is the *creativity* of the selection and arrangement that is granted copyright (as opposed to the public domain elements themselves), the choices and organization of the elements must be sufficiently creative. For instance, the alphabetical listing of data is not creative enough to warrant copyright protection, nor is the chronological ordering of data.

COPYRIGHT RIGHTS

For filmmakers and other authors, copyright law gives the copyright owner the *exclusive* right to take his work and:

- Make *copies* of it
- *Distribute* it
- *Perform* that work publicly
- Publicly *display* the work
- Make *derivative works* based on the original work

Anyone who, without the copyright owner's permission, performs any of these actions may be infringing the copyright. (See "Copyright Infringement," p. 353.)

IP

COPYRIGHT TERMINOLOGY

Many of the following terms are taken directly from the federal copyright statute itself and may be helpful in interpreting copyright law. More definitions can be found in the U.S. Copyright statute, 17 U.S.C. §101. See www.copyright.gov/title17/92chap1.html#101.

Author

The *author* is the original copyright owner of a work. For instance, if you write a screenplay by yourself and it is completely original with you and no one has hired you to write it, you are the author. However, under the work-made-for-hire rules, the author of the work is the person who commissions the writer to write the screenplay or the writer's employer, not the writer. (See "Work Made for Hire," p. 344.)

Audiovisual Works

Copyright law considers your film or video to be an *audiovisual* work:

> '*Audiovisual works*' are works that consist of a series of related images that are intrinsically intended to be shown by the use of machines or devices such as projectors, viewers, or electronic equipment, together with accompanying sounds, if any, regardless of the nature of the material objects, such as films or tapes, in which the works are embodied.[2]

Common examples include:

- Movies
- Television programs
- DVDs and videocassettes
- Streaming video
- Animation in whatever format

Derivative Work

A *derivative work* is a work based on one or more preexisting works, such as a translation, musical arrangement, dramatization, fictionalization, motion picture version of a book, sound recording, art reproduction, abridgment, condensation, or any other form in which a work may be recast, transformed, or adapted. A work consisting of editorial revisions, annotations, elaborations, or other modifications that as a whole represents an original work of authorship is a derivative work.[3]

Examples of derivative works in the film and television industry include:

- A movie script based on a play
- A movie is a derivative work of a script
- A television series based on a movie

IP

- An action figure based on a movie character
- A novel based on a movie
- The recording of a song composition

Motion Picture

"'*Motion pictures*' are audiovisual works consisting of a series of related images which, when shown in succession, impart an impression of motion, together with accompanying sounds, if any."[4]

Perform

"To '*perform*' a work means to recite, render, play, dance, or act it, either directly or by means of any device or process or, in the case of a motion picture or other audiovisual work, to show its images in any sequence or to make the sounds accompanying it audible."[5]

Publication

In copyright law, *publication* is the act of distributing a copyrighted work to the public. Specifically, it is "the distribution of copies […] of a work to the public by sale or other transfer of ownership, or by rental, lease, or lending."[6]

The date of publication is a critical one in determining whether a work is still protected by copyright.

> *Example:* Many films are works made for hire. For any work made for hire that you create today, copyright protection will last for 95 years from the year of first *publication* or 120 years from the year of creation, whichever expires first.

Publication of a motion picture publishes all the components embodied in it, including the music, the script, and the sounds. Thus, if a motion picture made from a screenplay is published, the screenplay is published to the extent that it is contained in the published work.

The performance itself of a motion picture (e.g., showing it in a theater, on television, or in a schoolroom) does not constitute publication. According to the U.S. Copyright Office,[7] a motion picture *is* published when:

- "One or more copies are distributed to the public by sale, rental, lease or lending, or when an offering is made to distribute copies to a group of persons (wholesalers, retailers, broadcasters, motion picture distributors, and the like) for purposes of further distribution or public performance."
- "Offering to distribute a copy of a motion picture for exhibition during a film festival may be considered publication of that work. For an offering to constitute publication, copies must be made and be ready for distribution."

IP

Public Domain

If a work is *not* protected by copyright, it is in the *public domain*. This means that it can be used by anybody without seeking permission from the original author. Some things are in the public domain by virtue of their nature—for example, facts, ideas, concepts, and works created by the federal government. (See Appendix A, "What Is Not Protectable Under U.S. Copyright Law?" p. 332.)

Even formerly copyrighted works can fall into the public domain for a number of reasons, including:

- *Expiration of copyright.* Copyrights have a life span. When that span runs out, the copyright dies and the artwork becomes part of the public domain, where it can enrich the work of other artists. It's the karma of copyright, man.

- *Copyright notice was not placed on the work.* Earlier versions of the copyright law required the © to be placed on the work when it was published. If a work was published prior to 1989 without proper copyright notice, the work may have fallen into the public domain. Be careful here; a number of exceptions to this rule apply. Don't automatically assume that a pre-1989 work published without notice is in the public domain.

- *Failure to renew the copyright.* Earlier versions of the copyright law required authors to renew their copyright registrations with the federal government. If a copyright was not renewed, it died.

- *Relinquished copyright.* Sometimes authors want their works to be public domain and have voluntarily given up their copyrights.

WHAT IS *NOT* PROTECTABLE UNDER U.S. COPYRIGHT LAW?

From screenplays to soundtracks, from dailies to final cut, copyright law protects the majority of the components used to make a film and television program. However, there is a host of things copyright law simply will not protect. In general, copyright law will not protect the "building blocks" required to make a work of art. For instance, though you can copyright a script, you cannot copyright a word. You can copyright a novel but not an idea. And so on.

BOTTOM LINE: Copyright protects the particular way an author has expressed himself; it does not extend to any ideas, systems, or factual information conveyed in the work.

Works That Have Not Been "Fixed in a Tangible Form" of Expression

IP

If you want to protect something by copyright, you have to write it down, record it, paint it, save it to a hard drive, and so forth.

> *Example:* If an actor improvises a speech on set, it will not be protected by copyright until it is captured on film or written down.

Titles, Names, Short Phrases, and Slogans

These are the domain of trademark law, not copyright law. Copyright will not protect them.

Example: You're trying to market your new vampire film using the phrase "The ultimate power drink—blood!" on all your posters and ad copy. Rather than turn to copyright law to protect that phrase, your best bet would be to try to register it as a trademark. Keep in mind that to be registered as a trademark, the phrase, word, or slogan would have to meet all the requirements of a trademark, such as identifying the source of a good or a service. However, the entire poster, phrase, and art work *combined* could be copyrighted.

Familiar Symbols or Designs; Mere Variations of Typographic Ornamentation, Lettering, or Coloring

In other words, you cannot copyright a plain blue triangle. As in the previous example, you may be able to get trademark protection for a symbol that would otherwise not be copyrightable.

Raw Data

Copyright protection is unavailable for raw data. For instance, you will not be able to protect:

• Mere listings of ingredients or contents

• "Works consisting entirely of information that is common property and containing no original authorship"

• "Standard calendars, height and weight charts, tape measures and rulers, and lists or tables taken from public documents or other common sources"[8]

Historical Facts and Theories

Despite the fact that the author may have invested a good deal of time and money researching a subject, historical facts and theories are also unprotectable under copyright law.

It might seem unfair, but just because you've spent time and effort laboriously researching a topic does not mean that you can copyright that research.[9] However, you certainly can copyright the text that contains that writing. As a result, you can't use copyright law to stop someone from reading your well-researched book or script and copying the facts and other data that you alone have uncovered. But you *can* sue for copyright infringement when that person copies the words, pictures, and structure that you've used to discuss your research.

Example: Dana Documentarian has spent the past 10 years researching her film *E.T. on the Grassy Knoll*, a groundbreaking documentary that demonstrates that

IP

John F. Kennedy was actually killed by extraterrestrials. Although her film may be protected by copyright, her actual theory is not.

Ideas, Themes, Concepts

Copyright law does not protect ideas. Let me state that again: **Copyright law does not protect ideas!** This is, perhaps, one of the hardest concepts for many artists to grasp. Copyright only protects an idea's *expression*, not the idea or concept itself.

One of the problems has always been how to determine where an "idea" stops and "copyrightable expression" begins. As one court pointed out: "The line [lies] somewhere between the author's idea and the precise form in which he wrote it down … protection covers the 'pattern' of the work … the sequence of events, and the development of the interplay of characters."[10]

> **Example:** The *idea* of a band of rebels who fight an evil Galactic Empire is not copyrightable. The fully expressed *screenplay* for *Star Wars*® is copyrightable, however. The former is merely a concept and is capable of being expressed in any number of ways. George Lucas's screenplay, on the other hand, is a collection of specific scenes, dialogue, detailed characters, plot, and a sequence of events, all of which form a unique and copyrightable whole.

Procedures, Methods, Systems, Processes, Principles, Discoveries, or Devices

Systems, processes, methods, procedures, and devices may be protected, but not by copyright law. You need to turn to patent or trade secret law, not copyright law, for help.

> **Example:** Fiona Filmmaker invents a great new system for preparing film budgets. She cannot use copyright law to stop other people from using her system.

Expired: Work in Which the Copyright Has Expired

Copyright protection expires after a certain amount of time. (See "Copyright Duration," p. 351.) Once a copyright expires, the copyright is in the *public domain* and anybody can freely use the copyrighted work without the permission of the former copyright owner.

Works Created by the U.S. Government

Works created by the U.S. government are not protected by copyright.[11] A work of the U.S. government is "a work prepared by an officer or employee of the United States government as part of that person's official duties."[12]

> **Example:** Jolene wants to use photographs from NASA's Hubble telescope as a background to her music video. She may do so without seeking NASA's permission because NASA is a federal agency and its images are generally

IP

not copyrighted. She must, however, be careful when using those images for commercial purposes, so as not to give the appearance that NASA is endorsing the particular product or service. Restrictions on endorsement fall outside copyright law and must be analyzed under right of publicity, trademark law, or particular federal statutes that may prohibit the appearance of commercial endorsement by a federal agency.

In contrast to U.S. government works, state government works may or may not be protected by copyright law. Nor does the law prevent independent contractors, working on behalf of the U.S. government, from owning the copyright to their works.

Be careful here. Even though the U.S. government cannot create a copyrighted work, it can hold the copyright assigned to it by others. This is why, when using material from the U.S. government, you should still verify that the material is not copyrighted.

Scènes à Faire

Scènes à faire (French for "scenes to be made") are common themes typical of an artistic genre and thus appear in numerous works. "*Scènes à faire* are unprotectable elements that follow naturally from a work's theme rather than from an author's creativity."[13] "Incidents, characters or settings which are as a practical matter indispensable, or at least standard, in the treatment of a given topic are *Scènes à faire*."[14] Furthermore, "thematic concepts … which necessarily must follow from certain plot situations" are not entitled to copyright protection.[15] In short, they're like ideas: "Under the *scènes à faire* doctrine, when certain commonplace expressions are indispensable and naturally associated with the treatment of a given idea, those expressions are treated like ideas and therefore not protected by copyright."[16]

> **Example:** Molly is filming a Western, and she wants to shoot a scene involving a showdown between a sheriff and an outlaw. Because this scene is so common to the Western movie genre, she need not be concerned that she will infringe the copyright of *High Noon*. But although the *scènes à faire* doctrine will allow her to use the concept of a showdown without fear of copyright infringement, she must be careful not to use the same dialogue, characters, or choice of shots that are used in another Western, since these may be protected by copyright.

FAIR USE

Among filmmakers, *fair use* is one of the most widely known and widely misunderstood copyright doctrines. Fair use is a defense to copyright infringement. (See "Copyright Infringement," p. 353.) It allows the taking of some part of the copyrighted work without needing to secure the author's permission. The trick is figuring out *what part* and *how much* of a copyrighted work one can take.

IP

TOP FAIR-USE MYTHS

- You can use *any* text under 2,000 words.
- You can use *any* music clip under 5 seconds.
- It's okay to use *anybody's* work in yours if you don't sell the final product.
- As long as you give the author credit, you *don't* have to ask for permission.

All of the above statements are *WRONG!* There are *no* bright-line tests for fair use. The distinction between fair use and infringement may be unclear and not easily defined. There is no specific number of words, lines, or notes that may safely be taken without permission. Acknowledging the source of the copyrighted material does not substitute for obtaining permission. Fair use is always determined on a case-by-case basis by the jury or the guy or gal in the black robe.

Categories of Fair Use

General categories of fair use include news reporting, criticism, comment, teaching (including multiple copies for classroom use), scholarship, or research. The 1961 *Report of the Register of Copyrights on the General Revision of the U.S. Copyright Law* cites examples of activities courts have regarded as fair use:

- "Quotation of excerpts in a review or criticism for purposes of illustration or comment;
- Quotation of short passages in a scholarly or technical work, for illustration or clarification of the author's observations;
- Use in a parody of some of the content of the work parodied;
- Summary of an address or article, with brief quotations, in a news report;
- Reproduction by a library of a portion of a work to replace part of a damaged copy;
- Reproduction by a teacher or student of a small part of a work to illustrate a lesson;
- Reproduction of a work in legislative or judicial proceedings or reports;
- Incidental and fortuitous reproduction, in a newsreel or broadcast, of a work located in the scene of an event being reported."[17]

Determining Fair Use

Courts must give weight to the following four factors in determining fair use:

IP

1. "The purpose and character of the use, including whether such use is of the commercial nature or is for nonprofit educational purposes;

2. The nature of the copyrighted work;

3. The amount and substantiality of the portion used in relation to the copyrighted work as a whole; and

4. The effect of the use upon the potential market for or value of the copyrighted work."[18]

Transformative Uses

In analyzing the first fair-use factor, a court will give greater weight to a defendant who is asserting a fair-use defense if she can show that her use is *transformative*. A transformative use "adds something new, with a further purpose or different character, altering the first with new expression, meaning, or message. ..."[19] So, if instead of merely slavishly copying a film clip, a producer modifies it using digital effects and uses the clip to comment on its original source, creating new expression or meaning, the court may be more likely to find fair use. Filmmakers should take note that merely removing objectionable content from an unlicensed film without adding anything new is generally not considered transformative enough to justify a fair-use defense.[20] To be transformative you have to do more than just repackage the old, unlicensed work into a new form. You have to use it to create new meaning, often by providing insightful commentary or criticism; otherwise the court may find that you're "free riding" on another's creations.[21]

Examples of Fair Use

Two examples illustrate how a court will analyze whether an unauthorized use is fair or infringement.

Scenario #1: Daniel, a television commercial director, makes a commercial for a local car dealership. He uses a film clip from *Star Wars* showing Darth Vader swinging his light saber and cutting down Obi-Wan Kenobi. Over this, he puts a voiceover saying, "We slash prices and kill the competition." The film clip is used without permission, and the commercial airs. Lucasfilm Ltd. sues for copyright infringement, and Daniel defends by asserting a fair-use defense.

- In determining whether his use was fair use, the court first looks to see "purpose and character of the use." Here, the court is analyzing what Daniel did with the clip he used. His use was clearly commercial and not educational, and therefore Daniel loses on this prong of the analysis.

- Second, the court turns to the clip itself and looks to "the nature of the copyrighted work." *Star Wars* is a work of fiction, not news or a documentary, and thus is afforded the highest protection under copyright law. This factor is also weighed against Daniel.

- Third, the court examines how much Daniel took and how important that clip was to *Star Wars* as a whole. Here, Daniel argues that his clip was only 5 seconds long—hardly significant given the movie's two-hour length. The attorney for Lucasfilm counters that though the clip may have been short, it was a critical moment in the movie, and thus its importance should not be judged by its length alone. The court will give weight to an argument like that one—and will look to see whether the "heart" of the work was appropriated. The court decides that this factor should also be counted against Daniel.

- Fourth, the court will look to see how Daniel's unauthorized use affects the market for the movie *Star Wars*. The court will take a look to see whether Daniel's use of the clip "usurps" the market for *Star Wars* clips.[22] The key here is whether the "defendant's use [acts] as a substitute for plaintiff's work in the marketplace."[23] Because Lucasfilm has licensed clips from *Star Wars* for use in other television commercials, this factor, like the others, is counted against Daniel. The court finds that Daniel has not made a successful fair-use defense and thus has infringed the copyright to *Star Wars*.

Scenario #2: Flaherty Filmmaker is shooting a documentary about the media's treatment of the issue of global warming and wants to use a few shots from an evening news story focusing on the world's biggest tire fire.

Flaherty tries to get permission from Nosey News Networks, Inc. (NNN), the company that produced the footage, but they turn him down. He decides to use it anyway, taking a 1-minute clip from the 6-minute story. The clip features a reporter who jokes about the impact on global warming the tire fire will cause, saying: "Will the fire warm the globe or just cause a few paranoid scientists to get hot under the collar ... over to you, Cathy." Flaherty adds "pop-up video"-style graphic bubbles with global warming statistics over the reporter's derisive commentary. The overall effect of Flaherty's editing and graphic additions makes the reporter seem extremely biased and ignorant of the issues. Even though Flaherty has been denied permission to use the clip, he nonetheless includes a copyright notice under the footage, properly attributing the clip to NNN.

Flaherty's documentary is released and he is sued by NNN. In court, he defends on the grounds that his use of NNN's clip was fair use. In its decision the court reasons as follows:

- In determining whether Flaherty's use was fair, the court first looks to see "purpose and character of the use." Flaherty used the clip as criticism of the news program and as social commentary. Furthermore, his use was educational. This factor is decided in his favor.

- Second, the court turns to the clip itself and looks to "the nature of the copyrighted work." News broadcasts, although protected by copyright, are themselves more prone to be used under fair use. As the U.S. Supreme Court has stated: "Copying a news broadcast may have a stronger claim to fair use than copying a motion picture."[24] This factor is decided in Flaherty's favor as well.

- Third, the court examines how much Flaherty took, and how important that clip was to the news broadcast as a whole. Flaherty took 1 minute of a 6-minute broadcast. The court decides that this was a substantial amount, and, because the clip contained the heart of the piece—the tire fire—the factor is decided in NNN's favor.

- Fourth, the court looks to see how Flaherty's unauthorized use affects the market for the NNN news segment. The court holds that because NNN does not license its clips, the nightly news market is NNN's primary market. Flaherty's use does not have any appreciable affect on the market, and this factor is decided in his favor as well.

- The court also points out that Flaherty's use was transformative—the "pop-up news bubbles" recast the clip. Furthermore, Flaherty acted in good faith by placing the NNN copyright notice below the clip.

- The court rules that Flaherty's unauthorized use was excused under fair-use principles.

> **CAUTION!** It is up to the court to decide—after the fact—whether a use is "fair use."

DE MINIMIS TAKING

De minimis is a fancy Latin phrase that means "of the least" or "of trifles." It refers to the taking of an insignificant amount of a copyrighted work—an amount so trifling that a court will rule that no harm was done even though what was taken was taken without permission. Although *de minimis* is a defense to infringement rather than an exception to copyrightability, it does underscore the fact that courts will rule that some infringement is just too harmless to worry about. Of course, it is up to the defendant to prove that the taking is *de minimis*. As the legal maxim goes, *de minimis non curat lex*—the law does not concern itself with trifles.[25]

> **Example:** Several years ago, a federal court was faced with the issue of potential copyright infringement within the movie *Seven*. In the movie there is a scene in which two police officers search a photographer's apartment, looking for clues to a murder. They enter the photographer's darkroom, which is filled with disturbing photographs. The copyrights to 10 of the photographs were owned by an artist who had never given his permission for the filmmaker to use them. However, in the final version of the film, the photographs are out of focus and only appear on screen for a matter of seconds. When the artist sued, the court ruled that the unpermitted use of the artist's photographs was a *de minimis* taking.[26]

The Legal Test for De Minimis Use

For films, the court pointed out that whether the use was *de minimis* is based on: "1) the amount of the copyrighted work that is taken, as well as [...] 2) the observability of the copyrighted work in the allegedly infringing work. Observability is determined by the length of time the copyrighted work appears in the allegedly infringing work, and its prominence in that work as revealed by the lighting and positioning of the copyrighted work,"[27] as well as factors such as focus and camera angles.[28] Fair use is usually asserted as a defense when a *de minimis* argument fails.[29] (See "Fair Use," p. 335.)

IP

> **CAUTION!** Whether a taking was *de minimis* is something only a court can decide–after you have been dragged into a lawsuit. Remember: Every time you're sued, you have to pay an attorney to defend you, even if you win. A better practice is to secure permission for all copyrighted works used in your film rather than rolling the dice and gambling on the fact that a court will find an unpermitted taking to be *de minimis*.

THE DOCTRINE OF INDEPENDENT CREATION

This is not an exception to copyright law but rather a rule that allows two people to have copyright ownership in what is essentially the same work. The way it works is this: If two authors come up with the same work independently of each other and neither has copied the other's work, both works will be entitled to copyright protection—even though the two works are substantially similar to each other. This is true because copyright is based on originality rather than novelty. As long as the work originated with an author and is not copied from another author, that author may claim a copyright.

> **Example:** Wendy Writer spent two years writing her script *The Platypus Papers*. Because she doesn't have any contacts in Hollywood, her script sits on her hard drive without being seen by anyone but her mother. To her dismay, she opens up the paper one day and sees an ad for the new film *The Platypus Diaries*, produced by Monotreme Pictures, Inc. When she goes to see the film, she is even more upset. The film is substantially similar to her screenplay—so much so that if she could prove that Monotreme Pictures had seen her script, she would have a great claim for copyright infringement. However, because she can't prove that anyone has seen her script—let alone copied it—she has no claim. She owns a copyright in her script and Monotreme Pictures has a copyright in their script and movie.[30]

COPYRIGHT OWNERSHIP

Who Is the Owner?

The person or entity who creates a copyrighted work is considered the *author*.

- If two or more people jointly create a work, they may be joint authors.
- In addition to people, companies can be authors.
- When an employee creates a work on behalf of a company, that company, and *not* the employee, is considered the author of the work. (See "Work Made for Hire," p. 344.)

IP

Joint Authors and Joint Works

> **JOINT WORK; JOINT AUTHORS**
>
> Copyright law defines a joint work as "a work prepared by two or more authors with the intention that their contributions be merged into inseparable or interdependent parts of a unitary whole."[31] The authors of a joint work are, not surprisingly, called *joint authors*.

When two or more authors work together to create a screenplay or film, copyright law may consider them to be *joint authors*. To be considered a joint author, each coauthor must:

- Contribute copyrightable elements to the joint work, and
- At the time the work was created,[32] intend to merge their own contributions inseparably or interdependently with the contributions of the other coauthors to form a unified whole.

Joint authors have certain rights under copyright law; if the authors want to change these rights, they need to do so by a contract between them, such as a writers' collaboration agreement. The contract must be in writing and signed by all authors.

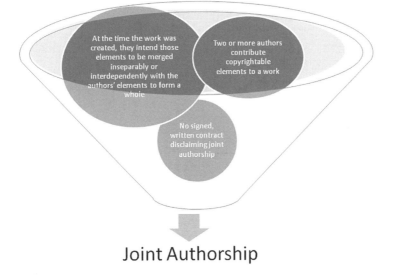

What Makes a Joint Author?

At the time the work was created, they intend those elements to be merged inseparably or interdependently with the authors' elements to form a whole

Two or more authors contribute copyrightable elements to a work

No signed, written contract disclaiming joint authorship

Joint Authorship

Copyrightable Contributions Required for Joint Authorship

Copyright law generally requires that each joint author's contributions must be copyrightable in its own right. If you have one writer and one "idea person," you

IP

have only one author—the writer—unless the agreement specifies otherwise. "To be an author, one must supply more than mere direction or ideas: one must 'translate [ ] an idea into a fixed, tangible expression entitled to copyright protection.'"[33]

As one court pointed out:

> […] the person with noncopyrightable material who proposes to join forces with a skilled writer to produce a copyrightable work is free to make a contract to disclose his or her material in return for assignment of part ownership of the resulting copyright.[34]

Example: Connor and Xander are working together on the screenplay *Hypno-Robot-Zombie-Vampires from Venus.* Connor just contributes the *idea* for the screenplay, and Xander does all the writing. Because ideas are not copyrightable, Connor cannot be considered a joint author. To share in the ownership of the copyright to the screenplay, Connor must enter into a contract with Xander.

What Are the Rights of a Joint Author?

When someone is a joint author, she has the following rights (again, unless a contract says otherwise):

* Each joint author is entitled to an equal and undivided interest in the copyright with the other joint authors. *Note:* The authors' contributions do not have to be equal; they will still share equally with other joint authors!
* Joint authors may grant nonexclusive licenses to the joint work. But *all* joint authors must agree to grant an exclusive copyright license to the joint work.
* Any joint author who sells or licenses the joint work must pay other joint authors an equal share of the money.
* Joint authors are not liable to each other for copyright infringement.
* Joint authors may have a duty to avoid destroying the joint work.
* Some courts require a signed contract to change a joint author's rights from those guaranteed by copyright law.

Example: Connor and Xander bring Natali in to write the screenplay with them—again, without a contract. This time Connor writes dozens of new pages, as does Natali. Everyone is a joint author. They are all excited and want to sell the screenplay. Connor and Xander go to Hollywood and submit the script to Big Film, Inc., a major Hollywood studio. Back at home, Natali gets a call from her uncle, the president of Fly-By-Night Pictures, a would-be production company whose only claim to fame so far has been the production of several cable-access television commercials for local car dealerships.

Fly-by-Night Pictures offers to purchase the motion picture rights to the screenplay for $100, and Natali accepts this offer over the phone without first talking to Connor or Xander. Can she do this?

IP

(cont.)

Unfortunately, yes, she can. Natali has granted a nonexclusive license to her uncle for $100. This means that he can make the picture. Of course, the other joint authors can also grant nonexclusive licenses to other production companies to make their own versions of the picture. However, the practical effect of Natali's grant is that Big Film, Inc., will never make the picture—no studio will invest money in a film as long as someone else has the right to make the exact same picture as well. It is no consolation to her coauthors that Sally must split the $100 three ways with them.

To avoid this disaster, the three of them should have had a contract that specified that any and all licenses must be granted only with the unanimous (or at least a majority) approval of the joint authors. (See "Writing Collaboration," p. 90.)

License That Destroys the Value of the Work

A joint author may be under a duty not to destroy the joint work. Some, but not all, courts have taken the view that a license that substantially reduces the value of a joint work constitutes a destruction of the work.[35] In the case of the motion picture industry, one could make an argument that any license of the motion picture rights to a screenplay destroys its value to be licensed for other pictures; no studio wants to make the exact same picture another studio is making at the same time. But even if one joint author sues another for destroying the joint work and wins such a lawsuit, the recovery of damages is only as good as the defendant author's ability to pay. No money can be recovered by the plaintiff author from the movie studio for the value of the destroyed work.

Is Everybody Who Contributes a Joint Author?

Not everyone who contributes to a movie is a joint author. In a case involving the authorship of the film *Malcolm X*, the 9th Circuit held that a technical consultant was not a joint author, even though he "helped to rewrite, to make more authentic" the script and the movie.

The court stressed that for a movie (in the absence of a contract), authorship was generally limited to the above-the-line cast and crew—in short, those who "mastermind" the movie:

> [The Author is] the person to whom the work owes its origin and who superintended the whole work, the 'master mind.' In a movie this definition, in the absence of a contract to the contrary, would generally limit authorship to someone at the top of the screen credits, sometimes the producer, sometimes the director, possibly the star, or the screenwriter—someone who has artistic control.

IP

[…] So many people might qualify as an 'author' if the question were limited to whether they made a substantial creative contribution that that test would not distinguish one from another. Everyone from the producer and director to casting director, costumer, hairstylist, and 'best boy' gets listed in the movie credits because all of their creative contributions really do matter. It is striking in *Malcolm X* how much the person who controlled the hue of the lighting contributed, yet no one would use the word 'author' to denote that individual's relationship to the movie. A creative contribution does not suffice to establish authorship of the movie.[36]

WORK MADE FOR HIRE

Normally the person who creates a work is considered the author and will own the copyright as well. *Not so for a work made for hire.* The copyright to a work made for hire is initially owned by the employer or other hiring party, *not by the artist who created it.*

For motion pictures, there are two ways a work gets to be a work made for hire[37]:

- **Employees.** Any copyrighted work created by employees within the scope of their employment is considered work made for hire and is automatically owned by the employer.

  Example: Artie the Animator is employed full-time by Rat Trap Productions, Inc., creating animations for the interstitial shorts they supply to the networks. Anytime Artie creates a work for his employers, the copyright to that work is automatically owned by Rat Trap. Even if Artie creates that work at home, if it is for a Rat Trap client the copyright will vest initially with Rat Trap. However, if Artie works on his own anime feature film—a project that is separate and distinct from any Rat Trap projects—he will initially own the copyright to that anime film. To be on the safe side, Artie may want to document that his anime project is not connected with any Rat Trap project, nor does it use any elements that he created in the course of working on any Rat Trap project.

- **Independent contractors.** For an independent contractor's work on a motion picture to be considered a work made for hire, he must sign a written agreement explicitly stating that the work is a work made for hire. Without both the signed, written contract and the clause that says the work produced is "work made for hire," the independent contractor's work is *not* a work made for hire.

  Example: Artie the Animator quits Rat Trap Productions, Inc., and works as an independent contractor for several animation facilities. He picks up a project from Gertie and McCay Productions, Inc., creating backgrounds for a children's cartoon series. He does the work at his home studio on his own equipment and, with the exception of the delivery date, on his own schedule. Artie is clearly an independent contractor.

IP

To own Artie's work product as a work made for hire, Gertie and McCay Productions better have a written contract with Artie, which Artie must sign. The contract must expressly state that any work he produces for them is considered work made for hire.

A CRITICAL ISSUE: WORK MADE FOR HIRE

This is one of the most important legal issues discussed in this book!

From a production company standpoint, *all* contributions of the artists, actors, writers, directors, other employees, and independent contractors should be created as works made for hire.

The contracts should do the following:

- Explicitly state that the work these employees or contractors are performing for the production company is being done as a work made for hire

- The contracts should be signed by that employee or contractor

- The contracts should be written *before* the work is created. Although it's true that some jurisdictions, such as New York (2d Cir.), allow the contract to be written after the work has begun *if and only if* that written contract memorializes an agreement that the parties discussed and consented to before the work was started, some jurisdictions require the written contract first. Better to be safe and get it in writing right before the creative juices start flowing.

No exceptions.

Work for Hire: Two Methods

The copyright in a Work For Hire is owned by the hiring party.

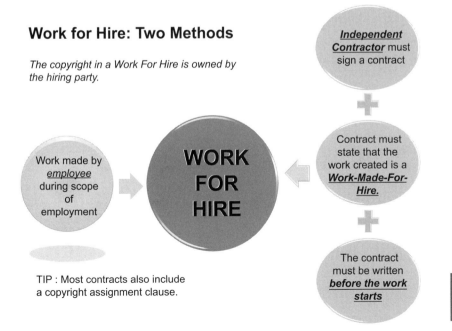

WORK FOR HIRE

Work made by *employee* during scope of employment

Independent Contractor must sign a contract

Contract must state that the work created is a *Work-Made-For-Hire.*

The contract must be written *before the work starts*

TIP : Most contracts also include a copyright assignment clause.

IP

Who Is an Employee for Purposes of Works Made for Hire?

Because an employee's work product is automatically a work made for hire, it is critical to determine just who is an employee. This might not be as easy as you think. Merely writing the word *employee* on a contract does not automatically create an employee/employer relationship.

In determining who is an employee for work-made-for-hire purposes, courts will look at the following factors[38]:

- The hiring party's right to control the manner and means by which the product is accomplished
- The skill required to make the product
- The source of the instrumentalities and tools
- The location of the work
- The duration of the relationship between the parties
- Whether the hiring party has the right to assign additional projects to the hired party
- The extent of the hired party's discretion over when and how long to work
- The method of payment
- The hired party's role in hiring and paying assistants
- Whether the work is part of the regular business of the hiring party
- Whether the hiring party is in business
- The provision of employee benefits
- The tax treatment of the hired party

Duration of Work Made for Hire

Works made for hire have a shorter copyright life span than do works that are not made for hire. For any work made for hire created after January 1, 1978, copyright protection will last for 95 years from the year of first publication or 120 years from the year of creation, whichever expires first.

Work Made for Hire/Copyright Assignment Clause

To be doubly sure that the copyright is effectively transferred from the creator to the hiring party, most work-made-for-hire agreements provide for an alternative copyright assignment. That way, if for some reason the work is not considered a work made for hire, the hiring party gets the copyright anyway by virtue of the alternate copyright assignment clause.

IP

Example: "Director acknowledges and agrees that all of his contributions to the Motion Picture, including, but not limited to writing, directing, storyboarding, gag creation, and any other result of the director's services provided under this contract (the 'Results and Proceeds'), are created as a 'Works Made For Hire,' with all copyright and other rights thereto vesting initially in the production company. Accordingly, the production company shall be considered the sole and exclusive author and copyright owner of the Results and Proceeds and of the Motion Picture. To the extent, if any, that ownership of the Motion Picture produced hereunder or the Results and Proceeds of Director's services do not immediately vest in production company by virtue of this Agreement, Director hereby immediately assigns to production company all rights (including all rights of copyright) of every kind and character in and to the Picture and the results and proceeds of Director's services. Director hereby waives all 'moral rights,' *'droit moral,'* and similar rights. All rights hereunder assigned shall be assigned in perpetuity, and such assignment shall be irrevocable. This effect of this clause shall survive any termination of this Agreement."

TIP: Include a copyright assignment clause in every work-for-hire agreement. To ensure that the copyright is fully transferred to your production company, make sure that the language of this clause transfers all material that was made for your film even *before* the contract was signed. A phrase such as "Writer assigns the copyright to the work performed under this Agreement" might not transfer a treatment written by the writer *prior* to the agreement being negotiated and signed.[39]

Type of Works That Qualify as Work for Hire

All work made by an *employee* within the scope of his employment qualifies as a work for hire. However, making matters more complex, only certain types of *independent contractor*-produced work qualifies as work for hire:

- Contributions to a collective work
- *Parts of a motion picture or other audiovisual work*
- Translations
- Supplementary works
- Compilations
- Instructional texts
- Tests or as answer materials for a test
- Atlases[40]

This means that if you've hired an independent contractor to create a type of work that is not on this list, it is *not* a work for hire, despite there being a written, signed, "work for hire" agreement.

If you're reading carefully, you've noticed that "part of a motion picture or other audiovisual work" is on that list, so as filmmakers, we're covered. However, if you want to have a make-up artist create zombie make-up for waiters serving finger

IP

sandwiches at your premier of *Hypno-Robot-Zombie-Vampires from Venus,* and you want to own the copyright to her makeup design,[41] you better have an alternate copyright assignment clause in her independent contractor's agreement.

Work for Hire and Employee Status

We've talked about the benefits of signing an independent contractor to a work-for-hire agreement. Now here's one potential drawback (at least in California). Under California law, when you sign an independent contractor to a work-for-hire agreement, *they become your employee.*[42] Yes, you read that correctly. If you sign a writer to an independent contractor work-for-hire agreement in California, you must treat him like an employee, which means you could be liable for unpaid taxes, disability payments, workers compensation, and other costs attendant on an employer/employee relationship. (See Appendix D, "A Filmmaker's Guide to Labor and Employment Law," p. 393.)

LICENSING AND ASSIGNING THE COPYRIGHT

A copyright license is the grant of a portion of the copyright (usually limited by time, geography, medium, etc.). The person giving the license is the *licensor;* the person receiving the license is the *licensee.*

> **Example:** Dingo Distributors, LLC, the licensor, grants a license to Bandicoot Broadcasting, Inc., the licensee, to broadcast *Wombats in Love* in North America for a period of three years or for a total of nine runs, whichever comes first.

- An *exclusive license*, also known as an *assignment*, is a license that gives the licensee the exclusive power to a certain right. It is a transfer of ownership of a copyright or any of the exclusive copyright rights. Even if it is called a *transfer of ownership*, that transfer may be limited in duration, scope, geography, or any other way you can think of. Once an exclusive license is granted, the licensor no longer has any power to grant another license to that right or to exercise that granted right herself. An exclusive copyright license must be in writing and signed by the licensor and the writing must clearly and unequivocally transfer the copyright.[43]

> **Example**: Pickled Piper Productions is negotiating a distribution deal for its film, *Pickled Petunias,* with Dahlia Distributors, LLC. The distribution agreement grants the distributor the exclusive right to distribute the film in North America for five years. This is an assignment, because the right to distribute a copyrighted work is an exclusive copyright right. The assignment is limited by territory (North America) and duration (five years). Because it is a copyright assignment, it must be in writing and signed by Pickled Piper Productions to be effective.

- A *nonexclusive license* is a license that may be granted to any number of licensees at the same time. A nonexclusive license may be granted orally or may even be implied from conduct. The holder of a nonexclusive license may not grant licenses to the work to others without the copyright owner's permission.

IP

TO TRANSFER A COPYRIGHT, YOU MUST GET IT IN WRITING

The Law

"17 U.S.C. § 204. Execution of transfers of copyright ownership

(a) A transfer of copyright ownership, other than by operation of law, is not valid unless an instrument of conveyance, or a note or memorandum of the transfer, is in writing and signed by the owner of the rights conveyed or such owner's duly authorized agent. ..."

As one court put it: "The rule is really quite simple: If the copyright holder agrees to transfer ownership to another party, that party must get the copyright holder to sign a piece of paper saying so. It doesn't have to be the Magna Carta; a one-line *pro forma* statement will do."[44] However that one-line statement must be unambiguous, clearly transferring the copyright.[45]

The Copyright License Request Letter

From literary characters to stock footage to musical recordings, some form of copyright license will be used in virtually every stage of the production's legal housekeeping.

The license and the *request letter* are the transactional workhorses of the production attorney. The two are often combined into one form—a letter of agreement that:

- Asks the owner's permission to use the copyrighted material
- Offers the owner licensing terms for the requested material's use

To accept the terms, the rights owner merely countersigns the letter and sends it back to the producer.

The request letter should be specific about how the producer intends to use the material, where the producer intends to exhibit the finished film or video, and the format of the film or video. Alternatively, depending on the owner's leverage, the producer may be sent the copyright owner's contracts and terms on a take-it-or-leave-it basis.

LICENSING TERMINOLOGY

Although copyright licenses differ depending on the type of material to be licensed, most licensing agreements share some common terminology:

- *The grant.* This is the critical clause of any licensing contract. It establishes exactly which material is being licensed and whether

IP

LICENSING TERMINOLOGY (cont.)

the license is exclusive. Because copyright is actually a bundle of rights—the right to reproduce a work, create derivative works, distribute copies of a work, perform a work publicly, or publicly display a work—a comprehensive license must outline the extent to which the licensee may exercise any of these rights.

- *The territory.* A description of where the film or video containing the copyrighted material can be performed or distributed.

- *The term.* The duration of the license. Most filmmakers want to have a license to use the material for the life of the copyright, including renewal terms, if any.

- *Advertising.* If the material the producer is licensing for the film will be included in the film's advertising, the producer will need to secure the right to include the work in the film's marketing and promotion.

- *Payments.* The rate of payment to the copyright holder and how it is calculated.

- *Credits.* How the copyright owner is to be credited in the film.

- *Representations and warranties.* Promises by the copyright owner that he has the right to enter into the license agreement and that nothing in the material infringes the rights of others. This section can be quite extensive.

- *Termination.* A statement that if the producer fails to pay the agreed-on rate or if the producer breaches the agreement in any other way, all granted rights revert back to the copyright owner.

Some other common terms include the right to audit a production company's accounts, a copyright owner's right to free samples of the finished work, and whether the licensee may, in turn, assign the rights it has been granted.

TERMINATION OF TRANSFER

One seemingly odd wrinkle in copyright law is the *termination of transfer* provision,[46] which allows a valid and otherwise irrevocable copyright assignment or license to be revoked after 35 years by the copyrighted work's author or her heirs. Once a copyright transfer has been terminated under this provision, no new derivative works can be made from the terminated copyright. However, works prepared while the copyright license or assignment was in effect can still be exploited as per the original agreement.

> *Example:* Xander assigns the copyright to his screenplay *Two-Fingered Bob* to Despot Pictures, which, over a 35-year period, makes a movie and a television

IP

series based on Xander's work. Even though the screenplay acquisition agreement between Xander and Despot explicitly states that the copyright transfer is irrevocable and lasts for the duration of the copyright, Xander can still revoke the copyright starting at the end of 35 years from when it was transferred! Despot can still exploit the movie and the television series it had made prior to the termination, in accordance with the terms of the screenplay acquisition agreement, but once Xander revokes the copyright, Despot can't make any more derivative works from the screenplay (video games, books, merchandise, etc.) without relicensing the copyright from Xander.

It is important to note that a work created as a work for hire is *not* subject to the termination-of-transfer provisions. This is simply another reason that, for production companies, it is better to get the copyright to the script as a work for hire rather than as an assignment.

Example: Connor is hired by Despot Pictures on a work-for-hire basis to write his screenplay *Lilly Liver with Onions*. Thirty-five years later, he hears about Xander's success in terminating the transfer for *Two-Fingered Bob*, as described in the earlier example. Connor tries to terminate the transfer of rights to *Lilly Liver* but fails; unlike Xander, who assigned the rights in his screenplay, Connor created his screenplay as a *work for hire* for Despot. When a work is created as a work for hire, the copyright originally vests in the contracting party (here, Despot Pictures). The law considers Despot Pictures the author of *Lilly Liver with Onions* from the moment of the script's creation. Since Connor never had any rights in the screenplay in the first place, he can't get the rights back.

COPYRIGHT REGISTRATION

To fully protect a copyright, it should be registered. The advantages of registration and the registration process are covered in the section "Copyright Registration" (p. 136).

COPYRIGHT DURATION[47]

A copyright has a life span, called a *term*. When that term expires, the work falls into the public domain, and anyone can use all or a portion of the copyrighted work without first seeking the permission of the copyright owner.

The life span of a copyright has changed many times over the last hundred years. For the majority of the 20th century, a copyright was given an initial term, which could then be extended if the copyright was properly *renewed* with the government. Although the copyrights of modern works no longer need to be renewed, the renewal status of a copyright may need to be researched when you're determining the life span of older copyrights.

How long the copyright lasts for a work is largely dependent on the following:

• When the work was made
• If the work has been published

IP

- If the work needed to be renewed and whether the work was, in fact, renewed
- When the author of the work died

Copyright Duration of Works Originally Created On or After January 1, 1978

- These works are protected the moment they are created and embodied in a tangible form.
- The copyright lasts until 70 years after the author dies.
- For joint works, the term lasts for 70 years after the last surviving author dies.
- For works made for hire, the duration of copyright is 95 years from publication or 120 years from creation, whichever comes first.

Copyright Duration of Works Originally Created Before January 1, 1978, But *Not Published or Registered* by That Date

- The duration is the same as in the preceding section. The life-plus-70-year or 95/120-year terms will apply to these copyrights as well.
- In no case will the term of copyright for works in this category expire before December 31, 2002.
- For works published on or before December 31, 2002, the term of copyright will not expire before December 31, 2047.

Copyright Duration of Works Originally Created and Published Between 1964 and 1977

- Protection started when the work was published with a copyright notice.
- The duration of protection is 95 years from date of publication with copyright notice.
- Copyright renewal was automatic.
- Registration was required.

Copyright Duration of Works Originally Created and Published Between 1923 and 1963

- Protection started when the work was published with a copyright notice.
- Protection is for 95 years from date of publication with copyright notice—but only if the copyright was properly renewed.
- Registration was required.

IP

Copyright Duration of Works Originally Created and Published Before 1923

- The work is probably in the public domain.
- Registration was required.

COPYRIGHT INFRINGEMENT

Anyone who violates any of the exclusive rights of a copyright owner may be liable for copyright infringement. Keep in mind that you don't have to *intend* to infringe a copyright to be liable for copyright infringement!

Proving Infringement

To prove copyright infringement, the copyright owner (the plaintiff) must prove both *ownership and copying:*

- *Ownership.* That he or she owned a valid copyright.
- *Copying.* That the defendant copied copyrightable elements of the plaintiff's copyrighted work.

There must be copying of *copyrightable* material. Copying of unprotectable elements is not enough. For instance, if all that was taken was an idea (which is not copyrightable), that would not be enough to prove copyright infringement, even if the plaintiff could show that the idea was directly taken from his or her copyrighted work.

Copying is composed of two parts: *access* and *substantial similarity:*

- *Access.* Although it's great if you can actually prove that the defendant copied your work, evidence of copying is usually hard to come by. Recognizing that, courts will accept circumstantial evidence of the defendant's *access* to the copyrighted work. A plaintiff proves access by showing that the defendant had the opportunity to view or to copy the plaintiff's work.
- *Substantial similarity.* In addition to access, the two works (the plaintiff's copyrighted work and the defendant's work) must also be substantially similar. The test for "substantial similarity" is "whether an average lay observer would recognize the alleged copy as having been appropriated from the copyrighted work."[48]

PLAGIARISM IS NOT THE SAME THING AS COPYRIGHT INFRINGEMENT

Plagiarism is an ethical violation, not a legal cause of action. It is possible for a filmmaker to be guilty of plagiarizing another artist's work without being legally guilty of copyright infringement. For

IP

> **PLAGIARISM IS NOT THE SAME THING AS COPYRIGHT INFRINGEMENT (cont.)**
>
> instance, plagiarism can occur when ideas are taken from a source without correct attribution. As indicated earlier, copyright law does not protect ideas.
>
> Plagiarism can be a very fuzzy concept. If what was taken was an idea, it can often be hard to draw the line between plagiarism and inspiration.

Penalties for Infringement

Courts have a plethora of punishments in store for the copyright infringer:

- *Damages and profits.*[49] A court may order an infringer to pay either:
  - The copyright owner's actual damages and any additional profits of the infringer, or
  - Statutory damages in a sum of not less than $750 or more than $30,000, as the court considers just.

For willful infringement the court, in its discretion, may increase the award of statutory damages to a sum of not more than $150,000.

- *Costs and attorneys fees.*[50] The court in its discretion may allow the recovery of full costs by or against any party… and the court may also award a reasonable attorney's fee to the prevailing party as part of the costs.
- *Injunctions.*[51] A court may issue injunctions halting the manufacture or distribution of infringing articles. (See Appendix C, "No Injunction," p. 387.)
- *Impounding and disposition of infringing articles.*[52] A court may order the destruction of all infringing copies of a copyrighted work. In addition to ordering the destruction of the copies, it can also order that the instruments that made the copies also be destroyed. This includes "all plates, molds, matrices, masters, tapes, film negatives, or other articles by means of which such copies or phonorecords may be reproduced."
- *Criminal penalties.* Courts may also sentence willful copyright infringers to jail for periods ranging from one to 10 years, depending on the severity and amount of their willful infringement.[53]

RIGHT OF PUBLICITY

WHAT IS THE RIGHT OF PUBLICITY?

IP

An offshoot of privacy law, the *right of publicity* is a person's right to benefit from the commercial exploitation of her own identity. Infringement of the right of publicity occurs from the unauthorized use of a person's identity (or likeness, voice, name, etc.) for commercial purposes (i.e., labeling goods and services with the unauthorized likeness or using the unauthorized identity in commercials and advertisements).

A celebrity's likeness is not the only part of her identity protected by her publicity rights. For instance, Johnny Carson won a suit against a company that was using the phrase "Here's Johnny" to advertise a toilet.[54]

Filmmakers tend to run into problems with right of publicity laws in two main areas:

- When they attempt to create merchandise, such as action figures, T-shirts, lunchboxes, and so forth, that feature an actor whose publicity rights have not been obtained

- When they create television commercials for products or services that use a celebrity's unlicensed likeness to help sell that product or service

DURATION

The duration and extent of right of publicity protection differs from state to state. Some states require a *signed writing* to convey the publicity right.

- In New York State, your right of publicity dies with you.

- In California, your right of publicity lasts for 70 years after your death; lawsuits for misappropriation of your right of publicity therefore can be brought by your estate.

- Some states do not recognize rights of publicity.

THE FIRST AMENDMENT AND THE RIGHT OF PUBLICITY

The First Amendment greatly limits the extent to which the right of publicity can control areas outside commercial exploitation of an image. Movies, television, some art, news, literature, and educational uses are usually not considered commercial use of a person's right of publicity. Even TV commercials and other advertisements promoting movies and television shows do not infringe the rights of publicity of the actors who perform in the movies and television shows being advertised.

That being said, outside of obvious commercial use, such as featuring an unauthorized likeness in a television commercial, courts and state laws are literally all over the map with regard to what triggers infringement.

For instance:

- A television news station broadcast an entire human cannonball act without the performer's permission. The court held that this may misappropriate the right of publicity.[55]

- A movie recreated and fictionalized the events of *The Perfect Storm* and based its characters on real people. The court held that this did not infringe the rights of publicity in the people depicted.[56]

IP

- A film portrayed Bobby Seales's participation in the Black Panthers without Mr. Seales's consent. In rejecting Mr. Seales's claim for infringement of the right of publicity, the court pointed out that a public figure had no exclusive right to his own life story. The court went on to state: "[I]n addressing right of publicity claims, courts have been mindful that the First Amendment provides greater protection to works of artistic expression such as movies, plays, books, and songs, than it provides to pure 'commercial' speech."[57]
- A commercial that depicted a robot turning letters in a game show violated Vanna White's right of publicity.[58]

One rule of thumb may be:

- "The use of a person's identity in news, entertainment, and creative works for the purpose of communicating information or expressive ideas may be protected [by the First Amendment], but
- "The use of a person's identity for purely commercial purposes, like advertising goods or services or the use of a person's name or likeness on merchandise, is rarely protected."[59]

TESTS TO DETERMINE INFRINGEMENT OF THE RIGHT OF PUBLICITY

The difficult part is determining where to draw the line between commercial and noncommercial use. Courts across the country have developed a variety of tests to determine whether a use is primarily commercial or primarily expressive.

- *Transformative test.* Does the work that allegedly infringes a person's right of publicity contain significant transformative elements, so that the value of the work does not derive primarily from the celebrity's fame?
- *Relatedness test.* Is the work that allegedly infringes a person's right of publicity directly related to that person, as in a life story? If so, it may be protected under the First Amendment. However, if the name or likeness is used simply to attract attention to that work and does not relate to the person himself, this may be a form of advertising and, therefore, it may require that person's permission.
- *Predominant use test.* Is the predominant purpose to exploit the person's right of publicity, or does it contain sufficient expressiveness so that it should be protected by the First Amendment?

When a filmmaker is dealing with the gray area of rights of publicity, the best practice, as always, may be to seek permission.

VIOLATION OF PRIVACY RIGHTS

IP

Producers need to be careful to avoid stepping on the privacy rights of people they film. The extent to which privacy rights are recognized differ drastically from state to state. What a producer may do freely in one state may be actionable in another. As with most torts, consent is a valid defense to these causes of action.

There are four basic kinds of invasions of privacy:
- Infringement of the right of publicity (previously discussed)
- Intrusion upon seclusion
- Public disclosure of private facts
- False light

INTRUSION UPON SECLUSION

Intrusion upon seclusion[60] is, perhaps, what is typically thought of when we think of invasion of privacy. For a filmmaker to be liable for intrusion upon seclusion, all the following elements must be present:
- The filmmaker intrudes, physically or otherwise, on the privacy, solitude, or personal affairs of his subject.
- The intrusion must be of a kind that is objectionable to a reasonable person.
- The intrusion must occur where the subject has a reasonable expectation of privacy.

> *Example:* Polly Producer is shooting a documentary about money laundering in the dry-cleaning industry. She tails Gus Grimes, CEO of Clean As A Whistle, Inc., a dry-cleaning chain. Hoping to get some dirt on his money-laundering activities, she sets up her camera in an apartment across the street from his house. Using a video camera with a powerful telephoto lens and a powerful microphone, she peers into the window of his house, recording his secret business dealings. Mr. Grimes may be able to sue Polly for the tort of intrusion upon seclusion. However, if Polly waited until Mr. Grimes was in a public park before photographing him, she might have a successful defense against his lawsuit; she would argue that there is no reasonable expectation of privacy for conversations that occur in a public place.

PUBLIC DISCLOSURE OF PRIVATE FACTS

A producer can be sued if he publishes private facts about the subject. For a filmmaker to be liable for *public disclosure of private facts*,[61] all the following elements must be present:
- The filmmaker shoots a film that divulges private facts about the private life of the subject.
- The filmmaker exhibits or shows the film to others (this is referred to as *publication*, even though it is a movie).
- The publication of these facts would be highly offensive to a reasonable person.
- There is no legitimate public interest in the disclosure of these facts.

> *Example:* Polly Producer wants her audience to know everything about Gus Grimes—including the fact that he is secretly a homosexual. Polly learned this

IP

fact from a friend of hers who works as a nurse in Mr. Grimes's doctor's office, where Mr. Grimes was tested last year for HIV. Polly photographs the lab report showing Mr. Grimes's medical condition and includes it in her movie. Once again, Mr. Grimes may be able to sue her for invasion of privacy, this time for public disclosure of private facts. However, if Polly had obtained facts concerning Mr. Grimes's sexual preference from a *public* record, she would have a good defense. Furthermore, if Mr. Grimes were a politician running on a platform in which he publicly attacked homosexuality, Polly would be able to defend the lawsuit brought against her on the grounds that "outing" Grimes and showing the hypocrisy of his platform was in the public interest.

Polly may have also violated the Federal HIPAA law,[62] which protects the privacy of medical records, and thus she may be looking at jail time.

FALSE LIGHT

False light[63] is similar to defamation in some respects. (See Appendix A, "Defamation," p. 359.) What is actionable here is publishing false information about somebody that attributes to that person viewpoints that he does not hold or actions that he did not take.

For a producer to be liable for the tort of publicly placing a person in a false light, all the following elements must be present:

- The filmmaker publishes *false* facts about the subject.
- A reasonable person would find these false facts highly offensive if the false facts were told about that person.
- The filmmaker had knowledge or acted in reckless disregard of the falsity of the published facts.
- If the published information is a matter of public interest or concerning a public figure, the producer must have acted maliciously.

In contrast to defamation, the false light tort requires a higher level of publicity not required by defamation. And unlike the requirements for defamation, a person placed in a false light does not have to show harm to his reputation but may only need to show that he suffered mental distress or indignity from the false publication.

> **Example:** Polly Producer has tailed Grimes for days. Her camera catches him heading into a McDonald's restaurant to use the bathroom. Knowing that Grimes is a strict vegetarian, she intercuts the shot of him going into the McDonald's with footage of hamburgers being fried and close-ups of a hand shoving a cheeseburger into a mouth. She finishes the sequence with a shot of Grimes leaving the restaurant and patting his stomach. People viewing her film assume that Grimes loves to stuff his face with cheeseburgers. When he discovers that people think he is a carnivore, Grimes suffers a nervous breakdown. The film is portraying him in a false light, and Grimes would be able to sue Polly yet again.

IP

HIDDEN CAMERAS AND MICROPHONES

In addition to the privacy laws we've listed, filmmakers can run into problems when they use hidden cameras and microphones. Federal law prohibits using microphones and cameras to eavesdrop on a conversation unless the filmmaker has the consent of at least one of the parties to that conversation.[64]

> *Example:* Polly Producer wants to catch Gus Grimes in the act of talking to his mob connection, Tony Turpentine. She hides a small video camera in a flower vase and puts it on the restaurant table of the secluded booth where the two are to meet for lunch. The camera records the conversation between the two evildoers and transmits it to Polly's laptop. Polly watches and listens to Gus and Tony's nefarious schemes while hiding in the restaurant kitchen.

Polly has violated federal law, despite the fact that Gus and Tony were discussing criminal activities.

Some states allow the use of hidden microphones if only *one* of the parties to the conversation consents.

> *Example:* Polly hides the microphone in a flower vase, but this time she has lunch with Tony and Gus and is part of their conversation. Here Polly might not have violated the law.

Be careful here! Some states—California, Connecticut, Florida, Illinois, Maryland, Massachusetts, Michigan, Montana, New Hampshire, Pennsylvania, and Washington—require *all the parties to consent* to having their conversations recorded.

> *Example:* Polly has lunch with Gus and Tony in a secluded luncheonette in Missoula, Montana. Unless she gets their permission to record the conversation, she may be violating Montana law—even though she would probably not be violating federal law.

LIBEL AND DEFAMATION

DEFAMATION DEFINED

There are two forms of *defamation:* slander and libel. *Slander* is the spoken form of defamation, and *libel* is a written, televised, or otherwise recorded form.

To be able to sue for defamation, the following elements must be present:

- A false and defamatory statement concerning another
- An unprivileged publication of that statement to a third party
- Fault amounting to at least negligence on the part of the publisher (fault amounting to "actual malice" in the case of a public figure; see Appendix A, "Public Figures," p. 361)
- Harm caused by the publication, or presumed harm because the statement falls within a special class of defamatory statements known as *defamation per se*[65]

IP

A film that contains false statements damaging to someone's reputation may expose the producer to claims of libel and defamation.

Defamatory Statement

A *defamatory statement* is one that is both false[66] and that tends to "harm the reputation of another as to lower him in the estimation of the community or to deter third persons from associating or dealing with him."[67] Usually statements that are "merely unflattering, annoying, irksome, or embarrassing, or that hurt only the plaintiff's feelings"[68] do not support a defamation claim, nor does humor or parody.

Some kinds of defamatory statements are considered especially harmful. Examples include:

- Accusations that the plaintiff has committed a crime.
- Statements that hurt the plaintiff's business reputation.
- Allegations that the plaintiff has a "loathsome disease."
- Accusations that the plaintiff has engaged in sexual misconduct.

Statements "of or Concerning Another"

To sue somebody for libel, a plaintiff must prove that the libelous statement was aimed at herself. The test, known as the *of or concerning another* test, looks to whether a reasonable person would assume the statement was made about or concerned the plaintiff.

> **Example:** A documentary film alleges that Provincetown pharmacist Robert Martin poisoned all his customers by filling prescriptions while he was drunk. If the allegations were false, any Provincetown pharmacist named Robert Martin could successfully sue the film company. However, it would be unlikely that a San Francisco pharmacist with the same name would win such a suit.

Defamation in Narrative Films

Although most people associate motion picture defamation with documentaries, narrative films can create problems for filmmakers as well. It may seem surprising that a work of fiction can give rise to a defamation claim—after all, unlike in a documentary, the author is not trying to say that the story is real. Trouble usually occurs when a filmmaker fictionalizes an actual person's life or creates a character that closely resembles an actual person. When faced with such a claim, a court may satisfy the "of or concerning another" test by asking whether a reasonable person seeing the film would understand that the fictional character was, in actual fact, the plaintiff acting as described.[69]

To establish a connection between the fictional character and the real person of the plaintiff, a court may compare a host of characteristics, such as the names, backgrounds, physical characteristics, ethnic backgrounds, personalities, and ages of

IP

the plaintiff and the character. A court may place emphasis on whether the filmmaker or author knew and had a relationship with the plaintiff. A disclaimer stating that the film is a work of fiction and is not intended to represent actual persons may be given weight by the court but is not conclusive.[70]

Producers take heart: In cases involving fictional characters, similarity of names between fictional characters and real people, by itself, is usually not enough to transform coincidence into defamation.

Publication of Defamatory Statement

For a statement to defame someone, the statement must be *published* to a third party. "Published" does not mean printed in a book, nor does "published" have the same meaning as it does under copyright law ("the distribution of copies of a work to the public by sale"). For a defamatory statement to be published, it must be seen, heard, read, and so forth by someone other than the person being defamed.

> *Example:* Franco Filmmaker videotapes himself saying, "Barney Banker steals from the cash drawer at the First National Bank to fund his Hummel porcelain box collection." The allegation is false and defamatory. Franco shows the tape only to Barney. Even though it is upsetting, Barney has not been defamed. But the moment Franco shows the tape to another person, Barney can sue for defamation.

Republication

If a defamatory statement is published again after its initial publication, it is considered *republished*. Generally, republishers may be sued for defamation as well. Filmmakers must be very cautious here! An interview in which a subject defames someone on camera may create republication liability when it is broadcast, when it is screened in theaters, and when it is reproduced on a DVD. Because the filmmaker has indemnified the broadcaster, exhibitor, and DVD manufacturer, those parties' legal claims and expenses will be passed on to the filmmaker.

There are exceptions to this rule of republication liability, but it is best to nip the problems in the bud by avoiding libel publication altogether.

PUBLIC FIGURES

A public figure is a politician, celebrity, or other individual who has voluntarily placed himself in the midst of a public controversy. Public figures have a much more difficult time proving defamation. To prove defamation, public figures must show that the alleged defamatory statement was made with *actual malice*.

Actual Malice

In the context of defamation, *actual malice* is the knowledge that the statement was false or was made with a reckless disregard for its truth.

IP

Example: Polly Producer shoots a "tell all" television documentary alleging rock singer Opie Um's decline into drug abuse. The program shows Opie's police record: He was arrested once for carrying a small amount of marijuana, and his friends give interviews saying that he routinely went on benders. The program's voice-over uses phrases like "Opie slid into the dark depths of drug abuse and despair" and "There was a monkey on his back—a monkey named Addiction!"

Opie sues Polly for defamation. He produces evidence that the marijuana bust was the first and last time he ever used illegal drugs and that he was far from an addict. He proves that the "benders" his friends referred to were actually stories cooked up by his agent to cover up the fact that he was in South America doing missionary work—a fact that would hurt his public image with his hard-rockin' fans. In short, Opie demonstrates that the statements made in the documentary were false.

Will Opie automatically win his suit? Not necessarily. Because he is a public figure, Opie will still have to show that the statements were made with knowledge that they were false or that they were made with a reckless disregard for the truth. This may be tough, considering the producer relied on police records of a drug arrest and interviews with Opie's friends.

DEFENSES TO DEFAMATION

There are a number of possible defenses to a charge of defamation:

- *Truth.* The most basic defense to defamation is truth. No matter how scandalous or injurious to a person's reputation a statement may be, it will not be considered defamatory if it is true.

  Example: Freddy Filmmaker shoots a documentary film titled *Prostitutes and the Policemen Who Love Them*, which features interviews with prostitutes naming the cops with whom they have had sexual congress. Sergeant Lou Scivious, named in the film, sues Freddy for libel. At trial, Freddy shows footage of Officer Scivious handing money to and entering a hotel room with the call girl in question. Freddy produces evidence showing that Officer Scivious was not engaged in an undercover vice operation targeting prostitution. The court will most likely find that the film's statements about the officer were true, and therefore Freddy will not be liable for libel.

- *Consent.* If someone consents to the publication of a defamatory statement, he will not be able to bring a claim for defamation. *This is why any time you film, videotape, or photograph somebody, you should get them to waive all claims of defamation.*

IP

Example: Freddy Filmmaker shoots an interview with Dusty Rinkle, the owner of a retirement home under state investigation. Prior to the interview, Rinkle signs an interview release form in which he waives the right to sue for defamation. The final film intercuts footage of Rinkle discussing the benefits of his retirement home with cartoons showing Rinkle burying little old ladies alive. If Rinkle sues, Freddy Filmmaker might win with a defense that Rinkle consented and waived his right to sue for defamation.

- *Humor or parody.* Humor and parody are generally protected by the First Amendment and are considered a form of protected opinion (see the "Opinion" bullet). There is no libel when the material is clearly understood as parody, satire, humor, or fantasy and is not capable of a defamatory meaning.[71]

    Example: Saturday Night Live does a sketch comedy routine about Gus Grimes, insinuating that he is a crook. Because this is a well-known humor and satire program, the skit will probably not be considered defamatory.

- *Privilege.* Certain types of communications, such as judicial and legislative proceedings, are considered privileged and therefore immune from claims of defamation.

    Example: Freddy Filmmaker films Congressional hearings in which Congressman Abe O'Lition accuses a tobacco industry lobbyist of having a second job of selling crack cocaine to children. The lobbyist sues the filmmaker. The filmmaker may successfully defend himself by the virtue of the fact that the statement was made during the course of a legislative proceeding.

- *Opinion.* Statements that reflect a point of view, or opinion, rather than specific allegations of fact are not considered defamatory. Also insulated from libel and slander are "vigorous epithets," "rhetorical hyperbole," "loose, figurative language," or "lusty and imaginative expressions."[72]

    Example: Freddy Filmmaker shoots a documentary about the history of New York pizza. In an interview with famous French chef, S. Cargo, the gourmet badmouths the owner of Pete's Za, a popular New York pizzeria. Cargo says: "Pete's pizza is the worst I've ever tasted. If you looked up the word 'disgusting' in the dictionary, you would find a picture of Pete. The man's an idiot!" Pete sues Freddy Filmmaker and Cargo for libel. The court will most likely find that Cargo's statements are opinion and, therefore, not actionable as libel.

Be careful here! Merely calling something an opinion does not insulate you from defamation. Whether a statement counts as an opinion depends on whether it is verifiable In other words, can the statement be proven true or false? The statement, "In my opinion, Pete Za lied when he testified under oath," if false, may be defamatory, notwithstanding the use of the word "opinion," because it accuses Mr. Za of the crime of perjury, and whether he lied might be proven true or false.

In determining whether a statement is an opinion and therefore not defamatory, a court will take a look at the context in which the statement was made and the customary way in which the words used in the statement are typically uttered. The court may apply a "totality of circumstances" test to determine whether the

IP

statement is fact or opinion. This test will take into account (1) the specific language used; (2) whether the statement is verifiable; (3) the general context of the statement; and (4) the broader context in which the statement appeared.[74]

Examples of statements found to be opinion:

- Union officials are "willing to sacrifice the interests of the members of their union to further their own political aspirations and personal ambitions."[75]
- An attorney was a "very poor lawyer."[76]
- A university vice president was the "Director of Butt Licking."[77]

- *Fair comment.* In matters of public interest, many states require that a reputation-damaging false statement be made with certain amount of malice before it can be considered libel. However, this privilege does not extend to material that defames another and is not reasonably necessary to the development of the subject matter of the film.

  Example: Jacob shoots a news story about a small dinner theater company's failure to pay the salaries it owes to its cast. He mistakenly says that dinner theater manager is "holding out" on the cast. In fact, the manager is withholding the money because the cast failed to show up for two shows, costing the theater money. The manager sues Jacob for defamation, claiming that the news story is one-sided. Since the story involves the public interest, if he can prove that he didn't shoot the story maliciously, Jacob may assert a fair comment defense.[73]

BOTTOM LINE: It may be counterintuitive, but the more inflammatory and hyperbolic a statement, the more likely a court will find it to be opinion and not defamatory language. So instead of saying, "Pete Za cheats on his taxes," you may be better off saying "Pete Za would cheat an orphan out of her last dime."

MATTERS OF PUBLIC CONCERN: GROSS IRRESPONSIBILITY TEST

Thanks to the First Amendment, matters of public concern are given greater leeway.

In New York, if the allegedly defamatory material is of public concern, the allegedly defamed person will have to show that a television news reporter, for example, acted with *gross irresponsibility* with regard to the accuracy of his or her reporting. Said one court:

Under this 'gross irresponsibility' standard, if an article is 'arguably within the sphere of legitimate public concern' or 'reasonably related to matters warranting public exposition,' the party allegedly defamed can recover only by establishing, by a preponderance of the evidence, that 'the publisher acted in a grossly irresponsible manner without due consideration for the standards of information gathering and dissemination ordinarily followed by responsible parties.[78]

IP

In determining gross irresponsibility, courts look to whether the producer:

- Followed "sound journalistic practices" in preparing the allegedly defamatory piece
- Followed "normal procedures," including editorial review of the piece
- Had any reason to doubt the accuracy of the source relied on and thus had a duty to make further inquiry to verify the information
- Could have easily verified the truth[79]

SPECIAL RULES REGARDING DEFAMATION

- You can't defame a dead person.
- "Defamatory statements" are not limited to words alone. Pictures, videos, and film may also contain defamatory material.
- A filmmaker can be held liable for defamation even if she did not intend to defame somebody. The only intent that is required is the intent to publish a particular statement.
- Defamation requires publication: the unprivileged dissemination of the statement to a third party. In other words, an otherwise defamatory statement made only to the person it allegedly defames is not defamation. However, for filmmakers, a motion picture containing defamatory statements shown or distributed to the public would be considered "published."
- The liability for defamation extends beyond the initial publisher. Even parties who disseminate the defamatory material can be held liable if they should have known of the defamatory content.
- Corporations may also sue for defamation when a film's false statements prejudice it in the eyes of the business community by accusing it of criminal business practices, dishonest conduct, or lack of integrity.
- Defamation law differs from state to state. Massachusetts, for instance, recently recognized an exception to the rule "truth is an absolute defense to libel." A federal court recently held that statements that are reputation-damaging but *true* can still give rise to a libel claim if they are made with "actual malice" (ill-will or malevolent intent). Although many attorneys, including yours truly, consider this a bad decision that flies in the face of years of contrary legal precedent, it is still the law… in Massachusetts.[80] However, federal constitutional law—primarily judicial interpretations of the First Amendment—sets limits to state defamation law.
- In general, a producer has greater leeway regarding the kinds of statements she may publish when the statements concern a public figure such as a politician or actor than when they concern somebody who is not in the public eye.
- Many states have *retraction laws* that allow the defaming party to retract her statements within a certain time period. If the statement is retracted, the defendant will be liable for fewer damages should she ultimately lose her case.

IP

- Groups of under 25 people can be libeled, and if so, they can each sue! For example, if you say "Lawyers are all thieves," that's not libel. But if you say "All the lawyers living in Kalawao County, Hawaii, are crooks," you may be open to a libel claim. At 13 square miles, Kalawao County is the United States' smallest county and probably has fewer than 25 attorneys (one would hope).

MORAL RIGHTS

Moral rights, sometimes referred to by the French name *droit moral,* are a collection of rights that allow the author of a work to have a say in how that work is used and whether it can be changed in any way.

Moral rights may include:

- The author's right to be credited for the film or to refuse to be credited
- The right of an author to prevent the film from being changed or altered in any way without the author's permission
- The author's right to determine how the film is shown
- The author's right to receive royalties from the film
- The author's right to stop the film from being exploited in any way that damages the author's reputation

In general, U.S. laws do not protect moral rights in and of themselves. They leave these sorts of protections to a combination of copyright, trademark, and unfair competition law. Other countries, notably France and other European countries, do protect moral rights; as a result, moral rights issues may come into play when the film is distributed in other countries.

Although moral rights generally cannot be transferred from one party to another, they may usually be waived (given up). To be on the safe side, production companies should include a clause that requires all writers, directors, actors, and other artists to waive their moral rights in their films.

A FILMMAKER'S GUIDE TO CONTRACT LAW

In this section you will learn the basics of contract law. Topics include:

- What is a contract? (p. 368)
- The elements of a valid contract (p. 368)
- Express and implied contracts (p. 371)
- Breach of contract (p. 371)
- Remedies for breach of contract (p. 372)

CONTRACT LAW: AN OVERVIEW

THE SCRIPT OF THE DEAL

A contract is a portrait of a transaction—the *script* of the deal. It is a legally enforceable agreement that spells out the rights and obligations of each contracting party.

- If one party breaches the contract, the other party may sue for *damages*, usually money. (See "Breach of Contract," p. 371.)
- If money is not sufficient compensation, *equitable remedies* may apply, such as injunctions, which are court orders compelling a party to do something or refrain from doing something. (See Appendix C, "No Injunction," p. 387.)

In the film industry, the subject of many contracts—the things being bought, sold, licensed, and protected—are intellectual property rights, such as the copyright to the film and the means of producing it (i.e., labor, materials, rentals, etc.).

> **LEVERAGE**
>
> *Leverage* is the amount of bargaining power a party has in a deal.
>
> ***Example:*** Amy Actress has won three Emmys® and an Oscar®, whereas Peter Producer is making his first feature film straight out of film school. Amy has the leverage over Peter in any deal they might try to make. As a result, Amy will probably be able to structure her actor's services contract in terms most favorable to her. She who has the leverage controls the deal.

WHAT IS A CONTRACT?

A contract is an agreement that a court will enforce. Not all agreements are contracts, and not all agreements are enforceable. In your filmmaking, you should have at least a rough idea of what constitutes a contract. Here are some examples:

- Producer says to Writer, "I'm going to try to make your movie." Writer cannot claim there is a contract at this point. There are no terms and no definite obligation on Producer's part.
- Rich Uncle says to Producer: "I'm going to give you $10 million to make your film. No strings attached." Wonderful news, but if Uncle reneges a couple of days later, Producer can't make him cough up the money. Promises to make a gift are generally not enforceable.
- Even if the parties are agreed on the key terms, if they are still negotiating there is likely no contract.[1]

THE ELEMENTS OF A VALID CONTRACT

If an agreement does not contain certain elements, it is not a valid contract and a court will not uphold or enforce it. So be careful—unless your agreement contains all the following elements, you might not have a contract! You need:

- An *offer* that is *accepted*.
- *Terms* that are definite and specific, not vague or ambiguous.
- *Consideration*—something that each party gives or gets for entering into the contract.
- *Legal capacity*—each party must be competent to enter into a contract.
- *Legal purpose*—a contract to do something illegal is no contract at all.

Here are examples of problems that can arise with each of these elements.

Offer and Acceptance

> *Example:* Freddy Filmmaker says he'll give Sammy Cinematographer $2,500 a week to shoot his film. That's an *offer*.

In an e-mail, Sammy writes back: "I'll do it for $3,000 a week." That's *not* an acceptance! It's actually a *counteroffer*.

Freddy does not respond to Sammy but hires Shelby Shooter instead. Sammy shows up on set and says, "I accept your offer of $2,500 a week—we now have a contract!"

Freddy rightly points out that Sammy's response, "I'll do it for $3,000 a week," was a counteroffer, which Freddy did not accept. He smiles smugly as two grips politely escort Sammy off the set.

LEGAL POINTS

- An *offer* is a promise to do something or to refrain from doing something in exchange for something of value.

- A *contract* is formed only when the offer is accepted.

- If an offer is *withdrawn* prior to its acceptance, acceptance of that offer will not form a contract unless the offer is made again.

- An acceptance of an offer that *changes* or *modifies* the original offer is actually a *counteroffer*.

Definiteness

Example: Freddy Filmmaker hires bestselling novelist Sara Scrivener to write a screenplay. In her screenplay services contract, Scrivener has stipulated that the "screenplay length, subject matter, and date of delivery are all at Sara Scrivener's discretion and subject to change at any time without notice." A court is likely to find Scrivener's obligations too vague, and the contract unenforceable.

LEGAL POINTS

- Key and material terms to the contract must not be vague.

- The obligations of each party must be definite and determinable. For instance, if one party retains an unlimited right to decide how and what constitutes performance of his contractual duties, the contract may not be enforceable.

Consideration

Consideration does not mean being nice to the person you're doing business with (although that almost always helps). In contract language, consideration is a thing of value that is bargained for. It can take the form of money, rights, or even a promise to refrain from doing something. A good way to think of consideration is, "What am I getting if I do this deal? And what do I have to give up or pay to get it?"

Example: Freddy Filmmaker offers Andrea Actress $3,500 a week to be in his film. Andrea's acting services are the consideration for Freddy's promise to pay her. The $3,500 a week is the consideration for Andrea's promise to perform as an actress on the film.

LEGAL POINTS

- Consideration is a requirement for all parties to a contract.

- In some states, it is acceptable in certain contracts to merely state that there is consideration for the contract—for example, as seen in the phrase "for good and valuable consideration, the receipt and sufficiency of which is hereby acknowledged."

Capacity

Example: Freddy Filmmaker corners Duncan Director at his favorite watering hole, the Teamster Tavern. Eager to sign the auteur to his new film, Freddy plies Duncan with one Appletini after another. Right before the drunken director's head hits the bar, Freddy pushes a director's services contract in front of him.

CONTR.

Duncan signs with a flourish—and passes out. Because he was intoxicated when he signed the contract, the court will not enforce it.

LEGAL POINTS

- To create a valid contract, you must have the legal capacity to do so. For instance, the signature of a minor, a mentally incapacitated individual, or a drunk may not create a binding contract.

- In each of these instances, you might need to secure the signature of their guardians, or if they're drunk, wait for them to sober up.

- Producers need to be careful here, since minors may void contracts—in other words, they can get out of a contract they signed as a minor. In some states, court procedures may be required to ratify a minor's contract so that the minor cannot void the contract. (See "Child Labor Laws," p. 400.)

Legal Purpose

Contracts to perform illegal acts are not valid.

> *Example:* Tony Soprano's contracts would not be enforceable in court, although he would probably have other ways of enforcing them.

WRITTEN AND ORAL CONTRACTS

Samuel Goldwyn supposedly once said, "An oral contract isn't worth the paper it's written on." Goldwyn's advice should be taken to heart as a sound business practice.

Technically, some contracts do not have to be written to be enforced. However, most of the contracts that producers deal with routinely *are* required to be in writing, because they deal with the transfer of copyright and intellectual property ownership.

- Any transfer of copyright ownership needs to be in writing and signed by the copyright owner.

- Additionally, if the contract cannot be performed within one year, it needs to be written to be valid.

(See Appendix A, "Licensing and Assigning the Copyright," p. 348.)

I have given the elements of a contract a brief treatment here, not because they are unimportant but because most contractual problems that filmmakers run into occur because the contract is valid ... and somebody has not met his or her obligations under the agreement.

Problems typically arise when a filmmaker or other contracting party:

- Didn't include provisions in the contract to deal with whatever circumstance has arisen and is now causing problems.

CONTR.

- Doesn't understand the provisions of a valid contract or disagrees on the meaning of those provisions.
- Ignores duties and obligations they are required by the contract to perform.

EXPRESS AND IMPLIED CONTRACTS

As a filmmaker, you'll be faced with two types of contract. The two flavors are the *express contract* and the *implied contract*. The second is the one that really causes unexpected problems.

EXAMPLES:

- Wanda Writer negotiates an option/purchase agreement with Penelope Producer for Wanda's script *Beige, the New Black*. Because the major deal terms are agreed on, the option/purchase agreement is an *express contract*.
- Penelope Producer asks Garry the Grip what his day rate is. Garry tells her, "$350." Penelope then says to Garry: "Hey, if you want to work on my film, come by the set tomorrow." Garry shows up and works a full day. At the end of the day, she hands him a check for $20 instead of the $350 he expects. She says, "Hey, I never said you'd get your day rate. I just asked you what it was." If Garry sues for breach of contact, a court would most likely find Penelope had an *implied contract* to pay Garry his day rate.

LEGAL POINTS

- An *express contract* is one in which all the elements of a contract (offer, acceptance, consideration, etc.) are specifically stated. An express contract is usually, but not always, in writing.
- An *implied contract* is an agreement that arises based on circumstances or by the actions or behavior of the parties. In other words, the contract may be created because the parties are acting as though a contract is in place, even though the terms of the agreement were not expressly discussed.

BREACH OF CONTRACT: TYPES OF BREACHES

Performance is the successful fulfillment of a contractual duty. If a party to a contract fails to perform his duties under that contract, he may have *breached the contract*.

There are two main kinds of breaches: *minor* and *material*.

A Minor Breach

A *minor breach* occurs when the damage to the aggrieved party is, well, minor. No surprise there. In the case of a minor breach, the contact still stands and the non-breaching party must still perform.

CONTR.

Example: A laboratory that is contractually obligated to deliver an answer print to a producer by noon delivers that film at 1:00 p.m. If the contract does not stipulate that "time is of the essence," the breach may be considered a minor one.

Remedy for Minor Breaches

The breaching party must remedy the particular breach and compensate the aggrieved party for any damages. For a minor breach, the aggrieved party, however, is not relieved of her duties under the contract.

Example: In the previous scenario, the laboratory that was late in delivering the film must pay any expenses resulting from the one-hour delay. However, the producer must still pay the laboratory the agreed-on fee (perhaps minus costs that the producer incurred as a result of the laboratory's delay).

A Material Breach

Unlike the minor breach, a *material breach* substantially affects the benefit the aggrieved party expected to receive from the contract. If there has been a material breach, the damaged party may consider the contract terminated, with no further obligation on their part to perform the duties they were obligated to perform. Furthermore, the damaged party may pursue contract remedies in court.

Example: In the previous scenario, if the film laboratory failed to deliver the answer print within a reasonable time, a court would likely find that a major breach of the contract had occurred. Other examples of major breaches might be an actor failing to show up for production as per her obligation under her performer's services contract, or a production company failing to pay a salary as per its obligation under a director's services contract.

REMEDIES FOR BREACH OF CONTRACT

A party that has been hurt because the other party to the contract has breached that contract may sue for *breach of contract*. The chief remedy for a breach of contract is the award of monetary *damages*. The primary kinds of damages awarded for breach of contract are *compensatory* and *consequential*.

Compensatory damages compensate the hurt party by paying her an amount of money that will:

- Put her in the position that she would have been in had the contract been performed as expected, or
- Put her in the position she would have been in if she had never entered into the contract in the first place (in other words, a repayment for any of the expenses she has incurred as a result of relying upon the contract).

Consequential damages compensate the damaged party for the reasonably foreseeable losses that occurred as a result of—as a *consequence* of—the breach.

Example: In the previous scenario, the reasonably foreseeable damages for the laboratory failing to deliver an answer print in a timely fashion might be the cost of booking a theater, if one had been booked. However, for consequential damages to be awarded, both parties must have been aware of the theater booking at the time that the laboratory contract is made.

IMPORTANT TIP: **Regardless of the specific duties and obligations of either party, keep in mind that there is an implied condition in *every* contract that the parties will behave in good faith toward each other.**

REMEDIES FOR BREACH OF EMPLOYMENT CONTRACTS

If the *employer* breaches an employment contract with its employee, the damages may be the full contract price.

If the *employee* breaches an employment contract, the damages may be the employer's cost to replace the employee. The employee may have a right to deduct from the damages owed to the employer the amount of money owed to the employee up to the date of the breach.

Example: Andy Actor goes on a drug-fueled bender and fails to show up on set for an entire week. As per Andy's contract (see "Performer's Services Agreement," p. 212), Paula Producer sends notice of default to Andy's agent. Andy still fails to show up, and the default is not cured. Rather than cancel the shoot and lose thousands of dollars, Paula Producer hires the only other available actor of Andy's caliber, David Drama. Unfortunately, David's fee quote is 10% higher than Andy's. When Paula sues Andy for breach of contract she may be able to recover the entire cost of hiring David, minus any moneys that Andy had earned to date.

In addition to damages, an aggrieved party may also be able to obtain injunctive relief. An *injunction* is a court order commanding something to be done.

Injunctions can also prevent something from being done. For example, a court can issue an injunction that compels a writer to transfer a copyright or that prevents a film from being distributed.

For employment and other service contracts, an injunction may not be used to force the employee who has breached the contract to continue to work for the employer. However, an injunction can be used to prevent the breaching employee from working for other employers during the term of the breached contract.

Example: For instance, in the earlier example, Paula Producer may seek an injunction against Andy Actor working on another film during the term of his contract with Paula. Paula may not, however, get an injunction that compels Andy to continue to work on her film.

Note: The damaged party has a duty to *mitigate* damages, which means that he must make an effort to keep down or reduce the amount of his losses.

Also note: Contract breaches, like most legal issues in this book, are incredibly nuanced and complex matters. If you are involved in a breach of contract or other litigation, seek the advice of an attorney.

THE CLAUSE COMPANION

We've taken a look at the issues that shape a contract. Now it's time to take a brief look at the contract clauses that address those issues.

A *deal point* is any major or important term in a contract. It may be helpful to think of a contract as having both *major deal points* and *supporting deal points.*

Major deal points are those issues that everyone must agree on or there is no point in negotiating the rest of the contract. These major deal points are usually the points the producer negotiates first.

Supporting deal points are those issues that shore up and protect the rights of the parties and lay out the rules of the business relationship. These supporting points are usually left to the lawyers to hash out. In the interest of space, this book will not go into great detail on the supplemental deal points of each contract. But make no mistake—you will need clauses that cover *both* main and supporting deal points in your final contacts.

The sequence of clauses in a contract is not fixed in stone: You may see supporting provisions mixed in with major deal points. Some contracts will have all the clauses shown in this book, other contracts only a few. Here the clauses are presented alphabetically for ease of reference.

TIP: You may want to bookmark this section.

MAJOR DEAL POINTS

These points should be negotiated and agreed on before the contracts are drafted. Examples of these points include compensation, kinds of rights being granted, term and duration, and creative control.

Approval

How will creative differences be resolved? For instance, who has final say over the final cut, hiring of key or cast or crew, or script changes? There are several different ways to create a mechanism for resolving creative differences:

- *Unilateral approval.* One party must approve the decision. This power is usually given to the producer or production company executive, and, unless the director is also the rights holder, this is the most common method of resolving differences.

- *Consultation.* This is generally toothless, as the party consulted does not have final say but only a right to "consult" with the decision makers.

- *Mutual approval.* Both parties must approve the decision; if there is no tiebreaker provision, it is difficult to resolve differences with this method.

- *Mutual approval with third-party tiebreaker.* Both parties must agree; if they can't agree, a predesignated third person decides which party prevails.

- *Mutual approval with one-party tiebreaker over certain types of decisions.* Mutual approval with one party (e.g., the director) having final say over creative decisions. The director's power is limited by the restriction that a tiebreaker decision in her favor cannot cause production budget overages.

The production company should designate particular persons (such as the producer and the executive producer) who are the sole representatives responsible for authorizing approval on behalf of the production company.

Compensation

This is obviously a critical section, since it specifies how people get paid. It is usually the most heavily negotiated section of any contract. It is often broken down into subsections that deal with types of payment, such as contingent compensation, deferred compensation, fixed compensation, residuals, bonuses, and so forth. Common forms of compensation include:

- *Fixed compensation.* This is the money the party will be paid regardless of whether the movie makes any money or even makes it into the can. It is the only money the party can actually count on.

- *Contingent compensation.* This is the money that a party will receive if the film is made and sold. Contingent compensation comes in many "flavors": deferred compensation, profit participation, residuals, and royalties. Bonuses can be contingent as well.

  - *Deferred compensation.* This is a fixed sum paid out when the film production company repays the costs of making the film, after it has received the Film's Net Profits from the distribution company. (See Appendix C, "Deferred Compensation," p. 377.)

  - *Profit participation.* This is money received from the Film's Net Profits. The definition of what constitutes net profits may be a closely negotiated issue. (See Appendix C, "Net Profits," p. 379.)

  - *Residuals.* These are fees payable to a performer when the motion picture is televised, broadcast, and so forth. Union contracts will set the minimum rate for these as well. On a nonunion production, companies often have the actors waive these fees.

  - *Royalties.* These are monies paid to a party when the film property is exploited in other media. For instance, a writer may receive royalties from the license of the film property to a video game company.

- *Bonus.* This is money paid to a party if a certain goal is reached, such as a script being filmed or box-office receipts reaching a specified target.

Audit and *accounting provisions* should always be included in any contract where one of the parties receives a net profit or other contingent compensation. (See Appendix C, "Audit and Accounting Provision," p. 383.)

Conditions Precedent

Requirements that must be satisfied, like the occurrence of an act or event, prior to a duty to perform arises. If the condition is not met, the promise by the other party does not have to be fulfilled.

> **Example:** Natali's performer's services agreement has as a condition precedent the requirement that she must pass a drug test on the first day of principal photography. If she fails the test, despite the existence of a pay-or-play agreement, the producers are not obligated to pay her and can treat her contract as though the contract had never been formed (subject, perhaps, to payment for any services she rendered prior to failing her drug test). (See "Pay or Play," p. 380.)

Credits

How credit is determined and the form it takes are integral parts of every film contract. This clause usually details when credit must be given; for instance, is the production company required to credit the party in just the film and its copies, or must the party's credit also appear in all paid advertisements for the film?

This clause may also specify the order in which the credit must appear and how large the credit must be in relation to the other credits. Production companies that are signatories to a union agreement, such as SAG's or the WGA's, need to make sure that they are complying with that union's crediting regulations.

Filmmakers should make sure that this clause prevents a party from suing them if there are any mistakes with the credits. The clause should expressly state that any failure of the credit provision is not a breach of the contract. The clause should also limit the injured party's sole remedy for a failure to provide credit on the film to a promise from the production company to correct the credits on future copies of the film.

Deferred Compensation

Many independent filmmakers attempt to save money for the production by deferring a portion of a worker's compensation. To quote Popeye's friend Wimpy, deferred compensation is like saying, "I'll gladly pay you Tuesday for a hamburger today." And just like Wimpy's hamburger IOU, deferred compensation may never be paid; it requires the film to be distributed and the production company to receive the Film's Net Profits prior to the compensation becoming due. (See

CONTR.

Appendix C, "Net Profits," p. 379.) There is no guarantee that all the deferred compensation will be paid out to the worker; after all, the film might not make *any* money at all.

When the deferred compensation is to be paid is also the subject of negotiation, and the priority of payment will be driven by a production company's prior obligations to its investors. Deferred compensation may be paid out from the first dollar into the production company from the Film's Net Profits, or, alternatively, once the investors have recouped a certain amount over their investment; it all depends on the production company's deferred compensation definition. Accordingly, if a large percentage of a worker's fee is deferred, that worker may feel entitled to a higher overall salary to offset the risk of not recouping his or her fee.

Engagement

This clause occurs in every *services* contract. A services contract is a contract in which somebody is hired or commissioned to do something, such as perform in a film or write a screenplay. The Engagement clause lists the specific duties required of the party being hired and how those duties must be accomplished. You might want to draft the Engagement clause in general terms, such as:

> Ari Flecks agrees to provide the services of camera operator and such other services as are customarily provided on first-class features films produced in the United States. In addition, Mr. Flecks agrees to perform those duties specifically listed in Rider A to this contract, if one is attached, and any other duties Production Company may reasonably require from time to time during Mr. Fleck's engagement.

Be sure to state any additional or unusual duties on a separate rider. For instance, if you need your camera operator to pick up the rest of the crew in the production van every morning, you should state this in the rider to avoid any confusion over job duties.

The Engagement clause usually contains the *term* of the agreement. The term provides the time periods during which the writer, director, performer, crew members, and so on are obligated to provide their services to the production company.

Favored Nations

A *Favored Nations* clause says that no other party can receive a better deal or a more advantageous position than the person who has favored nations status. The clause is tied to a particular deal point, such as compensation or credits.

For instance, if a production company grants a favored nations provision to a supporting actor with regard to his compensation, it will have to pay that supporting actor the same rate that it pays the principal actors, who presumably make more money.

Holdback Provisions

Reserved rights are often subject to holdback provisions. A *holdback provision* requires a copyright or other rights owner to refrain from licensing certain rights for a limited period of time.

For example, as mentioned earlier, although production companies typically try to acquire the greatest number and scope of rights from a screenwriter, the screenwriter very often reserves certain rights for herself, such as the right to turn the screenplay into a play for the theater. To ensure that the screenwriter does not execute her reserved rights in a manner that competes with the motion picture, the screenwriter's reserved rights are typically subject to a *holdback* period, which prevents the screenwriter from exploiting those rights for a certain number of years.

Key Person or Key Man Clause

Despite both the importance and prevalence of women in the film and television industry, this clause is often still referred to as a *Key Man clause*. It designates one or more people as essential to the production, such that their absence from the project is either a breach of contract or allows the deal to be terminated by the other side.

> **Example:** Shady Studios enters into a production services agreement with Poultice Productions in which Poultice will produce a 13-part medical documentary on the history of the use of leeches in medicine. Because Poultice producer Larry Lancet is known for his award-winning programming, Shady makes sure that Lancet is subject to a key man provision in the production services agreement. If Lancet quits the production, Shady Studios may void the contract or sue for breach, depending on the terms of the Key Man clause.

Kill Fee

Often a percentage of the full salary, a *kill fee* is a payment given to an employee (such as an actor, director, producer, etc.) if the project is cancelled in lieu of the money they would have made had the project gone forward. Once the kill fee is paid, the production company generally has no other obligations to pay the ex-employee. Kill fees are often offered as counterproposals to an actor or director seeking a pay-or-play deal. (See "Pay or Play," p. 380.)

> **Example:** Burt Breathless, last decade's Hollywood-hunk-o'-the-month, has been offered the part of Wedgewood the werewolf-mummy in *Moon Me*. He wants a pay-or-play deal, which would obligate the producers to pay his full salary even if the film doesn't go into production. The producers counter with an offer to pay Burt a kill fee of 10% of his negotiated salary if the film doesn't shoot.

Net Profits

For nonstudio-funded films, the *Film's Net Profits* are the monies that are given to the production company after the distributors have deducted their expenses and

CONTR.

have been paid their distribution fees. (See "Traditional Distribution," p. 289.) This is also the level at which investors and other net profit participants usually take their cuts. By contrast, the *Production Company's Net Profits* are what are left over after the production company has paid its investors, the profit participants (those people sharing in the net profits), deferred salaries, and other the costs of making and promoting the film. *Audit* and *accounting provisions* should always be included in any contract in which one of the parties receives a net profit or other contingent compensation. (See Appendix C, "Audit and Accounting Provision," p. 383.)

For an overview of the subject, see "Net Profits" (p. 379) and "The Money Pipeline" (p. 291).

Option on Future Services

If the film is successful, the production company may want the option to hire the same actor, director, cinematographer, or producer again at a salary rate they can lock in now. The employee will usually require any future service obligations to be subject to her "professional availability" and will try to negotiate a step-up in payment or the ability to negotiate in good faith for an increase in pay when the option is exercised. It is always better from the production company's point of view to negotiate and agree on future compensation rates, since a failure to do so may result in a "worthless option." (See "Screenplay Option/Purchase," p. 102.)

Parties

Every contract starts by listing who is bound by its terms. These are the *parties* to a contract. A party could be a person or a company. One special type of company, called a *loan-out company*, provides the services of a particular person, such as an actor or director, to work on a film. (See "Loan-Out Companies," p. 42.)

Make sure that your contracts include the proper spelling of the parties' names. For instance, if you are contracting with FilmCo., LLC, make sure that goes in the contract, not "FilmCo., *Inc.*" or just "FilmCo." Remember too that a contract can have more than two parties.

Make sure to get full contact information, including Social Security numbers for individuals and federal ID numbers for companies—these will be necessary when you're handling payroll and other taxes. Also include contact information about the parties' attorneys or agents, if they have them.

Pay or Play

The *Pay or Play* clause obligates the production company to pay the artist, actor, director, or crew member a certain sum regardless of whether their services are actually used. This clause is usually coupled with a *No Obligation to Produce* clause (see later).

CONTR.

Representations and Warranties

Representations and warranties are statements of fact and promises one party makes to another with the intention that the other party will rely on them. For instance, in a contract that transfers copyright from a screenwriter to a producer, one of the representations and warranties the screenwriter makes is that she has not infringed on anybody else's rights while creating the screenplay. For example, the writer promises that the screenplay is wholly original with her and that making it into a movie will not expose the production company to any claims of copyright infringement. (Representations and warranties for specific agreements can be found in the chapters that outline those contracts.)

The representations and warranties are usually coupled with an *Indemnification* clause so that a party who has misrepresented something must pay the other party's damages that stem from the misrepresentation.

Reserved Rights

The *reserved rights* are those rights that are *not* being granted under the agreement. For example, when granting the rights to a screenplay, a writer often reserves the right to adapt the screenplay to make a stage play. Because the stage rights are reserved by the writer, the production company, which may have the exclusive right to turn the screenplay into a film, does not have the right to make a play from the film.

Reversion of Rights

Screenwriters and other artists will want to get back those rights that they've granted if the production company has not exploited those rights within a certain period of time. This clause specifies how, if at all, those rights will automatically *revert* to the writer. This clause is often found in option agreements and provides that the rights will revert back to the writer or literary property owner if the option is not exercised within the option period.

Rights Granted

Rights Granted is one of the most critical clauses in any film contract because it does the work of transferring or licensing the intellectual property rights needed to create and protect the film property. (See "The Film Property," p. 24.) For instance, in a distribution contract, the filmmaker will assign the right to distribute the film (which is a copyright right) to the distributor. This clause occurs in virtually every single motion picture contract. For contracts with performers, crew, and creative staff, this section typically includes a Work-Made-for-Hire clause. (See "Work Made for Hire," p. 344.)

This clause should state:

- The rights granted—such as copyright, trademark, rights of publicity, etc.
- The territories (places) in which those rights can be used

CONTR.

- The length of time those rights are granted
- The media in which those rights are granted
- The manner in which those rights will be distributed (e.g., cable, satellite, or free over the air television)

Term

The *term* is the period of time that a contract is in effect. During the term of the contract, its conditions must be met and the parties' duties must be performed.

In a services contract, the term is the period of time during which the hired party must perform their duties as specified in the Engagement clause. For instance, in a performer's services contract, the term usually covers some preproduction time for rehearsals, the shoot itself, and period of time after principal photography to allow for reshoots, dubbing, and so on.

Work Made for Hire

Under copyright law, when a work is a work made for hire, the hiring party and not the writer is treated as the author. In the case of employees who create a work as part of the scope of their duties, work-made-for-hire status is automatic. In the case of independent contractors, however, a work will only be considered a work made for hire if there is a signed contract that expressly says so. (See Appendix A, "Work Made for Hire," p. 344.)

The clause that is typically used to create a work made for hire in film contracts usually does double duty: (1) It first attempts to create a work made for hire, and then, in the alternative, (2) it says that in the event that the work is not considered a work made for hire by a court of competent jurisdiction, the copyright to the work is assigned to the hiring party.

Although most film crew members should probably be treated as employees rather than independent contractors, the best practice is to put a work-made-for-hire/copyright assignment provision in every contract used to hire cast and crew.

In addition to dealing with copyright issues, the Work-Made-for-Hire clause usually attempts to give the hiring party the broadest grant of rights possible. For instance, the French intellectual property right *droit morale* is usually *waived* (given up) and "any and all other rights concerning the rights of authors" are typically *conveyed* (granted).

SUPPORTING DEAL POINTS

Some people refer to supporting deal points as the "boilerplate" terms. I don't. In fact, I hate that expression. It implies that the clause is not important or is a cookie-cutter one. Nothing could be further from the truth. These clauses, too often merely glanced at and forgotten, are quite powerful. For instance, they affect where you can sue the other party and what you have to do before you can sue them. They even determine whether you still have the right to sue in the first place—the clause may restrict the parties to using arbitration to settle disputes.

The point is that these provisions matter. The reason I've placed them in the "Minor Deal Points" section is because they are either (1) not heavily negotiated by the filmmaker and left instead for the lawyers to hash out or (2) subject to a fairly common industry standard.

Arbitration

Arbitration clauses are very common in entertainment contracts. They require the parties go to binding arbitration rather than to a court to settle contract disputes. Unlike a court decision, it is very difficult to appeal an arbitrator's decision.

Assignment and Delegation

This clause lays out the rules by which the parties can substitute new parties into the contract.

>*Example:* Pudgy Pangolin Productions, Inc. (PPP), has hired Walden Writer to write a screenplay. PPP may want to sell the film property to another production company, Angry Aardvark Associates (AAA). As part of that deal between PPP and AAA, PPP assigns Walden Writer's contract to AAA, according to the terms of the assignment and delegation provision of Walden Writer's contract with PPP. Now Walden must continue writing the script for AAA. The same terms apply to the Walden and Angry Aardvark relationship as applied to the relationship between Walden and Pudgy Pangolin—because it's the same contract. The only difference is that it has been assigned by one company to the other.

Typically production companies have the right to assign their contracts to other companies. Production companies, however, should prohibit the artists from being able to assign their contracts to other artists. It may seem unfair, but consider that each artist is unique. The production company does not want to be in the position of hiring a hot new director only to have the director assign the director's services contract to his brother, who is still in film school.

Audit and Accounting Provisions

Audit and accounting provisions specify how frequently the parties must provide each other with a detailed accounting of profits, costs, and revenue streams. It also regulates how often a party can send a certified public accountant (CPA) to perform an audit of the other party's financial records. This is especially important for a film's profit participants, who may need to audit the distributor to ensure that that the production company is receiving all monies due it by the distributor.

Choice of Law: Forum

This clause determines which state's laws apply to the contract and in which state the parties will bring any lawsuit or arbitration.

If a lawsuit is thought of as a battle, the *jurisdiction* is its battleground. Jurisdiction controls the location and kind of court that will hear a lawsuit. The laws can, and do, differ from state to state. Whether you sue in New York as opposed to Los Angeles may make the difference between winning and losing your case.

The *Choice of Law* or *Forum* clause in the contract is the parties' attempt to control the jurisdiction of the lawsuit. There are tremendous advantages in having a lawsuit brought in the jurisdiction of your choice. Often, it's the home-court advantage.

But sometimes it's the other way around. For instance, a production company that's based outside California and New York might still want California or New York law to apply to the contract. Because many films are made in New York and California, courts in those states have generated a lot of case law that applies to motion picture and television contracts. By choosing one of these jurisdictions, both parties may benefit from an established body of entertainment law. This allows all parties to anticipate, to some degree, how a lawsuit might play out in the courts, its possible outcomes, and the measure of damages the loser will have to pay.

In addition to determining which state's laws apply, the Choice of Forum clause often lists the *venue* in which any dispute must be brought. Venue is the geographic region—such as a county—over which a trial court has jurisdiction. The venue answers the question: Within this state, which trial court will hear the dispute?

> **CAUTION!** Forum clauses are not always enforceable; however, they are a strong factor in the court's decision to allow a lawsuit to proceed in a particular court.

Creative Control

It may seem odd to put a section on creative control in the "Minor Deal Points" section; it's here because it is a standard clause and is very rarely negotiated. Briefly, it says that the production company has creative control over all elements in the picture. The only time it is negotiated is when the director is vying for final cut. (See "Director's Services Agreement," p. 183.)

Default and Cure or Notice and Cure

A lawsuit can halt production—a scenario in which nobody wins. A *default-and-cure* provision gives the parties a chance to try to fix problems before they turn

CONTR.

into lawsuits. This provision usually requires the injured party to send a notice to the party doing the damage (called the *defaulting party*). The defaulting party then has a period of time in which to *cure* the default—in other words, they are given time to fix the problem. If the problem is not fixed within a certain specified time period, only then can a lawsuit be filed or arbitration started.

Defined Terms

Defined terms are terms that are defined in the contract for the purpose of understanding the contract. They are always capitalized and defined in a "Definitions" section of a contract or defined immediately after their first use.

Be careful here! Once a term is a "defined term," it takes on the defined meaning, which may not necessarily be the meaning in the dictionary. For example, if the contract says: "'Rutabaga' shall mean any motion picture sequel derived from the Screenplay," *any* use of the word *Rutabaga* in the contract will mean a sequel (note the uppercase "R"). It will not mean "a turnip with a large yellow root," (which is, of course, a rutabaga with a lowercase "r".)

Of course this is a silly example, but defined terms can be tricky, especially when the defined term is close to, but not exactly, the same as its dictionary definition. For example, everyone knows what a motion picture is, right? But what if a filmmaker uses the following definition in her contract: "'Motion Picture' shall mean the audio-visual feature film production, in whole or in part, produced by Film Prod, LLC, based on the screenplay *Script-o*, tentatively titled *Movie*, or any part thereof, and all derivatives of such production(s) and their or its parts, now or hereafter in existence, in any medium whatsoever, whether now known or hereafter in existence." Here the term *Motion Picture* means not just the film she's making, but any sequel to that film, any television series, graphic novel, video game, and so forth!

SNEAKY TIP: Watch out for the word *derivative*; it encompasses more than you may think. (See Appendix A, "Derivative Work," p. 330.)

BOTTOM LINE: If a term is not defined in the contract, a court may look to either: (1) the ordinary dictionary meaning of that term, (2) the meaning of the term as it is commonly used in the particular industry implicated by the contract (for our purposes, the film, television, or media industries, depending upon the deal), or (3) the meaning of the term in prior dealings between the parties.

Force Majeure

A standard provision in any production contract, the *force majeure* clause is also known as the "Act of God" clause. It lists the kinds of events that can stop production but are beyond the parties' control (e.g., floods, earthquakes, terrorist acts, fire, and riots). Among other things, this clause may determine how long the contract

CONTR.

is put on hold when *a force majeure* event stops production. (See also Appendix C, "Right to Suspend or Terminate," p. 390.)

Indemnification

Indemnification is the duty to compensate another person for his loss. It's kind of like saying, "Don't worry; I've got your back." Typically, rights holders and licensors (e.g., writers, filmmakers, and production companies) indemnify anybody who is licensing rights from them (called *licensees*). That way if a licensee is sued over something he has been indemnified against, the licensor must pay the cost of defending the licensee and any damages the licensee is ordered to pay.

A licensee will typically asked to be indemnified for:

- IP infringement lawsuits arising out of their use of the licensor's material
- Breaches of contract by the licensor
- Falsehoods in the representations and warranties made by the licensor

> *Example:* In a distribution agreement, Fatima Filmmaker indemnifies Dagmar Distributor against anyone suing Dagmar for copyright infringement stemming from Dagmar's copying and distribution of Fatima's movie. Fatima, however, used a pop song in her movie without getting permission from the song's copyright holders. The song's owners sue both Dagmar and Fatima. Because of the Indemnification clause, Fatima must pay to defend her own lawsuit, and because she has indemnified the distribution company, Fatima must pay Dagmar's legal costs as well.

Indemnification clauses are absolutely standard. No distribution company will pick up your film without being indemnified.

TIPS

If you are worried about your ability to indemnify a production company, you may want to try the following:

- Try to limit any knowledge-based indemnification to "best of knowledge and belief." For example, "To the best of Producer's knowledge and belief, Producer shall not include any infringing material in the program."
- Try to limit indemnification to payment of legal costs after the case has been lost and appeals exhausted. In other words, try to make sure you don't have to pay to defend frivolous lawsuits.
- Build in a cure period for those breaches that can be cured.
- Try to avoid absolute obligations ("Producer shall…") and replace them with good faith obligations ("Producer shall use reasonable business efforts to…")
- Make sure there is reciprocal indemnification; the production company should indemnify you as well!

CONTR.

Inducement Clause

This clause should be included in any contract between the production company and an artist's loan-out company. (See "Loan-Out Companies," p. 42.) Because the production company is contracting with the loan-out company and not the artist, the production company needs some assurances that the artist will abide by the terms of the contract between the production company and the loan-out company. This clause states that the artist will perform as though she (rather than her loan-out company) were the contracting party. It will also state that in the event of a default by the loan-out company, the artist will render services directly to the production company and indemnify the production company for any damages caused by the loan-out company.

Likeness Approval

Actors typically request some sort of approval rights over their likenesses prior to their image being used for movie posters or other publicity. This clause lays out how that approval is given and what percentage of photos, images, etc., the actor must approve. One typical formula is to require the performer to approve at least 50–75% of the images submitted to him by the production company.

Merger Clause

The *Merger* clause states that the written contract is the entire and complete agreement between the parties. In other words, if what you've been promised didn't make it into the written contract, don't sign the contract. Once you've put down your "John Hancock," the written agreement is what controls the relationship of the parties.

No Employment of Others

This clause prohibits the worker from hiring other workers (such as subcontractors) on the production.

No Encumbrances

Writers, directors, and other potential claimants to the film's copyright must promise not to "encumber" the copyright to a film. In other words, they will do nothing to impede or hamper the copyright or the clean transition of copyright from the production company to other companies to which the production company may be assigning the copyright.

No Injunction

An *injunction* is a court order commanding something to be done or preventing something from being done. For instance, a court could issue an injunction halting

CONTR.

distribution of your movie or ordering that a copyright registration be amended to include another author.

To obtain an injunction, the person seeking an injunction must show that money alone will not compensate the injury and that irreparable injury will result unless the injunction is granted.

In a film contract, a *No-Injunction* clause limits the parties' ability to seek an injunction. To prevent the disruption to the film caused by an injunction, producers should always include a No-Injunction clause in every cast and crew contract and specify that the person working on the film (actor, crew, etc.) agrees to waive the right to injunctive relief and limit her remedies, if any, to suing for money damages.

No Obligation to Produce

This clause makes clear that although the filmmaker may have been granted the right to produce a film, she is not *obligated* to produce that film.

No Third-Party Beneficiaries

A third-party beneficiary to a contract is someone who is not a party to a contract but who could nonetheless sue to enforce the contract. To become a third-party beneficiary, a person has to prove that the contract was made for his immediate benefit.

> **Example:** Acme Productions, Inc., is hired by the Poetry Channel to make a docudrama about Walt Whitman's little-known adventures as a gunfighter in the old West, entitled *Barbaric Yawp*. Acme hires Peter Performer to act in the program. In its performer's services contract with Peter, Acme specifies that Peter's services are for the benefit of the Poetry Channel. If Peter breaches his contract to Acme, the Poetry Channel, as a third-party beneficiary, may be able to sue Peter, even though the Poetry Channel is not a party to the contract.

The "No Third-Party beneficiaries" clause specifically states that no other parties are beneficiaries to the contract (other than the contracting parties themselves).

Notice

Notice provisions govern how the parties must communicate with each other about issues relating to the contract. For instance, the clause may say that communication sent via e-mail does not constitute sufficient notice.

In drafting the notice provision, it is important to have the proper legal names of the parties. If you are dealing with Pariah Pictures, LLC, don't call them Pariah Pictures, Inc. It may sound obvious, but sending a letter to an "Inc." when the proper business form is "LLC" may mean the difference between giving proper notice and not giving proper notice.

CONTR.

Publicity

Filmmakers like to keep a tight reign on the publicity for their films. Accordingly, they typically demand that all cast, crew, and other creative personnel associated with the film refrain from giving interviews or engaging in other publicity about the movie unless it is preapproved and organized by the production company. This means no unauthorized blogging or Facebook posts about the film!

The other side of the Publicity clause is the production company's right to use the biographies and likenesses of the cast, crew, and other creative personnel in the film's promotion. For lead cast members, the production company may also want the right to compel them to come to film festivals and premieres and to promote the film on press junkets (all on the production company's dime, of course).

Remedies

This clause details the remedies a party has if the other party breaches the contract. It usually severely limits the remedies for certain breaches, such as taking away any rights to injunctive relief a crew member or performer may have.

Right of First Negotiation

Whoever holds the *right of first negotiation* is saying, "You have to deal with me first!" For instance, if the owner of a copyright wants to sell or license that copyright, this clause requires the copyright owner to first negotiate the sale of the copyright with the party who holds the *Right of First Negotiation.* If after good-faith negotiation the parties can't reach an agreement or if the holder of the right of first negotiation doesn't want to buy the copyright, the copyright owner is free to try to sell the copyright to others. The Right of First Negotiation clause is often found in writers' agreements, screenplay options, and directors' and actors' services agreements.

> *Example:* Neville the novelist has transferred the right to make a motion picture from his novel *Two-Fisted Tales of Actuarial Science* to Paulina, a producer. Under the literary acquisition agreement he signed with Paulina, Neville reserves the right to make a play based on his novel. However, Paulina has a right of first negotiation with respect to these theatrical rights. Bentley, the Broadway financier, has offered to purchase the rights to make a stage musical from Neville's novel. Before Neville can negotiate any deal with Bentley, he must first negotiate in good faith with Paulina, giving her the first opportunity to try to strike a deal with Neville. If Paulina passes or she and Neville cannot reach an agreement after good-faith bargaining, Neville is free to sell the rights to Bentley.

Right of Last Refusal

In a way, the *Right of Last Refusal* clause is like a bookend to the right of first negotiation (see previous discussion).

CONTR.

Effectively, the right of last refusal gives one party the last bite at the apple. Like the Right of First Negotiation, this clause comes into play when the owner of copyright or any other rights wants to sell or license those rights.

After the copyright owner has negotiated a deal for the sale or license of the copyright, the owner must first offer those same deal terms to the person who holds the right of last refusal. The holder of the right of last refusal is given a time limit, typically two weeks to 30 days, in which she must accept the offer or the offer will be deemed refused. Only after the holder of the right of last refusal has rejected the offer may the copyright owner sell or license the copyright to the party she was negotiating with originally. Like the Right of First Negotiation, the Right of Last Refusal clause is often found in writers' agreements, screenplay options, and directors' and actors' services agreements.

> *Example:* Paulina the producer has a Right of Last Refusal clause in her literary acquisition agreement with Neville the novelist. Neville has negotiated with Bentley the Broadway financier for the sale of the rights to his novel to make a Broadway play, and Neville and Bentley have agreed on price and other terms; Bentley now has a firm offer off the table to Neville. Before Neville can accept Bentley's offer, he must first go back to Paulina and give her a chance to purchase the stage rights on the same terms as those that Bentley offered.

Right to Suspend or Terminate

This clause details how and when a production company may suspend or terminate a crew member, performer, or other worker's contract. Essentially, it allows the production company to put the worker's contract "on hold" for a certain period of time for events beyond the parties' control (such as *force majeure)*. If the worker is ill, is incapacitated, engages in unprofessional behavior, or commits a crime, this clause also allows the production company to cancel the worker's contract altogether.

Right to Withhold

This clause gives the production company the right to withhold taxes and other legally authorized deductions from the worker's paycheck.

Savings Clause

A *Savings clause* allows certain provisions to survive the termination of a contract. For instance, a production company will usually insert a Savings clause in the "Rights Granted" paragraph. This Savings clause will state that if the contract is terminated for any reason, the rights transferred to the production company under the agreement will remain with the production company.

CONTR.

Security Interest

A *security interest* is a property interest in collateral pledged to secure a loan or other obligation. For example, when you buy a car on credit, the loan company has a security interest in your automobile.

Often filmmakers are required to grant a security interest in their films as collateral for a loan. Sometimes filmmakers must grant a security interest to secure other obligations. For instance, producers who have agreed to work under Screen Actor's Guild (SAG) rules are required to grant a security interest in their film to SAG. If the production company fails to pay the performers' salaries, residuals, or other fees, SAG can seize the film, sell it, and repay the production company's debt to the actors. (See "SAG," p. 205.)

Severability

If any clause in the contract violates the law, the Severability clause allows the offending paragraphs to be deleted from the contract without destroying the validity of the contract. The offending clause simply falls out of the contract and the contract is interpreted as though the clause had never been included in the first place.

Step Payments

Production companies working with first-time writers or problematic scripts will often pay the screenwriter in incremental steps for each stage of the writing process. That way, if either the screenplay or the writer is not working out, the production company has not paid the full price of a completed screenplay. This deal is often referred to as a *step deal*. This clause outlines the stages and the amounts to be paid during each stage.

Waiver

This clause allows a party to a contract to be able to *waive*—to give up a legal right—guaranteed by the contract without waiving all the rights granted under the contract. It usually stipulates that all waivers must be in writing.

THE BOTTOM LINE: Your final contracts should contain BOTH main and supplemental deal points.

A NOTE ON "LEGALESE"

We attorneys take a lot of flak for confusing laypeople with our "legalese." It can be quite frustrating: A business person might make an offer to "sell" a widget, but a lawyer will "sell, convey, transfer, and assign all the rights in and to the widget,

CONTR.

in perpetuity." You'd think we were being paid by the word. Quite honestly, some lawyers do use extraneous words. For instance, in this example, the single word "sell" would probably work just fine.

For most purposes, using clear, simple language in the contract is the best way to draft. In fact, there are very few "magic" legal words that are required in contract law. Much of the time, if you can express the party's intentions in plain language, it will do the trick.

However, there are times when a lot of seemingly duplicate words are necessary. Remember, the contract lawyer's job is to take the broad deal points and to render them as precisely as possible. The best contract is one that is *both* clear and precise. This is especially true for contracts dealing with intellectual property, such as those in the film industry. There are many different ways a copyright can be transferred from one person to another. It can be mortgaged, it can be sold, it can be licensed, it can be assigned, security interests can be granted in the copyright, and so on. And all those transfers are *not* the same.

When a lawyer is drafting a contract, her greatest fear is that if she fails to be precise enough, that lack of precision will create a loophole that will be exploited when the parties decide they can no longer play nicely with each other. A contract that says only that "Mr. Jones hereby licenses the copyright to his screenplay to Mr. Smith" does not say anything about whether Mr. Jones may borrow money from a lender and use the copyright as collateral for the loan. If Mr. Smith wants to prevent that from happening, he needs to insert language into the contract that talks about mortgages, security interests, and so forth.

A FILMMAKER'S GUIDE TO LABOR AND EMPLOYMENT LAW

As a general premise, a producer or production company is an employer, an actor or cameraperson is an employee or independent contractor, and a movie set or location is a workplace. The laws that govern employers, employees, and independent contractors are complex;[1] a brief overview of these laws would fill an entire book. This appendix, therefore, is designed to highlight a few areas of employment law critical to filmmakers. It is not a detailed guide to all the laws you need to be aware of. It is highly suggested that before hiring anybody, the production company work closely with its attorney to make sure that state and federal laws are being strictly adhered to.

Topics presented here include:

- Employee or independent contractor? (p. 393)
- Employer's responsibilities (p. 399)
- Child labor laws (p. 400)

EMPLOYEE OR INDEPENDENT CONTRACTOR?

Whether a worker is classified as an employee or independent contractor has a huge impact on the working relationship. Different sets of laws apply to each classification, and a production company has different responsibilities toward employees than it does toward independent contractors.

EMPLOYEE

- *Federal regulations.* Employees have a host of federal laws to protect them. These laws govern:
  - Benefits
  - Minimum wage and overtime
  - Family and medical leave
  - Health and safety in the workplace
  - Discrimination

- *Taxes.* Employers must withhold federal and state income taxes, Medicare, and Social Security from an employee's paycheck. Employers must also contribute to Social Security and Medicare for each employee. The employer must keep track of the employee's annual gross earnings and withholdings, reflected in a W-2, which must be sent to the employee.

- *Workers' compensation.* Employers must have workers' compensation insurance and possibly disability insurance when they have employees.

- *Unemployment.* Employers must make contributions to the state's unemployment insurance fund and pay federal unemployment taxes.

INDEPENDENT CONTRACTOR

- *Federal regulations.* Independent contractors are treated as separate businesses. Overtime, minimum wage, and other laws may not apply.

- *Taxes.* Employers do not have to withhold anything from an independent contractor's check, nor do they have to send a W-2 form. If the independent contractor has been paid more than $600 in one year, the employer should send them a 1099-MISC Form with a copy to the IRS.

- *Workers' compensation.* Workers' compensation insurance is generally not required in dealing with independent contractors. To be on the safe side, the production company may want to confirm that an independent contractor has his own insurance to cover workplace injuries.

- *Unemployment.* There is usually no requirement to pay unemployment contributions or taxes for independent contractors.

As you can see, a production company has a lot more work on its hands if the worker is an employee and not an independent contractor. So why doesn't a production company simply hire independent contractors?

Many try to do just that. Unfortunately, whether a worker is an independent contractor or an employee—in other words, the worker's status—is not determined simply a matter of writing the words "independent contractor" on a contract. To make matters worse, there are penalties for misclassifying a worker as an independent contractor if he should be classified as an employee. To top it all off, a worker must be properly classified as either an employee or an independent contractor for both federal and state agencies.

DETERMINING A WORKER'S STATUS

Federal Test

The Internal Revenue Service (IRS) looks at three primary factors to determine whether a worker is an independent contractor or an employee:

- *Behavioral control.* If the production company has the right to direct and control how the worker accomplishes her job, the worker is most likely an employee.

The more instructions a worker is given on how the work should be done, what steps the worker must perform, and what tools she must use, the more likely it is that the worker is an employee.

- *Financial control.* The more a worker has a financial stake in the business, shares in its profits and losses, or pays for supplies and materials without reimbursement, the more likely it is that a worker is an independent contractor.

- *Relationship of the parties.* How the worker and the employer perceive their relationship is also taken into account. Does a written contract specify that the worker is an independent contractor? If so, that tips the scales in favor of independent contractor status. Does the employer pay employee benefits? In that case, the worker is more likely to be an employee.

IRS RESOURCES

For more on how the IRS determines a worker's status, see its brochure, "Contractor or Employee?" at http://www.irs.gov/pub/irs-pdf/p1779.pdf

For information on an employer's tax responsibilities, see "Employer's Supplemental Tax Guide" at http://www.irs.gov/pub/irs-pdf/p15a.pdf

---

TIP: **The IRS may be more likely to find that loan-out companies are independent contractors and their principals, the actors or crew members who run them, are not employees of the production company.**

In addition to the federal test for whether a worker is an independent contractor or an employee, the production company should also double-check the working relationship under the appropriate state law. For reference, the law of two big moviemaking states, California and New York, is provided.

Independent Contractors and Employees

CALIFORNIA

As is true in most states, there is no simple definition for who is an independent contractor in California. In determining a worker's status, the California Division of Labor Standards Enforcement (DLSE) applies the "economic realities" test, which is a multifactor test.[2]

The most important factor in the test is whether the hiring company "has the right to control as to the work done and the manner and means in which it is performed."[3] The more control a worker has, the more likely that he should be classified as an independent contractor.

Other factors the agency may consider are:

- "Whether the person performing services is engaged in an occupation or business distinct from that of the principal (or employer).
- "Whether the work is a part of the regular business of the principal or alleged employer.
- "Whether the principal or the worker supplies the instrumentalities, tools, and the place for the person doing the work.
- "The alleged employee's investment in the equipment or materials required by his task or her employment of helpers.
- "Whether the service rendered requires a special skill.
- "The kind of occupation, with reference to whether, in the locality, the work is usually done under the direction of the principal or by a specialist without supervision.
- "The alleged employee's opportunity for profit or loss depending on her managerial skill.
- "The length of time for which the services are to be performed.
- "The degree of permanence of the working relationship.
- "The method of payment, whether by time or the job.
- "Whether the parties believe they are creating an employee–employer relationship may have some bearing on the question, but is not determinative, because this is a question of law based on objective tests."[4]

However, even if the production company does not control the work details, the worker will be classified as an employee if:

- The production company "retains pervasive control" over the operation as a whole.
- The worker's duties are an integral part of the operation.
- The nature of the work makes detailed control unnecessary.

WORK FOR HIRE AND EMPLOYEE STATUS

California has shown some exceptions to the general rules and factors above that are seemingly unique to California:

- *If you have a work-for-hire agreement with an independent contractor, you must treat the contractor like an employee*! If the contract is made in California or subject to the laws of California, the independent contractor is treated as an employee for the purposes of the workers' compensation rules.[5]
- A worker who works from home on his own equipment and sets his own hours may still be an employee if employee independence is customary in the relevant industry. "[T]he custom of the community as to the control ordinarily exercised in a particular occupation is of importance."[6]

As you can see, there is a lot of leeway for the state to classify a worker as an employee.

For more on the California laws regarding a worker's status, see the California Independent Contractor FAQ at http://www.dir.ca.gov/dlse/faq_independentcontractor.html

NEW YORK

In New York, as in California, the presumption is that a worker is an employee, but this presumption is rebuttable. New York takes a different approach from California to the common law tests of supervision, direction, and control.

The New York Department of Labor provides guidelines for determining worker status in the performing arts. The guidelines list "indicators of independence" that make a worker an independent contractor and "indicators of employment" that make a worker an employee. However, even though the presumption that a worker is an employee is rebuttable, the guidelines say "[i]n most film and theatrical production cases, performers would not be determined to be independent contractors."[7]

Under New York law, if the following factors are true of a worker, it indicates that she may be an independent contractor and not an employee:

- "Having an established business.
- "Advertising in the electronic and/or print media.
- "Maintaining a listing in the commercial pages of the telephone directory.
- "Using business cards, business stationery, and billheads.
- "Carrying insurance.
- "Maintaining a place of business and making a significant investment in facilities, equipment, and supplies.
- "Paying one's own expenses.
- "Assuming risk for profit or loss in providing services.
- "Determining one's own schedule.
- "Setting or negotiating his or her own pay rate.
- "Providing services concurrently for other businesses, competitive or noncompetitive.
- "Being free to refuse work offers.
- "Being free to hire help."[8]

On the other side of the equation are the factors that, if true about the production company, indicate that the worker is an employee and not an independent contractor.

"[The production company]:

- "Determines when, where, and how services will be performed.

- "Provides facilities, equipment, tools, and supplies.
- "Directly supervises the services of the worker.
- "Stipulates the hours of work.
- "Requires exclusive services.
- "Sets the rate of pay.
- "Requires attendance at meetings and/or training sessions.
- "Requires oral or written reports.
- "Reserves the right to review and approve the work product.
- "Evaluates job performance.
- "Requires prior permission for absences.
- "Reserves the right to terminate the [worker's] services."[9]

Because New York starts with the presumption that a worker is an employee, the fact that any one factor in the tests is absent does not necessarily make a worker an independent contractor.

In addition to the preceding tests, for performers there are nine indicators of employment[9]:

- "The performer is paid at a rate established solely by the production company or organization.
- "The production company or organization makes standard withholdings from the performer's pay, e.g., income tax, Social Security, and so forth.
- "The performer is covered under the production company or organization's Workers' Compensation policy.
- "The production company or organization retains artistic control of the performance.
- "The performer is paid to attend or is required to attend rehearsals.
- "The production company or organization provides substitutes or replacements if the performer is unable to provide services.
- "Attire is dictated by the production company or organization.
- "The production company or organization establishes breaks.
- "The performer is provided with music or other materials for the performance (e.g., props, equipment, etc.)."

For more on how New York state classifies performing artists, see "New York Guidelines for Determining Worker Status: Performing Artists" at www.labor.state.ny.us/ui/pdfs/ia31817.pdf

EMPLOYER'S RESPONSIBILITIES

If you are an employer (e.g., a production company) hiring an employee, your responsibilities include paperwork.

- You must have the employee complete the following forms:
  - *Form I-9.* This is an immigration status form required by the US Bureau of Citizenship. You can find the form here: http://www.uscis.gov/files/form/i-9.pdf
  - *IRS Form W-4.* This is a federal tax withholdings form. You can find the form here: http://www.irs.gov/pub/irs-pdf/fw4.pdf
  - *IRS Form SS-4.* The form for the production company to apply for an employer identification number (EIN). You can find it here: http://www.irs.gov/pub/irs-pdf/fss4.pdf
  - *You may be responsible* for additional state forms, such as a New-Hire Reporting Form.
  - *W-2 Forms* must be sent to the employee each year. You can find a copy of the form here: http://www.irs.gov/pub/irs-pdf/fw2.pdf
- Some of the taxes the employer must withhold or pay are as follows:
  - Federal income tax withholding
  - Social Security taxes
  - Federal unemployment taxes
- The production company/employer will have to comply with the following laws:
  - *Title VII of the Civil Rights Act.* This statute protects against illegal discrimination in the workplace and hiring and firing practices.
  - *Occupational Safety and Health Act (OSHA).* This law sets workplace safety standards. Both state and federal OSHA laws must be adhered to.
  - *Workers' compensation insurance.* Determined by state law, this is mandatory insurance for all employers. It provides income and medical payments for employees injured on the job.
  - *Disability insurance.* Some states require employers to have disability insurance as well as workers' compensation insurance.
  - *The Americans with Disabilities Act (ADA).* This protects against job discrimination against an individual who is disabled or is regarded as disabled. It applies to businesses that have had 15 or more employees for 20 or more weeks of either the current or previous year.
  - *The Fair Labor Standards Act (FLSA).* This regulates minimum wage and overtime requirements. Many film professionals are exempt from overtime and minimum wage requirements.

- *The Family and Medical Leave Act (FMLA).* If your production company has more than 50 employees you may be required to provide unpaid medical and family leave.
- Other applicable state and federal laws.

CHILD LABOR LAWS: CALIFORNIA AND NEW YORK

Child labor laws are extensive, cumbersome, and complex. As a rule, hiring and employing a child or minor is more regulated by federal and state law than hiring and employing an adult. Special permits must be obtained, and money must be withheld in a special trust. A producer might want to consider whether an actual minor, someone under the age of 18, is required when an adult who can "play" younger would suffice.

CALIFORNIA CHILD LABOR LAW

"California employers who are bound by contractual arrangements made in California to employ minors residing within the state to work on location outside of the state, must comply with all California regulations, including the use of studio teachers."[10] Under California Child Labor Law,[11] a minor "means any person [aged 15 days[12] to 18 years] who is required to attend school under the provisions of the education code and includes minors under age six."

Permits Required to Employ a Minor in California

- In California, a producer who wants to hire a minor to act in a film must first obtain from the Division of Labor Standards Enforcement a Permit to Employ Minors in the Entertainment Industry (PEMEI) or file an Application for Permission to Employ Minors in the Entertainment Industry (DLSE form 281) and be granted one. You can find the form at http://www.dir.ca.gov/dlse/DLSE-Forms-CL.htm.
- The parent or guardian must apply for an Entertainment Work Permit (DLSE form 275) (EWP) by completing an Application for Permission to Work in the Entertainment Industry (DLSE form 277; APWEI). You can find the form at www.dir.ca.gov/dlse/DLSEForm277.pdf.
- Permits are required even when the entertainment is noncommercial.[13] The Division issues individual permits and blanket permits. Individual "Entertainment Work" permits last for six months and are specific to the minor named in the permit.

- For the Division of Labor Standards Enforcement to issue a PEMEI, the producer/employer must show proof of workers' compensation coverage. The PEMEI has no expiration date; however, it may be "denied, revoked, or suspended for any violation of law or regulation or any discrimination against a studio teacher for performing duties authorized or required by law and regulation for the protection of their minor charges" (8 CCR 11758 and 11758.1).

Work Hours for Minors in California

As a general rule, "[m]inors in the entertainment industry may not work more than eight hours a day or more than 48 hours in a week … may only work between the hours of 5 a.m. and 10 p.m. or to 12:30 a.m. on days preceding a nonschool day."[14] There is an exception to this rule. "Upon the Labor Commissioner's approval following a written request (submitted 48 hours in advance), a minor aged eight to [eighteen] may continue … her part past 10 p.m. up to 12 midnight preceding a school day in a presentation, play, or drama which begins before 10 p.m. *This exception may never be construed to allow the minor to be at the place of employment more than the maximum number of hours permitted in law or regulation."*

On-Set Teacher Requirements in California

California requires a state-certified studio teacher and a nurse to be provided by the production company in certain circumstances:

- "All minors aged six months to 16 years must be provided with one studio teacher for each group of 10 or fewer minors when school is in session and for each group of 20 or fewer minors on Saturdays, Sundays, holidays, or during school vacations. In addition to the studio teacher, a parent or guardian must always be present."[15]

- For very young minors the restrictions are very specific. For example, infants aged 15 days to six months "may be at the place of business for one period of two consecutive hours, which must occur between 9:30 a.m. and 11:30 a.m. or between 2:30 p.m. and 4:30 p.m. Actual work may not exceed 20 minutes under any circumstances. Infants may not be exposed to light exceeding 100 foot-candles for more than 30 seconds at a time. A studio teacher and nurse must be present for each three or fewer infants aged 15 days to six weeks. A studio teacher and a nurse must be present for each 10 or fewer infants aged six weeks to six months. A parent or guardian must always be present."[16]

- California may assess civil penalties of up to $1,000 for each and every violation and criminal penalties "punishable by fines ranging up to $10,000 or by confinement in the county jail for periods up to six months, or by both fine and imprisonment," for a violation of California's child labor laws. … [t]he employer, never the minor, is liable for child labor violations."

Mandatory Trust Fund

In addition to the aforementioned restrictions and requirements, a parent or guardian and every employer must comply with the Coogan Law, named for the actor Jackie Coogan. Coogan was a child performer who shot to stardom in 1921 at the age of seven, staring opposite Charlie Chaplin in *The Kid*. He had earned $4 million by the age of 13. However, in 1935, when he demanded his money from his mother and stepfather (who had been his manager), they refused. He filed suit, and the court held that under California law he had no right to the money he earned as a minor. Because of the notoriety of this case, California passed the Child Actor's Bill in 1939 to protect a child performer's income for his future use. The law, which became known as the Coogan Law, has been amended several times since 1939, most recently in 2004. (Jackie Coogan later went on to play Uncle Fester in the television show *The Addams Family*.)

The law applies to all minor actors[17] and to any contract in which a minor and "a person agrees to purchase, or otherwise secure, sell, lease, license, or otherwise dispose of literary, musical, or dramatic properties, or use of a person's likeness, voice recording, performance, or story of or incidents in his or her life, either tangible or intangible, or any rights therein for use in motion pictures, television, the production of sound recordings in any format now known or hereafter devised, the legitimate or living stage, or otherwise in the entertainment field."[18]

- The current California law requires that 15% of a minor's gross income be put into a trust in California,[19] called a Coogan Trust Account,[20] that is established no later than seven business days after the contract is signed by the parties.[21] The trustee is the parent or guardian who is entitled to physical custody of the minor, but a court may appoint a trustee if needed.

- Next, within "ten business days after the minor's contract is signed by the minor and the employer, the trustee must prepare a written statement under penalty of perjury that shall include ... [all the] information needed by the employer to deposit into the account the portion of the minor's earnings."[22]

- The employer "shall deposit or disburse the funds within 15 business days of receiving the trustee's statement ... pending the receipt of the trustee's statement, the employer shall hold for the benefit of the minor the percentage ... of the minor's gross earnings.[23] And, "once the minor's employer deposits the set-aside funds. ... [in the trust], the minor's employer shall have no further obligation or duty to monitor or account for the funds."[24]

- However, if the parent or guardian fails to provide the employer with the trust information after 180 days of the minor's beginning employment, the employer must transfer 15% of the minor's gross income to the Actor's Fund of America. Upon receipt of those forwarded funds, The Actors' Fund of America shall become the trustee of those funds, and the minor's employer shall have no further obligation or duty to monitor or account for the funds.

Avoiding Disaffirmance of a Minor's Contract in California

Most states have laws that allow a person to get out of contracts that he made when he was a minor (called *disaffirming* a contract). This can be extremely problematical for filmmakers who find that the contracts they have with their minor performers are no longer valid. In California, however, if an entertainment contract is approved by Superior Court, it cannot be disaffirmed.[25]

Any party can seek court approval, and the approval extends "to the whole contract and all of its terms and provisions, including, but not limited to, any optional or conditional provisions contained in the contract for extension, prolongation or termination of the term of the contract."[26]

Details on California's child labor laws and their application to filmmaking can be found in the pamphlet "Child Labor Laws 2000," at http://www.dir.ca.gov/dlse/cllpamphlet2000.pdf.

NEW YORK CHILD LABOR LAW

Permits Required to Employ a Minor in New York

New York requires that a minor who is employed as a performer have a special employment permit. The permit is required even if the minor is not a New York resident or the work is unpaid. If the performance or the location is in New York, the permit is required. You can find the form at http://www.labor.state.ny.us/workerprotection/ellsformsandpublications.shtm#Child Performer.

A parent or guardian must obtain a Child Performer Employment Permit form from the State Department of Labor before employment begins (the permit is valid for six months and must be renewed 30 days before it expires). New York now allows new applicants to fill out forms online to obtain a one-time only permit that is valid for fifteen days. This is to allow the child to work while the parent submits the required documentation from the child's school. The website may be found at https://www.labor.state.ny.us/secure/welcome.asp. The forms must be printed out at the end of the online process.

Before employing a child in New York, an employer must obtain a Certificate of Eligibility to Employ Child Performers. You can find the form at http://www.labor.state.ny.us/formsdocs/wp/LS550.pdf.

More information can be found in this FAQ provided by the New York State Labor Department: http://www.labor.ny.gov/workerprotection/laborstandards/secure/ChildPerformerFAQ.shtm.

New York Mandatory Trust Funds

New York has its own Coogan Law, called the Child Performer Education and Trust Act of 2003, which is nearly identical to the California law. New York will recognize a Coogan Trust Account set up in California as sufficient compliance with New York's Child Performer Education and Trust Act. However, there are some distinctions between the two laws:

- Within 15 days of the start of employment, a parent or guardian must establish a child performer's trust account unless one that complies with New York exists.[27] Within 15 days of the start of employment, the parents must give the production company all necessary information to make a transfer of at least 15% of the child performer's gross earnings[28] (including residuals) to the trust account. If a parent or guardian fails to establish a trust account, the state will not renew or issue a new child performer's permit until the parent demonstrates that he or she has complied with the law.[29]

- If the parent/guardian or custodian has not provided the necessary information within 15 days of the start of employment or no such account has been established, [the employer must] transfer the money together with the child performer's name and last known address to the state comptroller for placement into the child performer's holding fund.[30]

Avoiding Disaffirmance of a Minor's Contract in New York

In New York, as in California, any party to a minor's contract may ask a court to approve a minor's contract so that it cannot be disaffirmed by the minor on the grounds "of infancy or assert that the parent or guardian lacked authority to make the contract."[31] New York requires that:

- "The custodial parent provide to the court written acceptance of the contract to be approved;

- "The contract term, including any extensions or options, must not be for more than three years from the date of the approval of the contract. But if the minor is represented by a qualified attorney who is experienced in the entertainment industry laws and practice, the contract term may be for seven years. The court retains discretion to approve any contract even though the term is longer than three or seven years as long as the court finds it to be reasonable."[32]

On-Set Teacher Requirements in New York

Unlike California, in New York "there is no minimum age for child performers at theatrical, radio, or television performances."[33] But minors have restrictions on working hours based on age and if they are required to attend school.[34]

The employer is required to "provide a teacher, who is either certified or has credentials recognized by the state of New York, to such child performer to fulfill educational requirements pursuant to the education law ... when the child performer is not receiving educational instruction due to his or her employment schedule."[35]

OTHER STATES

Every state has labor laws that apply to working children, but so far only a few have passed laws specific to child performers or require special work permits. Currently California, Louisiana, New York, and New Mexico require work permits for child performers and a Coogan Trust or Blocked Trust Account to be set up to receive a percentage of the child's earnings. Since the release of the first edition of this book, several states have passed new child labor laws or strengthened existing laws because of public reaction to the bad working conditions on certain productions.

For more information on key child labor legislation for the entertainment industry in Florida, Louisiana, and New Mexico, see this book's online supplement at www.thepocketlawyerforfilm.com.

KEEP CURRENT

Regardless of your politics and whether you believe that health insurance reform is good for the United States, all employers and producers need to be aware of how the new health care regulations and requirements will affect their productions. It is a good idea to stay informed as the new rules and regulations are put into effect. *Keep your information current by regularly checking the websites of state and federal departments of labor.*

STATE FILM COMMISSION OFFICES

Every state has a film commission whose function is to encourage in-state film and television production by helping filmmakers find local crew and supplies, recommending production-oriented state policy and legislation, and providing information on state permits, production incentives, and public land location regulations. Prior to shooting in a particular state, give that state's film commission a call; they are extremely valuable resources.

ALABAMA
ALABAMA FILM OFFICE
401 Adams Ave., Suite 616
Montgomery, AL 36104
(334) 242-4195
(334) 242-2077 Fax
www.alabamafilm.org

ALASKA
ALASKA FILM OFFICE
550 W. 7th Avenue, Suite 1770
Anchorage, AK 99501
www.alaskafilm.org

ARIZONA
ARIZONA FILM COMMISSION
1700 W. Washington St. #600
Phoenix, AZ 85007
(602) 771-1100
(800) 528-8421
www.azcommerce.com/film

ARKANSAS
ECONOMIC DEVELOPMENT COMMISSION
900 West Capitol
Little Rock, AR 72201
(501) 682-7676
(501) 682-3456 Fax
www.arkansasedc.com
http://www.arkansasedc.com/arkansas-film-commission.aspx

CALIFORNIA
CALIFORNIA FILM COMMISSION
7080 Hollywood Blvd. #900
Hollywood, CA 90028
(800) 858-4749
(323) 860-2960
(323) 860-2972 Fax
www.film.ca.gov

COLORADO
OFFICE OF FILM TELEVISION & MEDIA
1625 Broadway, 27th Fl.
Denver, CO 80202
(303) 592-4065
(303) 722-1158 Fax
www.coloradofilm.org

CONNECTICUT
DEPARTMENT OF ECONOMIC AND COMMUNITY DEVELOPMENT
505 Hudson St.
Hartford, CT 06106-7106
(860) 256-2800
(860) 256-2811 Fax
www.ctfilm.com

DELAWARE
DELAWARE FILM OFFICE
99 Kings Highway
Dover, DE 19901
(800) 441-8846
(302) 739-4271
(302) 739-5749 Fax
http://dedo.delaware.gov/
http://dedo.delaware.gov/Film.shtml

DISTRICT OF COLUMBIA
OFFICE OF MOTION PICTURE & TELEVISION DEVELOPMENT
2025 M St., NW, Suite 600
Washington, DC 20036
(202) 727-6608
http://film.dc.gov

FLORIDA
FLORIDA FILM COMMISSION
Governor's Office of Film and Entertainment
Executive Office of the Governor

The Capitol, Suite 2001
Tallahassee, FL 32399-0001
(850) 410-4765
(877) FLA-FILM
(850) 410-4770 Fax
www.filminflorida.com

GEORGIA
GEORGIA FILM & VIDEO TAPE OFFICE
75 Fifth St. NW, Suite 1200
Atlanta, GA 30308
(404) 962-4052
(404) 962-4053 Fax
www.georgia.org
http://www.georgia.org/GeorgiaIndustries/Entertainment/FilmTV/Pages/
default.aspx

HAWAII
HAWAII FILM OFFICE
1 Capital District Bldg
250 S Hotel St. 5th Floor
Honolulu, HI 96813
(808) 586-2570
(808) 586-2572 Fax
www.hawaiifilmoffice.com

IDAHO
IDAHO FILM BUREAU
700 W. State St.
Boise, ID 83720
(800) 942-8338
(208) 334-2470
(208) 334-2631 Fax
www.filmidaho.com

ILLINOIS
ILLINOIS FILM OFFICE
100 W. Randolph St. 3rd Floor
Chicago, IL 60601
(312) 814-3600
(312) 814-8874 Fax
www.illinoisbiz.biz/film/index.html

INDIANA
INDIANA FILM COMMISSION
One North Capitol Ave. #700

Indianapolis, IN 46204-2288
(317)-232-8888
(317)-232-4146 Fax
www.filmindiana.com

IOWA
IOWA DEPARTMENT OF ECONOMIC DEVELOPMENT
IOWA FILM OFFICE
200 East Grand Ave.
Des Moines, IA 50309
(515) 725-3100
(515) 242-4795 Fax
http://www.iowalifechanging.com/film/

KANSAS
KANSAS FILM COMMISSION
1000 S.W. Jackson St. Suite 100
Topeka, Kansas 66612-1354
(785) 296-2178
(785) 296-3490 Fax
www.filmkansas.com

KENTUCKY
KENTUCKY FILM OFFICE
500 Metro St.
2200 Capital Plaza Tower
Frankfort, KY 40601
(800) 345-6591
(502) 564-3456
(502) 564-7588 Fax
www.kyfilmoffice.com

LOUISIANA
LOUISIANA FILM AND TELEVISION DEVELOPMENT
1051 N. 3rd St.
Baton Rouge, LA 70802
(888) 665-0447
(225) 342-8150
(225) 342-5389 Fax
www.lafilm.org

MAINE
MAINE FILM OFFICE
59 State House Station
Augusta, ME 04333

(207) 624-7631
www.filminmaine.com

MARYLAND
MARYLAND FILM OFFICE 401
East Pratt St., 14th Floor
Baltimore, MD 21202
(800) 333-6632
(410) 767-6340
(410) 333-0044 Fax
www.marylandfilm.org

MASSACHUSETTS
MASSACHUSETTS FILM OFFICE
10 Guest St., Suite 280
Boston, MA 02135
617.423.1155
617.423.1158 (fax)
www.mafilm.org

MICHIGAN
MICHIGAN FILM OFFICE
300 N. Washington Sq., 4th Fl.
Lansing, MI 48913
(800) 477-3456
(517) 335-2693
(517) 241-0867 Fax
www.michiganfilmoffice.org/

MINNESOTA
MINNESOTA FILM and TV BOARD
401 N. 3rd St., Suite 440
Minneapolis, MN 55401
(651) 645-3600
(651) 645-7373 Fax
www.mnfilmtv.org

MISSISSIPPI
MISSISSIPPI FILM OFFICE
501 North West St., 5th Floor
Jackson, MS 39201
(601) 359-3297
(601) 359-5048 Fax
www.filmmississippi.org

MISSOURI
MISSOURI FILM OFFICE
301 West High St., Suite 720
Jefferson City, MO 65101
(573) 522-1288
www.mofilm.org

MONTANA
MONTANA FILM OFFICE
301 S. Park Ave.
Helena, MT 59620
(800) 553-4563
(406) 841-2876
(406) 841-2877 Fax
www.montanafilm.com

NEBRASKA
NEBRASKA FILM OFFICE
P.O. Box 98907
Lincoln, NE 68509-8907
(402) 471-3746
(402) 471-3238 Fax
www.filmnebraska.org

NEVADA
NEVADA FILM OFFICE
555 E. Washington Ave. #5400
Las Vegas, NV 89101
(877) 638-3456
(702) 486-2711
(702) 486-2712 Fax
www.nevadafilm.com
or
NEVADA FILM OFFICE (RENO & TAHOE)
108 E. Proctor
Carson City, NV 89701
(775) 687-1814
(775) 687-4497 Fax
www.nevadafilm.com

NEW HAMPSHIRE
NEW HAMPSHIRE FILM OFFICE
20 Park St.
Concord, NH 03301
(603) 271-2220

(603) 271-3163 Fax
www.nh.gov/film

NEW JERSEY
NEW JERSEY MOTION PICTURE AND TELEVISION COMMISSION
153 Halsey St., 5th Fl.
P.O. Box 47023
Newark, New Jersey 07101
(973) 648-6279
(973) 648-7350 Fax
www.njfilm.org

NEW MEXICO
NEW MEXICO FILM OFFICE
418 Montezuma Ave.
Santa Fe, NM 87501
(800) 545-9871
(505) 476-5600
(505) 476-5601 Fax
www.nmfilm.com

NEW YORK
NEW YORK STATE GOVERNOR'S FILM OFFICE
633 Third Ave., 33rd Fl.
New York, NY 10017
(212) 803-2330
(212) 803-2339 Fax
www.nylovesfilm.com

NORTH CAROLINA
THE NORTH CAROLINA FILM OFFICE
301 N. Wilmington St.
Raleigh, NC 27601
(866) 468-2273
(919) 733-9900
(919) 715-0151 Fax
www.ncfilm.com

NORTH DAKOTA
NORTH DAKOTA FILM COMMISSION
1600 E. Century Ave.
Bismarck, ND 58501
(701) 328-2525
(701) 328-4878 Fax
http://www.ndtourism.com/industry/media-links/

OHIO
OHIO FILM COMMISSION
77 South High St., 29th Fl.
Columbus, OH 42316
(800) 230-3523
(614) 644-5156
(614) 466-6744 Fax
www.discoverohiofilm.com

OKLAHOMA
OKLAHOMA FILM and MUSIC OFFICE
120 N Robinson Ave., Suite 600
Oklahoma City, OK 73102
(800) 766-3456
(405) 230-8440
(405) 230-8640 Fax
www.oklahomafilm.org

OREGON
GOVERNOR'S OFFICE OF FILM & TELEVISION
1001 SE Water Ave., Suite 430
Portland, OR 97214
(503) 229-5832
(503) 229-6869 Fax
www.oregonfilm.org

PENNSYLVANIA
PENNSYLVANIA FILM OFFICE
Commonwealth Keystone Bldg.
400 North St., 4th Fl.
Harrisburg, PA 17120
(717) 783-3456
(717) 787-0687 Fax
www.filminpa.com

PUERTO RICO
PUERTO RICO FILM COMMISSION
355 F. D. Roosevelt Ave. #106
Hato Rey, Puerto Rico 00918
(787) 758-4747
(787) 756-5706 Fax
www.puertoricofilm.com

RHODE ISLAND
RHODE ISLAND FILM & TV OFFICE
One Capital Hill

Providence, RI 02908
(401) 222-3456
(401) 222-3018 Fax
www.film.ri.gov

SOUTH CAROLINA
SOUTH CAROLINA FILM OFFICE
1205 Pendleton St., Rm. 529
Columbia, SC 29201
(803) 737-0490
(803) 737-3104 Fax
www.scfilmoffice.com

SOUTH DAKOTA
SOUTH DAKOTA FILM COMMISSION
711 East Wells Ave.
Pierre, SD 57501
(800) 952-3625
(605) 773-3301
(605) 773-3256 Fax
www.filmsd.com

TENNESSEE
FILM, ENTERTAINMENT, & MUSIC COMMISSION
312 Rosa L. Parks Ave.
Tennessee Tower, 9th Fl.
Nashville, TN 37243
(877) 818-3456
(615) 741-3456
(615) 741-5554 Fax
www.state.tn.us/film/

TEXAS
TEXAS FILM COMMISSION
PO Box 13246
Austin, TX 78711
(512) 463-9200
(512) 463-4114 Fax
www.governor.state.tx.us/film/

UTAH
UTAH FILM COMMISSION
300 N. State St.
Salt Lake City, UT 84114
(800) 453-8824
(801) 538-8740

(801) 538-1397 Fax
www.film.utah.gov

VERMONT
VERMONT FILM COMMISSION
10 Baldwin St.
Montpelier, VT 05601
(802) 828-3618
(802) 828-0607 Fax
www.vermontfilm.com

VIRGINIA
VIRGINIA FILM OFFICE
901 East Byrd St.
Richmond, VA 23219
(804) 545-5530
(800) 854-6233
(804) 545-5531 Fax
www.film.virginia.org

WASHINGTON
WASHINGTON FILMWORKS
1218 Third Ave., Suite 1709
Seattle, WA 98101
(206) 256-6151
(206) 256-6154 Fax
www.filmwashington.com

WASHINGTON, D.C.
OFFICE OF MOTION PICTURE & TELEVISION DEVELOPMENT
2025 M St. NW, Suite 600
Washington, DC 20036
(202) 727-6608
http://film.dc.gov

WEST VIRGINIA
WEST VIRGINIA FILM OFFICE
90 MacCorkle Ave. SW, #143
S. Charleston, WV 26303
(800) CALLWVA
(304) 558-2200
(304) 558-1662 Fax
www.wvfilm.com

WISCONSIN
WISCONSIN FILM OFFICE
648 N. Plankinton #425

Milwaukee, WI 53203
(414) 287-6235
http://www.filmwisconsin.net/

WYOMING
WYOMING FILM OFFICE
1520 Etchetape Cir.
Cheyenne, WY 82007
(800) 458-6657
(307) 777-3400
(307) 777-2877 Fax
www.filmwyoming.com
www.wyomingfilm.org

BIBLIOGRAPHY AND RESOURCES

STARTING AND RUNNING A BUSINESS

Robert W. Emerson *et al., Business Law* (Barren's Educational Series, Inc. 1997).
Anthony Mancuso, *Form Your Own Limited Liability Company* (Nolo Press 2002).
Anthony Mancuso, *Your Limited Liability Company, an Operating Manual* (Nolo Press 2002).
Fred S. Steingold, *The Employer's Legal Handbook* (Nolo Press 2005).

FILM FINANCE

John W. Cones, *43 Ways to Finance Your Feature Film* (Southern Illinois University Press 1995).
John W. Cones, *Film Finance and Distribution: A Dictionary of Terms* (Silman-James Press 1992).
Bill Daniels *et al., Movie Money: Understanding Hollywood's Creative Accounting Practices* (Silman-James Press 1998).
John Durie *et al., Marketing and Selling Your Film Around the World* (Silman-James Press 2000).
Jeremy Juuso, *Getting the Money* (Michael Wise Productions 2009).
John J. Lee, Jr., *The Producer's Business Handbook* (Focal Press 2000).
Louise Levison, *Filmmakers & Financing* (Focal Press 2001).
Mark Litwak, *Risky Business: Financing and Distributing Independent Films* (Silman-James Press 2004).
Schuyler M. Moore, *The Biz: The Basic Business, Legal, and Financial Aspects of the Film Industry* (Silman-James Press 2002).
Regulation D can be found on the SEC website at www.sec.gov/divisions/corpfin/forms/regd.htm#exemption3.

FILM AND TELEVISION LEGAL: CONTRACTS

Dina Appleton & Daniel Yankelevits, *Hollywood Dealmaking: Negotiating Talent Agreements* (Allworth Press 2002).

Stephen F. Breimer, Esq., *The Screenwriter's Legal Guide* (Allworth Press 1999).

John W. Cones, *The Feature Film Distribution Deal* (Southern Illinois University Press 1997).

Mark Litwak, *Contracts for the Film and Television Industry* (Silman-James Press 1998).

Mark Litwak, *Dealmaking in the Film and Television Industry* (Silman-James Press 2002).

FILM AND TELEVISION BUSINESS AND LEGAL

Gunnar Erickson *et al., The Independent Film Producer's Survival Guide* (Schirmer Trade Books 2002).

Jon M. Garon, *The Independent Filmmaker's Law and Business Guide*, 2nd ed. (Chicago Review Press 2009).

Philip H. Miller, *Media Law*, 4th ed. (Focal Press 2003).

Jon Reiss, *Think Outside the Box Office* (Hybrid Cinema 2010).

INTELLECTUAL PROPERTY

Donald S. Chisum *et al., Understanding Intellectual Property Law* (Matthew Bender Publishing 1996).

Stephen Elias *et al., Patent, Copyright & Trademark* (Nolo Press 2001).

Stephen Fishman, *The Public Domain: How to Find & Use Copyright-Free Writings, Music, Art & More* (Nolo Press 2006).

Craig Joyce *et al., Copyright Law* (Lexis Publishing 2000).

Bruce P. Keller *et al., Copyright Law: A Practitioner's Guide* (PLI Press 2005).

Marshall Leaffer, *Understanding Copyright Law* (Lexis Publishing 1999).

Arnold P. Lutzker, *Content Rights for Creative Professionals* (Focal Press 2003).

Thomas J. McCarthy, *The Rights of Publicity and Privacy*, 2nd ed. (Thomson West 2006).

Melville B. Nimmer *et al., Nimmer on Copyright* (Matthew Bender 2006).

Richard Stim, *Copyright Law* (West Legal Studies 2000).

Richard Stim, *Getting Permission: How to License and Clear Copyrighted Materials Online and Off* (Nolo Press 2000).

Richard Stim *et al., Nondisclosure Agreements* (Nolo Press 2001).

MUSIC LAW

Al Kohn *et al., Kohn on Music Licensing* (Aspen Publishers 2002).

WEBSITES

Attorneys

Attorney Thomas A. Crowell, Esq.: www.thomascrowell.com; www.sclawpartners.com

Attorney Ivan Saperstein, Esq.: www.sclawpartners.com

Attorney Matthew Savare, Esq.: www.lowenstein.com/msavare/

Entertainment attorneys by state from Findlaw.com: http://lawyers.findlaw.com/lawyer/practice/Entertainment,-Sports-&-Leisure-LawCopyright, Intellectual Property, Public Domain.

Law firm of Saperstein & Crowell, LLP: www.sclawpartners.com

Copyright, Intellectual Property, and Public Domain

The United States Copyright Office: www.copyright.gov

The United States Patent and Trademark Office: www.uspto.gov

Search the copyright office website for works registered or renewed since 1978, here: www.copyright.gov/records/

Copyright Registration Short Form PA: www.copyright.gov/forms/formpai.pdf

Copyright Registration Standard Form PA: www.copyright.gov/forms/formpas.pdf

Copyright Office "Circular 45: Copyright Registration for Motion Pictures Including Video Recordings." www.copyright.gov/circs/circ45.pdf

Copyright Office Circular 12: recording copyrights and transfers: www.copyright.gov/circs/circ12.pdf

AUCSM fair use website: www.centerforsocialmedia.org/resources/fair_use/

AUCSM's *Documentary Filmmakers' Statement of Best Practices in Fair Use:* www.centerforsocialmedia.org/resources/publications/documentary_filmmakers_statement_of_best_practices_in_fair_use/

National archives: www.archives.gov/research/formats/film-sound-video.html

Entertainment Unions and Societies

Writers Guild of America: www.wga.org

WGA "Screen Credits Policy": www.wga.org/subpage_writersresources.aspx?id=171

The International Alliance of Theatrical Stage Employees, Moving Picture Technicians, Artists and Allied Crafts of the United States, Its Territories and Canada: www.iatse-intl.org

The National Association of Broadcast Employees and Technicians-Communications Workers of America: www.nabetcwa.org

For info on SAG low-budget contracts: www.sagindie.org/contracts2.html

Casting Society of America: www.castingsociety.com

Legal: General

www.whichdraft.com

Lenders

Three Point Capital: www.3pointcapital.com

Music

ASCAP: www.ascap.com
ASCAP's "ACE" title search: www.ascap.com/ace/
BMI: www.bmi.com
SESAC: www.sesac.com
American Federation of Musicians: www.AFM.org
National archives: www.archives.gov/research/formats/film-sound-video.html

Labor and Employment Law

California laws regarding a worker's status: See the California Independent Contractor FAQ at www.dir.ca.gov/dlse/FAQ_IndependentContractor.html

For more on how the IRS determines a worker's status, see its brochure: "Contractor or Employee" at www.irs.gov/pub/irs-pdf/p1779.pdf

For information on an employer's tax responsibilities, see "Employer's Supplemental Tax Guide" at www.irs.gov/pub/irs-pdf/p15a.pdf

NOTES

CHAPTER 1

[1] See 17 U.S.C. § 102(a)(2010).

CHAPTER 3

[1] *Texas Integrated Conveyor Systems, Inc. v. Innovative Conveyor Concepts, Inc.,* 300 S.W.3d 348, 368 (Tex. App.-Dallas, 2009) ("Under the doctrine of respondeat superior, a principal or employer may be vicariously liable for the tortious acts of an agent or employee if the acts are within the course and scope of employment").

[2] *Celia Hendricks v. Pepperidge Farm, Inc., Holiday Supermarkets, Hellendale Distributors, Inc., and Gale Grunigen,* 16 Phila.Co.Rptr. 164, 167 (Pa.Com.Pl. 1987) ("in order to hold a master vicariously liable for the negligence of a servant, it must be shown that the master has the right to control not only the results of the servant's work but also the very manner in which the work is to be done").

[3] N.Y. LLC. LAW § 206.

CHAPTER 5

[1] Section 2(1) of the Securities Act of 1933, as amended.

[2] *SEC v. W.J. Howey Co.,* 328 U.S. 293 (1946).

[3] www.sec.gov/answers/rule504.htm.

[4] www.sec.gov/answers/rule505.htm.

[5] www.sec.gov/answers/rule506.htm.

[6] www.sec.gov/info/smallbus/secg/formdguide.htm.

CHAPTER 6

[1] See the Hawaiian Film Office website: www.hawaiifilmoffice.com/incentives-tax-credits, accessed March 5, 2010.

[2] www.michiganfilmoffice.org/cm/files/film-Incentive-Combined-FAQs.pdf.

[3] www.michiganfilmoffice.org/cm/files/film-Incentive-Combined-FAQs.pdf.

[4] www.illinoisfilm.biz/index.php?option=com_content&view=article&id=73&Itemid=57.

5 www.filminmaine.com/files/mafi_explained.pdf.

6 However, see www.entertainmentpartners.com/Content/ProductionIncentives/Jurisdictions/US.aspx for more information on individual state information.

7 See New York State Film Production Credit & New York City Made In New York Film Production Tax Credit Instructions for Initial Application Guide, p. 8 (www.nylovesfilm.com/tax/Instructions2009.pdf), downloaded on March 5, 2010.

8 See Michael Cieply, "State Backing Films Says Cannibal Is Deal-Breaker," *New York Times*, June 15, 2010, at A1 (referencing Michigan state production incentive legislation). Online at www.nytimes.com/2010/06/15/movies/15credits.html?emc=eta1.

9 Id.

10 Although *The Women* was able to shoot in Massachusetts using that state's tax incentives. See *NY Times* Media Decoder, July 20, 2010, "Come to Massachusetts: We Love Cannibals!" by Michael Cieply.

11 Internal Revenue Code: Sec. 181: Treatment of Certain Qualified Film and Television Productions.

CHAPTER 7

1 *Nadel v. Play-By-Play Toys & Novelties, Inc.*, 208 F.3d 368 (2d Cir. 2000).

2 See *Charity Group LLC v. Absolut Spirits Co.*, 92 U.S.P.Q.2d 1844 (2009) ("In contract-based submission-of-idea cases in New York, the critical inquiry is the novelty to the recipient.")

3 For definitions and explanations of common contract clauses, see Appendix C, "The Clause Companion," p. 375.

4 *Montz v. Pilgrim Films & Television, Inc.*, WL 2197421, C.A.9 (Cal.), June 3, 2010.

5 *Alliance Sec. Products, Inc., v. Fleming and Co.*, 290 Fed.Appx. 380 (2nd Cir. 2008). ("When 'an idea consists in essence of nothing more than a variation on a basic theme ... novelty cannot be found to exist.'")

6 *Rodriquez v. Heidi Klum Co.*, No. 05 CV 10218, 2008 WL 4449416, at *4 n.11 (S.D.N.Y. Sept. 30, 2008).

7 *Hollywood Screentest of America, Inc., v. NBC Universal, Inc.*, 151 Cal.App.4th 631, 646, 60 Cal. Rptr.3d 279, 290 (Cal.App. 2 Dist., 2007)

8 *Murray v. NBC*, 844 F.2d 988 (2d Cir., 1988).

9 *AEB & Assocs. Design Group, Inc., v. Tonka Corp.*, 853 F.Supp. 724, 734 (S.D.N.Y. 1994) (internal citations and quotation marks omitted).

CHAPTER 8

1 WGA Separation of Rights Guide: www.wga.org/subpage_writersresources.aspx?id=114.

2 WGA Credits Survival Guide: www.wga.org/content/subpage_writersresources.aspx?id=153#1.

3 WGA Screen Credits Policy: www.wga.org/subpage_writersresources.aspx?id=171.

CHAPTER 10

1 www.copyright.gov/circs/circ23.pdf.

2 Circular 22, "How to Investigate the Copyright Status of a Work"; see www.copyright.gov/circs/circ22.pdf.

3 Copyright Office Circular 1, "Copyright Office Basics": www.copyright.gov/circs/circ1.pdf.

[4] See 17 U.S.C. 407 (2010).

[5] U.S. Copyright Office Circular 3, "Copyright Notice," www.copyright.gov/circs/circ03.pdf.

[6] 17 U.S.C. § 205 (2010) Recordation of transfers and other documents. [...] (d) Priority between Conflicting Transfers.—As between two conflicting transfers, the one executed first prevails if it is recorded, in the manner required to give constructive notice under subsection (c), within one month after its execution in the United States or within two months after its execution outside the United States, or at any time before recordation in such manner of the later transfer. Otherwise the later transfer prevails if recorded first in such manner, and if taken in good faith, for valuable consideration or on the basis of a binding promise to pay royalties, and without notice of the earlier transfer.

[7] www.copyright.gov/docs/fees.html.

[8] www.copyright.gov/circs/circ12.pdf.

CHAPTER 11

[1] According to Variety.com, accessed March 10, 2010; www.variety.com/index.asp?layout=slanguage_result&slang=backdoor+pilot&x=0&y=0.

[2] Yes, I know a contract contains *legal* requirements as well; the legal/contractual distinction I draw here is merely a rhetorical device.

CHAPTER 13

[1] See California Fair Employment and Housing Act: www.fehc.ca.gov/act/default.asp.

[2] *S. G. Borello & Sons, Inc., v. Dept. of Industrial Relations*, 48 Cal. 3d 341 (1989).

[3] See California Labor Code Section 3351.5.

[4] California Labor Code Section 3700.5.

[5] *Yellow Cab Cooperative v. Workers' Compensation Appeals Board*, 226 Cal. App.3d 1288 (1991).

[6] *Toyota Motor Sales v. Superior Court*, 220 Cal. App. 3d 864, 877 (1990).

CHAPTER 15

[1] Directors Guild of America Master Bargaining Agreement, Article 7, §7-101.

CHAPTER 17

[1] According to a search of www.IMDB.com conducted on March 22, 2006.

CHAPTER 18

[1] *Clark v. ABC*, 684 F.2d 1208 (6th Cir. 1982).

[2] *Psenicska et al. v. 20th Cent. Fox Film Corp et al.*, Summary Order No. 08-4604-cv.

CHAPTER 20

[1] *Woods v. Universal,* 920 F. Supp. 62 (SDNY 1996).

[2] The Copyright website: www.benedict.com/Visual/Monkeys/Monkeys.aspx, accessed June 26, 2010.

[3] 17 U.S.C. § 107 (2010).

[4] 17 U.S.C. § 120 (2010). "Scope of exclusive rights in architectural works: (a) Pictorial representations permitted. The copyright in an architectural work that has been constructed does not include the right to prevent the making, distributing, or public display of pictures, paintings, photographs, or other pictorial representations of the work, if the building in which the work is embodied is located in or ordinarily visible from a public place."

[5] See 17 U.S.C. §301(b)(4) (2010).

[6] Lanham Act § 43(a).

[7] *Allen v. National Video, Inc.,* 610 F. Supp. 612, 627, 226 U.S.P.Q. 483 (S.D.N.Y. 1985).

[8] *Facenda v. NFL Films,* 542 F.3d 1007 (3rd Cir Pa. 2008).

[9] *Rogers v. Grimaldi,* 875 F.2d 994, 10 U.S.P.Q.2d 1825 (2d Cir. 1989).

[10] *Rogers v. Grimaldi,* 875 F.2d 994, 10 U.S.P.Q.2d 1825 (2d Cir. 1989).

[11] *Waits v. Frito-Lay, Inc.,* 978 F.2d 1093, 23 U.S.P.Q.2d 1721, 1733 (9th Cir. 1992).

[12] N.Y. Civ. Rights Law §§ 50–51 (McKinney 1992).

[13] *Burke v. Mars, Inc.,* 571 F.Supp.2d 446, 452 (2008).

[14] 15 U.S.C. § 1125(a)(1).

[15] Under the Lanham Act (15 U.S.C.).

[16] *Warner Bros. Entm't Inc. v. Ideal World Direct,* 516 F.Supp.2d 261, 268 (S.D.N.Y. 2007).

[17] See 15 U.S.C. §1115(b)(4) (2010).

[18] *Caterpillar Inc. v. Walt Disney Co.,* 287 F. Supp.2d 913, 922 (C.D. Ill. 2003).

[19] *Caterpillar Inc. v. Walt Disney Co.,* 287 F. Supp.2d 913 (C.D. Ill. 2003).

[20] *Hormel Foods Corp. v. Jim Henson Productions, Inc.,* No. 95 Civ. 5473, slip op. at 4, 1995 WL 567369 (S.D.N.Y. Sept. 22, 1995).

CHAPTER 22

[1] *Waits v. Frito Lay,* 978 F. 2d 1093 (9th Cir. 1992).

[2] *Bridgeport Music, Inc., et al., vs. Dimension Films,* 2004 Fed App. 0297P (6th Cir.).

[3] *Lennon v. Premise Media Corp.* 556 F.Supp.2d 310, 323 (S.D.N.Y., 2008).

[4] *Lennon v. Premise Media Corp.* 556 F.Supp.2d 310, 323 (S.D.N.Y., 2008).

CHAPTER 25

[1] The owner of the copyright has the exclusive right "… to distribute copies or phonorecords of the copyrighted work to the public by sale or other transfer of ownership, or by rental, lease, or lending." 17 U.S.C. § 106(3) (2010).

CHAPTER 26

1 www.oscars.org/awards/academyawards/rules/rule12.html.

2 https://www.createspace.com/pub/l/general_amazon.do?rewrite=true&utm%5Fid=4603& ref=404248.

3 https://www.createspace.com/Products/DVD/.

4 Paragraph 7(g), Create Space Member Services Agreement, accessed November 24, 2010, (https://www.createspace.com/Help/Rights/MemberAgreement.jsp).

5 Paragraph 7(e), Create Space Member Services Agreement, accessed January 12, 2010, (https://www.createspace.com/Help/Rights/MemberAgreement.jsp).

6 www.youtube.com/t/youtube_rentals.

7 www.youtube.com/t/partnerships_benefits.

8 www.youtube.com/t/terms. Section 4E.

9 https://www.google.com/adsense/login/en_US/.

10 https://www.google.com/adsense/support/bin/answer.py?answer=73987.

11 http://drhorrible.com/.

APPENDIX A

1 17 U.S.C. §102(a), (2010).

2 17 U.S.C. §101, (2010).

3 Id.

4 Id.

5 Id.

6 17 U.S.C. §101.

7 U.S. Copyright Office Circular 45, "Copyright Registration for Motion Pictures Including Video Recordings," www.copyright.gov/circs/circ45.pdf.

8 U.S. Copyright Office Circular 1, "Copyright Office Basics," http://www.copyright.gov/circs/circ01.pdf

9 See *Miller v. Universal Studios*, 650 F.2d 1365 (5th Cir. 1981).

10 *Hogan v. DC Comics*, 48 F.Supp.2d, 298 (S.D.N.Y. January 26, 1999).

11 See 17 U.S.C § 105, (2010). Subject matter of copyright: "United States Government works: Copyright protection under this title is not available for any work of the United States Government, but the United States Government is not precluded from receiving and holding copyrights transferred to it by assignment, bequest, or otherwise."

12 17 U.S.C §101 (2010).

13 *MyWebGrocer, LLC, v. Hometown Info, Inc.*, 375 F.3d 190, 194 (2d Cir. 2004).

14 *Williams v. Crichton,* 84 F.3d 581, 587 (2d Cir. 1996).

15 *Reyher v. Children's Television Workshop*, 533 F.2d 87, 91 (2d Cir. 1976).

16 *Swirsky v. Carey*, 376 F.3d 841, 848 (9th Cir. 2004).

17 http://www.copyright.gov/fls/fl102.html.

18 17 U.S.C. §107 (2010).

19 *Campbell v. Acuff-Rose Music, Inc.,* 510 US 569, 579 (1994).

[20] *Clean Flicks of Colorado, LLC, v. Soderbergh*, 433 F.Supp.2d 1236, 1241 (D.Colo., 2006).

[21] Judge Pierre N. Leval, "Toward a Fair Use Standard," 103 *Harv. L. Rev.* 1105, 1116 (March 1990). "The first fair use factor calls for a careful evaluation whether the particular quotation is of the transformative type that advances knowledge and the progress of the arts or whether it merely repackages, free riding on another's creations."

[22] *Lennon v. Premise Media Corp.*, 556 F.Supp.2d 310, 327 (S.D.N.Y., 2008) ("In considering the fourth factor, [the] concern is not whether the secondary use suppresses or even destroys the market for the original work or its potential derivatives, but whether the secondary use usurps the market of the original work. The market for potential derivative uses includes only those that creators of original works would in general develop or license others to develop").

[23] Patry on Copyright, §10:150, Westlaw, (2010).

[24] *Sony Corp. of America v. Universal City Studios, Inc.*, 464 U.S. 417, 455 n.40 (1984).

[25] *Gottlieb Development LLC v. Paramount Pictures Corp.*, 590 F.Supp.2d 625, 632 (2008).

[26] *Sandoval v. New Line Cinema Corp.*, 147 F.3d 215 (2d Cir. 1998).

[27] Id.

[28] *Gottlieb Development LLC v. Paramount Pictures Corp.*, 590 F.Supp.2d 625, 632 (2008).

[29] Patry on Copyright, §10.10, "dismissal of the plaintiff's case on the ground it failed to establish a prima facie case on *de minimis* grounds avoids the more complicated fair use."

[30] Or as the famous Judge Learned Hand put it: "If by some magic, a man who had never known it were to compose anew Keats' 'Ode to a Grecian Urn', he would be an author, and, if he copyrighted it, others may not copy that poem, though they might of course copy Keats." *Sheldon v. Metro-Goldwyn Pictures Corp.*, 801F.2d 49, 54 (2d Cir. 1936).

[31] 17 USC 101.

[32] *Janky v. Lake County Convention And Visitors Bureau*, 576 F.3d 356, 362 (C.A.7 (Ind.),2009).

[33] *Gaylord v. U.S.*, 595 F.3d 1364, 1377 (C.A.Fed., 2010).

[34] *Childress v. Taylor*, 945 F.2d 500, 507 (2d Cir. 1991).

[35] Nimmer on Copyright, §6.10[c].

[36] *Aalmuhammed v. Lee*, 202 F.3d 1227 (9th Cir. 2000).

[37] 17 U.S.C. §101 (2010).

[38] *CCNV v. Reid*, 490 U.S. 730 (1989).

[39] *Gladwell Gov't Servs, Inc., v. County of Marin*, No. 05-17327, 2008 U.S. App. LEXIS 2291 (9th Cir. January 28, 2008).

[40] 17 U.S.C. §101.

[41] *Carell v. Shubert Organization, Inc.*, 104 F. Supp. 2d 236, 243–244 (S.D.N.Y. 2000).

[42] Cal. Labor Code §3351.5.

[43] *Weinstein Co. v. Smokewood Entertainment Group, LLC*, 664 F.Supp.2d 332, 341 (S.D.N.Y.,2009) ("the intention of a copyright owner seeking to transfer an ownership interest must be clear and unequivocal").

[44] *Effects Associates, Inc., v. Cohen*, 908 F.2d 555 (1990).

[45] *Weinstein Co. v. Smokewood Entertainment Group, LLC*, 664 F.Supp.2d 332, 341 (S.D.N.Y.,2009).

[46] 17 U.S.C. §203.

[47] For more on copyright duration, see the U.S. Copyright Circular 1, "Copyright Office Basics," www.copyright.gov/circs/circ01.pdf, and Circular 15a, "Duration of Copyright: Provisions of the Law Dealing with the Length of Copyright Protection," www.copyright.gov/circs/circ15a.pdf.

[48] *Warner Bros. Inc. American Broadcasting Companies*, 654 F.2d 204, 208 (2d Cir. 1981).

[49] See 17 U.S.C. §504 (2010).

[50] See 17 U.S.C. §505 (2010).

[51] See 17 U.S.C. §502 (2010).

[52] See 17 U.S.C. §503 (2010).

[53] See 17 U.S.C. §506 (2010); 18 U.S.C. § 2319 (2010).

[54] *Carson v Reynolds*, 48 CPR (2d) 57 (1980).

[55] *Zacchini v. Scripps-Howard Broadcasting Co.*, 433 U.S. 562 (1977).

[56] *Tyne v. Time Warner Entertainment*, 336 F.3d 1286 (11th Cir. 2003).

[57] *Seale v. Gramercy Pictures*, 949 F. Supp. 331, 337 (E.D. Penn. 1996).

[58] *White v. Samsung Electronics America, Inc.*, 971 F.2d 1395 (9th Cir. 1992).

[59] *Twist v. TCI Cablevision, Inc.* SC84856 (2003).

[60] Restatement (Second) of Torts §652B.

[61] Restatement (Second) of Torts §652D.

[62] 42 U.S.C. 1320d-6.

[63] Restatement (Second) of Torts §652E.

[64] 18 U.S.C. §2511(1).

[65] Restatement (Second) of Torts §558.

[66] Although some states, such as Massachusetts, allow libel for harmful statements published with "actual malice." See *Noonan v. Staples, Inc.*, 556 F. 3d 20 (1st Cir. 2009).

[67] Restatement (Second) of Torts §559.

[68] Robert D. Sack, Sack on Defamation, §2.4.1, 2–12, (3d ed., PLI 2005).

[69] *Bindrim v. Mitchell*, 92 Cal. App. 3d 61, 78 (1979). The test of whether a fictional character so closely resembles an actual person as to satisfy the "of and concerning" test is "whether a reasonable person, reading the book, would understand that the fictional character therein pictured was, in actual fact, the plaintiff acting as described."

[70] For more on defamation in fictional characters see Matthew Savare's excellent article, "Falsity, Fault, and Fiction: A New Standard for Defamation in Fiction" (Fall 2004). *UCLA Entertainment Law Review*, 12 (1).

[71] *Salek v. Passaic Collegiate School*, 255 N.J. Super. 355 (App. Div. 1992).

[72] Robert D. Sack, Sack on Defamation, §4.2.4, (3d ed., PLI 2005).

[73] *Bichler v. Union Bank & Trust Co. of Grand Rapids*, 745 F.2d 1006, 1012–15 (1984).

[74] *Milkovich v. Lorain Journal*, 497 US 1 (1990).

[75] *Gregory v. McDonnell Douglas Corp.*, 552 P.2d 425 (1976).

[76] *Sullivan v. Conway*, 157 F.3d 1092 (7th Cir. 1998).

[77] *Yeagle v. Collegiate Times*, 255 Va. 293, 26 Media L. Rep. (BNA) 2337 (1998).

[78] *Chaiken v. VV Publishing Corp.*, 119 F.3d 1018 (2d Cir 1991).

[79] Id.

[80] *Noonan v. Staples, Inc.*, 556 F. 3d 20 (1st Cir. 2009).

APPENDIX B

[1] *Weinstein Co. v. Smokewood Entertainment Group, LLC,* 664 F.Supp.2d 332, 346 (S.D.N.Y., 2009). ("It is fundamental to contract law that mere participation in negotiations and discussions does not create binding obligation, even if agreement is reached on all disputed terms.") However, a court can find that parties have entered a preliminary agreement to negotiate in good faith based on the following factors: "(1) the language of the agreement; (2) the context of the negotiations; (3) the existence of open terms; (4) any partial performance; and (5) the necessity of putting the agreement in final form, as indicated by the customary form of such transactions." *Weinstein* at 356, internal citations omitted.

APPENDIX D

1. Special thanks to Sheafe B. Walker, Esq., for his hard work in helping to prepare this section.
2. Independent Contractor versus Employee, www.dir.ca.gov/dlse/FAQ_IndependentContractor. html at 1 citing *S. G. Borello & Sons, Inc., v. Dept. of Industrial Relations*, 48 Cal. 3d 431(1989).
3. Other agencies such as the Division of Workers' Compensation (DWC) may use the "control test" which may result in a different determination, that is, (IC under one statute and an EE under another).
4. Independent Contractor versus Employee, www.dir.ca.gov/dlse/FAQ_IndependentContractor.html at 1 citing *Yellow Cab Cooperative v. Workers' Compensation Appeals Board*, 226 Cal. App 3d 1288 (1991).
5. California Labor Code §3351.5 (c).
6. *Justmed, Inc., v. Byce*, 600 F.3d 1118, 1128 (2010), FN 7, citing Restatement (Second) of Agency §220, comment e.
7. See New York Guidelines for Determining Worker Status: Performing Artists, www.labor.state. ny.us/ui/pdfs/ia31817.pdf.
8. Independent Contractors, www.labor.state.ny.us/ui/dande/ic.shtm.
9. Id.
10. 8 CCR 11756.
11. See California Child Labor Guide, Section 9, http://www.dir.ca.gov/dlse/CLLPamphlet2000.pdf.
12. "No infant under the age of one month may be employed on any motion picture set or location unless a licensed physician who is board-certified in pediatrics provides written certification that the infant is at least 15 days old and ... is physically capable of handling the stress of filmmaking, and the infant's lungs, eyes, heart and immune system are sufficiently developed to withstand the potential risks." CLC §1308.8(a).
13. CLC §1308(a)(5).
14. "All travel time between the studio and a location counts as work time. Up to 45 minutes travel from on-location overnight lodging to a worksite is not generally considered worktime": www.dir. ca.gov/dlse/CLLPamphlet2000.pdf at 39.
15. However, "minors under 16 do not require the presence of a studio teacher for up to one hour for wardrobe, makeup, hairdressing, promotional publicity, personal appearances, or audio recording, if these activities are not on the set, if school is not in session and if the parent or guardian is present." Id at 39.
16. For a complete chart: www.dir.ca.gov/dlse/MinorsSummaryCharts.pdf.
17. "[i]ncludes, but is not limited to, services as an actor, actress, dancer, musician, comedian, singer, stuntperson, voice-over artist, or other performer or entertainer, or as a songwriter, musical producer or arranger, writer, director, producer, production executive, choreographer, composer, conductor, or designer." CFC §6750(a).
18. CFC §6750(b).
19. See §6752(d) for statutory requirements of the trust.
20. CFC §6753(a).
21. Id. Only one "Coogan Trust Account" is required for a minor. However, if none exists, one must be established under the aforementioned regulations.
22. CFC §6753(c).
23. CFC §6753 (4).
24. CFC §6752(c)(6).
25. CFC §6751(a).

[26] CFC §6751(c).

[27] New York Law will accept a Coogan Trust Account, but New York requires that once the trust's balance is $250,000, a trust company must be appointed custodian for the account. NYEPTL Article 7P7 § 7-7.1(2)(b).

[28] The statute defines as "the total compensation prior to taxes, deductions, or commissions payable to a child performer pursuant to a contract." New York Labor Law Article 4-a §150(5).

[29] New York Labor Law Article 4-a §151(4)(a).

[30] New York Estates, Powers, and Trusts Law Article 7 §7-7.1 (2) (a).

[31] New York Arts and Cultural Affairs Law Article 35 §35.03 (1)(b).

[32] New York Arts and Cultural Affairs Law Article 35 §35.03 (2)(d).

[33] See New York Labor Law Article 4 §130 (2)(a).

[34] See "Permitted Working Hours for Minor in New York": www.labor.ny.gov/workerprotection/laborstandards/workprot/hrswork.shtm.

[35] New York Labor Law Article 4-a §152(2)(a).

INDEX

A

ABL lending process, 70–71
Above-the-line costs, 48
Accountants, 47–48
Accounting
   for Director's Services Agreements, 188
   for Performer's Services Agreements, 219
   for Producer's Services Agreement, 175
   under content aggregator deal, 319
   under Screenplay Purchase Agreements,
      107
Accredited investors, 58–59
Actors, 203–225. *See also* Performer's
      Services Agreements; Screen Actors
      Guild (SAG)
   agents and, 222–223
   auditions for, 223
   likeness approval for, 387
   Performer's Services Agreement for, 203,
      212–222
   quotes for, 224
   SAG for, 6, 205–212
Actor's Fund of America, 402
"Additional insureds", 50
Advertising
   and DIY distribution, 308
AFM. *See* American Federation of
      Musicians
AFTRA. *See* American Federation of
      Television and Radio Artists
      (AFTRA)
Agents, 222–223
Agreements. *See* Assumption Agreements;
      Collective Bargaining Agreements;
      Composer's Services Agreements;
      Co-production agreements; Crew
      Services Agreements; Director's
      Services Agreements; Distribution
      agreements; Distribution Rights
      Acquisition Agreements; Film Clip
      License Agreement; Life Rights
      Consent Agreements; Literary

Property Acquisition Agreements;
      Low-budget agreements; Master
      Bargaining Agreements; Modified
      Low-budget agreements; Music
      Licensing Agreements; Negative
      Pickup Agreements; Nondisclosure
      agreements; Performer's Services
      Agreements; Producer's Services
      Agreement; Production-Financing/
      Distribution Agreements; Screenplay
      Purchase Agreements; Service
      Agreements; Short film agreements;
      Ultra-low budget agreements; Writer's
      Collaboration Agreements; Writer's
      Services Agreements
Amazon.com, 315–316
American Cinematographers Manual, 3
American Federation of Musicians (AFM),
      271
American Federation of Television and
      Radio Artists (AFTRA), 167
American Society of Composers, Artists and
      Publishers (ASCAP), 265
American University Center for Social
      Media (AUCSM), 246
Approval rights, under Performer's Services
      Agreements, 217
Arbitration
   for deal points, 383
   under contract law, 31
Architectural copyrights, 246–247
Artwork licenses, 248
   E&O insurance and, 256–257
   infringement under, 255
ASCAP. *See* American Society of
      Composers, Artists and
      Publishers
Asset-backed lender (ABL), 69
   working with, 70–71
Associate producers, 171
Assumption Agreements,
      210, 304

Attorneys, 43–47
  copyrights and, 134
  fees for, 45–46
  Volunteer Lawyers for the Arts
    Organization and, 46
AUCSM. *See* American University Center
  for Social Media
Audiovisual works, 330
Auditions, 223
Authors. *See also* Joint authorship, of
  screenplays; Screenwriters
  under copyrights, 330

B

Backdoor pilot, 152
"Bankable" star, 163
Below-the-line costs, 48
BMI. *See* Broadcast Music, Inc
Bonus compensation, 107
  under Writer's Services Agreement, 114
Box office, percentage of, 310
Breach of contract, 31, 371–374
  injunctions from, 373–374
  material, 372
  minor, 371–372
  remedies for, 372–374
Broadcast Music, Inc. (BMI), 265
Budget
  and DIY distribution, 308
Budgets, for productions
  above-the-line costs, 48
  below-the-line costs, 48
Buyouts, 29

C

C. Corporations, 40
  taxation for, 40
California
  child labor laws in, 400–403
  DLSE in, 395
  independent contractors in, 395–397
Canadian tax credits, 70
Casting directors, 223
Cease-and-Desist letters, 46–47
Certificate of Authorship, 142–143
Chain of title, 131–143. *See also*
  Copyright(s)
  Certificate of Authorship as part of,
    142–143

definition of, 131
  in screenplay clearance reports, 135–136
Chaplin, Charlie, 402
Child Actor's Bill. *See* Coogan Law
Child labor laws, 400–404
  in California, 400–403
  Coogan Law, 403
  disaffirmance of, 403
  in Louisiana, 405
  mandatory trust funds under, 403–404
  in New Mexico, 405
  in New York, 403–404
  PEMEI and, 401
  permit requirements, 400–401, 403
  teacher requirements under, 401, 404
  work hours under, 401
Child Performer Education and Trust Act,
  New York (2003), 403–404
Children. *See* Minors
Cinematography. *See* Pick-up shots;
  Principal photography; Second-unit
  photography
Clauses. *See* Favored-nations clauses;
  Inducement clauses; Merger clauses;
  Morals clauses; Savings clauses
"clean states", 72
Clearances, on set, 244
Collective Bargaining Agreements, 146
Companies. *See* Corporations; General
  partnerships; Limited liability
  companies; Limited partnerships;
  Loan-out companies; Production
  companies; Sole proprietorships
Compensation. *See also* Contingent
  compensation; Deferred compensation;
  Fixed compensation; Net Profits; Per
  diems; Residuals
  for artwork licenses, 249
  as deal points, 376–377
  bonuses as, 29, 107
  buyouts as, 29
  contingent, 29, 110, 114
  deferred, 29, 114
  distribution rights as, 29
  extension payments as, for Option
    Agreements, 104
  fixed, 29, 110, 113–114
  licensing fees as, 29
  net profits as, 29
  option prices as, 29

rental fees as, 29
royalties as, 29
under Composer's Services Agreements, 274
under Crew Services Agreements, 198–199
under Life Rights Consent Agreements, 129–130
under Literary Property Acquisition Agreements, 120
under location agreements, 240
under Producer's Services Agreement, 174–175
Compensatory damages, 372
Completion bonds, 50–51
completion guarantor for, 50
Composers, 272
Composer's Services Agreements, 272–278
compensation under, 274
composers under, 272
credits under, 274–275
E&O insurance under, 276
inducement clauses in, 277
publicity under, 275
terms of, 273
Cones, John W., 4
Confidentiality obligations, 177
Consequential damages, 372
Content aggregator, 317–318
Content aggregator deal, 318–320
accounting, 319
exclusivity, 319
fee, 318
grant of rights/territories, 318
no assignment, 319
power of attorney, 319
representations and warranties/indemnification, 319–320
reservation of rights, 318
term, 318–319
Contingent compensation, 29, 110, 114
as deal point, 376
under Performer's Services Agreements, 215
under Producer's Services Agreement, 174
under Screenplay Purchase Agreements, 110
Contract law, for films, 22, 27–32, 367–374
arbitration under, 31

clauses under, 27
compensation under, 29
damages under, 367, 372–373
deal memos under, 27
deal points in, 27–28
elements of, 368
financing under, 29
intellectual property rights under, 28
leverage in, 367
parties under, 28
physical property under, 29
services under, 28–29
Contracts, 368–374. *See also* Breach of contract; Contract law, for films; Deal points; Form contracts; Investment contracts; Services contracts
breach of contract, 31, 371–374
capacity in, 369–370
consideration in, 369
definiteness in, 369
elements of, 368
express, 371
implied, 371
legal purpose of, 370–371
Contractual restrictions
on product placement and endorsements, 162
Coogan, Jackie, 402
Coogan Law, 402, 403
Co-production agreements, 53
Copyright infringement, 353–354
penalties for, 354
proof of, 353–354
Copyright law, 13, 23–26
distribution under, 24
doctrine of independent creation and, 340
exclusive rights under, 24
fair use under, 234, 245–246, 255, 336–339
film properties under, 24–26
ideas under, 334
joint authorship of screenplays under, 94, 96–97, 342–344
licensing under, 25
protections under, 23, 332–335
under Distribution Rights Acquisition Agreements, 303
"work" defined under, 137
Copyright License Request Letter, 349–350

Copyright notices, 139, 285
  disclaimers and, 285
Copyright(s), 13, 329. *See also* Idea rights
  architectural, 246–247
  assignment/transfer of, 139–140
  attorneys and, 135
  for audiovisual works, 330
  Certificate of Authorship and, 142–143
  clearing for, 132
  constructive notice for, 140
  Copyright License Request Letter for,
    349–350
  costs for, 88, 138
  de minimis for, 339–340
  derivative works under, 330–331
  development and, 76
  duration of works and, 331, 352–353
  during post-production, 262
  infringement of, 353–354
  licensing of, 348–349
  for music licensing, 263–266
  notice of, 139
  on film sets, 245–248
  ownership of, 340–343
  public domain and, 132, 332
  recordation of, 140, 142
  referenced, 135
  registration of, 136–139, 351
  rights under, 329
  scènes à faire and, 335
  in screenplay clearance reports, 135
  searches for, 133–134
  short form assignment of, 141
  terminology for, 328–332
  under Distribution Rights Acquisition
    Agreements, 303
  under Film Clip License Agreement,
    283
  under Literary Property Acquisition
    Agreements, 119
  under Screenplay Purchase Agreements,
    106–107
  work made for hire and, 344–348
  Writer's Collaboration Agreements and,
    92–93
Corporations, 35, 37, 40
  C., 40
  Subchapter S., 40
CreateSpace, making money with, 316
CreateSpace contract, 317

CreateSpace eStore, 316
Creative control
  as deal point, 384
  in Director's Services Agreements, 186
Credits
  artwork licenses and, 249
  as deal point, 377
  location agreements and, 241
  under Composer's Services Agreements,
    274–275
  under Crew Services Agreements, 199
  under Director's Services Agreements,
    188–189
  under Distribution Rights Acquisition
    Agreements, 299
  under Film Clip License Agreement, 282
  under Life Rights Consent Agreements,
    130
  under Literary Property Acquisition
    Agreements, 121
  under Music Licensing Agreements, 269
  under Performer's Services Agreements,
    216
  under Producer's Services Agreement,
    175–176
  under Screenplay Purchase Agreements,
    108
  under Writer's Services Agreements, 116
  WGA policy for, 98–99
Crew Services Agreements, 183, 195–201
  compensation under, 198–199
  credits under, 199
  exclusivity during, 198
  inducement clauses in, 201
  per diems under, 198
  perquisites as part of, 201
  publicity under, 199
  reimbursements under, 198
  rights assignment under, 199
  termination of, 200
  terms of, 197–198

D

Damages, 367, 372–373
  compensatory, for breach of contract,
    372
  consequential, 372–373
  under contract law, for films, 367
Deal memos, 27

in Performer's Services Agreements, 212
Deal points, 27, 375–391
 approval as, 375–376
 arbitration for, 383
 choice of law in, 384
 compensation as, 376–377
 conditions precedent, 377
 creative control as, 384
 credits as, 377
 default-and-cure provision as,
  384–385
 deferred compensation, 377–378
 delegation of, 383
 engagement, 378
 favored-nations clause as, 378
 force majeure and, 385–386
 future services, option on, 380
 holdback provisions as, 379
 indemnification as, 386
 inducement clauses as, 387
 "key man" clause, 379
 kill fee in, 379
 likeness approval as, 387
 major, 375–382
 merger clauses as, 387
 net profits as, 379–380
 option on future services, 380
 parties, 380
 pay or play as, 380
 precedent conditions, 377
 publicity as, 389
 remedies, 241
 representations and warranties, 381
 reserved rights as, 381
 residuals as, 376
 reversion of rights as, 381
 right of first negotiation/last refusal as,
  389–390
 rights granted, 381–382
 royalties as, 376
 savings clauses as, 390
 security interest as, 391
 supporting, 382–391
 termination of, 390
 terms of, 382, 385
 third party beneficiary in, 388
 waivers to, 391
 work made for hire and, 382
Defamation, 359–366
 actual malice in, 361–362

 defenses to, 362–364
 in depiction releases, 229
 in films, 360–361
 gross irresponsibility and, 364–365
 libel as, 359
 parody and, 363
 publication of, 361
 of public figures, 361–362
 republication of, 361
 retraction laws and, 365
 slander as, 359
 statements of, 360
Default-and-cure provisions,
  384–385
Deferred compensation, 29, 114
 as deal point, 376
 under Director's Services Agreements,
  188
 under Performer's Services Agreements,
  215
 under Producer's Services Agreement,
  175
 under Writer's Service Agreements, 114
Deliverables, 154–155, 301–302
 legal/business, 302
 physical, 302
De minimis (of the least), for copyrights,
  339
Depiction releases, 229–232
 defamation in, 229
 E&O insurance and, 230
 invasion of privacy in, 230
 for minors, 231–232
 notice releases and, 232
 right of publicity in, 229
Derivative works, 330–331
Development, of film properties, 7, 10–11.
  See also Copyright law; Idea rights
 acquisition as part of, 10
 copyright protection as part of, 76
 idea rights as part of, 77–86
 Option Agreements and, 105
DGA. *See* Directors Guild of America
Directors. *See also* Director's Services
  Agreements
 DGA and, 183
 Director's Services Agreement for,
  183–193
Directors Guild of America (DGA), 183
 MBA for, 189

Director's Services Agreements, 183–193
accounting for, 188
compensation under, 187–188
conditions precedent in, 173
creative control as part of, 186
credits under, 188–189
delivery standards under, 190–191
exclusivity as part of, 185
festivals/premieres and, 192
inducement clauses in, 192
net profits under, 193
pay or play under, 190
per diems under, 187
perquisites as part of, 193
post-production services under, 190
publicity under, 189–190
reimbursements under, 186
right of first negotiation/last refusal in,
192
rights assignments under, 189
termination of, 191
terms of, 184–185
Disclaimers, 285
Discrimination, under employment
law, 165
Distribution, 289–306
agreements, 4
as compensation, 29
deals, 290–291
exclusions in, 293
expenses during, 293, 304–305
fees, 293, 298
film festivals and, 306
forms of, 289
gross receipts from, 293
licensing and, 25
money pipeline, 291
residuals and, 293
rights to, 8, 12–13
subdistributors and, 289
under copyright law, 24
Distribution agreements, 4, 290. *See
also* Distribution rights acquisition
agreements
deliverables under, 301–302
distribution rights acquisition agreements,
290, 295–303
negative pickup agreement, 290
production-financing/distribution
agreement, 290

Distribution fee, 291
Distribution rights acquisition agreements,
290, 295–303
Assumption Agreements as part of, 304
copyrights under, 302
credits under, 299
E&O insurance under, 303
laboratory access letter as part of,
303–304
recoupable expenses under, 299
rights assignments under, 296
territories under, 298
Distributor's rentals, 292
Division of Labor Standards Enforcement
(DLSE), in California, 395
DLSE. *See* Division of Labor Standards
Enforcement
Doctrine of independent creation, 340
Documentaries, fair use in, 246
*Documentary Filmmakers' Statement of Best
Practices in Fair Use*, 246
"Doing business as" (d.b.a.)
certificates, 38
Do-it-yourself (DIY) distribution, 307
content aggregator deal, 318–320
DVD distribution, 307, 314–317
four-wall agreement, 311–314
online distribution, 307, 317–318
steps in, 308–309
theatrical distribution, 307, 309–311
YouTube, 320–321
Droit moral. *See* Moral rights
Duplication vs. replication, 315
Duration of works, for copyrights, 330,
351–353
DVD distribution, 307, 314–317
CreateSpace, making money with, 316
CreateSpace contract, 317
DVD duplication on demand,
315–316
fulfillment companies, 314–315
DVD duplication on demand, 315–316

E
E&O insurance. *See* Errors and Omissions
insurance
Employment law, 393–405. *See also*
Independent contractors
discrimination under, 165

during pre-production phase, compliance with, 165
  employer responsibilities under, 399–400
  IRS and, 394–395
  for minors, 166–167, 400–404
  taxation under, 394
  work status under, 394
Engagement/production services, 150–151
Equity investment, 55
  indie film net profits, 56
  net profits, 55–56
Equity investments, 55–56
  in LLCs, 55
Errors and Omissions (E&O) insurance, 49
  artwork licenses and, 256–257
  depiction releases and, 230
  under Composer's Services Agreements, 276
  under Distribution Rights Acquisition Agreements, 303
Escrow accounts, 44
Exclusivity
  under content aggregator deal, 319
Executive producers, 171
Exhibitors, 292
Exhibitor's net, 292
Express contracts, 371
Extension payments, under Option Agreements, 104
Extras, 229
  notice releases and, 232
  under SAG, 229
E-Z tabs, 9

F

Fair use, 277
  categories of, 336
  in documentaries, 246
  legal determinations of, 336–337
  transformative determinations for, 337
  under copyright law, 234, 245–246, 256, 335–339
False endorsement, 250–251
False light, 358–359. *See also* Defamation
Favored-nations clauses
  as deal point, 378
  in Performer's Services Agreements, 224
Fees

attorney, 45
  distribution, 293, 298
  licensing, as compensation, 29
  rental, 29
  for shooting permits, 237–238
  subdistribution, 293
  under content aggregator deal, 318
50/50 net deal, 290–291
Film(s)
  defamation in, 360–361
  video *v.*, 5
Film bookers, 309–310
Film Clip License Agreement, 281–283
  copyrights under, 282
  credits under, 282
  rights assignment under, 281–282
Film clips, 279–283
  Film Clip License Agreement for, 281–283
  quitclaim licenses for, 281–282
Film festivals
  Director's Services Agreements and, 192
  distribution and, 306
  Producer's Services Agreement and, 180
Film properties. *See also* Screenplays
  financing of, 10, 53–61
  under copyright law, 24–26
Film tax credits, and production incentives, 63–64
  asset-backed lenders, working with, 70–71
  credits into cash, 69–70
  eligibility requirements, 64–65
  good tax credit state selection, 72–73
  production tax credits, types of, 66–67
  state tax credits application, 67–69
Film's net profit, 57, 305
Financing, 10, 53–61. *See also* Loans; Promissory notes; Securities laws
  with co-production agreements, 53
  equity investment as, 55
  securities laws and, 56–60
  through credit cards, 53
  through loans, 53, 54
  "out of pocket", 54
  through promissory notes, 55
  under contract law, 28–29
First Amendment (U.S. Constitution)
  life story rights and, 125
  right of publicity and, 355–356

Fixed compensation, 29, 110, 114
    caps on, 180–181
    as deal point, 376
    under Director's Services Agreements,
        187–188
    under Producer's Services Agreement,
        175
    under Screenplay Purchase Agreements,
        110
    under Writer's Service Agreements, 114
Force majeure (acts of God), 178, 191, 200
    deal points and, 385–385
Form contracts, 4
Four-wall agreement, 311–314
    advertising, 312
    box-office receipts/income, 312
    engagement, 311
    four-wall fee, 311
    parties, 311
    permissions, 312
    publicity, 312
    representations and warranties, 312–313
    rights, 312
    services, 311
    shipping costs, 312
    tips and tricks, 313–314
Fulfillment companies, 314–315

G

General partnerships, 38–39
    duties under, 38
    for joint authorship of screenplays, 95
    liabilities under, 38
Gilliam, Terry, 243
Good tax credit state selection
    federal incentives, 72–73
    film content, 72
    incentives, 72
    location, 72
    nature of, 72
    office set up, 72
    recapturing, 72
Grant of rights/territories
    under content aggregator deal, 318
Grantor
    artwork, description of, 249
    assignment of rights in, 249
    compensation for, 249
    credits andcopyright, 249
    film, title and description of, 249
    remedies, 250
    waivers in, 250
Gross receipts, 291
Gross rentals, 291

H

Holdback provisions, 379
House nut, 292

I

IATSE. *See* International Alliance of
    Theatrical Stage Employees
Idea rights, 77–86. *See also* Nondisclosure
    agreements
    NDAs and, 77–79
    "novelty" requirement for, 82–84
    Submission Releases and, 77–79
Implied contracts, 371
Independent contractors, 165–166, 394
    in California, 395–397
    in New York, 397–398
    taxation for, 394
    for Unemployment insurance, 394
    for Worker's Compensation insurance,
        394
    work made for hire and, 344
Indie film net profits, 56
Inducement, 192
Inducement clauses, 42
    in Composer's Services Agreements,
        277
    in Crew Services Agreements, 201
    as deal point, 387
    in Director's Services Agreements, 192
    in Performer's Services Agreements, 219
    in Producer's Services Agreement, 172,
        179
Injunctions, 354, 373
Insurance, 49–51
    "additional insureds" as part of, 50
    completion bonds, 50
    E&O, 49
    general liability, 49
    location agreements and, 238–239
    packages, 49
    unemployment, 394
    Worker's Compensation, 49
Intellectual property clearances, 156

Intellectual property law, 22–23, 29–32. *See also* Contract law, for films; Copyright law
  definition of, 23
  joint authorship of screenplays under, 90–91
Intellectual property rights, license of, 159
Internal Revenue Service (IRS), 394–395
International Alliance of Theatrical Stage Employees (IATSE), 167, 195
Intrusion upon seclusion, 357
Invasion of privacy, 135
  in depiction releases, 230
Investment contracts, 57–58
IRS. *See* Internal Revenue Service

J

Joint authorship, of screenplays, 90–97. *See also* Writer's Collaboration Agreements
  general partnerships for, creation of, 95
  intellectual property under, 95
  joint ventures and, creation of, 95
  LLCs and, 95
  under copyright law, 94, 95, 343–345
  value reduction from, 343
  Writer's Collaboration Agreements for, 91–97
Joint ventures, 39
  for joint authorship of screenplays, 95

L

Laboratory Access Letters, 303–304
Laws. *See* Child labor laws; Contract law, for films; Coogan Law; Copyright law; Employment law; Intellectual property law; Law suits; Privacy laws; Retraction laws; Securities laws
Law suits, 46–47
Legal deliverables, 154–155
Legislative restrictions
  on product placement and endorsements, 161–162
Letters of intent (LOI), 203–205
Libel, 135, 359. *See also* Defamation
Licensing. *See also* Artwork licenses; Music licensing
  artwork, 248–250
  compensation and, 29

of copyrights, 348–349
distribution as part of, 25
duration of, 25–26
music, 263–278
in specific mediums, 25
territorial, 26
under copyright law, 25
Life Rights Consent Agreements, 124, 127–130
  compensation under, 129–130
  credits under, 130
  grantors for, 127
  producers rights under, 127
  releases and waivers under, 124, 128–129
  reserved rights under, 128
Life story rights, 124–130. *See also* Life Rights Consent Agreements
  definition of, 124
  estates and, 126
  First Amendment and, 125
  Life Rights Consent Agreements for, 124
  state laws and, variation among, 125–126
Likeness approval, 387
Limited liability companies (LLCs), 35–37, 40–41
  Articles of Organization for, 40
  equity investments in, 55
  features of, 40–41
  for joint authorship of screenplays, 95
Limited partnerships (LPs), 35–37, 39
Line producers, 171
Literary Property Acquisition Agreements, 117–123
  compensation under, 119
  copyrights under, 119
  credits under, 121
  first negotiation/last refusal under, 120
  producer's rights under, 119
  publicity under, 121
  reserved rights under, 119
  reversion of rights under, 120
  Screenplay Purchase Agreement *v.*, 117
Litwak, Mark, 4
Loan-out companies, 42
  inducement clauses and, 42
Loans
  personal, 54
  secured, 54
  unsecured, 54

Location agreements, 238–241
  compensation under, 239
  credits and, 241
  insurance as part of, 241
  trade dress under, 239
Locations, 235–242. *See also* Location
    Agreements
  location agreements for, 238–241
  nuisances on, 237
  privacy laws and, 236
  shooting permits for, 237
  trespass to chattel at, 236
  trespass to land and, 235–236
Low-budget agreements, under SAG, 206
Lucas, George, 334

M
Mandatory trust funds, under child labor
    laws, 403–404
Manufacturer/advertiser, 157
Marketing
  and DIY distribution, 308
Massachusetts tax credit program, 72
Master Bargaining Agreements, 167
  for DGA, 189
Master Use Licenses, 264
  in Music Licensing Agreements, 266
MBA. *See* Minimum Basic Agreement
Merchandising rights, under Literary
    Property Acquisition Agreement, 118
Merger clauses, 387
Miller, Philip H., 4
Minimum Basic Agreement (MBA)
  under SAG, 206
  under WGA, 97–98
Minors
  depiction releases for, 231–232
  under employment law, 166–167
Modified low-budget agreements, under
    SAG, 208–209
Moral rights, 366
  under Performer's Services Agreements,
    216–217
Morals clauses, in Performer's Services
    Agreements, 221–222
Moviegoer, 292
Music licensing, 263–278. *See also*
    Composer's Services Agreements;
    Music Licensing Agreements

AFM and, 269
ASCAP and, 265
BMI and, 265
for commissioned works, 271–272
Composer's Services Agreements for,
    272–277
for compositions, 263
copyrights for, 263–264
Master Use Licenses, 265–266
Music Licensing Agreements for,
    267–271
Performance Licenses, 264
performance rights societies for, 264–265
for prerecorded songs, 263–264
for recordings, 263–264
for rerecording, 266–267
royalty-free music and, 270–271
SESAC and, 265
Synchronization Licenses, 264
Videogram Licenses, 264
Music Licensing Agreements, 264
  credits under, 269
  Master Use License in, 268
  Performance Licenses in, 268
  Synchronization Licenses as part of, 268
  Videogram Licenses in, 268

N
NABET-CWA. *See* National Association of
    Broadcast Employees and Technicians-
    Communication Workers of America
National Archives, 279, 283
  stock footage from, 279, 280
National Association of Broadcast
    Employees and Technicians-
    Communication Workers of America
    (NABET-CWA), 195
NDAs. *See* Nondisclosure agreements
Negative Pickup Agreements, 290
Net profits, 29, 55–56
  as deal point, 379–380
  and DIY distribution, 308–309
  under Director's Services Agreements,
    193
  under Performer's Services Agreements,
    221
  under Producer's Services Agreement,
    181
  under Writer's Services Agreements, 116

Network problems, 155
Network selection
    under production services agreement,
        149–150
New York
    child labor laws in, 403
    Child Performer Education and Trust Act
        in, 403–404
    independent contractors in, 397–398
Non-accredited investors, 58–59
Nondisclosure agreements (NDAs), 77–79,
        81–82
    confidentiality under, 81
    costs of, 84
Nonrefundable and nontransferable credits,
        66–67
Notice releases, 232
Nuisances, as property harm, 237

O

Online distribution, 307, 317–318
Option Agreements, for screenplays,
        103–105
    development during, 105
    duration of, 104
    exercising an option during, 104–105
    extension payments under, 104
    option prices within, 104
    producer's rights under, 103
    Screenplay Purchase Agreements and,
        103–104, 110
    writer's rights under, 103–104
Option Extension Payments, 110
Option prices, 29
    in Option Agreements, 104

P

Parody, 362. *See also* Fair use
    of trademarks, 253–254
Payments. *See* Compensation
Payment schedule/acquisition price,
        151–152
Pay or play
    as deal point, 380
    under Director's Services Agreements, 190
    under Producer's Services Agreement, 177
    under Writer's Services Agreements, 115
PEMEI. *See* "Permit to Employ Minors in
    the Entertainment Industry"

Per diems
    in Producer's Services Agreement, 174
    under Crew Services Agreements, 168
    under Director's Services Agreements,
        187
    under Performer's Services Agreements,
        216, 220
Performance Licenses, 264
    in Music Licensing Agreements, 268
Performance rights societies, for music,
        264–265
    ASCAP, 265
    BMI, 265
    SESAC, 265
Performers. *See* Actors
Performer's Services Agreements, 203,
        213–225
    accounting for, 219
    approval rights under, 217
    availability dates under, 214–215
    compensation under, 215–216
    credits under, 216
    deal memos as part of, 213
    favored-nations clause in, 224
    inducement clauses in, 219
    letters of intent (LOI), 203–205
    moral rights under, 217
    morals clauses in, 221
    net profits under, 221
    options on future services under, 221
    per diems under, 216
    perquisites as part of, 216
    publicity under, 218
    residuals under, 215
    rights assignments under, 216–217
    SAG compliance and, 219–220
    suspension of, 217–218
    termination of, 217–218
    terms of, 213–215
Perks. *See* Perquisites
"Permit to Employ Minors in the
    Entertainment Industry" (PEMEI),
        400–401
Perquisites. *See also* Per diems
    definition of, 220
    under Crew Services Agreements, 201
    under Director's Services Agreements,
        216
    under Performer's Services Agreements,
        216

Personal loans, 54

Pick-up shots, 228

Post-production phase, 8, 12
copyrights during, 262
Director's Services Agreements for, 185
liens during, 262
staffing for, 261–262

Power of attorney
under content aggregator deal, 319

Pre-production phase, 11. *See also*
Development, of film properties;
Service Agreements
Collective Bargaining Agreements
during, 167
employment law compliance and, 165
Master Bargaining Agreements during,
167
services agreements as part of, 146
union compliance during, 146

Principal photography, 228

Privacy laws. *See also* Right of publicity
false light and, 358
hidden cameras/microphones and, 359
intrusion upon seclusion and, 357
locations and, 236
public disclosure and, 357–358
right of publicity and, 356
violation of, 357–359

Producers. *See also* Producer's Services
Agreement
associate, 171
executive, 171
Life Rights Consent Agreements and,
127–128
line, 171
Literary Property Acquisition Agreements
and, rights under, 117
Option Agreements and, rights under,
103
Producer's Services Agreement for,
171–181
Screenplay Purchase Agreements and,
rights under, 105–106

Producer's Services Agreement, 171–181
accounting for, 175
compensation under, 174–175
conditions precedent in, 173
credits under, 175–176
festivals/premieres under, 180
inducement clauses in, 179

net profits under, 181
pay or play under, 177
per diems as part of, 174
production companies and, 172
publicity under, 176
riders in, 173
rights assignments under, 176
termination of, 178

Product endorsement, 162

Production companies, 6, 10, 35–42, 157.
See also Attorneys; Corporations;
Distribution agreements; Financing;
General partnerships; Insurance;
Limited liability companies; Limited
partnerships
accountants as part of, 47–48
attorneys as part of, 43–47
corporations, 35, 37, 40
equity investments in, 55
formation of, 35
general partnerships, 38–39
insurance for, 49–51
joint ventures, 39
as legal person, 35
liability limitations of, 35–36
LLCs, 35–37, 41–42
loan-out companies and, 42
LPs, 35–37, 39
NDAs and, 81–82
Producer's Services Agreements and, 172
Respondeat Superior doctrine and,
36–37
Service Agreements and, 167–168
sole proprietorships, 37–38

Production company fee, 151

Production company's net profits, 57

Production-Financing/Distribution
Agreements, 290

Production incentives, definition of, 63–64

Production phase, 8, 11–12
depiction releases as part of, 229–234
locations during, 235–242
on set clearances during, 244
stages of photography during, 228

Production services agreement, 149
approvals/required elements, 152–153
delivery requirements, 154–155
engagement/production services,
150–151
intellectual property clearances, 156

network problems, 155
network selection, 149–150
parties, 150
payment schedule/acquisition price,
  151–152
production specifications, 152
representations and warranties, 155
right of first refusal, 152
rights, 151
Production tax credits, types of, 66–67
Product placement agreement, 157
  agencies, 163
  approvals/manner of depiction, 159
  "bankable" star, 163
  contractual restrictions, 162
  credit, 161
  experienced media lawyer, placement
    with, 162
  failure to place products, 158
  insurance, 160
  intellectual property rights, license of, 159
  legislative restrictions, 161–162
  loss and damage of product, 161
  monetary payment, 158
  parties, 157
  placement, 158
  publicity, 160–161
  remedies, 161
  representation and warranty and
    indemnity, 160
  restricted uses, 160
Project requirements, 176
Promissory notes, 55
  definition of, 55
  noteholders, 55
Prop rental houses, 255
Public domain, works in, 132–133
  artwork, 255
  copyrights for, 132–133, 332
  definition of, 332
  U.S. government works as part of,
    334–335
Publicity
  as deal point, 389
  in depiction releases, 229
  under Composer's Services Agreements,
    275
  under Crew Services Agreements, 199
  under Director's Services Agreements,
    189–190

under Literary Property Acquisition
  Agreements, 122
under Performer's Services Agreements,
  218
under Producer's Services Agreement,
  176
under Screenplay Purchase Agreements,
  116
under Writer's Services Agreements,
  108–109
Purchase price/compensation, 107
Purchase Price Payments, for screenplays,
  120
  contingent compensation, 110
  fixed compensation, 110

Q
Qualified production expenses, 64
  and loan-out companies, 65
Quitclaim licenses, 280–281
Quotes, for actors, 224

R
Rate Schedules (for WGA), 107
Rebates, 63
Refundable tax credits, 66, 69
Reimbursements
  under Crew Services Agreements, 198
  under Director's Services Agreements,
    186–187
Rental fees, 29
"Rent-a-theater" distribution. *See* Four-wall
  agreement
Replication vs. duplication, 315
Representations and warranties/
  indemnification
  under content aggregator deal, 319–320
  under production services agreement,
    155
Reservation of rights
  under content aggregator deal, 318
Reserved rights
  as deal point, 381
  under Life Rights Consent Agreements,
    128
  under Literary Property Acquisition
    Agreements, 117–118
  under Screenplay Purchase Agreements,
    106

Residuals
as deal point, 376
distribution and, 291
under Performer's Services Agreements, 215
under SAG, 209
Respondeat Superior doctrine, 36
Retraction laws, defamation and, 365–366
Reversion of rights, 107
Riders, in Service Agreements, 169
in Producer's Services Agreement, 173
Right of First Negotiation/Last Refusal
as deal point, 389
in Director's Services Agreements, 192
Right of first refusal
in production services agreement, 152
Right of publicity, 354–356
definition of, 354–355
duration of, 355
First Amendment and, 355–356
infringement on, 356
predominant use test for, 356
relatedness tests for, 356
transformative tests for, 356
Rights. *See* Approval rights; Copyright
law; Copyright(s); Distribution,
rights to; Idea rights; Life story
rights; Literary Property Acquisition
Agreements; Merchandising rights;
Option Agreements, for screenplays;
Reserved rights; Right of First
Negotiation/Last Refusal; Screenplay
Purchase Agreements; Separated rights;
Television rights; Trademarks; Writer's
Collaboration Agreements; Writers
Guild of America; Writer's Services
Agreements
Rights, reversion of, 107
Royalties, 29
as deal point, 376
Royalty deal, 290
Royalty-free music, 270–271
Rule 504 (security law exemption), 59
Rule 505 (security law exemption), 59
Rule 506 (security law exemption), 59

S

SAG. *See* Screen Actors Guild (SAG)
SAG Minimum Basic Agreement, 206

Savings clauses
as deal point, 391
under Writer's Services Agreements, 115
Scènes à faire (scenes for action), 335
Screen Actors Guild (SAG), 6, 205–212. *See
also* Performer's Services Agreements
definition of, 206
extras under, 229
low-budget agreement under, 209–210
MBA under, 206
modified low-budget agreement under,
208–209
Performer's Services Agreements and,
219–220
residuals under, 208
security interest under, 211
short film agreement under, 207–208
signatories to, 206, 211
student film contracts under, 207
ultra-low budget agreement under, 208
Screenplay adaptations, 117
Literary Property Acquisition Agreement
for, 117–123
Screenplay clearance reports, 135–136
chain of title in, 135–136
copyright issues in, 135
invasion of privacy issues in, 135
libel issues in, 135
trademark infringement in, 136
Screenplay Purchase Agreements, 102–103,
105–111
accounting under, 107
compensation under, 107, 110
copyrights under, 106–107
credits under, 108
Literary Property Acquisition Agreement
v., 117
Option Agreements and, 102–103,
110–111
producer's rights under, 106–107
publicity under, 108–109
reserved rights under, 106
reversion of rights under, 107
for WGA members/non-members, 108
Screenplays, 87–99, 101–130. *See also* Life
story rights; Option Agreements, for
screenplays; Purchase Price Payments,
for screenplays; Screenplay adaptations;
Screenplay clearance reports;
Screenplay Purchase Agreements;

Screenwriters; Writer's Collaboration
  Agreements; Writers Guild of America
  acquisition of, 10, 98
  adaptations, 110, 117
  clearance reports for, 135–136
  joint authorship of, 90–97
  life story rights for, 124–130
  Option Agreements for, 103–105
  Purchase Price Payments for, 110
  Screenplay Purchase Agreements for,
    103–104, 105–106
  sole authorship of, 87–89
  U.S. Copyright Office and, 88–89, 96
  WGA and, 97–99
Screenwriters. *See also* Joint authorship, of
    screenplays; Writer's Collaboration
    Agreements; Writers Guild of America;
    Writer's Services Agreements
  Option Agreements and, interests under,
    103–104
  reserved rights for, 106
  Writer's Services Agreements for,
    112–117
Scripts. *See* Screenplays
Second-unit photography, 228
Secured loans, 54
Securities laws, 56–60
  accredited investors under, 58–59
  compliance with, 60–61
  definitions under, 57
  fraud and, 60
  investment contracts and, 57–58
  non-accredited investors under, 58–59
  offering under, 60
  registration exemptions to, 59–60
  Rule 504, 59
  Rule 505, 59
  Rule 506, 59
Security interest
  as deal point, 391
  under SAG, 211–212
Self-booking, 310
Separated rights, 97–98
  WGA and, 98–99
Service Agreements, 167–169
  Crew Services Agreement, 183, 195–200
  Director's Services Agreement, 183–193
  major elements of, 150–151
  Performer's Services Agreements, 203,
    212–222

Producer's Services Agreement, 171–181
  production companies and, 167–169
  riders in, 169
Services contracts, 146
SESAC. *See* Society of European Stage
    Authors and Composers
Sets, for films, 243–257. *See also* Artwork
    licenses
  artwork licenses for, 248–250
  copyrights on, 245–248
  prop rental houses and, 255
  trademarks on, 250–254
Settlement transactions, 292
Seven, 339
Shooting permits, 235–238
  fees for, 237–238
  requirements for, 237–238
Short film agreements, under SAG, 207
Short form copyright assignment, 141–142
Signatories
  to SAG, 206, 211–212
  to WGA, 98–99
Slander, 359. *See also* Defamation
Society of European Stage Authors and
    Composers (SESAC), 265
Sole proprietorships, 37
  DBA certificates for, 38
Star Wars, 334, 337
State tax credits application, 67–69
State tax incentives
  tips for, 65
Step deals, 111
Stock footage, 279, 281
  companies for, 279
  from National Archives, 279, 283
Student film contracts, under SAG, 207
Subchapter S. corporations, 40
Subdistributors, 289
Submission Releases, 77–79
  costs of, 84
  provisions of, 80
Synchronization Licenses, 264, 268
  in Music Licensing Agreements, 265

T

Taxation
  for C. corporations, 40
  for independent contractors, 394
  under employment law, 394

Tax credit brokers, 66
Technical deliverables, 154
Television rights, under Literary Property
    Acquisition Agreement, 118
Term
    under content aggregator deal, 318–319
Termination agreements, 93
Termination of transfer, 350–351
Term sheet, 71
Theatrical distribution, 307, 309–311
Theatrical exhibition agreement, 310
Trade dress, 239, 250
Trademark clearance letters, 254–255
Trademarks
    clearance letters for, 254–255
    false endorsement, 250–251
    on film sets, 250–251
    informational uses of, 250
    parody of, 253–254
    in screenplay clearance reports, 135
    tarnishment of, 252–253
    under Literary Property Acquisition
        Agreement, 118
Traditional distribution. *See* Distribution
Transferable tax credits, 66
Trespass to chattel, 236
Trespass to land, 235–236
12 Monkeys, 243

U
Ultra-low budget agreements, under SAG,
    208
Underages, 151
Unemployment insurance, 394
    for independent contractors, 394
Unions. *See also* American Federation of
    Television and Radio Artists; Crew
    Services Agreements; Directors Guild
    of America; International Alliance of
    Theatrical Stage Employees; National
    Association of Broadcast Employees
    and Technicians-Communication
    Workers of America; Performance
    rights societies, for music; Screen
    Actors Guild; Writers Guild of
    America
AFTRA, 167
Collective Bargaining Agreements with,
    167

DGA, 183
    during pre-production phase, compliance
        with, 165, 167
IATSE, 167
Master Bargaining Agreements with, 167
NABET-CWA, 195
SAG, 6, 205–213
WGA, 11, 94
Unsecured loans, 54
U.S. Copyright Office, 26. *See also*
    Copyright law; Copyright(s)
    registration through, 136–139
    screenplays and, 88–89
    searches through, 133–134
U.S. Customs Service, 137

V
Video
    digital, 53
    film *v.*, 5
Videogram Licenses, 264
    in Music Licensing Agreements, 266
Volunteer Lawyers for the Arts
    Organization, 46

W
Waits, Tom, 267
Waivers
    in artwork licenses, 250
    to deal points, 391
WGA. *See* Writers Guild of America
Woods, Lebbeus, 243
Work made for hire
    and employee status, 348
    independent contractors and, 347
Work made for hire, 344–346
    copyright assignment clauses for, 345
    copyrights and, 344–346
    deal points and, 382
    definition of, 344–346
    duration of, 346
    independent contractors and, 344, 394
    Worker's Compensation insurance, 49,
        394
Writers. *See* Screenwriters
Writers Guild of America (WGA), 11, 88
    credits policy for, 98–99
    MBA and, 97
    Rate Schedules for, 106–107

Screenplay Purchase Agreements and, for
 members/non-members, 109
screenplays and, 90, 97–99
separated rights and, 97–98
signatories to, 97–98
Writer's Collaboration Agreements and,
 91–92
Writer's Collaboration Agreements, 90–96
 ownership of copyrights under, 92–93
 termination agreements for, 93
 WGA and, 94
Writer's Services Agreements, 112–117
 compensation under, 113–114
 credits under, 116
 delivery period as part of, 113

net profits under, 116
option period as part of, 113
pay or play under, 115
product forms in, 113
publicity under, 116
reading period as part of, 112, 113
right of first negotiation under, 114
savings clause under, 115
step deals as part of, 111–112
Writing partnerships. *See* Joint authorship,
 of screenplays

Y
YouTube, 320–321